Our Life Beyond MKUltra:
Then and Now

by Elisa E

LOGOSOPHIA

OUR LIFE BEYOND MKULTRA: THEN AND NOW
by ELISA E

LOGOSOPHIA, LLC

Logosophia LLC
90 Oteen Church Road
Asheville, NC 28805
https://logosophiabooks.com
logosophiabooks@gmail.com

First Edition
Library of Congress-in-Publication Data available upon request.
Non-Fiction
E, Elisa
Our Life Beyond MKUltra: Then and Now
ISBN 978-1-7350432-3-4

ARTWORK: Front cover collàge "Piece of Mind", back cover collage "Mormon Sin", and all interior collàges created by Elisa E.

BACK COVER: The Mystery of the Grail, The 7th Seal, Anthroposophy. Astral experience which renders the universal meaning of human evolution. **Cube** represents space. **Two serpents** represent the lower human powers that grow out of cube, these bring forth out of themselves the purified higher spiritual nature, represented by the **world spirals**. The upward growth of these higher powers makes it possible for a human being to become a recipient, or chalice, of purely spiritual cosmic being, expressed in the **dove**. Thereby humanity becomes the ruler of spiritual cosmic forces, portrayed in the **rainbow**.
– from https://anthroposophy.eu/w/images/thumb/b/b4/FMC00.259.jpg/2000px-FMC00.259.jpg

Our Life Beyond MKUltra: Then and Now

Caveat lector!
If you think you may have been a victim of *total mind kontrol (tmk)* programming, I strongly suggest that you read the following material with a safe support person in place with whom you can dialogue as **TRIGGERING MAY OCCUR.**

Dedication

May the world awaken to the reality of mind control *en masse* now affecting
all of humanity and the environment.
This is nothing short of genocide and ecocide;
the permanent alteration of humanity and the Earth.

May each of you awaken to find true Sovereignty
and come to know the realities in which you live
and play a never-ending role.

To Russ Dizdar, a man who truly walked the path of Spiritual Warrior
and offered to others his strength of spirit and fighting knowledge.

Acknowledgements

My deepest Love and appreciation to Lynn and all who have followed in his footsteps with support and faith in me. Without you, I would not be here to tell what *we* know. No judgment, just Unconditional Love.

Thank you to Elana for giving me hours of editing and remaining ever-patient with my constant questioning, all the while knowing this story needed to be told.

Many thanks to Elida Hanson-Finelli as well for the photography work on my colláges.

A special thanks to Ron Patton and the staff of *Paranoia* magazine. Additionally, I thank all of those internet radio hosts who encouraged my going public and supported my presentations.

I am extremely grateful to predecessors who have gone public. Their willingness to come forward has provided validation and corroboration for much in my own alter downloads and conscious experience memories, as well as assisted in my struggle to break free of my doubt programming. Their courage has inspired me.

Thank you to all the amazing researchers out there who have helped explain the seemingly impossible and advanced technologies that are actualized and being applied to myself and others like me...*for decades*.

And on it goes...

TABLE *of* CONTENTS

BOOK 1

Foreword for the 2nd Edition

The assassination of President Kennedy was, in the final analysis, a nation-wide MK-ULTRA project designed to inflict massive trauma on the entire country and to thereby affect a significant change in the collective conscious-ness of the American people.

— David McGowan, "Ruminations on Littleton, Mind Control, and JFK", September 2000

During the years I spent digging through disinformation and the occasional sudden Freedom of Information Act revelation as to what happened to the United States after World War Two, I discovered many disparate answers that, with diligence, finally fit together to reveal a picture of terrible intention and purpose.

My research also led me to remarkable individuals victimized during the Cold War, now morphed into the techno-fascist Third Reich no doubt envisioned by the transplanted Paperclip Nazis in league with homegrown rightwing extremists. The remarkable individuals I learned of had clawed their way out of brutal mind-soul control and therefore constitute the canaries in the coal mine crying out to us, our children and grandchildren, to warn us of the *Transhumanism* and engineered humanity now upon us.

Elisa is one of these intrepid people whose *Our Life Beyond MKUltra: Then and Now* meticulously records her struggle.

That organized religions like the Mormon Church are engaged in incest, pedophilia, mind control, and Satanism should come as no surprise. Dying institutions whose once good intentions have fled often devour their young.

I think of Elisa as a third-generation MK-ULTRA survivor. Cathy O'Brien, author of the first book about MK-ULTRA I read, *Trance Formation of America* (1995), was a first-generation post-war MK-ULTRA survivor who testified before the Texas Justice Council in Dallas, Texas on June 11, 1996 regarding the terrible intention and purpose of engineered mind control as per the Mormon/CIA/Jesuit "merger":

It was in Mackinac Island that I first met then-Prime Minister of Canada Pierre Trudeau, a professed Jesuit. Through conversations that I overheard between him and Governor Romney, I learned how the CIA and the Catholics were merging their information for NWO [new world order] controls.

Michigan's Governor George Romney was very much interested in implementing mind control of the masses. He wanted to bring the Satanic rituals of child abuse that were proliferating in the Catholic Church into the Mormon Church. He wanted a robotic society growing up within the Mormon church so that they would give more money to the NWO effort.

One of the things that he instructed me to do was to attend the Muskegon Catholic Central High School—which was very much involved in this CIA/Jesuit merger of mind control information. Through implementation of trauma in the school system, a person such as myself would photographically record whatever I was taught. I got all A's but I didn't gain any information I could use. I couldn't think to use anything that I had learned, but I was recording facts and that's what they were interested in...

Governor Romney was also interested in an early version of the Global Education 2000 Program (Outcome-Based Education) that's infiltrated our school system. It was designed to increase our children's learning capacity while decreasing their ability to critically analyze. As a result, the Michigan education system ranked first in the nation for many years, but the devastation to the children was horrible.

– Cathy O'Brien, *Sex, Lies and Mind Control*

Unbelievable? Not really. From 1975 to 1977, the U.S. Senate Select Committee on Intelligence and Subcommittee on Health and Scientific Research of the Committee on Human Resources (the Church Committee) Joint Hearing tangled with the same out-of-control CIA that President John F. Kennedy and his brother Attorney General Robert F. Kennedy did. After two years of testimony and ten large boxes of documents labeled "MK-ULTRA, 1952-62", the public went back to sleep until a brief awakening during the 1995 President's Advisory Committee on Human Radiation Experiments under President Bill Clinton—himself an MK-ULTRA victim—then fell asleep again.

Historical accounts insist that MK-ULTRA ended in 1973, but the truth is that it has continued under one name or another, moving from trauma-hypnosis-drugs to remote electromagnetic mind control. Robert

Duncan, author of *The Matrix Deciphered* (2006) and *Project: Soul Catcher* (2010), calls it remote neural monitoring (RNM), EEG cloning/EEG heterodyning. Access to MK-ULTRA cutting-edge technology for no-touch torture and slavery has expanded beyond its original federal military and intelligence agency gatekeepers to defense contractors like Lockheed Martin and Raytheon to other transnational corporations, police departments, criminal cabals, cults, churches, NATO, Satanic corporate (Illuminati) families, etc. Now, MK-ULTRA is coming of age under the Transhumanist phase of nanotechnology and brain-computer interface (BCI) to be entirely run by artificial intelligence (AI).

Elisa tells her tale in all its horror and pathos in *Our Life Beyond MKUltra: Then and Now,* speaking from the reality of multiple personalities ("alters") who also have a say, given that each of them holds memories that Elisa must eventually hear and know in order to *deprogram*. To speak as "I" is to speak as a singular individual, which Elisa admits is not her condition.

Her vantage point for telling the tale is that of the programmed twilight zone, which makes this book valuable to professionals grappling with programmed clients and valuable to victims struggling to come to terms with their own twilight of alters living their lives inside their psyche—alters they must build a relationship with in order to learn their secrets.

Elisa is a proponent of the fact that programming provides access to realms normally unattainable. Given our era of quantum entanglement, parallel dimensions, and the manmade Metaverse, accessing other realms or "realities" should not sound far-fetched or "made up".

Hopefully, *Our Life Beyond MKUltra: Then and Now* will stimulate a long-overdue public dialogue about MK-ULTRA and pedophilia in Hollywood, child trafficking, Satanic ritual, secret societies, and the questionable American obsession with entertainers who are little more than throwaway slaves dominated by contracts and handlers.

A terrible intention has shanghaied the United States of America. Learning about mind control is a good first step to increasing a wakefulness that might lead to actual public action.

– Elana Freeland, April 1, 2022

Elana Freeland is the author of the Sub Rosa America: A Deep State History *series that can be purchased at Amazon. She is also the author of a definitive trilogy on what Geoengineering really is, the final book being*

Geoengineered Transhumanism: How the Environment Has Been Weaponized by Chemicals, Electromagnetism & Nanotechnology for Synthetic Biology (2021). *Her website is* elanafreeland.com, *and she posts daily at her one facebook site EMF Planetary Engineering, plus* gab.com *group "Geoengineered Transhumanism with Elana Freeland."*

Second Edition Introduction

It has been some years now since I began what I refer to as deep de-programming. Despite years—more like two decades—of memories and searching it would not be until I was 46 years of age that I finally met two men who would help me begin the process of not only recovery of memories in a more cohesive fashion, yet to begin to understand what my life had truly been as an MKUltra mind controlled victim.

It is 2022, a year I never thought I would be around to see, yet here I am, 60 years old and still going thanks to a level of Sovereignty I also once believed I could never attain.

What is most striking to me are the proclamations, as well as predictions, that some of my alter personalities repeatedly *cried from the pulpit* so to speak to anyone who would listen back then. I am here to witness some of them manifesting in a much earlier year than imagined. With the CV-19 psychological operation in full swing, the mind control success (for far too many) can be witnessed by those with the ears to hear and eyes to see.

The loudest proclamation of one of my alters (or more likely more than one alternate personality coming together to proclaim such) was this: *They are riding the technology into everyone.* No truer words as witnessed today. She/they would go on to explain that this involved entities who are against the Divinely-intended and assisted evolution of humanity and are attempting to divert such by creating a false evolutionary path. It is true that there are humans working for these dark entities on the physical plane, hoping to receive a reward for their efforts, namely immortality. I am here to say they are desperately wrong. One of the absolutes in this Game of Life is that the dark ones are only in it for themselves. All are expendable when it comes to humanity, save the ones they ultimately want to own lock, stock and barrel.

Ironically or not, "National Socialism" as described by Yuri Bezmenov in *The Four Stages of Ideological Subversion* interview in 1984 (https://www.youtube.com/watch?v=yErKTVdETpw), is very pertinent to our times.

v

Notice the **Twilight Language** of that interview date? (For definitions of **boldfaced** terms throughout, please turn to the Lexicon at the back of the book.) This is indeed what we are in the midst of globally as of 2022.

These proclamations also stated that humans would one day rise to live their lives as on any other day, yet without the realization they had lost all free will. Mind control technologies at their finest.

What I have witnessed over the past couple of years with the false "pandemic" is the beginning, at least the beginning of this level, of that agenda. I am reminded of what is known as End-Time programming (more on this later) and witnessing such in many of the events of these current years. One aspect of that is MKUltra slaves set loose on the populace to wreak havoc in a pre-determined, programmed-in, organized agenda. Some of this activity may appear haphazard, but it is not. Much of this was evident to me with the Black Lives Matter and Antifa destruction in various cities, as well as those in positions of authority making decisions for the populace. Not to mention the gender neutral push towards Transhumanism. Many of these poor souls are MKUltras working at the behest of those the populace will likely never come to know, or even apprehend to exist. No one will ever convince me MKUltra did not play a major role in this "Chaos". (Much of this book was written years ago, long before the current psychological operation, bio-weapons attack began.)

In addition, nanotech is being introduced via needle into the arms of a large percentage of the unwitting global population. What is in that injection (which is *proven* to not be a vaccine) is the "next level" beyond decades of chemtrail and GMO food delivery of some of the very same ingredients, as well as dire advances. This includes nanotechnology for the ultimate surveillance/control machinations now and in the coming decades, rolling into the future human condition: *Trans*-human (Human 2.0). And let us not forget the sacrifices offered to the malevolent gods in the form of genocide victims already at the hands of this "jab," and those still to come. Yet behind even this is an agenda on the level of Spirit that is the desired result. Much of this can be found in the lectures and writings of the Anthroposophical genius Dr. Rudolph Steiner.

Life today is nothing of what it was even four or five years ago. It has been forever altered and there will be no return to "normal". There never was a normal, that too was an illusion. I know, I lived in the darkness of the "real" world agenda. That false sense of "normal" has since passed and it is now a time of individual responsibility. Yes, this can and will morph into communal efforts, however, now is the time for each man and woman to stand for themselves. To choose. Will I go along and not think for myself, not question, not pay attention, not notice the outrageous inconsistencies in the world around me and who is promoting them? Or will I choose to engage my Divine mind and heart to reveal the truths that will allow me to continue on my God-given path of evolution? The latter does not mean it must be done alone, however, unless one willingly and consistently pursues such a path, one will indeed feel as though they are alone. In the determined and disciplined seeking, one finds the assistance and guidance one needs…but not beforehand.

My journey over the last couple of decades has gifted me for my efforts. I have indeed found I was never alone, yet my responsibility was to commit to a life of truth no matter the outcome. No easy task in this world. The unknowns were just that, and faith would see me through. The revelations I found by acting in that faith have been tremendous. It is my belief that knowing what's ahead individually may slow us down if not completely halt our efforts. Trusting in oneself and those that are there to assist along the way can bring great insight.

This edition is intended to open up what followed the early years of deep deprogramming. There will be corrections in the original manuscript, as well as some elaborations on what is there thanks to a clearer mind of who, what and where "we" have been. I no longer speak in the plural, nor do I live in it, though I am uncertain I can claim I experience life even now the way another without having had alternate personalities does. I find I often have access to a deep understanding of the esoteric agenda playing out. I attribute this to my history as well as my current commitment to the Light side of workings.

I no longer classify myself solely as a "survivor", due to learning how now to thrive rather than just survive. Surviving continued for me for many years into deep deprogramming due to not really knowing anything else. I've had to teach myself to take responsibility for cultivating the genuine desire and belief that I can indeed *thrive*. It is a work in process and I am ever so grateful for the opportunity.

I have met many people along the way who have played a part in renewing a trust in life and others. A trust I am uncertain I was ever able to fully experience in the past. Additionally, and perhaps the precursor to what I just referred to, was a slowly building trust in beings of the Light side. I had a life of interacting with entities of the dark, and it took some years into deprogramming to come to experience, often in full consciousness, those assisting me on the Light side. For me, this was the pivotal point in my recovery of self: body, mind, soul and spirit. A journey, not momentary, but a journey of reward and grief and doubt, born into something inexplicably real. The words that come to mind are love, safety, peace, and a journey begun. Strength. Purpose beyond just me and my survival. And a knowing that this path was not about being virtuous and deserving, but the path I *had* to go down. The very reason I am here. What else could I do as my heart and mind were drawn into my destined path? The outcome wasn't the matter, the course was. Show up and let it unfold before you, bit by bit, day by day, year by year. Trust.

I have found and continue to find Sovereignty outside of what "they" do or don't do. As a result, I have seen things in the way of interference against them by the Light side, right before my eyes…on more than one occasion. Like last year when "they" came for me again.

Since writing my books over a decade ago, I am indeed a Christian, yet rather an esoteric one. I was initiated into darkness involuntarily, now I have been initiated into the Light of Christ. I began to understand that much of what they did, much of what I knew due to my alters and programs, could now be used to my advantage, against them.

I reached a point a few years back where I lost the fear of them and I chose to become a "watcher" and reporter of their technologies as related to what they were doing to me. I felt an empowerment after that and the effect they sought lessened on my end.

I am a Divine being with rights that supersede what insane people do in the physical. This has to be taken in so deeply and consistently, no matter what occurs outside, until one knows it body, mind, soul and spirit, without any hesitation whatsoever. I came into this life for a reason, and that reason isn't just to suffer and/or die at the hands of psychopaths. It is to find my way back to Christ with everything I am, here, now, to the best of my ability on any given day. The more I understand about this world, this magnificent Cosmos we call home, the better off I am no matter what these lost souls do. As it is said, I am in this world, but not of it. I am taking myself back no matter "their" plans. They don't have me anymore. This does not make me invincible, it makes me a Sovereign being here and hereafter. And believe me, they now know they do not *own* me anymore, no matter what they attempt, I will never be theirs. For me, that is where the **Christ Impulse** comes in.

I recall a time when someone had to tell me to hold on, don't give up, no matter what, and they promised me it would change. I did not have to believe in it, they believed in it for me…and it has, beyond belief. The change isn't a result of the perpetrators changing their ways, it is because I have changed, inside. I have love, faith, compassion and a passion for bringing the truth out to any who want to know. My goal is to assist in any way I can our Divinely intended human future, in this world and beyond it.

I have combined books 1 and 2 into a single version. Below you will find the two books in succession as they originally were published with a few edit changes as well as updating to cover further understanding in deprogramming for over a decade.

Though I no longer refer to myself in the plural, I have left alone the original versions that are written as such to reflect my alternate personalities. This is an important part of understanding what multiplicity is like before any form of integration. A scattered and ungrounded state of being. I will change a few plurals to first person where I believe it reflects my current outlook in life and does not harm the multiplicity narrative. Keep in mind that these books were written in 2010 through 2013 and reflect early deep deprogramming in process. Therefore, when you see I, me, my, mine without italics, it is now the truest part of me that was recovered in my deprogramming efforts. These will be current updates as of the publication date of this second edition in 2022.

Blessings and Love to you all.
Elisa E

BOOK 1

First Edition Introduction, 2013

It was not until April 2008 that *we* came to consciously understand that *we* are a multi-generational bloodline, satanically ritually abused, trauma-based, *total mind kontrol* slave (*tmk* slave). *We* often referred to ourselves as "high-level" due to some of the people involved in *our* programming and subsequent use being in positions of recognition. Prior to 2008, *we* remained under the kontrol of *our* programmers even as *our* programming was severely breaking down. Through much struggle and heartbreak, *we* slowly came to realize who and what *we* were and were able to take up the ongoing process of gaining control over *our* own lives.

First of all, *we* **front alters** use the words *i*, *me*, *us*, *we*, *our*, and *our-selve*s to denote all or several of *our* personalities (found in italics in this edition). Thus the use of italics for *our* personal pronouns, as well as for the names of certain alters. When *we* began writing, *we* were finding ourselves switching between using *i* and *we*, still very much in the lifelong discovery process. *We* decided to go back and replace almost all *i*'s with *we* so that the reader would be less confused. *We* realize that this takes away from expressing, in a word, the part of the process that *we* have to go through in order to move toward some degree of wholeness, but at least less confusion will encourage readers to read *Our Life Beyond MKUltra: Then and Now* in full.

Our Life Beyond MKUltra: Then and Now is a partial collection of *our* memory downloads spanning a lifetime—several lifetimes, if you consider all of *us*. Where possible, *we* have not gone into unnecessary violent details, only into what *we* feel is necessary to those for whom this text is written.

We have encountered many personalities within *us*, some full, others fragmentary. Full personalities can interact with the world at large, if necessary, while fragments seem to be completely unaware of the world at large and exist only within a particular programmed act. Fragmentary personalities never age or mature.

The **alters** who have consciously become known to *us* thus far collectively cover a broad range of programming. The majority are fragmentary personalities with very specific programmed "tasks". So far, *we* have *seen* and *felt* more than two hundred alters and fragmentary personalities, some of whom are named, most of whom are not, due to being parts of systems. Hundreds fall into sub-groups under larger systems. For example, the *crystal system* is a grouping of sex alters who perform sexual acts for whoever can access them. *We* hope to make this process clearer as *we* continue.

Many personalities have appeared without staying around or giving their names. One—a young adult—consciously presented for the first time in a **download** as recently as a few days ago. Some alters have normal names and many do not—or if they do, *we* front alters are unaware of that name. Some seem to be associated with numbers, some with animals. In most cases, *we* believe it is how they are known to whomever it is that knows them.

Another aspect that is confusing to *us* is that *i* am not yet sure about who *i* am, but *i* do know that *i* am part of the **frontline alter system** and that *i* am not the original self. Often, *i* realize that *i* am a front alter programmed for other alters who need to come through. At times, *i* seem to forget (or be forgotten) until alters show *me* again. Thus, the process of writing *Our Life Beyond MKUltra: Then and Now* has been one of internal struggles.

Upon editing *Our Life Beyond MKUltra: Then and Now*, *we* clearly saw that different parts of *us* were writing at different times. Alter perspectives are varied, particularly when information is coming from several alters but presented by one alter working as a conduit for the others. *Our* main front alter is not the one who holds the memories or information about our "systems"; they are presented by many.

Try to understand *our* need for excessive italics and quotation marks for the exact words *we* see in *our* head. In many cases, *we* believe them to be specific programming words. In April 2012, *we* edited as much as *we* could, focusing particularly on utilizing capital letters and removing excessive quotation marks while still maintaining the truth. This was a difficult task as *our* inclination was to leave it as originally recorded, due to the possibility that it might resonate with other victims.

Our downloads are usually experienced as the presenting alter's consciousness as well as one or more of our front alter's simultaneous consciousness, now that *we* are in what *we* refer to as our **deep deprogramming**.

Often, more than one alter is providing download details as more than one alter was present during the experience. When this occurs, it is clear to *us* that one alter's memory stops as another's starts.

It took *us* a while to understand and get used to the personality switches taking place within the original occurrence. *Our* alters present their memories to *us* from within their own characteristics, abilities, frames of reference, timeframes, and levels of safety. The information is their memories from their life experiences—memories that have never been lost, only separated and sequestered away with the alter by walls within *our* shared mind.

When *we* use the words *see* and *feel* to describe our downloads, *we* are denoting a knowing between *our* front alters and other alters within *us*. That knowing may be physical, emotional, mental, spiritual, or all, and it is nearly impossible to describe the power of it in words in that it involves body, mind, and spirit. It is not that *we* are remembering so much as the alter is showing us their memory due to the fact that *we* were not present at the time of the original occurrence. *Our* body was there, but it was the mind of the other alter/alters that was present.

There are huge gaps within *our* conscious memory, often spanning many years. With what *we* refer to as *our* deep deprogramming, some of these gaps have given way to a flood of memories spanning a year or two.

Downloads of experiences have come in many ways, including photographic flashbacks and fragments during full waking consciousness or dream/rest time. *We* are uncertain if *our* state of sleep/rest is the same as that of a non-multiple personality, given that *we* have alters who never sleep. Our cells reveal body memories as well as intense emotional and physiological downloads. *We* have ongoing conversations between *our* alters, an internal process that can and usually does involve at least one of our front alters; hence *our* awareness either as a participant or as an observer. Often, when *we* find someone *we* can share with, as in someone seriously researching **total mind kontrol** (**tmk**) or another healing victim of *tmk*, *we* find validation and corroboration for many of our experiences.

After two and a half years of deprogramming backed by a minimal support group, *we* are attempting to live a life on *our* own and function within reasonably acceptable parameters within a society that appears to know nothing about *tmk*. We have gained a degree of management over *our* lives, though it remains an ongoing process as *we* continue to struggle with a labyrinth of masterful internal programs programmed into *us* since infancy, and against individuals sent to interfere with *our* process of de-programming. At times, *we* are still accessed by *our* kontrollers, given that programs can and do still run inside of *us*. As the main front alter, *i* can say that there is still much for *us* to discover and learn.

The words *entities, demons, aliens, beings,* and *others* are used inter-changeably as they are the true programmers, kontrollers, and handlers. *We* ask readers to suspend judgment until they have read *Our Life Beyond MKUltra: Then and Now* in its entirety.

And last but certainly not least, there are the colláges throughout both books contained in this edition. In the summer of 2009, *we* began col-lecting material for them as well as their actual construction. This was a collaborative effort by the many of *us*. The collection process alone took several months during which some of *our* front alters did not know why certain images were being gathered. *We* had no idea how profoundly pow-erful this work would be for *us* in our heart, mind, body, and spirit. Each page reveals things that some of *us* are still coming to understand.

At the outset of the work, several of *us* asked all of those of *us* who would be willing to participate in this effort to please do so, assuring them that no one would ask questions of them regarding it—a necessity for many of *us* in order to come forward and be willing to help create what is contained in this book. In the more than three years of deep deprogram-ming, *we* have noticed that most of those inside are very guarded about their identities, and rightfully so. *We* are learning to honor that, no matter what. So it is the many of *us* who put their memories and understandings into this work. The colláges appear throughout.

[The colláges had to be laminated due to the glue failing over the years, hence the photography by Elida Hanson-Finelli involved much time, ef-fort and skill.]

Prelude

Rudolf Steiner describes this setting in the latter part of the 15th Century. A small gathering of Rosicrucians stand before an altar in reverence and solemn manner in a ritual acknowledging human knowledge of the stars. This is what is said:

> We resolve to feel ourselves responsible at this moment not only for ourselves and our community, or our nation, nor even only for the people of our time; we resolve to feel ourselves responsible for everyone who has ever lived on Earth; we resolve that we will feel ourselves as belonging to the whole of humanity, and we feel that what has really happened with the human being is that he has deserted the rank of the Fourth Hierarchy and has descended too deeply into matter (for the Fall into Sin was understood in this sense) and in order that humanity may be able to return to the rank of the Fourth Hierarchy, may be able to find for ourselves of our own free will what in earlier times Gods have tried to find for us and with us; now let the higher knowledge be offered up for a season.

Baby Parts

1
Shattering a Young Mind: The Early Years

We would be well into *our* forties before becoming consciously aware that other parts of *us* were personalities and that *we* had **Multiple Personality Disorder (MPD)**. The main front alter could not figure out these wounded and terrible parts of *us*, nor how and when such things had occurred and how *i* could do such things, nor why *i* had these parts that wanted to do such terrible things.

In the 1960s, *we* lived as a small child with *our* family in New Jersey in an area that many years later would be revealed to have strong connections to *total mind kontrol* programming (*tmk*). Due to how *we* were to be used by *our* programmers, kontrollers, and handlers in subsequent years, *we* were systematically sexually abused from infancy through adulthood. *We* are still being sexually abused, though the explanation for this needs to be left until later in the book after the reader has grasped how *tmk* programming affects *our* own continually running internal programming along with program access via external forces.

From infancy on, *we* were consistently abused and sexually traumatized to create early alters who would participate in a willing manner with their abusers. Such willingness is a direct result of systematic victimization by *our* programmers. There have been many, many downloads in which *our* alters—child, adolescent, teen, and adult—were not only participating but were instigating sexual acts and engaging enthusiastically *after* being triggered by *our* abusers. This is how programming works: once successfully triggered, the alters are in kontrol of *our* mind and body, having been completely programmed at a young age to perform sex acts that normal children don't even know of, let alone perform with enthusiasm and skill. (More on this later, though due to its integral nature in *our* programming, *we* wish to give it the necessary introduction here.)

Thus *our* formative years were shaped by perverse acts of sex with *our* father and at least one of *our* brothers (as well as outsiders). From the crib

1

years forward, these sexual acts were combined with systematic physical, emotional, mental, and spiritual trauma and torture (electroshock, drugs, rape, drowning, suffocation, *alien* encounters and abduction, near death experiences, etc.) to seal them as programming as well as creating my psychic access to other realms. Such techniques of what today is known as *trauma-based mind control* allowed *our* programmers to fragment and split *our* mind into alters that could then be programmed to be used to do their bidding. (These sophisticated techniques were implemented at various locations including military bases as well as unknown locations.)

We still deeply struggle to dismantle the programs that transform repetitive pain into pleasure (sadomasochism or S&M) and extract *ourselves* from the grip of *our* programmers, kontrollers, and handlers. This struggle is very intense and difficult due to the complex nature of the internal programming *we* are still under. Even within *our* deep deprogramming, *we* continue to struggle with the disabling programmed behaviors and desires of *our* alters as they present to *us*, all the while having to thwart direct interactions with those still being sent to access *our* programming in an attempt to continue to kontrol *us*.

The Infant

Our first conscious memory of abuse is as a preverbal infant, when *our* original or core self was splintered off, followed by an experience that designed the *rabbit* personality at three years old. This is the earliest experience memory thus far presented to *us* by alters attempting to show *us* the original *us* or at the very least someone closely associated with her. What *we* now attempt to relay is the body memory with a full **abreaction** coming from *our* preverbal infant who is co-existing with others of *us* so she can relay her trauma involving suffocation, followed by the memory of a trauma inflicted to split a three-year-old involving men in Navy issue clothing. Within this memory, *we* switched back and forth between the alters presenting while at the same time remained consciously aware of the collective of alters. Body memories are so numerous throughout *our* life that *we* are aware of their surfacing prior to their presentation, as was the case here.

We were just finishing a long distance voicemail download to one of the men supporting *our* attempts in deep deprogramming when *we* began to cry: a body memory was being brought to *us* by several alters. After

2

hanging up the phone, *we* reclined on *our* bed as the front alters became aware of another alter holding *our* body as *our* body moved into a position that *we* would later realize was *us* in an infant's body, the infant manifesting *pre-verbal* arm and leg movements as well as consciousness.

Through the sobs and contortions of her in *our* adult body in the here and now, *we* experienced the infant's pain and screams from long ago, still very present within *us*. Her mouth was stretched as wide as it would go and *we* were trying to scream, yet no sound was coming out. The pain was everywhere without her knowing *Why?* After her mouth was momentarily free, *we* sobbed and rolled about, then again she was holding *our* body, her mouth again blocked from screaming and breathing, stretched as wide as it would go.

We do not know how long this went on, time not being felt. *We* became aware that *we* were *seeing* and *feeling* through her as she stared blankly at one spot on the ceiling, completely empty inside. *We* were making a movement with *our* mouth, creating a sound from within her small body, on her back, her arms and legs held in that infant way. It took *us* several minutes to realize it was the end of what had happened to her and she was now adrift somewhere, empty, dissociated, staring at the ceiling, smacking her lips to alleviate the feeling there.

Then a sound issued from *our* mouth, a familiar sound that occurs often after body memories in deprogramming—not very loud, but a subdued release of air as though gently holding it from escaping to prevent it from creating too much noise, allowing *us* to go unnoticed—a constant, continuous, soft hum that creates a vibration in *us* that becomes the total focus of *our* mind—a sound that *feels* pleasant to *us* in that nothing prior to it exists.

[This sound was from another child alter, though I do not know her age I would continue to encounter this sound occasionally throughout deep deprogramming as awful memories surfaced. She was providing this in the here and now as a participant in this revelation, hoping to help ease the pain for all of *us*.]

Within the hours following this memory experience—including a full abreaction—*our* alters presented information to *us* through *jacked*, a neuter alter who is the presenter for several other alters with much to tell *us*. *Jacked* also will talk to someone it trusts who is sincerely interested and knows that what has happened to *us* is real. The man that works

3

with *us* in *our* deep deprogramming has received many downloads from *jacked*. *Jacked* provided *us* with understanding that this infant was part of *our* original self—a reflection, so to speak, of our original self. The main front alter did not fully understand this until *our* alters holding this information revealed it because she was part of what disappeared within *us* so long ago when she was associated with *our* core before *our* mind was fragmented.

Rabbit

The memory of the experience that designed the *rabbit* personality at three years old was shown to *us* by the three year old alter herself. We *see* her as a *rabbit*, what she is in *our* consciousness and what *we* visually see her as. She never speaks verbally and so by thought transference, she said that this experience designed her.

The memory begins with *us* looking down at a 20° angle on a man with blond hair and blue eyes some fifteen feet or so away in a very large warehouse. *We* feel nothing at all in this part of the memory—a common dissociated state for many of *our* alters. *We* are evidently above where he is standing next to a metal cot with a bare mattress, no linens. *We* can still *see* the thin, pale red pinstripes on the cream-colored fabric with fabric-covered buttons creating indentations. Behind him are long, high rows of large metal shelves of three or four levels. It is difficult to see exactly what these are, though sometimes *we feel* deeply that some of *us* cannot bear to know.

He is chained to the cot by a roughly six-foot metal chain attached to a device screwed into his head. *We* can hear the chain against the metal frame of the cot as he moves. Blood seeps from his head. He has been badly beaten and his clothes are bloody. He is wearing Navy-issued denims and has a blank stare on his face as if he is totally gone, dissociated.

Immediately, *we* are aware of voices and sounds of men approaching from *our* right and know what is going to happen, thanks to another alter sharing a part of the memory of what is to come. *We* turn *our* head as four men in Navy denims come around the tall metal shelf-like structure behind the man chained to the cot. The men are talking to one another in a jovial, normal day sort of way, even laughing as they approach. *We* see that whatever these metal shelf type structures are, *we* are on the same, having rows of each on either side of the cot.

[I have come to understand these as small cages stacked one upon another in rows. This is rather common in facilities that contain and harvest **adrenochrome**, as well as supply mind controlled children and adults to pedophiles and human traffickers, including those practicing Satanism.]

The memory ends there for *rabbit*, yet *we* know that the chained, beaten man is finished off in front of *us*. *Rabbit* was designed by this experience.

Rabbit would show *us* another memory of when *we* were in bed with *our* father sleeping with his back to *us*. *We* were very young and small and the bed seemed so big with him on the left side and *us* as far to the right as *we* could get without falling off. Down the side of the bed on the floor next to the bed is *rabbit* who doesn't talk but *we* know what she needs. She is very hungry and thirsty and the kitchen is not far, yet *we* are afraid to leave the bed. *We* have to get her water, so *we* look at the back of the sleeping man and decide to very quietly go and get a small dish of water for her. *We* do this with terror in *our* heart because *we* do not want to awaken the man. The bottom drawer of the nightstand is open, it has two drawers, and there is some type of natural fibers in there that *rabbit* has started to eat.

[My father was my sexual abuser for the early years and well into young adulthood, with my victimized brother having an incestuous relationship with me into our early teens as I understand it. Much of the horrific abuse came from outsiders in the military/intelligence and private sectors. I still do not know the circumstances of my being handed off to military/intelligence from my family. Clearly the ONI (Office of Naval Intelligence) was a significant part of early programming and into teen years.]

The next childhood memory *we* have occurred at five years old. It takes place in Tennessee, *our* second home. *We* are uncertain at what age *we* moved there.

Childhood Aliens

We are standing outside along the edge of the street a few houses down from ours in an altered state. Our older brother is playing in the street while we stand in the gutter looking across the street over the houses at a brilliant ball of light far away in the clear blue, cloudless, high noon sky. We know it is coming to us but feel no fear. Our brother has not yet seen it, though we only notice his unaware state in our peripheral vision because we can't take our eyes off the brilliant ball of light coming very quickly but getting smaller as it nears.

By the time it is over the house across the street, it is no longer a ball of light but a 3D *orb* moving gently, angularly, and gracefully—with intention. In a soft, intentional motion, it crosses the street and comes to a stop inches from *our* face. Inside it, various subdued colors are swirling—creams, tans, browns, and blues with a faint iridescence showing now and then. *We* know it is alive. *We* are also aware that *our* brother is now standing to *our* left, very close and silent, looking at the orb. Then the conscious memory ends.

Years later, *we* would discover that this town in Tennessee is a region in which other *tmk* victims as well as "*alien* abductees" have reported heavy encounters. *We* want to be clear: with *our* extensive personal encounters of this type throughout *our* life, *we* do not know of any of these beings to be Benevolent in nature. *We* can and will only write of *our* personal encounters and abductions. They are certainly connected to our *total mind kontrol* programming.

[This has changed significantly in deep deprogramming. There have been encounters of a very different kind with clearly Benevolent energies. We understand these beings to be related to Christ and those who work for the good of humanity.]

But this is not the only conscious memory *we* have while living in this home in Tennessee. The next occurs when *we* are six years old. *We* would be in *our* early thirties when *we* would finally be shown by *our* alter what actually occurred that evening, a memory that came flooding up because of the circumstances preceding the abduction, namely catching fireflies at dusk with *our* eldest brother. It was a profound memory, one that *we* remembered with much emotion.

We are standing in the woods behind *our* house at dusk catching and releasing fireflies with an old mayonnaise jar with the screw-top lid. While looking at *our* smiling eldest brother, *we* get hit with a blinding light so intense that *we* immediately have a severe headache and are unable to see anything other than blinding brightness. *We* knew as a child that this light was extraordinary in that it could penetrate *us* and yet *didn't leave a shadow.*

6

The next thing *we* recall is that *we* are sitting in a room on a table of some sort, with *our* feet dangling off one end. *We* are alone. The first thing frighteningly apparent to *us* is the incredible silence in the room, a deafening silence—an oxymoron *we* know, yet are afraid to speak at first. What *we* knew, though *we* do not recall how *we* knew, was that someone was going to come through the door and *we* were very frightened by who that was going to be. *Our* fear got the best of *us* and *we* began calling out for *our* brother, saying aloud, "I want my jar; where is my jar?"

Next, *we* realize that someone is close to *us* to *our* left, someone shorter than an adult, given that *we* are a six year old up on a table looking at a slight angle down. *We* glanced and saw the back right side of a head that frightened *us* so terribly that *we* quickly looked away and stared into *our* lap at *our* hands, trying desperately not to acknowledge what *we* had seen. *We* can still clearly see that it was not a human head but bulbous just above where the head meets the neck. An exaggerated dimple similar to but larger than what humans have between the tendons was at that point, the skin translucent white with visible blue and pink veins and capillaries. The conscious memory ends there.

In *our* early thirties, a hypnotherapist who *we* believe was actually, wittingly or unwittingly, reprogramming *us* for *our* programmers, kontrollers, and handlers tried to access more of this memory. Repeated attempts to find out what occurred between the blinding light hitting *us* and being in that room were to no avail and all *we* got was an excruciating headache.

A very telling circumstance at this time in *our* life is that the elder brother present at the time of this abduction in the woods had previously drawn, while in New Jersey, an elaborate underground tunnel system with machines and equipment and soldiers moving about. *We* would not recall his drawing until *our* programming began to severely break into *our* conscious front alter's mind in *our* early thirties.

During the first few months of *our* deep deprogramming in April 2008, *we* would experience the flashing of a brilliant white light *inside* *our* head as *our* young child sex alters surfaced with their memories. As of October 2010, *we* are certain that this particular abduction was not an *"alien* abduction" per se, but a sex ritual in the woods behind *our* home during which *we* were raped and sodomized. The latter brutality to such a small child is the direct cause of the blinding white light that *we* were experiencing in *our* head alongside an instant debilitating headache as new alters were created to cope with the pain and trauma. *We* believe *"alien*

7

abduction" screen memories were used to prevent *us* from remembering certain things. However, *we* believe this traumatic event pushed *our* consciousness into another realm. Screen memories would be programmed into *our* young mind over the years during and after trauma and torture that would come. Additionally, various parts of *us* were being designed to reach beyond this world as a needed capacity for use later. More will be written about what was truly occurring as opposed to what was to be remembered.

[This type of activity during trauma and torture can and has revealed other beings of other timelines and "places." It is utilized in MKUltra methods to open such abilities. These encounters would continue into deep deprogramming, not only as memory, but as current experience. Another factor to consider is the use of **Optogenetics** in mind control.]

There are more memories associated with this neighborhood, including a man who lived down the street—memories that involve life-threatening fear and a great malevolent darkness, as well as fire.

Missing Time

At eight years old, *our* father moved *our* family yet again, putting us near the military installation of MacDill Air Force Base in Tampa, Florida that was infamous for *tmk*. There, *we* would be programmed throughout *our* teens. (See Resources for more on programming sites.)

In *our* second grade classroom at the end of school one day, *we* had a missing time experience. Thanks to corroborating witnesses, namely *our* mother and father, *we* can write of this experience.

We can still *see ourselves* erasing the chalkboard, then all goes blank, the next conscious memory being of walking home alone and later in the afternoon than usual. *We* knew this even at the time of this experience because of anxiety about middle schoolers getting out later and being verbally abusive to us younger ones as we passed their school, a location we would walk by each day on *our* way home. *We* were alone, uncertain of where *our* schoolmates had gone. Just as *we* neared the middle school, *our* father pulled up in the car, opened the door, and shouted, "Where the hell have you been? Get in this car!" *We* were fearful of his temper and at a loss as to why he was angry.

8

We got in the car and began to tell him *we* had been with *our* teacher Mrs. Smith, and that she had asked *us* and Laurie (another female student) to stay after school to help clean the chalkboards and erasers. *We* thought nothing of it as Laurie and *i*, a young front alter, were teacher's pets. But he said it was late afternoon, *we* had been missing for several hours, and that he and *our* mother had called the school only to be told that all of the students and teachers had gone home. He told *me* that they had called the police and that *our* mother was at home vomiting because she knew *we* were "gone"—her word that *i* would hear later in life. This fear had plagued her since we children were small—probably a belief instilled in her by her mother. Her fear that *we* would be "taken" (her word) ran deep.

The missing time was never resolved, nor do *we* recall any attempt by *our* parents to do so, nor if they really had called the police. *I* have no memory of how *we* were back then, even the front alters, due, *i* believe, to all of the switching between alters that went on in *our* childhood and adolescence.

However, during *our* time in second grade, *we* were extremely fearful of going to school—terrified and living with a non-ordinary level of anxiety associated with *our* demise. Some of *us* were certain *we* would die there. Part of *our* terror was of another eight year old's ongoing sexual advances during class and caused *us* unbelievable confusion and panic over what presented as his and *our* sexual relationship—real even to *our* front alters because of what we believe was abuse occurring at this time for both *us* and him at school.

Our opinion is that both of us were being abused and this was breaking into *our* and his front alters, terrifying *us* as well as causing *us* to have to deal with the crossover, a tremendous burden to *our* various parts. Later in *our* high school, *we* would encounter this same boy, having not seen him since second grade, and go into a severe state of PTSD triggered by *our* alter's memory—something *we* can readily identify with since so many of *our* alters deal with fragments of other parts' lives, even into *our* deep deprogramming.

We front alters had no conscious memory of being engaged in any sexual relationship with this young boy's alters, perhaps because it was sequestered with *our* other young parts. *We* lived in an unknown childhood terror while *our* young front alter presentations were of a somewhat disturbed little girl with high anxiety only at times apparent to those around *us*. *Our* programming made sure of this.

9

[While living in Tennessee, we twisted the hair off of our head on one side. This was usually done while sucking our thumb. My mother said I had long blonde locks on one side and stubble on the other. This would carry well into adulthood, yet with carpet fuzz instead of hair (thank goodness!) I recall flashes of finding carpet fuzz and rolling it up between my thumb and forefinger well into my late twenties, possibly even my thirties. This gave me a subtle sense of peace. I see this as an unconscious acting out of what was being kept from my conscious mind due to the amnesiac walls separating our alter's memories.]

Alien Abduction?

This experience also took place when *we* were eight years old. *We* were sleeping in the recliner chair in the living room of the apartment *our* family lived in. *We* had slipped and fallen at the apartment complex pool earlier that day and *our* back was hurting. *We* awaken in the dark and know that *they* are here.

Immediately in front of *our* face inches from *our* nose is the face of a gray *alien* with big black eyes. *We* feel completely relaxed while looking at him. (As an adult, *we* would like to note here that the feeling was the equivalent of being heavily drugged.) Trusting it completely, *we* are engaged in telepathic communication as levitation begins. Being young, *we* did not check to see if *we* were leaving *our* body, but it felt like *we* were levitating in *our* body. *We* still have vivid memories of the feeling like tiny bubbles under *our* skin as *we* became lighter and lighter and began to lift out of the chair. The memory then fragments and *we* see the nighttime sky.

Next, *we* are lying in a room with several of these beings around *us*, including the one who came for *us*, *our* friend. They stuck something up *our* left nostril that hurt and *we* began to cry and demand to go home. All of a sudden, *our* friend is at *our* right side again close to *our* face and *we* start to feel good again. Next, *we* are returning to the chair in the living room and the weight of *our* body becomes heavy, dense, and suffocating.

Years later, *we* would describe it as the feeling of putting on a sweater that is far too small. At that point, the *alien* face is again inches from *our* face. *We* giggle because *we* are told not to tell *our* mother, though nothing is said about telling *our* father—strange until one realizes he is one of the ones who has been abusing *us*; that he is one of *our* main abusers is *our* secret. But whose secret, really? *Ours* and the *alien*'s? *Ours* and *our* father's?

And it wasn't just the two of us present in this memory; others were there. Who? The memory fragments end there for this alter.

The profound feeling of becoming weightless and then returning to the incredible heaviness of *our* body is still with *us*. Leaving the body, dissociating as well as what *i* believed was levitating ("flying")—both seemed real experiences to *us*. Also, what would strike *us* later as an adult is that this friend with the *alien* face seemed rather two-dimensional. Nor did *we* see a spaceship, as was also true in the abduction at six years old in a previous entry. It is possible that this particular abduction, like several others, was rife with holograms or some type of virtual reality known to *us* now as screen memories.

However, almost two years after *we* began *our* deep deprogramming, *we* learned that accessing the pineal gland up through the nasal cavity can "awaken" certain latent abilities. What *we* knew by the time *we* heard this is that *we* have some exceptional abilities within the physical world and beyond the physical world as most know it, and that these abilities can be accentuated and utilized by *our* programmers, kontrollers, and handlers.

("*Alien* abductions" are often screen memories installed within programmed alters to obscure what is really occurring: esoteric occult rituals of which many of *us* have fragmented memories—terrible rituals involving sex, human sacrifice, and cannibalism. And yet *we* do indeed believe at this time that the programmers and kontrollers are very *alien*, meaning *demonic* and malevolent, the two being practically one in the same. There are other memories of human perpetrators accompanied by beings of another realm.)

Breathing Underwater

In *our* late forties, *we* would finally read about Navy experiments to create amphibious soldiers—*tmk* slaves with unusual abilities. *Our* connections to the Navy were already there, including members from both sides of *our* parents' families. As *our* programming broke down over the years, *we* would have more pool downloads, including one by an alter who as a teenager was in a very deep pool with two other people. (See Chapter 2, "The Teen Years", *The Breathing Pool*.)

While living in Florida in the apartment with the swimming pool, *we* told *our* mother that *we* were able to breathe underwater. She dismissed this as fanciful and yet cautioned *us* not to try it in the apartment pool. Of course *we* did repeatedly, but always came up coughing, baffled as to why it didn't work. *We* clearly remembered having done it there before, even how *we* had to breathe in the water slowly at first. Years later, *we* would realize that the original water of *our* memory had been slightly thicker than regular water—not something an eight year old would pay a lot of attention to. Obviously, the apartment pool was a cover or screen memory and not the actual setting for the lesson in breathing underwater.

In 1990, *we* would have *our* first exposure to others' reports of "breathing pools" during alien abductions in *Secret Life: Firsthand Documented Accounts of UFO Abductions* by David Jacobs (1993). When I turned the page to the chapter titled "BreathingPools", it sent me into an abreaction just by seeing the words. [I have recently looked at the table of contents of this book online, and see no mention of a chapter titled such. Perhaps this has been edited in recent years? The adult memory while deprogramming is quite clear. Perhaps it was another book?] *We* wound up locking the front door to the retail store where *we* were working at the time, and curling up in the back in the bathroom until *we* could compose ourselves.

Secret Life also contained experiences of a person we'll call "L" to whom *we* would eventually become very close when *our* major programming was breaking down in *our* early thirties and *we* were looking everywhere for help. She told us she worked directly with Dr. Jacobs attempting to deal with her own memories. *I* surmised she was a victim of *total mind kontrol* herself, possibly sent as containment to lock down *our* memories, and succeeded in postponing *our* deprogramming and assuring *our* continued use. It appears from *our* alter's memories that "L" was a part of *our* programming as early as in *our* teens (with perhaps even earlier than that).

[I would also find out in the 1990s that she had worked in New Jersey for years for the military contractor Siemens in an administrative position. The apparent memories of her from our teens could have been placed in after we started to have program breakdown. Her presence in our early memory retrieval is valid, and I believe she had no idea that she was assisting in our continued use.]

As difficult as it must be for those living outside the life of a *tmk* slave, in *our* deep deprogramming *we* cannot deny the reality of the many abilities *our* alters have. Even *our* front alters have difficulty with this, despite having seen enough firsthand high strangeness in *tmk* programming to recognize the need to at least keep an open mind. *Our* conclusions are that abilities like underwater breathing are desired by certain covert black projects and that what was done to *me* was some part of that as evidenced in the drowning tortures during programming. *We* can still hear in *our* head *Stop holding your breath* while *we* were underwater with more than one man standing over *us* looking down at *us* while *we* were unable to surface.

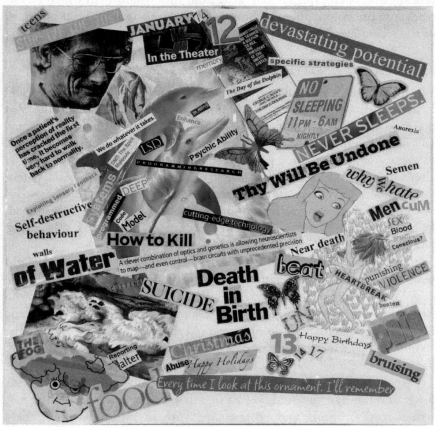

Devastating Potential

[To this day, in 2022, it still seems a possibility due to all the research that has surfaced while in deep deprogramming regarding this topic. This drowning or near drowning technique relates to splitting the mind as well as pushing the psyche into other realities. I am aware of our ability to access places and beings living in other realities, as well as timelines. I am reluctant to label those other realities since I have no real evidence of what and where they are. However, that they exist in a very real way, I've no doubt. In deep deprogramming I consciously experienced some of them, and in one case a being resembling a Greek god statue, though quite alive and surprised by my seeing him in what I call my mind's eye (sixth chakra/ pineal gland open), quickly retreated from the "window" in which he entered into my vision. These abilities and behaviors devoid of fear are many of the techniques I now use to thwart them when they reach out.]

Black Patent Leather and Nancy the Cheerleader

While at work one day in the late 2000s in the New Mexico, *we* would have another conscious download from *our* alters of programming that occurred at the age of eight. *We* were idly watching foot traffic in the small village in which *we* worked when across the street a woman exited a small cafe carrying a large black patent leather handbag. Immediately, a child alter's memory surfaced of *us* in a cheerleading costume and black patent leather boots with heels. Both the alter and *we* remember clearly *our* days as a cheerleader for *our* father's and brother's Little League football team in Tennessee. But that front alter cheerleader wore white tennis shoes, not black patent leather boots with heels.

The rest of the memory surfaced later that night. There *we* were at eight years old in black patent leather boots and a cheerleading costume made of gold light-weight corduroy with black trim seducing an older man who was not *our* father and singing Nancy Sinatra's "These Boots Were Made for Walking" in a manner no eight year old should know, let alone do. The song would play in *our* head for days during *our* alter *Nancy*'s presentation, named no doubt for Nancy Sinatra, the song's original performer.

By this time in *our* deep deprogramming, many child alters with sex programming had surfaced, yet to this day *we* have not become accustomed to discovering and experiencing with them. Understand: these alters were under years of extreme programming and had little sense of right or wrong, their pleasure and participation due to malevolent programming.

Once Upon a Time

2
The Teen Years

These years are so fragmented, *we* initially wondered if they existed at all. *We* have detailed fragments as *we* do for the late teens and early twenties, and with time these fragments are connecting and allowing huge gaps to be filled. Slowly, *we* have come to understand why alters chose to remain hidden for so long, the teen years being a time *we* needed to protect *ourselves* from remembering, when *we* were under the full kontrol of *our* programmers, kontrollers, and handlers, *our* programming locked in.

Unhappy Birthdays

Through several alters' memories, *we* have realized that *our* birthdays were not celebrations for *us*. Instead, they were times for programming and use and keeping *us* bound to them through the idea that they kontrolled *our* birth and death. Throughout *our* adult life, *we* have never enjoyed birthdays or holidays, and now *our* front alters understand why: calendar observations were often occasions for major programming. Thus *we* have chosen to not celebrate cultural occasions as *our* affirmation to choose, choice being something *we* are learning to assert while attempting to not hide any longer. It has been part of *our* front alter's programming to deny what *we see* and *feel* and act otherwise. Never have *we* felt connected to the "world of man" around *us*, and birthdays and holidays are just one of many examples why.

The next memory seemed rather benign, as some do until they are seen in the context of the rest of *our* life. *Our* memory in *our* front alter is of going to a movie with *our* friends for *our* birthday.

Innocent enough? It is *our* 12th birthday and *we* are with several other girls about *our* age in a theatre watching the 1973 movie *The Day of the Dolphin*. The strange thing is *we* cannot identify the girls with *us* in the theatre, except for one, a friend from a large Catholic family. All *we* can remember is that *our* mother is with us, the exception being flashbacks of movie details. From *our* seat, *we* can partially *see* a group of girls numbering about half a dozen. *We* cannot recall if there were other people in the theatre or not. Like the fireflies memory, this innocent-appearing experience has a profound effect on *us*.

During *our* adult deep deprogramming research, *we* began to wonder about Dr. John C. Lilly due to his connections to research into sensory deprivation, dolphins, and *The Day of the Dolphin*. *We* were immediately back in that theatre on *our* 12th birthday. *We* could remember George C. Scott in the film, yet not the storyline.

As *we* read the storyline of *The Day of the Dolphin* in the Lilly article, it talked of things undeniably linked to *tmk* programming and *our* particular use. *We* were now sure that the birthday memory was a screen memory. The baseline of *our* childhood programming was very pertinent to *our* subsequent use by *our* programmers. *Our* birthday was not a birthday party in the conventional sense but a day of programming with other girls *our* age. *Our* birthdays would show up again and again as occasions for programming. Dr. Lilly's work was used in *our* programming.

[See the film *The Day of the Dolphin* online to study how it could be used to program, as well as Lilly's possible associations to *tmk* programming techniques, "Programming and Metaprogramming in the Human Biocomputer", http://johnclilly.com/metaprog.html.]

The next memory is difficult to describe, particularly its effect on *our* main front alter. This will be the first time the main front alter *sees*, *hears*, and *feels* the events. It is also important to understand that the most disturbing memories continue to result in re-fragmenting *our* mind. According to some mental health professionals this is known as a full abreaction. This occurred here. The memory was revealed the day before *our* 2009 birthday.

Our front alter's encounter with the experience memory went something like this: In the early morning hours of present day, *we* were fully conscious in the present while seeing in *our* mind's eye a girl in her late teens lying in the grass below, her face covered with hair matted and stringy, red with blood and white with wads of a clear fluid in great quantity. *We* instantly recognized this fluid as semen. She appeared only semi-conscious, not moving except for the slightest movement of her head. She was badly abused and incapacitated. *We* couldn't see her face due to the hair.

Over the course of the next several seconds, alters who were present at the original experience showed *us* this scene. Others of *us* were now present to *see* and *feel* it for the first time. *We see* her and ask, *Who is that?* Then *we* can *see* her blue eyes in *our* minds eye, but not physically, due to the bloody hair covering her face. It is then that *we* realize that she is *us*. Due to the severity of the abuse, more than one alter holds this memory, more than one alter being necessary within the original experience. *We* are above and out of *our* body, so dissociated that *we* do not even think it is *us* at first, hence asking, W*ho?*

We are lying on *our* right side, arms and legs slightly bent. The intensity of the fear and pain experienced during and within this memory is debilitating. *Our* alter let *us* know *we* were brutalized and raped and men ejaculated in *our* hair. *We* were told that the blood was not *ours*. She showed *us* the age *17*. Then *we* saw *14*, followed by *13*, telling *us* that this was a recurring event—*our* birthday "celebration".

This experience memory falls into the category that can never quite be filed away. Most of *our* alter's memories that surface are deeply disturbing, yet some just never seem to stop hurting, and making peace with them will take years, if ever. This is one of those. *Our* abreaction to this experience memory lasted for weeks. To this day, it brings a deep sadness accompanied by someone's desire within *us* to die.

"Female", Not a Woman

This memory seemed surreal until many years later *we* came to understand who and what *we* are. *We* are walking through the living room in the home where *we* spent most of *our* adolescent and teen years. As *we* near the sliding glass doors on the south side, *we* realize it is night. *We* are dressed in a flannel nightgown and carrying a stuffed animal in *our* right arm held close to *our* chest while *our* left hand holds the hand of a wide-eyed little boy. (Over the years, more than 25 stuffed animals were given to *us* by *our* father—reinforcements to *our* programming and representative of some of *our* alters.) The wide-eyed little boy is listening to *us* telepathically as *we* ask him to take care of *our* stuffed animal so precious to *us*. Telepathically, he assures *us* that he will.

At this point in the experience, *we* know that the wide-eyed little boy is a small *alien being* with very large eyes and that *we* are going with them. *We* have always been able to see these *beings*, but it is safer for some of *our* young alters to *see* a little boy.

18

We release the stuffed animal to him and let go of his hand as *we* walk out of the already open sliding glass door and onto the grass in *our* back-yard. *We* stop and look up into the night sky and see a human-looking "female" flying about. *We* know that *we* are to join her, so *we* close *our* eyes and begin to concentrate, focusing on being with her as *we* begin to lift slowly off the ground—something in *our* programmed youth that *we* are quite familiar with and *we* know how to do because they taught *us*.

Let Your Dreams Take Flight

[Obviously, this is astral projection, otherwise known as leaving the body. Even in my youth I had the ability to dissociate easily thanks to all the trauma. They are the ones who taught us it is "flying". Astral programming and reinforcement is extensively used by the humans and the malevolent *beings* involved. They are involved in technologies in current times beyond the comprehension of most. That the black projects are 50+ years ahead (I find it to be farther along than that quite honestly) of anything above ground is true in my experience. This in many aspects is due to the esoteric practices of the groups that truly run things. (See *Our Invisible Bodies: Scientific Evidence for Our Subtle Bodies* by Jay Alfred, 2007 to understand more about subtle bodies.]

Our thoughts waver and *we* begin to descend, so *we* refocus on being with her and not just thinking about her. For this young alter, it is a very visual experience and she *sees* herself up there with this "female". She lifts off with a tremendous amount of focus, partly due to having already learned how to "fly". Then *we* are moving about in the air with this "female". *We* look down to the yard. There is a man, *our* father, yet to this alter he did not *feel* like her father standing in the yard looking up with a blank expression on his face, frozen in time. To *us*, he looks sad, so *we* swoop down towards him, yet he remains unresponsive. She feels a deep sadness for him.

Next, *we* are seated at a long narrow table like the ones with the foldout legs you see at conventions, the top made of a faux wood, the legs metal, with simple metal folding chairs—very "earthly" furniture, with the "female" seated across from *us*. To the right of her directly in front of *us* is seated a "woman" with brunette hair, her back to *us*, her head leaning on her arm on the table. *We* never see her face. *We* feel emotionally detached, *we* are being taught. The "female" looks at *us* as *we* stare at the back of the head of the "woman", then at the "female" whose hair is blond like *ours*.

Looking into her eyes, *we* hear in *our* head, *You are a female like me, not a woman. Do you understand?*

We completely understand, as if in that moment *we* knew and understood on a cellular level what was and was not stated. As if *we* had always known this, *we* telepathically respond, *Yes, i understand. Yes, i remember.* *We* recall the whole body sensation with a visual and mental understanding of all that this implied for *us*. *We* felt no emotion at all while remembering that *we* would never live the life of a "woman," ever. *We* were different and would have a different life.

(*We* had already been programmed for many years for that different life and for this alter at this time there was not even a question to be asked.

We did not reason or ask such things of these alters. There had always been something that *we* knew about *us* that *we* could not explain and she was reminding *us* of it. This was all part of dissociating *me* from everyone in the world around *us*. This in time would lead to much better use of *us* for what was intended.)

The "female" then parted her lips so *we* would see her incisors longer than a human's. *We* clearly understood that this would be something *we* would come to understand more fully at another time, but now it was clear to *us* that *we* were a "female", not a "woman".

There are many things *we* now know about this, things that would not surface until *we* began a more intense breakdown of *our* programming in *our* early thirties. The "female" represented here was a screen cover for the being and/or humans involved in this program session. This person shown to *us* would be a part of *our* front alter's life in the years to come, more than a decade after this programming experience. The presentation of the incisors were part of this alter's conscious indoctrination into vampirism, the ingestion of human blood in particular. More on this later.

Brutality to the Young

This alter experience download would be one that would leave *us* with an understanding of why so many of these experiences were compartmentalized within *our* fragmented mind. Their presentations to *our* front alters were always devastating, yet in *our* deep deprogramming *our* understanding of the necessity for many of these alters to present to *us* for some level of freedom to take place was enhanced.

We are standing a couple of feet from a cinder block wall inside an emotionless alter of the teen years who is very dissociated. (The cinder block wall is a wall within *our* own mind due to fragmenting. Breaching this wall is the alter's memory.)

Over the top of the wall a teenage girl falls towards *us* with *us* thinking she is learning to "fly" on the other side of the wall as *we* were taught to "fly" by *our* programmers. She is badly beaten and bloodied, with a compound fracture to her right arm so extreme that part of the forearm and hand are dangling.

There is a rush of confusion over who this teenage girl is. This is an attempt to decide if she is one of *us* or not. She did not look like *us*, however, at other times we don't look like *us* either (*rabbit, crystal sex alters*, etc.), often even changes occur in our physical human body (eye color, shape of

21

face, etc.) It quickly becomes clear it is not one of us and this girl's imminent death is apparent.

She is incapable of speech. Her eyes meet *ours*. *Help me*, she pleads
telepathically.

Our dissociated, emotionless thought responds, *I cannot help you*.

It is *our* understanding that she indeed was not *us* and that one of *us*
was present at her demise. With *our* heart pounding, the *entity* presence
at the time of this resurfacing memory was very strong. Though a low
level *entity*, its effect on *our* emotional and physical state required much
prayer effort to eliminate its *demonic* presence from the room the memory
resurfaced in. At last, *we* succeeded and were left with much sadness over
the poor young teenage girl's demise. *Our* lack of compassion and ability
to assist her, due to *our* own programming under this alter, continues to
haunt *us*.

The Deep Breathing Pool

An alter that *we* refer to as *the breathe underwater alter* showed *us* another
experience memory in a very deep, very large breathing pool in which *we*
were not alone. The pool may have been one hundred feet long and twenty
to thirty feet deep at its deepest end, the floor being a gradual descent.

The deepest end is where she, *our* alter, is submerging herself feet first
with her arms, easily and calmly holding her breath. When she hits the
bottom, she turns her head to the left and sees two other individuals in the
distance in dark outer wear standing on the bottom, one in the shallower
end, the other roughly in the middle. *Our* alter then looks forward and
gently begins to inhale the water, filling *our* lungs with breath. As when
we were younger, this *breathe underwater alter* draws it in very gently, her
consciousness showing *us* that she was taught this by *them*, those *we* had
come to know as *alien beings*.

As time has progressed, *we* understand these *others* to be one and the
same as the *entities* and *demons* that *we* have encountered throughout *our*
life since *our* first consciously remembered experience at five years old.
(See Book 1, Chapter 1, "Shattering a Young Mind: The Early Years",
Breathing Underwater.)

We have also come to realize in *our* deep deprogramming that several
aspects of *our* programming came into play in this experience. *We* have a
recurring body memory of drowning and other memories, including a tank

22

of water with men above *us* telling *us* to stop holding *our* breath. *We* are certain this was part of the trauma perpetrated on *us* several times by *our* programmers to facilitate the fragmenting of *our* mind.

In *our* deep deprogramming, *we* have also found references to programmers attempting to create an "amphibious human" able to breathe underwater. This ability and two other abilities that *we* have (according to alter downloads) are supposed to be physical impossibilities in this three dimensional world. But *we* know, beyond any doubt, that *our* alters can do these things without *our* front alters being able to explain how.

[It is my contention still, almost fifteen years into deprogramming, that what can and cannot be done in the physical human body is subject to esoteric arts. In this case, black esoteric arts. I still cannot explain these memories (abilities?), however, as mentioned previously there is much evidence of deep research into making humans "**Übermensch**", or superhuman. It is also still my contention that the black esoteric sciences and technologies born of such are used in MKUltra and have been for decades and that current technologies are light-years ahead of above ground systems known to the general public. There is ample evidence of covert military/intelligence organizations researching this. See the declassified document below from 1969. Additionally, as explained previously in *Breathing Underwater*, this is used to create abilities that reach beyond the physical world as we know it. See Appendix B: "The Feasibility of Liquid Breathing in Man," 1969 document.]

We acknowledge that this may sound like a rationalization for *our* surviving drowning torture; however, the cross-dimensional *demonology* aspect of programming must be understood and considered when speaking of such matters.

Nowhere to Hide

Another late teens experience seemed strange until *we* realized that others who have been *tmk* slaves had been reporting having similar experiences with almost identical verbal messages.

The experience occurs in the home in Florida near MacDill Air Force Base in which *we* underwent programming from adolescence until *we* turned 18. When the conscious download of this experience memory

23

starts, *we* are running about the living room, dining room and kitchen in ambient lit darkness, alone and terrified: a dark helicopter is hovering silently in the backyard, yet *we* can hear the sound of the air in the blades, an intermittent *whoosh! We* see it in slow motion, probably due to the terror making *us* dissociate. *We* are running from hiding place to hiding place—a corner in the dining room, under the dining room table, up against the lower cabinets in the kitchen, between the sofa and coffee table in the living room—while men in black fatigues surround the house, armed with semi-automatics emitting red laser light. When *we* sit still, *our* heart pounding, *we* realize that anywhere from three to six red laser dots are trained on *our* chest, hearing in *our* head, *There is nowhere you can hide that we can't find you and kill you.* The words in a male voice are spoken calmly and matter-of-fact.

When *we* jumped up and ran to another spot, *we* experienced the same. Here, the conscious memory ends.

Later during deep deprogramming, *we* read an account of something so similar in Brice Taylor/Susan Ford's 1999 book, *Thanks for the Memories: The Truth Has Set Me Free* that *our* alters became physically ill at the implication. According to her account, this is a hunting game for the programmers and a program reinforcement for *tmk* slaves. Her version took place outdoors. *We* can assure the reader that the recurring message *nowhere you can hide* worked and continues to do so to this day.

Is it any wonder that *our* front alters spent so much of *our* life believing *we* must be crazy, while at the same time knowing that *we* needed to hang on a bit longer until someone would know what was happening to *us*?

Brought Together

This experience memory was presented in three segments by *our* alter along with other alters who know what she does not. The first segment of this memory involved two members of *our* biological family, one being *our* mother, the other a brother, and *our* mother is also present in the third segment, the most important here. The second segment is a flashback that *we* feel is unnecessary to relay here, though it involves both *our* alter and the man to whom it appears *we* are programmed. The first memory will also be left out.

Our interaction with this alter has been extensive, yet the main front alter did not realize that *we* had not visually *seen* her until this memory download. (Alters can present many revelations and yet also remain se-cretive. In the case of this alter, *we* had not *seen* her fully until this pre-sentation. I refer to this as *seeing* in my minds eye, the third eye.) This is quite real and detailed. She is in her teens and lovely to *us*. Her innocence is palpable, due to having no knowledge of programming, no memories of trauma, torture, or *entities, aliens*, or *demons*. During those times, other alters take over and allow her to stay in an innocent, devoted state to the one she devoutly loves, in what *we* believe is some sort of spiritual program binding. She has no idea that she, and possibly the one to whom she is devoted, is under *total mind kontrol*, nor that either of them are possessed by *entities* due to their placement during programming.

She and the other alters presented this memory, the trigger being the one known to *us* as "Cain". *Our* alter is possessed/utilized by Cain, *we* are told, a very powerful malevolent *being*.

The Secret Life of an American Teenager

[Cain seemed to play a significant role in my programming by these malevolent beings. Having relationship to more than one of my alters. This programming and reinforcement occurred mostly in an altered state, often in the astral plane and most often at night. It is my contention that this type of programming is even more common and frequent than the technological programming done at various locations by human perpetrators. During the night, when one is easily accessed, reinforcing programming also easily occurs.]

According to *our* downloads, the person *we* would be bound to is allegedly possessed by Cain and is apparently in intimate relationship with this alter and another one, *Alter 14.*

The third segment is key to the memory download. *Our* innocent alter is standing outdoors in the grass on what feels like a summer day with leaves on scattered trees rustling as a breeze blows. She is dressed in a long gown of pale golden yellow and green layers of chiffon with a v-neckline supported just below the breasts by a bodice. There are ruffles on the sleeveless shoulders made of the same chiffon. *We* look upon her and *feel* her innocence.

She is attempting to adjust the dress because it is now a little too big. She doesn't remember that she has lost weight, this time in *our* life being a time of excessive trauma with weight loss one of many side effects. In fact, she doesn't know why she is feeling physically unwell, lethargic and out of it, having no memory of what was done to *us* the night before due to other alters having been there for that. From within *our* deep deprogramming, *we* experience the pain *our* alters endured.

Her thoughts are only for *him.* He is coming today so they can be brought together. She is standing in the grass thinking of him. Off to her left is a long table covered with an abundance of food in the open field. The occasion is to bring them together. Several people are present that she refers to as family, yet *we* are only aware of *our* biological mother being present and do not know who the other family members are.

She reaches up and feels around her neck and ear lobes, realizing with a slight disappointment that she forgot to wear jewelry. But the out-of-it state she is in has dulled her concern for anything but *him.*

Just then, he walks out onto the grass with two men and sits between them on chairs. *Our* alter's heart is filled with utter devotion, he being the sole object of her programming.

This memory explained a lot to the rest of *us* about her undying utter devotion to this person and *our* relationship with the Cain *entity*.

[The degree of this devotional programming will be explained further under "More On Task" where I go further into this person's seeming personal-sexual use of one of my kill alters with heavy sexual programming. There will be updates on my alters and him in Book 2 as well.]

This event—including the night-before trauma—are part of being brought together in some sort of spiritual program binding, a binding *we* are now trying to break through deep deprogramming. The feelings that she still has for him run very deep in *us*. According to *our* memory downloads (programming) by more than one alter, the relationship with this person spanned more than two decades.

As of September 2010, *we* are still uncertain whether or not *our* relationship with this person—due to the very real relationship with the *demon* Cain present within this person—is strictly a programmed-in memory so this alter might be utilized with, by, or against this person, or if this relationship actually did exist in the physical contact world. *Our* inner world of programming is very real to many of *us*, just as real, if not more so, than the "world of man" going on around *us* to which *we feel* no significant connection due to extreme dissociation.

[Much of my life in my front alter consciousness always felt contrived. Meaning, even there I was aware that I did not understand many of the things going on around me and felt fraudulent. I would observe others and their reactions and emotions and in many instances I was trying to discern and imagine what was going on with them. I was painfully aware I was not like them. That I was deeply defective. On the outside looking in. The mind control programming creates and reinforces this each and every day.]

At what seemed great risk during deep deprogramming, we went to a talk given by this person who is a public figure. We believe him to be programmed as well for the very public persona he is. Remember, disinformation contains much truth to be believed, but it is half-truths which are very misleading and can be more destructive than full-out lies.

We still struggle with *our* programmed feelings for him, though it has lessened greatly, thanks to *our* willingness to interact with alters who at least appear to know him intimately.

As of October 2010, *we* thought it prudent to acknowledge that in the first year of *our* deep deprogramming *we* were shown a download by one of *our* kill alters—*alter 14*—of a program to kill this man while he spoke at a public event, a program revealed repeatedly over several months by *alter 14*. This kill alter has also downloaded to the rest of *us* her apparent sexual relationship with this man. (See Book 1, Chapter 8, "More On-Task", *Mutual Handling*.)

Greer's Girl

Our point here is that *we* are still uncertain of the true nature of *our* relationship to this man, though there are other pieces of information inclining *us* to believe that this is more than solely a programmed relationship taking place only in *our* mind, and that physical interaction with this man has also possibly taken place during *our* years of use. It remains unresolved at this time, nor do *we* consciously have the details of what took place out in that field that day to bring *us* together with that man.

[As regards this particular programming/binding episode, I believe that it was on the astral level, likely during our rest state at night, rather than in the physical realm. I have several reasons for believing this, but cannot say for certain. That there may indeed have been physical contact with this man in the subsequent years, remains a real possibility, though that could be a case of encountering him in programming sessions rather than actual interaction elsewhere. There are additional "encounters" with him and *alter 14.*]

3
"18"

"18" for *us* was an age when all hell began to break loose inside, due to their use of *us*. Things were done to *us* and by *us* under the kontrol of *our* programmers, kontrollers, and handlers. *We* were sent out to do their bidding which has not once been presented to *us* by *our* alters as anything other than terrible.

Torture, Programming, Guns, and Reptiles

We become aware, as opposed to waking up or opening *our* eyes. The awareness is a struggle, a very foggy state in which *we* at first are still very lost. Due to being heavily drugged, *our* alter is very groggy but trying to think, the struggle being to get through the fog in *our* head enough to even think.

We realize *we* are lying down, though at this point *our* eyes have not opened. *Our* body slams into a rigid, outstretched position, all of *our* muscles tightened, *our* head forced back and chin up in the air. This lasts for *we* don't know how many seconds when *our* body goes limp again.

Our ability to begin to ask what is happening to *us* arises. *We* open *our* eyes and try to look about, but are unable to move. Confusion arises. All is blurry, yet *we* *see* and *feel* that men are there. An excruciating pain slowly creeps into all of *our* nerve endings with an intensity that is frightening. *Our* alter hears a man's voice: "Three more rounds." *Our* body again goes rigid as it is forced into this position by whatever is being used on *us*. Once again *we* are released from this rigidity.

Though drugged and confused, *our* alter is aware of a pleasant, warm feeling between her legs. *We* become conscious of the fact that *we* are naked and cold and that the warmth between *our* legs is *our* own urine. *We* become somewhat cognizant of the fact *we* are in a terrible situation at the hands of others, *But who?*

Still fighting the heavy fog in *our* head, *we* become aware of a few things: *We* are naked and cold, lying on a table, and *we* have urinated on *our* self. To *our* right are two men, one in a white lab coat, the other in a khaki military uniform. Behind them are at least two men, maybe more, in this rather small, brightly lit room. Beyond *our* feet is a door off to the left guarded by another man with something long (rifle? baton?) in his hands. These men are shocking *us* and *our* alter is baffled and terrified. The excruciating pain is increasing and unbearable as *we* again go rigid. All goes black.

For years *our* main front alter was sure *we* were going crazy due to what *we* saw while lying on that table: To *our* left very close to *us*, we saw a dinosaur, its eye looking directly into *our* left eye. *We* could see his head, skin, and snout. It was reminiscent of the dinosaurs *we* had seen is in the movie *Jurassic Park*. (That comparison would come later, since the movie was not out in 1980.) When *we* finally told this occurrence to the two men helping to support *our* deprogramming years later, they said that they had heard similar first-hand reports from others and assured *us* that *we* were not crazy. The sheer terror felt within *us* while it was staring at *us* is some-thing others of *us* have felt over and over. That being's presence would continue through the years.

The second thing *we* saw in our head during this programming torture was a triangle made of blue light—a *delta*-shaped triangle set against the solid black background with a grid inside and "s" curves coming off the two bottom corners. What *we* were uncertain of was whether or not it came from inside *our* head or was put in there by them.

Next, *we* again become aware (as opposed to awakened or opening *our* eyes) that *we* are elsewhere and more lucid but still completely unable to move, including *our* eyes. *Our* lucidity makes *us* even more fearful. *We* are painfully aware that the men in military uniforms have no real concern for *us* and that *we* may die here, yet *we* are also aware that they are not *trying* to kill *us* but doing their jobs.

Alters hold different parts of our life experiences in memory. Memories surface one event at a time, separate and presented by different alters, often months and years apart. Years later, one of the things that became clear to our front alters was that as long as none of the fragmented events touched one another, we would survive in a programmed sort of way, as in not becoming completely non-functioning. In other words, the amnesic walls between events kept most of us from knowing what and who we are.

In this next fragment, *we see* directly in front of *us* a man's leg and brown boot with black tread, brass eyelets, and brownish-gold laces under khaki pants. He is standing astride and he is about two to two and a half feet in front of *us*. *We* cannot move *our* eyes but can see *our* periphery and *see* and *feel our* position on the floor. *We* are on *our* left side, knees and right arm bent, *our* left arm under and behind *us* parallel to *our* body. The floor is cold, smooth concrete, and *we* seem to have been lowered to the floor without any concern for *our* position. The man in front of *us* is facing the two men behind *us* who are talking, though *we* cannot make out what they are saying while the man in front of *us* waits for them to finish, after which he is going to take *us* away. *We* are clearly in and out of *our* body during this time due to *seeing* things that are even beyond *our* peripheral vision, such as *our* position from above and the two men behind *us*. It is no surprise to *us* that this is the case, given the circumstances: out-of-body.

We see that *we* are in a huge structure that looks like an airplane hangar minus airplanes. People are moving about and it is very well lit. No one here feels that a young, naked, incapacitated woman on the floor is of concern. *Our* alter realizes that *we* would probably die at their hands in this place and no one would feel a thing. Again, they aren't *trying* to kill *us*, yet if they do, too bad. This was palpable and completely incomprehensible. Once again, it all goes black.

When *our* alters began to show and tell *us* what they had experienced, *we* realized how much at times *we* could *see* and *feel*. Several parts have much of the information and are now able and safe enough to share with *our* front alters what they know. This is basically the process *we* call *our* deep deprogramming: *we* had begun to deprogram long before *we* actually had anyone to really talk to about *total mind kontrol* and *our* alters, except amongst *ourselves*.

This is what *we* know regarding this experience: *We* were in a military atmosphere that *we* have long believed to be MacDill Air Force Base in Tampa, Florida, having apparently been taken there on more than one occasion. Things were being taken out of and put into *our* mind, though the alters present had no conscious knowledge of "mind kontrol" during this experience nor during its revelation to *our* front line alter system later. *We* just knew that these people were in *our* head messing around and realized that other frightening things were taking place—being with people with a total disregard for *our* life, encountering what looked like a dinosaur, etc. *We* had been abducted, tortured, and did not know why they had been in *our* mind.

32

One of the most prominent elements of this experience was that an overwhelming amount of sexual energy was in and around the event. In the parts *we* remembered, there was no sexual rape per se, yet *we* could clearly *see* and *feel* that they had used *our* sex against *us*. This was one of the aspects that continued to disturb *us* for years until *we* acquired more conscious recall of events during which *we* were raped. The use and severe abuse of sexual energy is paramount in programming and reinforcing programming and is truly one of the most difficult aspects to deal with in deprogramming. It haunts one while hidden, as well as when it is revealed.

For example, since *our* late teens *we* repeatedly relived men in military uniforms engaging in various sexual acts with *us*. (There were men in non-military clothing as well, yet here *we* wish to address men in military uniforms.) Again, the physical, emotional, and mental aspects of using *our* sex against *us* was overwhelming, yet in the fragments from the airplane hangar event, the act of sexual rape wasn't presented to *me*. *We* have come to believe understanding their use of *our* sexual energy against *us* plays a significant role in *our* deep deprogramming.

At this point in *our* life, *our* main front alter as well as other parts of *us* were consciously unaware that *we* are a *we* and all that this means. Obviously *our* main front alter was deeply disturbed and confused due to her unawareness of being in alters during these rapes in which *we* appeared to be complicit directly due to the alter's programming triggered by these men. For an unaware front consciousness, it reinforced the *we are crazy* program. This was and is part of the psychological torture.

A particular memory has played over and over for decades: *We* are on *our* knees in front of a small three-man group in black fatigues. *We* are performing oral sex on the leader who is holding a black handgun against *our* cheek. Despite the obvious threat, *we* are completely focused on this act with fervor. Until *our* front alter came to understand that *we* are a *we*, these memories haunted her and prevented *us* from getting the help *we* needed. Guilt and shame are by far the most difficult emotions to deal with when memories surface with no understanding of *tmk* programming.

When *our* 24-hours-a-day downloads began once it was safe for *our* alters to speak up, the things *we* re-experienced were devastating. In far too many memories, *we* had become a perpetrator directly out of *our* victimization. *We* were doing their bidding under *total mind kontrol* without consciously knowing *we* were under *total mind kontrol*. That is exactly what they do so well. It is the "why" of what they do.

For *us* to be able to initiate *our* deep deprogramming enough to really start to be able to heal, *we* front alters had to allow the other alters to show and tell their lives to *us*. *We* had to come to the understanding that *we* are a *we* and how *we* became such. *Our* alters had been with *us* off and on all of *our* lives, *we* just consciously did not understand who and what they were. The main front alter just kept trying to figure out these hideous memories and what was wrong with her. She was the one who predominated in our daily consciousness.

Years later, even the aspect of the man in fatigues holding the gun against *our* cheek during this act of oral sex made sense. After finally telling someone who was helping *us* deprogram that *we* have inexplicable and unusual reactions to handguns, *we* would read accounts of other *tmk* slaves who also had what one researcher called "gun fever". *We* now know that *we* have alters who were programmed to guns in very disturbing ways.

Piece of Mind

Binding Possession

For years, *we* have viewed this experience as an *alien* union, having no other context within which to understand it. *We* now understand it as an *entity* binding—all part of *our* generational programming.

The experience begins at night in *our* bedroom in the home *we* lived in during the *our* years of adolescent and teen programming. *We* are standing in *our* bedroom in front of the door that is closed. *Our* eyes are unwillingly closed, but *we* are not frightened as *we* are in alter. *We* can *feel* that someone is standing in front of *us*. Telepathically, *we* ask him if *we* may open *our* eyes to look at him. He responds in the affirmative as though the concept of "yes" is relayed to *us* telepathically.

We open *our* eyes and gasp, *feeling* many emotions at once. His physical beauty is astounding; seeing him simultaneously evokes fear and desire. Starting with *our* eyes at the top of his head, *we* slowly work *our* way down, taking in as much as *we* can, awestruck. He is humanoid, yet clearly not human. He is not much taller than *us*, his skin tan, his eyes amber with vertical pupils like a cat. He has no hair on his head or body (at least to the waist), and though he is small in stature, his musculature is very pronounced. Nothing is wasted on him; his skin is taut over frame and muscle with not an ounce of fat. His facial structure is strong and angular, his ears so close to his head they are barely noticeable from the front. A nose, lips, a square jaw. At the neck and chest, the exaggerated muscle development, and rounded muscular shoulders and arms. His pectoral and ab muscles are very developed, however there are no nipples or belly-button. His v-shape leads to the smallest waist *we* have ever seen with highly developed muscles. *We* want to touch him, to run from him screaming, to engage in sex with him, all the while feeling repulsed by him. *We feel* him as father, brother, friend, lover, and god; *we* are euphoric.

When *we* reach his waist, all goes black, followed by a visual landscape of desolate desert plains and mountains of red sand. At this point, "union" takes place, as though *our* soul unites with his. It is not sex between a man and a woman as *we* know it; it is much more for this alter.

We become obsessed with him and *our* memory of him, the way he looked, the way *we* felt when *we* looked at him, and most of all, the deeply felt emotional connection that accompanied what repeatedly played in *our* head: that *He and i are kin*; that *He and i come from the same place, the red place*…that he had shown *us*.

35

Years later at a UFO conference, *we* would see this body neck down on a sculpture made by a self-proclaimed *alien-human hybrid abductee. We* would also see the exact same facial structure with vertical pupils on an *alien hybrid reptile* painted by Zulu shaman Credo Mutwa. (David Icke did several interviews years ago with this man. https://www.youtube.com/playlist?list=PL459F8F86F9163EA6.)

At 18, *we* joined a health club via a *tmk* family involved with *our* family through *our* father. Years later, *we* realized that *our* upper body workouts were geared towards trying to emulate the shoulders *we* saw on him that night. Why? Was it because our "union" meant he possessed *us?* Was he inside of *us?*

We now consciously understand him as one of many ruling *entities* within *us* running *our* programs, or perhaps more appropriately *our* alters. *We* have come to see these *entities* as *our* 24 hours-a-day handlers, the ones running *our* programs, with him being one of the more powerful ruling *entities* that have been and continue to be in possession of *us* and allowing the ongoing programmed use and abuse of *us* on both the physical and astral planes—complete ownership through total deception and programming.

[It became clear with time that this entity was a significant handler regarding my kill alters and programming. Even the weight lifting and training, which at one point in my life led to very developed musculature on our body, was significant to that usage. Strength can come from any size individual when entity possession is present. However, this musculature did indeed play a role in my use.]

However, *we* now have the ability to affect this condition, at least in degrees. It is *our* devout opinion that programming is not possible without the presence of these *entities*, this being the key to success in programming *us*. During deep deprogramming, *we* painfully discovered the extent of their possession of *us* and their ability through astral access to wage 24-hour warfare against *us* in order to maintain or even regain kontrol over *us*, once *we* began to attempt to exorcise them with assistance from *our* support group. *We* know these "aliens" (*entities/demons*) intimately, yet not nearly as well as they know *us. Our* attempt to free *ourselves* from them is a daily struggle, due to the depth and complexity of *our* programming.

A Taste for Beauty

The Mormons

The sundress *we* were wearing during the following encounter tells *us* that this occurrence took place at the age of 18 or 19. *We* are getting into a car with a man in a gray suit. *Our* alter is under the misconception that *we* are going to a business convention for a "job interview" with a "family-type company", *our* hope being to become a "team member" and part of the "family".

As usual, *our* questioning and reasoning capacity within *our* alter is almost non-existent. This alter does not ask who this man is nor what it is *we* will be doing for this "company". *We* ride in the front seat with him, both he and *we* silent until we arrive at a complex of buildings which *we* recognize as a hotel in a tropical setting. (The alter who is showing this to *us* is not the same alter who told *us* that it may not be the tropics. *We* believe it is a tropical theme hotel possibly in Las Vegas, Nevada, or even in Florida where *we* were living at the time. *We feel* more strongly that it is the former.)

The man pulls up to a covered sidewalk-walkway as opposed to a parking space in the large lot and the man and *we* get out of the car. It is daytime, feeling like late morning light. Maybe six men and women are waiting there for *us*, one whom *we* know as "the daughter," a petite woman with short dark hair making up in energy what she lacks in stature. In her late twenties, she is confident and competitive and roughly *our* height, though she is wearing heels. *Our* alter reads "the daughter" immediately; many of *our* alters have an ability to read people and their *entities*, a programmed ability geared to the success of the alter's programming, not to save *ourselves*.

Everyone is professionally dressed, "the daughter" and another woman in dark skirt suits. As soon as we get out of the car, everyone starts walking down a sidewalk walkway covered with an aluminum top with aluminum poles holding it up at the sides every ten feet or so. There are no introductions, *we* just know to follow everyone. "The daughter" is on *our* right, the man who brought *us* on *our* left a few steps back, the others scattered and walking with us. *We* become aware that *we* are in a sundress and everyone else is dressed professionally and briefly wonder about this, yet no one seems to notice or comment, so it slips from *our* mind.

To *our* right and between the buildings is a somewhat large open foliage area with tropical plants like palm fronds. Beyond is a white building. To *our* left is only about eight or ten feet of foliage and then the white stucco wall of a building. The walkway is leading into this complex of buildings. *We* see no signs. Though *our* alter is unable to reason things out, *we* are aware that *we* are nervous because these people are unscrupulous. The thought in *our* head is, *Be careful or they will chew you up and spit you out.*

The next memory fragment is *us* indoors entering a room through auditorium-type double doors with a long bar handle. Our small group is following "the daughter" into a very large room with a stage and seating for 150 to 200 people. A tall man who is "the father" to "the daughter" that *we* are with is standing up front just below the stage on a wooden parquet floor that resembles a dance floor measuring roughly 30 by 40 feet. The rest of the room is carpeted.

The chairs are in rows in a u-shape around the parquet dance floor area. As we enter, *we* just keep following. The tall man is holding a microphone and begins to speak to other men and women in professional attire as we enter and continue to walk down the carpeted aisle towards the front. Before *we* even saw the tall man, *we* were aware that he was "the father" of "the daughter" and that he would be speaking today. *We* were also aware that there is another "daughter" present though *we* don't recall seeing her in the room, yet *we* know what she looks like, just not how *we* know. She looks very different from "the daughter" *we* are with—more fair, with long dark blond hair and fair eyes. *We* are also aware that "the father" began talking to the group just when *we* arrived. Even *our* alter realizes they were waiting for *us* and fears these people, yet *we* are incapable of figuring out why.

The man who picked *us* up peels off to the left into a row near the back. *We* hesitate, uncertain if *we* too should sit, yet there is no empty chair next to him. It is obvious to him that *we* are confused, so he says, "I don't like to sit up front" and motions with his head for *us* to follow "the daughter" who has not broken stride. So *we* continue behind her.

She takes *us* all the way down to the front and around the right side of the u-shape to two seats along the dance floor right in front of the tall man with the microphone who is looking intently at *us* as he speaks to the group. She sits down in one of the chairs and *we* step past her to sit to her left. The tall man is talking about *the company...Family...being a team member...welcoming our new member...all working together for a common goal...*(Words in italics heard by our alter at the "interview".)

Within seconds of *us* sitting down, the tall man—his eyes locked onto *us*—begins idly walking towards *us* while talking into the microphone, his left arm and hand palm up outstretched. *We* begin to shake as he nears and respond by taking his hand with *our* right hand as he gently pulls *us* up and out onto the parquet floor, continuing to talk and look into *our* eyes. He turns *us* toward the center of the u-shaped group and releases *our* hand, then turns away and steps further onto the dance floor.

[I am certain this *eyes-locked*—a common part of trigger series used on me in different situations—combined with what he was saying, which I do not recall, were the triggers to get me to introduce myself to the group present.]

We know *we* are supposed to introduce *ourself*, so *we* do, shaking and twitching as we use *our* given name. *Our* front system is made up of several alters with the same name so no one would notice that *we* are a *we*, including most of *us*. Three times, once towards each of the three sections of the u-shaped crowd, *we* say, "Hello, *i* am Elisa," then return to *our* seat and sit down. *We* hear murmurs and subdued laughter and are again unable to determine why *we* are as fearful as if *we* were in a roomful of sharks. Often *we feel* that something is going on but are unable to figure out what, then even that thought slips away, at which point *we* break into a *profuse* sweat—not perspiration, but a full, dripping sweat.

We look at "the daughter" who seems to not notice or care. Everyone, including "the daughter", reaches under their seats, so *we* too look. Sure enough, there is a thick stack of folders. "The daughter" pulls out the top one, so *we* do the same, but the first page seems to be in gibberish and *we* cannot read it. It doesn't look like English or any language *we* recognize.

Confused, *we* look at her and she returns *our* look with a very dismissive comment while scrunching up her nose and slightly shaking her head, saying, "This is only for the presidents." *We* put it away, assuming she meant the "presidents" of the "company", yet it seemed that everyone has them. Are there that many "presidents" in this "company"? At this point, confused and uncomfortable, feeling very alone in this group, *we* wish *we* could leave.

The conscious download of this experience stops there, but here is what *we* know to be true about this encounter:

In 1980 or 1981, *we* were being presented as a "new member" of the Network to which *we* are a slave to be utilized by the Mormon church. Later in *our* forties, *we* realized that the tall man up front was the current Prophet of The Church of the Latter Day Saints back *before* he became President/Prophet. *Our* alter's memories show *us* that *we* were used by the Mormons in various ways over the years.

As with many alter experiences, *we* were aware that everyone in that room except *us* knew who and what *we* were. It was not a "job interview" but the presentation of *us*, a *total mind kontrolled slave* to the "presidents" of the Church. It would not be until 2008 that a person well versed in the Mormon-LDS Church and its structure informed *us* that *our* alter's estimate of attendance was roughly the equivalent of "stake presidents" within the Church.

We have also found references to mission and temple presidents, both of whom attend stake conferences. *We* were frightened because even though in alter, there was enough of a programming breakdown occurring to try and warn *us* of the danger *we* were in, including the profuse sweating. This also explains why no one was concerned about *our* casual attire nor *our* profuse sweating. The reason *we* can remember neither what was said as well as why *we* couldn't read the paper is that *we* were programmed to not be able to. Parts of memories can be photographic, a total blank, or blurred, such as faces. *We* know what is occurring, but cannot get at the specifics. It is possible that the papers the "presidents" read were in code, but it is much easier to believe *we* were programmed to not be able to read it.

We have conscious memories of trips to Las Vegas, Nevada as well as Salt Lake City, Utah over the years, yet no conscious memory of why *we* went and only fragments of what *we* did while there. *We* also have memories of locales in Salt Lake City that *we* were able to locate after memory downloads with no front alter conscious memory of having been there. In these memory downloads, there are also places *we* have yet to locate, some of which—due to the nature of why *we* were in these places—*we* will probably never locate.

We are presenting what *our* alters presented to *us*, not making a judgment about The Church of the Latter Day Saints congregation. Instead, *we* are showing that Latter Day Saints *at the highest levels* are involved in *total mind kontrol* slave use.

The Little Black Dress

4
Killing

An alter from when *we* were 18 years old gave *us* an experience memory that began to explain things *we* had known for a long time but which *our* main front alter hadn't understood.

It is here that *we* must now reveal with much difficulty that *our* main use was as a killer for members of the Network. *Our* extensive sexual programming was often used in conjunction with *our* kill programming, very often according to *our* downloads as well as independent of it. It is *our* understanding that *we* had many uses, though *our* heaviest programmed uses were sex and killing. Within the following downloads are more than one presenting alter, each showing a part of the experience they were present for.

Alpha and Omega: First and Last Solo

There are two parts to this memory, two different occurrences for this particular alter. The first part was the *alpha*, the second the *omega*. In other words, this download contained her *first* on-task in which she would be on her own for the kill but under the watchful eye of her handler at the beginning. The download also contained her *last* on-task as well as some of the programming involved. She was showing *us* the beginning and end of her use.

Alpha

We are walking calmly and confidently through a narrow area in a casino, not the wide open main room. Poker tables are to *our* right. *We* are eighteen years old in a mid-thigh black dress with black hose and black high heels, *our* blond hair down to the middle of *our* back. To *our* left, a man dressed in a long dark coat, dark slacks and large dark sunglasses is at one of four black and silver pay phones on the faux wood wall. He holds the phone to his right ear as he faces the room, his head moving

43

with *us* as *we* pass. *We* are relieved to see him there and feel the same sexual connection to him that he feels toward *us*. *We feel* him deeply, like a life force, yet if anyone would ask this alter who he is, she would not have been able to answer. *We* did not seem to know who he was, yet *we* knew him *very* well. Within this alter's consciousness, this paradox was not a concern; she did not ask who, where, why, how. These were not things she could think about unless they were programmed as part of her on-task; she simply recognized him in a *feeling* that felt deeply good to her. He is *our* handler.

We are also aware that *we* should not continue looking at him. *We* avert *our* eyes to the target at the last poker table in a row of five tables, deeply aware that the man on the phone will not take his eyes off of *us* as *we* continue with *our* task. A dealer faces *our* direction while the man *we* are to go to has his back to *us*. The target is wearing a two-piece gray suit with a white shirt and no tie. His hair is gray to white. *We* sit in the chair to his left and swivel it so *we* are facing him. He has now turned toward *us* and *we* look him in the eye silently and cross *our* left leg over *our* right. He smiles and leans in toward *us*, looking deeply into *our* eyes as he places his hand palm down on *our* inner left thigh. *Our* eyes follow his hand. (To this day, *we* can *still* see his hand on *our* black panty hose.) *We* return *our* eyes to his and he says, "*Place a bet* [on it]," *place a bet* being part of a combination of actions that trigger access to the appropriate sex alter. *We* have switched alters.

We then went up to his room, engaged in sex with him, and killed him. This was her first on-task kill program by herself. *We* can still *see* his nameless face but know nothing about him except that he was willingly engaging in sex with a very young woman.

Much changed for us during this year of unbearable use. Memories of *my* front alter life show serious signs of self-harm, self-abuse, and wishes of death. Clearly it is not intended for a child of God to kill another and this being what it was, involuntary *mind kontrol*, made it all the more un-bearable. It went against everything that is *our* very nature. *We* were made into what is abhorrent to the Divine soul within *us*; *our* eternal freedom depends upon *our* deep recognition of this. *We* often wonder how much program reinforcement was necessary to keep *us* functioning properly. There would be periods of reprogramming in the years to come and *i* sus-pect *our* use had a lot to do with that necessity.

Omega

The second part of this download occurred in fragments and flashes. At one point, *we* are moving through a city's downtown; at another point, in a semi-industrial zone with residences off to one side. It refers to the same alter who is not to survive the last programmed on-task: the *omega*. Whether this means the alter will die or all of *us* are slated to die during or after the on-task is uncertain. (As in via a suicide program of which I discovered several.) The *omega* for one alter, or for the entire system and end of *our* physical life? *Our* alter is programmed to not even question if *she/we* will die.

What *we* do know, thanks to researchers out there, is that this is what is known as *End-Time programming*. (See Resources, particularly *How the Illuminati Create an Undetectable Total Mind Controlled Slave* by Fritz Springmeier and Cisco Wheeler, 2008.)

Ten months after this conscious memory download, *we* intuitively went to the exact area in the suburbs of Salt Lake City without ever having been there in *our* front alters. The two areas involved, in addition to Salt Lake City, were West Valley City and West Jordan.

In the download, *we* see several green street signs with white letters at intersections and consciously remember *Parkway* and *Athens*, though there were more *we* could not retain. *Our* alter does not think about what she is doing but moves through these areas knowing what to do next as she comes upon the next trigger such as *Bangerter*, she knows to, *Turn right now to get back to downtown,* and does just that.

A memory gap and then she is in a very expensive, elegant building. Inside are granite tiles, water fountains, plants and a lot of glass, with something else that would later seem so out of place, outside of program reasoning. *We* are entering an area that the alter thinks is a mall food court, though *we* see no restaurants or food of any kind.

She descends tile steps, the atmosphere new and very expensive. A curious group of gray- and white-haired men and women are seated at round tables to *our* right. Even to this alter, they seem out of place, but they are waiting for her, looking at her, some smiling. She begins to see through the scene but lacks the unprogrammed reasoning to decipher it. She looks at them, then to *our* left where bright red cursive writing is lit in a "Cinema" marquee high up like something out of the 1970s or 1980s.

The men and women begin to speak to *us*. It feels wrong, but the alter cannot get at what is wrong. Their statements and questions are odd,

45

their smiles and familiarity even more odd. Are they testing *us*? They ask seemingly innocuous questions to see if she remembers them, but she does not. As can and repeatedly does occur, *our* alter is perceiving beyond her programming but not enough to get very far. Like other kill alters within *our* system, she has a lot of high alert programming for use within the programmed on-task, but unfortunately it does not allow *our* alters to decipher these programming sessions at the time of their occurrence. She listens and responds with head nods or shakes, and then the memory fragments. She goes through a door beyond the group. Another gap in the download.

Next, *our* alter is in a garden atmosphere on a walkway. She stops to look at a "snake" about five feet long on the walkway with mucous all around it, like a slug trail but much larger and thicker. A gray-haired woman walks up and raises her foot to step on the head of the snake. *We* stop her and say, "No, it is life." She stops, as does the download.

Here is what *we* know: The city is Salt Lake City, the semi-industrial area in the southwest suburb called West Valley City is on Parkway Boulevard, with the, *Turn right now to get back to downtown,* being at Bangerter Highway while heading west. *We* are to deliver something, possibly bio-weapons—but that is uncertain—to someone or a group of people in this area. *We* would later find Athens Drive south of West Valley City in another suburb of Salt Lake City called West Jordan. Since going to West Jordan and being on Athens Drive, *we* also understand that the National Guard Reserve base within a mile or two of Athens is involved, yet *we* are unable to state how.

The "mall food court" is not a food court but the interior of The Church of the Latter-Day Saints Conference Center in downtown Salt Lake City near Temple Square. The group of gray- and white-haired men and women are a "council" within *our* programming, perhaps even an actual three-dimensional human council present during *our* programming, *feeling* however, like an internal council within *our* system that has shown up repeatedly in memory downloads. (See Fritz Springmeier's works on creating an illuminati *total mind control slave* for an explanation of "internal councils". The systems are what *we* are, a compilation of alters with programming, a system of alters, and *we* have more than one system.)

[I suspect this may have been another astral programming session as I have come to understand the technology. This programming occurred in the early 2000s. It is possible, if not likely, that this *entire* encounter, including the "council", took place with everyone present inhabiting alternate bodies occupied by their astral bodies, from their original self. Yes, that is indeed what I said. Something about this never felt like a purely physical experience, however, I did not have the understanding I do now. The level of black technology used in these covert operations is far, far beyond anything anyone has imagined it is. There will be more on this later and information will be available in the Resources at the end of the book.]

The neon "Cinema" sign was a screen memory to throw *us* off if *we* begin to remember *our* location as The Church of the Latter-Day Saints Conference Center, plus reinforcement of *our* extensive movie programming. The alters with End-Time programming would tell us that *The Dark Knight* film was a major trigger for *our* End-Time programming, *The Dark Knight* being representative of a group of alters in *us*, various characters in the movie reinforcing various alters and their End-Time programming in *us*—the End-Time program referred to here being associated with the Mormon LDS Church hierarchy.

Obviously, *we* were not to make connections to the Mormon Church. Snakes are part of *our* programming both in content and as the *entities* themselves, as well as what *we* believe really occurred in the garden on top of the Center after the programming was tested to be in place, and the Church of the Latter-Day Saints Conference Center was at least in part the location of programming. (We would also like to refer people to a book by Ron Alan, a targeted individual, titled *21st Century MK-Ultra Slave, a Vintage Transhuman Tale*. The snake may indeed take on a whole new meaning.)

Again, this section was the *omega* for this alter as well as being one of *our* End-Time programs within *our* system. This download was so profound it would lead *us* to Salt Lake City to see these areas. In January 2009, ten months after *our* deep deprogramming began, *we* found them. On the next trip to Salt Lake City, *we* found Athens in West Jordan, not far from West Valley City. Finding these locations triggered a tremendous amount of fear and paranoia as self-destruct programming kicked into full gear, but it also allowed *us* to finally accept that *we* have indeed been involved with the Mormon Church (FBI, CIA, etc.), and that the Mormon Church is deeply involved in *total mind kontrol* programming and the use of *total mind kontrolled* slaves.

Another very disturbing element that surfaced with this download is that The Church of the Latter-Day Saints Conference Center's construction was not completed until April 2000, which means *we* were programmed there between 2000 and 2007.

Mormon Sin

Shiny Purple and the Actor

Here *we* will address a download for which it is difficult to determine *our* age, though *we* choose to put it here due to the age of the woman *our* front alters would meet in the physical world in *our* early thirties, which was not the first meeting with this woman for others of *us*. In this experience memory, this woman appears to be in her forties and when *our* front alters met her, supposedly for the first time in the physical world in *our* early thirties, she was in her sixties. (See Book 1, Chapter 2, "The Teen Years", *Alien Abduction?* and *"Female", Not a Woman*.) The other possibility is that the use of this woman's appearance is cover being used by the *being* performing astral programming on *us*. This technique has been used in other circumstances, and *we* were only able to understand this with time.

She appears to be an ongoing presence in *our* programming years and different alters know her as different things. Ultimately, it appears that she was involved with *us* since *our* youth, exactly how young *we* are unsure. When *our* front alters met her in *our* early thirties, they did not consciously recognize her at that time.

[I wonder at this. Is it possible that during my early attempts at deprogramming and the attempts years later, did my controllers use her likeness to confuse me? If so, it worked.]

This download begins with *us* driving up to a small building with white flowing yoga and lounge wear clothing hanging out front that draws *us* in with its purity and white, flowing motion. Next, *we* are inside a health club in a section where they sell exercise, yoga and lounge wear clothing. *We* are standing in front of a round clothes rack, aware of the colors, particularly *shiny purple*. *We* can *see* and *feel* the shiny purple, though shiny pink, green, blue, silver, gold, and white are also present. It is the shiny purple that *we* are to focus on. On the other side of the rack is this woman. She is looking intently at *us* as *we* take in the shiny purple and then return her gaze. *We* feel very uncertain about what is happening here, at which she says to *us*, "Though it is not at all what you thought, it's more than okay, you *must* continue. It's still beautiful." Though *we* still feel uncertain, *our* alter is aware of her commitment, so *we* agree.

Note on health clubs: *We* have come to understand that *we* were actually programmed in some health clubs around the United States, being triggered as well to go to them on *our* own. Additionally, it appears that sometimes an illusion of health club atmosphere was presented during programming so *we* could not determine our actual location if the programming began to surface. Much like the "Cinema'" sign used in the LDS Conference Center. Years after this memory surfaced and five months into writing this work, *we* would find articles by ex-programmer Svali mentioning private workout facilities for programmers ("Illuminati"

49

in her vernacular) and other members of the Network with access who wished to keep fit. Could these facilities also be used for programming *tmk* slaves?

Next, *we* are in the workout area of the health club crouched by a counter next to what appears to be actor Danny Glover as gunmen brandishing handguns enter the health club. *Our* alter feels no fear and is very systematic, doing what is before her with confidence and no emotion. She tells the actor to stay put, that she will take care of it, and heads toward the gunmen.

Now it is night and *we* are standing on the sidewalk outside the aforementioned building facing the street wet with a recent rain. *We* still *feel* nothing, and Glover is standing in front of *us*.

[At this point in the current download, I am aware that this is a programming memory for an actual on-task, and that the person in front of me was not Glover at all but someone who looked like him for programming purposes. My alter does not know this, nor even question who this is or isn't. She does not know him as an actor, nor who he is at this time, only as someone in the scenario that she just encountered—in fact, as the target she is to interact with in a particular way. Therefore the need to have it look like Danny Glover for face recognition.]

The street is dimly lit with brick on the front of the building. *We* can *see* and *feel* lust coming from the person playing the actor. With both hands, he cups *our* face and pulls *us* to him as he forcefully kisses *us* and shoves his tongue deep into *our* mouth. *Our* alter feels nothing; she does not want him. He realizes this and says to *us*, "I'd like to get a glass of wine or orange juice." The code he delivered to *us* was either out of date or delivered improperly. Emotionless, we tell him, "We will not have sex."

He then points to a 1970-something dark Ford Fairlane parked under a street light on the opposite side of the street about 150 feet away. *I* cannot tell what the color is, yet when *our* alter looks at it, she immediately remembers, knows and *feels* exactly this concept; *the time of the darkness becoming a physical presence within our life*. It is as though she is consumed by those words and that all resistance is futile, as though death itself is upon her. She knows that she will give herself to him and do whatever he wants, now and always. The "always" that *we* refer to is a result of *no time* in the alter's conscious reality. To her, now is "always".

The alter being triggered by the car, the color, a combination of several things, comes out, painfully aware in *feeling* that her programming has been triggered out. She is aware that extreme sexual pain is coming because that is what she takes. She can *feel* how much he wants to hurt her that way and she will let him. She is one of the most despondent, resigned alters that *we* have experienced to date. What she is programmed to give is ruinous.

We were being programmed to be part of a *team* kill.

Here is what *we* know: This programming involved the woman that *our* front alters would meet years later in *our* early thirties when *our* programming began breaking down. It was a kill program targeting the actor with the person playing the actor gaining access to a sex alter who takes severe, sexual pain. Years later in *our* deep deprogramming, *we* would discover that Danny Glover was a high-profile political activist who eventually became a real thorn in the side of the Bush administration with his support of Venezuelan leader Hugo Chavez:

> [Danny] Glover sits on the advisory board of Telesur, the state-owned television network owned by Chavez's government, and has frequently appeared on Chavez's own show. This friendship is forged by anti-Americanism and support for the neo-Communist ideology of Chavez. Glover's friend and fellow actor, Harry Belafonte, said during a trip to Venezuela he took with Glover that "no matter what the greatest tyrant in the world, the greatest terrorist in the world, George W. Bush says, we're here to tell you: Not hundreds, not thousands, but millions of the American people...support your revolution." It doesn't get much more Red than that. (Ryan Mauro, "Danny Glover: Hero to the Media, Villain to the Intelligent", *PJ Media*, 19 April 2010.)

[In addition, we have a conscious flashback of going to see this actor while he was filming one of the Lethal Weapon movies at a marina in Clearwater, Florida. This was a series of movies he did with Mel Gibson back in the 1980s and 1990s. So it was either the first one (released 1987) or the second one (released 1989) in the series. I was out somewhere public with some people, it was late at night, and I recall excusing myself. I drove to Clearwater Beach, parked, got out of the car and walked to the marina. I stood there for maybe 5 minutes before Danny Glover, followed by Mel Gibson, came walking out from where they had just filmed. He was no

51

more than 15 or 20 feet away. I watched him walk by, turned and left. I was completely emotionless, in alter, and it was very timely. It was down right creepy upon recall years later.]

Words to Remember

5
Twenties: More Sex and More Killing

By the time *we* were 20 years old, things were slipping into *our* conscious mind and forcing *our* front alters to have to deal with undeniable, disturbing facts.

Our frontline system being a compilation of alters designed to deal with any difficulties that might slip through to *our* conscious mind, *we* believe *our* front alters would have to be some of the strongest alters in *our* system. Imagine personalities that have to deal with sexual perversion, occult ritual, killing, cannibalism, severe trauma, and the actual real-time physical conditions for which the front personalities have no recall, fragments that slip into their everyday life while consciously they never know that they are part of a multiple personality disorder system whose parts perform unspeakable "tasks" at the bidding of their programmers, kontrollers, and handlers while under the threat of self-destruction and death programming if they remember.

The following are some experiences from *our* twenties. Sometimes, *we* know *our* actual age, sometimes only that it occurred within a range of years. Except for front alters, *our* alters don't age, so whether the memory is from twenty years ago or yesterday, certain alters look the same to *us*.

Broken Bones

Most of the 1980s have been missing from *our* conscious frontline system most of *our* life, as were *our* childhood, adolescent, and teen years, though many pieces have begun to return, often with major experience memory downloads of occurrences spanning the better part of two years, and often all at once. This particular experience was always present in the physical reality of *our* front alter's consciousness, admittedly deeply tucked away due to its inexplicability, but *our* frontline system was aware of it when *we* arose the day after it occurred. Thus it has haunted *us* for years, forever altering *our* conscious life.

53

We awoke one morning in a lover's bedroom, *our* right hand and forearm in great pain. The sunlight shining into the room said it was late morning. *Our* arm was still under the sheets. *We* pulled it out and were shocked at the swelling and bruising distorting the forearm, wrist, and hand. Everything was blue, purple, and green and so swollen the skin looked as if it might rip open. The pain was excruciating. As adrenaline rushed through *our* body, *we* heard in *our* head, *Something is very wrong,* referring not only to *our* arm and hand, but resonating into areas of *our* life that *we* could not consciously reach. This was alter chatter that *we* knew for so long as others in *us* tried to reach the front alters.

Our mind raced to try to find an explanation, but found none. To *our* left was the back of a sleeping man, a lover as well as a handler from a *tmk* family *we* were heavily involved with. *We* were bartending in lingerie at the *tmk* family's restaurant and sleeping with both sons. He was sound asleep, so *we* again looked at *our* arm, trying desperately to figure it out, consciously knowing that he would never do such a thing, he was not like that. *Our* mind raced through *our* conscious memory of the night before. *Our* lover and *we* had gone dancing at a club in a city about 30 miles from where he lived—the same city near MacDill Air Force Base, where *we* had been programmed—after which *we* came back to his place and had sex. That was all *we* remembered, the programming at MacDill being sequestered in *our* alter's memory.

We reached over and woke him, showed him *our* arm, and asked him what happened the previous night. He looked sleepily at it, then grew wide-eyed, responding with profanity that he had no idea. His sincerity appeared genuine. *We* believe he too was a multiple and consciously unaware of what had occurred the night before, though at this time *we* are uncertain as to his particular use other than as *our* handler.

We looked at each other, fear in our eyes, though not for long. You learn to cover for things that slip into your front alter's consciousness because allowing them to linger is often far too disturbing to your other "selves". We got up, talked a bit about it, and decided he would take *us* to a doctor. He suggested a walk-in clinic to avoid emergency room questions.

We still remember the doctor looking at *us*. Something was clearly not quite right about our story, plus the obvious delay in seeking help apparent in *our* hand and arm. *Why would anyone wait so long to treat such numerous fractures? We* could *see* and *hear* his disbelief when *we* looked into his eyes.

Over the next six weeks, *we* became an ambidextrous bartender, using *our* left hand to pour while *our* right arm was in a cast. Every time someone asked about it, *we* felt the fear of not knowing, yet covered with lies that went on long after the cast was removed. Over and over, one of *our* front alters asked how in the hell *we* broke *our* hand? *What could we have hit and not remembered? And why?* How hard *we* must have hit whatever it was.

We still cannot claim to have the answer in *our* conscious mind, but there is a visual fragment that plays over and over since that morning. It is of *us* attempting to fight *our* way out of a small room with at least three men in it, punching *our* way out. The room is similar to rooms from other downloads—a simple room with a table and chairs, a small room with men *we* did not wish to be in with, a room in which *we* had been receiving instructions in *alter*.

Hanging On through the Heavy Use Years

The age of 18 marked the beginning of *our* decades-long main use by *our* programmers, kontrollers, and handlers. *We* were stunned when *we* heard of other *tmk* victims reporting heavy use beginning at 18 and running on into their twenties—for particular tasks, anyway. Eighteen and twenty-two had always been extremely significant ages and numbers to *us*, long before *we* even consciously knew that *we* are a *we*. After the experience at the military base detailed under *Torture, Programming, Guns And Reptiles*, *we* knew that 18 and 22 were very significant, though uncertain if it was from 18 to 22 years old, or at 18 for 22 years, which would put *us* at *our* death age of 39.

[It would turn out that that particular torture session—the specific programming of select splits would come later—resulted in 22 splits or mind fragments and it was directly related to the delta triangle they put inside of our head. I believe that night a system of kill alters was installed.]

Our downloads show that *our* use continued well beyond 22 and even beyond 39. The length of *our* use provokes discussions during deep deprogramming about programmers extending the efficiency of their programming to extend the life of a *tmk* slave's use. *Our* uses certainly shifted as needed over the years, yet one of *our* main uses certainly did not end in *our* twenties or even our thirties.

55

Our early twenties were fraught with brief breaks in *our* programming that allowed *us* to know that something was terribly wrong while unable to get at it due to the success of *our* programmers, or retain it briefly, then it was gone again. *We* very clearly recall episodes of complete breakdowns in *our* early twenties during which *we* could not function or leave the house, curling up into a ball in the corner of a room, hysterical. Programmers are working on eliminating such problems.

These weren't missing memories, though *we* would find out that collectively *we* have hundreds of missing memories held by alters. The breakthroughs were conscious memories that *we* tucked away so that *our* front alters would be able to consciously survive without going completely insane. To *us*, insanity is losing all ability to function in the everyday world, and *we* were consciously and painfully aware all *our* life that *we* were teetering on that edge, hiding *ourselves* away, yet the why and what of that was never clear to *us*, even with many details of *our* programming and "on-tasks" in *our* conscious mind.

If you can understand the degree of fear *our* perpetrators instilled in *us*, you can begin to see the lifelong deterioration that *we* as a *tmk* slave went through. Though the programming may still be holding, the physical, mental, emotional and spiritual deterioration started very early and is directly related to *our* particular use. *We* appeared to age slowly, yet inside *we* were dealing with a 24-hour-a-day adrenaline push, despite the compartmentalization and walls between *our* alters—alters whose entire existence were the very same programs that were abhorrent to *our* Benevolent Spirit because they were killing *our* body, mind and spirit, and *we* mean that literally.

This is what *we* knew: anxiety escalating to terrifying panic; being at *our* jobs in the "world of man" and having to lock the door and spend *we* don't know how long curled up in the corner of the bathroom, sobbing with terror over things not remembered but *felt* and *seen* in flashes; the sense that *we* would die at any moment never leaving *us*, nor the desire to.

It is difficult to explain how the lives of *our* alters are experienced by those of *us* separated from them in *our* internal mind as well as body. When *our* programs broke through, *we* could *see* and *feel* the other lives but not remember them, at least not in the way most people experience memory. It is relived in fragments or flashes in the consciousness of other alters and often re-fragmenting *us*, like abreactions in deep deprogramming.

Body Memories

By *our* early twenties, *our* body began trying to tell *our* front alters what was occurring. *We* began having body memories, often without *our* conscious mind *seeing* what the cause of these memories was. For *us*, these body memories were terrifying and painful, as if the experience was occurring right then and there, yet only sometimes did *we* have a visual during them. There were things *we* understood about these body memories that made them all the more surreal—sex, torture, murder, and more—all of which would kick *our* doubt programming into high gear and debilitate *our* ability to understand who and what *we* were. After all, *i* the main front alter had not been consciously present during these experiences. *We* knew *we* were suffering and going to die in them, yet here *we* were, still alive, *our* fragmented mind at a total loss to explain it. And yet *we* knew it was more real than the life *we* appeared to be leading.

During these years, *we* had very little conscious recall of these experiences, *our* alters still feeling far too unsafe to bring the information forward. Besides, without support, if *we* had been subjected to what we had done thus far, coming fully to *our* conscious mind, *we* would probably have taken *our* own life as per *our* programming.

The Bordello Years

Under *Broken Bones,* *we* wrote of two lovers, the two sons of the *tmk* family that owned a small restaurant and bar franchise based out of a well known city in Florida. The one sleeping beside *me* was the unmarried son, the other one married. *We* worked out of the franchise south of the original location in another developed city with many *tmk* ties, as *we* would learn years later.

While the wife, two sons and daughter-in-law worked in the restaurant and bar, the husband/father was pastor of a local fundamentalist church. The wife and daughter-in-law were classic *tmk* slaves, but under *tmk ourselves,* *we* could tell something was very wrong with them but were no more capable of determining what that was than that *we* were a multiple personality. Consciously, *we* knew that the married son was sleeping with his wife and *us*, and that *we* were sleeping with him and his brother.

S.W. had brought *us* into this family business, initially offering *us* to the two sons for their personal sexual use. *We* clearly remember being told that the married son was tired of another young woman working for them and that *we* could have both sons. *We* took this other woman's place in the married son's bed and behind the bar, as well. *We* also remember being repelled by the father, yet could not figure out why. *We* know for a fact that he acted out his perversions with various other girls working for him, despite his jolly, kind father and pastor persona. It sickens *us* even now. Happily, *we* may have escaped his attentions, given the pretty young blond twin girls and their adventures in a local motel room at which *we* are pretty certain *we* were not present, thank goodness. The wife and the daughter-in-law both behaved as if they were unaware, except that the pastor's wife was a heavy drinker and prescription drug taker.

Demo-ed in New York

After working for them for some time, *we* were told that *we* were to go to New York with the franchise creator and owner, J., and one of "her girls" from her restaurant. The story was we were going to Wall Street to seek investors. J. owned and ran another restaurant out of another city in Florida. *Our* front alters thought nothing of this journey, but from this point onward what occurred is fragmented and at points frightening.

We went to meet J. and "her girl" D., another blue-eyed blonde, and recall *nothing* about this Florida trip of a few hundred miles, nor of being in the restaurant in which they worked. *We* are uncertain if *we* flew there, though *we* think *we* did. Then we all flew to New York, though *we* don't remember flying; instead, it is known and shared by one of *us* without presenting the actual memory of the plane.

[I have since recalled a split second flash of memory of being in J's restaurant in north Florida.]

We were greeted at the airport by a man with dark hair in a suit, roughly 45, maybe close to 50. We were then driven to the Roosevelt Hotel where *we* stayed—at least *we* consciously recall being in the lobby of this historic hotel, yet remember absolutely nothing about the rooms, including if *we* shared a room with someone or were alone? Nothing!

From this point on, *we* have flashbacks of being in a yellow cab racing very fast down a narrow street. *We* recall eating out at a restaurant and being served a seven-course meal at a large, long table with J., D., and the man in the suit from the airport, as well as other people that *we* do not know. *We* also recall being in a small Italian restaurant where the waiters and waitresses took time out to sing at a microphone. *We* have flashbacks of walking in downtown New York, as well as being inside Saint Patrick's Cathedral and sitting on the steps outside watching people go by. It was cold, so *we* are guessing it was fall or early spring, though not full winter.

[I recall I wore a rabbit fur coat during that trip (as well as for several years) given to me by a "fiancé" from a family associated with my father through business. There is quite a bit more related to this family and my family provided further on, though much of it remains lost to me. The irony of wearing a "rabbit fur" coat is not lost to me. A way to reinforce *rabbit's* programming and the potential threat of things to come.]

Of all the flashbacks, the flashback of what *we* were told was a building on Wall Street frightens *us* the most. *We* recall going into a dressing room of some kind with D. to change into in corsets, hose, and heels. Two young Florida girls in their twenties, tanned and smiling, half-naked. *We* then entered a room filled with approximately twenty men in suits. A wall of windows looking out onto the city indicated it was midday and we were several floors up. We walked among them being "charming, yet not too talkative", our instructions from J. The men looked us up and down and enjoyed the alcoholic drinks we served.

This scenario has haunted *us* due to a clear memory of a terrible *feeling* as well as the last recalled fragment of this event. As within many alter experience memory downloads, this alter tells *me* that something was happening that she was not aware of. It's as if a part of *us* knows something else is occurring, but *we* cannot even inquire within *ourselves* enough to figure it out. As soon as the *feeling* appears, it slips away and *we* continue *our* program. This entire experience *feels* that way, and the last piece made *us* feel very frightened:

We are standing still in the center of the room holding *our* tray and smiling. A man in a gray suit in his thirties or forties, slightly shorter than *us* as *we* are in heels, is walking around *us*, looking *us* up and down without speaking. The alter had the distinct feeling that he was choosing *us*, *But for what?*

The download ends with no conscious recall of leaving Wall Street, going back to the Roosevelt Hotel, or flying back to Florida—*nothing more of the entire trip*! However, *i* still *feel* anxious and sick at this memory, even after four years of deprogramming. *We* are also certain that while standing in that room being circled by the man in the final memory fragment, *we* switched alters per programming.

Uptime

The FBI

We are now sure that D. and *we* were being demoed on Wall Street and that investors were indeed being sought, but possibly for a very different agenda than was told to *us*.

As a manager, *we* helped this *tmk* family open two more locations within a tri-county area. By the time they had established the third location, FBI presence was apparent. *We* were told by one of the sons that wiretaps had been installed with the cooperation of their father. Maybe he got caught with his hand in the cookie jar and was being used by the FBI in some way, or *we* were being told a lie to explain the FBI presence, or a faction of the FBI was trying to gain information about this particular arm of the *tmk* Network, given that all high-level organizations have *tmk* factions. *All*. *We* do not recall any court appearances or judgments involving law enforcement regarding the *tmk* family.

We have since come to understand that FBI presence regarding the *tmk* family's restaurant and bar franchise went farther than *we* originally suspected. Due to *our* inability to prove involvement by certain individuals, they shall remain nameless, though not so in *our* personal support system conversations. Included is a high-level FBI official who, despite claims to have "retired" in the 1970s, we believe continued to work for this Network, possibly under duress. *We* contend that he had connections to this restaurant and bar and its programming and use of *tmk* slaves, including his possible personal sexual involvement with slaves out of a Manhattan Beach, California location.

It would not be the first or last time *we* encountered men in suits claiming to be FBI while not displaying any identification, since the men *we* were being handled by were involved in drug trafficking and prostitution. It is difficult to determine which handlers came first and likely that the number of people involved with *our* various alters at that time were numerous. From 18 through *our* early twenties, *we* consciously remember being run by several handlers, one running a very large county in the aforementioned tri-county area, trafficking drugs and running a prostitution network. He may also have been engaged in gun trafficking, due to some of the other people who show up in *our* alter memories. A man presenting as FBI warned *us* about him while he was in the restroom in a nightclub in Clearwater, Florida. *We* recall *our* front alters becoming frightened by his activities, yet do not recall the circumstances of *our* eventual split from him.

Through most of these years of heavy use, *we* officially lived in Florida and were most definitely associated with and utilized by what is known as "the Octopus". (See Resources: *The Last Circle: Danny Casolero's Investigation into the Octopus and the PROMIS Software Scandal.*)

The Island and Shiny Purple

Another fragmented memory from *our* sex and kill program alters puts *us* in what *we* believe are the Bahamas, a location *we* have fragmented conscious memory of going to in *our* early 20's on several occasions with handlers. *Our* memory is in more than one part, each a segment of the same event, within hours of each other.

In the first segment, it is daytime and *we* are seated in a slightly raised section of the restaurant at a small, round, wooden table with two dark -haired men, one being a lawyer and the other possibly *our* handler. They are facing away from *us*, looking out the open slatted wooden shutters painted a light color toward the water and beach beyond the restaurant. A wall is behind *us*, to *our* right and left. We are in an alcove. Just beyond the shutters are fronds of potted palms hanging slightly over into the opening and framing *our* view. The shiny wooden floor has two steps down to the main floor of the restaurant where there are other small tables and chairs, after which it opens out onto a beach of white sand.

We are in what *we* call *holding pattern*, a void alter of *ours*. *We* can acutely *see* and *hear* the surroundings and yet *we* are empty inside in this alter. This is an actual personality, but designed as empty and waiting—an alter between alters, a place where *we* are put to await the next switch. Within this *holding pattern*, *we* are as usual devoid of the ability to ask questions even of *our* own mind, devoid of the capacity to reason. *We* simply are. Yet we can mentally record what is happening.

The two men are engaged in conversation about where they would like to dine tonight. They wish to eat at a nice restaurant. *We* are not a part of what they are discussing, nor do *we* exist at this moment for them. In fact, the most predominant awareness *we* have in this segment of memory is that *we* are observing without any feelings or thoughts.

The second segment is later. *We* become aware that *we* are in a white hotel room walking over to clothing hanging on the outside of a closed closet door made of slatted, white shutters near the room's front door. Hanging there are shiny purple, satin pants with a hand-written note saying, "Wear this to dinner." *We* are in the *holding pattern* alter until *we* read the note. The combination of the clothing, colors, and written words initiate a switch into a sex alter who knows she is to go to the lawyer's room to seduce him. As *we* move from the *holding pattern* alter into the sex alter for the sexual encounter, it feels good to *us* and her. There is an almost inexplicable *relief* when *we* are released from the *holding pattern* due to the profound void and emptiness that *we* feel in that alter, as well as clearly experiencing the *feel* of sex *coming into us* and are very pleased by the thought and feel of going to his room to seduce him. This is the alter's life and to her it is not only okay—it is natural per her programming. *We* are not going to dinner, as the note says; *we* are to go to his room without even putting on the outfit. This alter is to go to his room for a sexual encounter, that is all she is programmed to do.

This is where it is difficult for *us* because *we* know that the lawyer was killed after *our* sexual encounter with him began. *We* can *see* and *feel* that it is *us* who was responsible for his death. *Our* alters have shown *us* that, yet *we* cannot consciously tell you how he died because it is not what this sex alter knows.

[Some time after first publishing this book, we had a resurfacing of a most horrific memory. The encounter was with an alter named *She 29th*, a kill alter programmed to be much like our programmers: devoid of compassion and lusting for sex and death. In the memory, I experienced the killing of a man during sex through S&M. At the point of erotic asphyxiation, my alter took this man's life while he was tied to the bed. It will appear later on in this manuscript under *S&M and the Lawyer*. I suspect it may have been this encounter, however, in the *holding pattern*, I do not recall the detail of the faces of the two men I was with and then the later encounter in another alter.]

Bodies on the Beach

The first flashback presented by *our* alter regarding this on-task occurred approximately eight months prior to another experience memory download that came in several segments, all pertaining to this occurrence. For *our* front alter, it was only yesterday that we found this first download written last year in *our* deprogramming journal and realized that it too pertained.

In the first download, the alter is very sexual in a young adult body, fully developed, yet emotionally childlike. Due to several downloads *we* realize she is part of *our* kill programming. *We* call her *the wild one*. *We* are still uncertain about her exact role in this kill, but she was clearly known to the couple in this home before returning to them in an on-task and participating in some capacity in the death of the man and the adolescent son.

To backtrack: In the first download, *the wild one* is playfully and innocently flirting (in her consciousness, anyway) with the man in front of his wife. Both of them act a little surprised, which this alter quickly interprets as them feeling sorry for her. They certainly do not overreact.

The very next flashback presented in this first download is of *our* alter making her way down to a beach at a 45° angle from a rugged precipice above. *Our* alter *feels* the danger *we* often *feel* when kill alters are present.

From the two experience memory downloads, it is apparent that this middle-aged couple knew *us* in some capacity and that *we* were later responsible for the death of the man and adolescent son which had been planned for when the wife/mother was not around, after which she would be shown their bodies on the beach, her fear and hysteria being the desired effect *our* kontrollers and handlers intended.

In this case, it is possible that *our* alter broke programming, but there is no evidence except for *our* suspicion.

The other flashback from the second download regards this same location in *my* observation, given the house on the bluff and the beach below. If this is the same location as that of the other two memory downloads of two other alters (the flirting encounter and the other one of making *our* way down to the beach with a sense of danger), it puts *us* there at least three times, allowing *us* to recognize this may have been a regular location of *our* use.

Our adult un-childlike sex alter is wearing a yellow skimpy string bikini and getting ready to exit the house to go down to the beach to "entertain" several men waiting for her.

This experience download is in three segments, all presented by more than one alter. The first segment *we* will not present here due to it being unnecessary. The second and third segments *we* understand to be at different points in time within the same incident. *We* will present them in the order they were presented to *us*. If this is the order in which they occurred, it may mean the woman was killed after her husband and son were shown to her.

[I am presenting this for the purpose of showing how much energy and focus goes into understanding through these alter downloads what my life has been. The only way to truly come to see this is to record everything regardless of it making sense, or not, at the time of its presentation. If you think it is confusing to read, imagine living it and attempting to recover your mind, spirit and soul.]

Having exited an expensive house up on a remote bluff, we are walking in a sandy area. Sea oats stretch out toward the ocean before we reach the drop off up ahead. *We* sense this is the California Coast. *We* are above the shoreline and approaching a drop off down the bluff. An early fifties blond woman is walking on *our* left just a couple of footsteps behind *us*. *We* are leading her and *feel* nothing, no emotions at all: *we* are on-task.

As *we* reach the rise a couple of hundred or so feet out of the back of her house, *we* look down at two bodies rocking slightly in the shallows, the shore protected from some kind of break from the open ocean, or it is at low tide. This is clearly a protected area, private beach. The bodies are brownish-green in color, as if in a degraded condition or coated or covered in something. Ropes are tied around their necks that run about six or eight feet up onto the shore where each is secured to a small heavy metal pole like rebar. *We* feel they have possibly been in this water for several days.

The woman reaches the rise and looks, emitting a muffled scream and clasping her hands over her mouth. *We* do not look at her but at the bodies as she tries to contain her grief over the bodies and fear of *us*. This alter feels nothing but realizes in a detached way that the man and child were very close to her. It is a very intellectual observation. The woman tries to control her uncontrollable emotions so *we* are not angered. That the deaths do not affect *us* is creating additional fear of what *we* will do next. *We* know this, *we* can read her. *We* turn away from her and look at the back of the house. *We* feel a tightening of *our* stomach, *But why?* This is not something this alter usually feels.

Our programming was briefly breaking due to the nature of *our* relationship to what had occurred. But this alter's programming does not allow for emotions, so the break disappears quickly.

This experience memory download breaks and then continues with *us* in *the wild one* propped up on *our* elbows and lying naked on the floor on *our* stomach, legs bent at the knees, ankles crossed, feet up in the air. The location is the house on the bluff. *The wild one* is humming and looking at *our* hands. *We* are in an adult body, late teens or early twenties, *our* long blond hair pulled up in a ponytail. Something has occurred in this room and *we* are facing away from it, the "consequences" behind *us*.

("Consequences" are what they are to this alter—dead bodies she has killed.) There is a man close to *our* right side facing away from *us*, squatting down, doing something to the "consequences". *We* do not look at him, yet know that he glances back at *us*. *We* know him and he knows *us* very well.

We have much difficulty with this memory, including severe physical reactions during *our* first attempt to record it in writing. *We see* more than *we* can write and know more than *we* have said. Eventually, *our* front alters will address it as is needed, it just takes time.

What *we* will write is that the man squatting near *us* is a dark-spirited man doing something to the dead bodies, either the man and adolescent or the woman. (*We* strongly suspect that *the wild one* wound up killing the wife/mother though she was not originally supposed to per her instructions and program, and that the alter who led the woman out of the house to show her the bodies, was clearly not *the wild one*. As well, *our* alters are generally very meticulous about the details and timing of memory downloads; hence *our* confusion over why *we* would be shown this segment after being shown the emotionless alter presenting the bodies to the woman unless the "consequences" are now the woman herself. *The wild one* successfully distracted herself and *us* while lying there on the floor. When *we* later drew a picture of this scene, the dark-spirited man squatting behind *us* was drawn completely in solid black.)

[Note: In late summer 2010, information came my way to help me understand why the bodies were presented as they were to the woman. My kill alter was just following her programming without any information other than what she needed to know, and my front alters had no conscious knowledge of Masonic traditions and codes. The shallow water's edge and ropes around the victims' necks were to send a message to others in the Network that, *If you step out of line, we will kill you*—crystal clear to me. I would discover this information thanks to David Icke's book, *Tales from the Time Loop: The Most Comprehensive Exposé of the Global Conspiracy Ever Written and All You Need to Know to Be Truly Free*, 2003.]

Alter 14's Right Hand Grip

Alter 14 gave the following experience memory download to *us* with her lack of emotion, systematic execution of skill, and program-initiated thoughts occurring at the moment of assault. Someone else in *us* would become conscious in the aftermath of what occurred in the parking lot and would have to face what *alter 14* left for *us* to see, which was why *we* returned from this memory download to *our* front alter consciousness yelling aloud. For those of *us* who are not in any way killers, it was surreal and devastating. With every presentation by *alter 14*, *we* are amazed by her lack of fear, her precision in *our* body and mind, and her power. She frightens *us* and yet she belongs to *us* as well. She does what she is programmed and trained to do, nothing more, and absolutely nothing less.

Alter 14's download starts in a parking lot at night. A light on a tall pole is near where *we* are. She is approaching a man. Off to *our* left about 25 to 30 feet away near a delivery truck is a woman with another man who just exited the truck. The truck is like an old bread delivery truck. *Alter 14* gives *us* the impression that these two men are planning to abduct the woman and *alter 14* has come to stop that from happening.

In a split-second move, *alter14* steps towards the man in front of her and grasps his windpipe in a fingers and thumb grip. The man seems to know what *alter 14*'s intention is and succeeds in knocking *our* right arm from his throat. Both are moving quickly and intently, *alter 14 completely* focused and not taking *our* eyes off of his windpipe, thinking the whole time, *finish this quickly* because she clearly knows that each passing second is a second closer to not succeeding in crushing his windpipe and once the target knows what is happening, the chance of success is limited.

This is *our* view during download, the view through *our* alter's eyes. To this day, *we* can still *see* his windpipe as well as *feel* the emotionless thoughts of *alter 14*. Her calm, powerful confidence is most certainly not *ours*, it is indeed hers.

He is moving backwards in an evasive dance, yet not taking his eyes off of *us*, as she is aggressively making intermittent contact with his throat but not maintaining the grip. She is not only envisioning crushing his windpipe, but of crushing it and ripping it from the throat. She is not angry, only motivated solely by being on-task, something that must occur.

A blackout—for lack of a better term—occurs at this point in the download. Others of *us* become conscious as it continues with a woman's scream. *We* are now standing in the parking lot as *we* come into the consciousness of another alter, no longer *alter 14*. *We* see the woman off to our left about to be abducted screaming hysterically and looking in *our* direction. There is a body in front of *us* motionless on the blacktop: the man *alter 14* was pursuing. *We* are responsible. As with other downloads about *our* kills and other kills for which *we* were present, *we* often don't have the actual kill in *our* conscious mind. *We* would like to say that *we* never know it occurred, yet that is not the case.

Warlords, Guns & Money

6
Ritual Use, Ritual Death

The ritual experiences are difficult to assimilate into *our* front alter consciousness. They were kept in *our* alter's memory for good reason, and more often than not they are held by several alters. They did not present more than *we* could handle, but much like *our* killing experiences, the effect when they surfaced was often debilitating. At times, *we* would get just a part of the experience from one alter while other alters presented other parts of the experience and left *us* physically, emotionally, and mentally devastated for days, weeks, even months.

Part of the reason was *we* had not yet come to realize how many of *us* there were, nor that these horrible things had occurred to or been perpetrated by *us*. *We* who are part of the frontline system were terribly confused as to *our* age then and how it could still be happening "now". *We* were haunted for days, weeks, months and years as the memories surfaced, incapable of consciously grasping them, let alone assimilating them. Full physical, mental, and emotional abreactions are still common.

By far, these experiences are the most profound when it comes to triggering *our* suicide programming.

There Be Dragons

We are in a kitchen with an adult male who is an *entity/demon*. Also here are a little boy and a little girl who are "creatures", not children, allowing *our* other alter to remain somewhat detached from them. One of *our* alters *sees* "creatures" in order to buffer *our* psyche while *we* see children. The door leading outside is open and to *our* left; beyond it, the screen door is shut. Outside, a Komodo Dragon looking creature steps slowly into view. It is taller than *us* and looking inside, moving ever so slowly. Terror rises in *us*: the screen door is not latched. Slowly, *we* reach out to close it, knowing that *we* and the little ones with *us* are in danger.

Instantly, the standing Komodo Dragon is inside the door next to *us*, towering over *us*. *We* are frantic now and attempt to pick-up the little boy and girl off the floor to get them out of the Dragon's reach. The little ones do not realize the danger and innocently continue to move about on the floor out of *my* reach. *We* are now hysterical inside, yet trying to remain silent.

The Dragon and the adult male then begin a frenzied fight, thrashing about wildly. The little ones are ripped to shreds in moments, their limbs torn off. *We* scream hysterically, even in *our* front alter consciousness as *we* return to the here and now. This memory would leave *us* feeling desperate and suicidal for weeks. As with others, it was difficult to put away this recall, as there was no place to put it.

Cassandra

Monatomic Gold

The following memory returned amidst repetitious **loop programs** running all night long, accompanied by a low-grade fever and body aches—what *we* once called *delirious sleep*, a night state in which sleep never comes amidst ongoing physical symptoms. It is a common, recurring state, day in and day out, while experience memories surface, past and present. *We* felt drugged in the original experience, which is partially why it felt so surreal.

We are in a room with a fog that *we* believe is coming from *our* drugged mind. A dozen or so men are there with *us*. A gold bowl is sitting on top of a table or surface of some kind. The bowl is about a foot and a half across and about eight inches deep, thick and roughly hewn stone or ceramic, with an ancient, pitted surface. It is empty except for three small white cylindrical pills with a small amount of a pink substance around their edges, sitting just inside below the rim. Oddly, the white pills are not resting on the bottom of the bowl, as if defying gravity. *Our* alter stops downloading there and another alter takes over to tell *us* that these men used *us* sexually and that blood was added to the bowl containing the white pills, which the men then ingested. Semen was on *us* as well.

We cannot recount this experience without weeping and gagging. After this memory first resurfaced, despair and *our* suicide programming plagued *us* for weeks.

We were at a loss to explain the gravity-defying pills, but were certain someone may someday be able to explain it. *We* have since learned of a weightless substance called *Monatomic Gold* greatly desired by certain humans and *entities* alike. Its multi-dimensional properties make it more and more weightless as the amount is increased. *Our* source alchemically produced it, claiming that some was stolen from his heavily secured lab and that the thieves did not set off the alarm system (a system that ran in the five figures to procure). Since in deep deprogramming, *we* have had a small jar of it in *our* hand. It is a tangible, physical substance that does not belong to our physical realm alone. It defies many of the accepted physical laws of our daily reality.

[This substance should not be utilized by anyone. Its promises of health-building and youth are outweighed by what is given access to ones physical and subtle bodies, therefore affecting ones spirit and soul. It actually makes humans more susceptible to being accessed by these malevolent entities.

71

Malevolence uses humanity's ignorance against them. The recognition that many of the alchemical processes and results that were once understood through proper training have been lost to the subdued consciousness man lives under currently. This is what makes certain things untenable in our time, though I suspect with the continued proper evolution forward, much of this knowledge will return. It is not simply a matter of this or that is good for you, but under what circumstances and methods it is and isn't. Man of today knows nothing of this.]

Human Flesh

We present the next experience because it is integral to *our* programming and use, part of *our* training being to dispose of bodies after kills. But the fragment *we* share here is very disturbing. *We* share only what *we* deem necessary to create an understanding of what it was like under programming and help people grasp what a true miracle it is every time a *total mind kontrolled* slave begins to sincerely heal with the assistance of Benevolent, Unconditional, Creative Love.

The memory download entails dark-skinned, human female body parts (including pubic hair) tangled up inside of a black trash bag amidst blood and other body fluids. Additionally, there are memories of consuming human flesh and blood.

Our programmers sought not only to successfully create kill alters, but to dissociate *us* in the most extreme ways possible from *our* humanity. Thus *our* alters were programmed to undergo and then subsequently perpetrate many horrendous abuses.

We are standing over a stainless steel sink in a kitchen. The water is running full force from the faucet and overflowing onto the floor because the drain is blocked. A man is standing behind *us*, watching. He is one of them. *We* are projectile vomiting liquid containing small chunks of human flesh and blood into the overflowing sink. *We* step back only to realize that the floor is covered with water mixed with the human flesh and blood. This memory is lucid, vivid, and horrendous.

Since *our* programming began breaking down in *our* early thirties, *our* front alters realized that *we* were no longer consuming the flesh of animals because *we* could not handle its texture in *our* mouth. This is still true to this day, now that the rest of *us* know consciously what *we* were programmed to do.

Subjecting *us* to this trauma had several purposes for various parts of *us* as well as the *demons* that inhabited *us*. For some of *our* alters, it separated *us* from all other humans and made *us* believe for many years that *we* are more like *our* programmers. Certain alters thus believe they are not human because the ones *we* truly serve are not human. The double bind is that *we* are *one of them, always and forever*, due to no human ever being able to love *us*. Additionally, *my* human part will never forgive what *we* have done and is thus buried so deep within *us*. It has created an isolation that is still so omnipresent that *we* wonder if it will ever really be possible to *see* and *feel* that *we* are indeed like others around *us*. Hence, *our* strong need to be able to associate with other slaves who are sincerely healing, particularly those who were programmed to be utilized the way parts of *us* were.

The *demons* themselves participate in such activities on a regular basis; hence those *entities* running the alters inside *us* drive those same alters to such deeds. These *entities* are the handlers within, creating **cult-loyal alters** with programming reminiscent of the personalities of the very *demons* themselves, though much more a human alter that is despondent and empty of spirit. Thus binding *us* to them mind, heart, and soul—until from *our* soul the Benevolent, Unconditional, Creative Love that *we* are first and forever pushes through the lies of the unforgivable.

7
All in a Night's Work

This particular experience memory is a combination of torture, program-ming, and use all in one night. It also shows the extent a full abreaction can have when it surfaces within deprogramming.

Full Abreaction on Halloween

This download is definitely the most severe abreaction in *our* deep depro-gramming thus far, meaning that its effect on *us* during and after reliving it lasted for days. Because of the intensity involving overwhelming physical, emotional, and mental symptoms, *we* thoroughly believed that it occurred on the night of October 30th and early morning hours of October 31st of the year 2008, but the reality was that it was an experience memory from years ago.

We will now relate the fragmented memory download, followed by parts of *our* journey in the days following. What *we* know from hundreds of experience memory downloads is that the dates that *our* alters choose to download are not random; they repeatedly choose the day or date that the experience actually occurred and can even present it repeatedly each year on that date until resolved by *our* wholeness.

The part of the experience now in *our* conscious mind began with it being night and *we* are in the backseat of a light-colored late 1970s, early 1980s model Suburban vehicle. The driver is a man in his late thirties, average build, dark blond hair; *we* are clearly blocked from remembering his face. This is quite common: *we* often remember intricate details such as the designs on clothes, but faces remain in a fog or non-existent, as if *we* never saw them.

We pull up to the door of an industrial shop outside which another man is standing and looking at *us*. He is about the same age as the driver and is blond with blue-green eyes. *We* know him as "Jones" and remem-ber his face. "Jones" brings up a wild image: Jones is unpredictable and aggressive to one or more of *our* alters. *We* are in an alter that is innocent and totally oblivious to any danger, neither able to think of why she is there nor able to fear it.

[This alter appears in many different downloads, apparently used to move me about without any need to be concerned I would try to escape. Using programming to hypnotize the mind from being able to perform everyday tasks such as moving the limbs, and in another case with me, even moving my eyes, is quite common. If one were to look into **Targeted Individual (TI's)** research, one would find these physical tortures plaguing citizens worldwide in the millions nowadays.]

The driver turns the engine off and exits the Suburban, walking around the back to pass where *we* are seated in the back seat on the passenger side, the front and back being bench seats. He looks in at *us* as he passes on his way to Jones. *We* watch him as *our* alter attempts to exit the vehicle, baffled that she cannot move her hands or feet. She feels twisted up, yet cannot figure out why. And yet she is not afraid, but is rather content to believe that the driver will get her out. It is then that *we* realize how unaware of her situation this alter really is, perhaps because fear is not even possible for her. *We* see no physical bonds around her hands or feet and believe she is *bound within her mind*—programmed to not be able to move or break free because she does not even know she is programmed.

When the driver reaches Jones, *we* hear Jones say, "I've had her." Both are looking at *our* alter in the backseat. Jones has not taken his cold stare off of *us* since we pulled up. The driver too is cold throughout the entire scenario.

The memory fragments here, though *we* know *we* were taken into the shop, tortured, and raped, the latter involving a cattle prod, an object used on *us* repeatedly over the years. *We* also know that drugs were used. Additionally, *we* know that this experience was about torture, programming, and use all wrapped up in one night. The *degree* of this experience is what puts it in a category all its own, there being many aspects of what is locked in *our* mind and body that *we* do not know how to let out. *Our* inability to capture or define it makes it *feel* separate, something other than or beyond occurrences written about so far. It also occurred on more than one occasion.

The real confusion for *us* began in the early morning hours of October 31, 2008, partly due to the fact that *we* were alter-awake most of the night. *We* were accustomed to looking at *our* watch that *we* kept next to *us* at night to record times, as the memory patterns were ongoing and often repetitive. On heavy alter download nights, all sense of time is lost.

According to *our* bedside watch, *we* arose with awareness at 3:30 a.m. with a great deal of nausea, even getting up to get plastic bags to keep next to *us* for vomit. *We* tried to lie down, yet were up and down until 7:00 a.m. when *we* finally just stayed up. *Our* bowels repeatedly evacuated. Homeopathic remedies didn't alleviate *our* symptoms. *Our* sense of time was so distorted that *we* couldn't understand how the events of the previous night/early morning hours could have occurred. Even though the time seemed in short supply, *we* never really trusted *our* sense of time, given that most of *our* life spanning years had been lost, so *we* didn't trust *our* judgment of time within this particular event at all.

What *we* awakened to in the morning were physical and emotional symptoms that would worsen over the next few hours and continue for days. Heart palpitations were more severe than usual, though not uncommon in extreme experience memory downloads, particularly when electricity had been used on *us*. As *our* chest fluttered throughout the day, *we* wondered if *we* might have a heart attack. Due to years of trauma, electricity, and drugs, *we* were aware in deep deprogramming that *our* heart was not very strong. *We* were sick to *our* stomach and running a fever with severe body pain.

Our abdomen swelled due to the cattle prod rape, and by late morning, *our* womb, lower back, kidneys, and entire pelvic region were filled with pain—a condition that recurs throughout *our* life. *Our* front alters are unable to explain it, though it often comes on the heels of vaginal and anal penetration memories.

In this download, the emotion was just as intense. *We* wept almost continuously, despairing that *we* had so many more fragments. At this time, *we* were staying about twenty miles from a small town in someone's home while they were gone. Thus *we* were alone. But *we* felt *we* had to go into town and pushed *ourselves* to go. *Our* ability to do this never ceases to amaze me, *our* capacity to dissociate still alarming to *our* conscious mind. During the town trip, *our* physical and emotional abreaction symptoms worsened. *We* had several conversations with various alters while triggers all about *us* had a profound effect due to *our* vulnerability. *We* couldn't see that *we* were pushing *ourselves* much too far because *we* were so accustomed to pushing beyond *our* physical, emotional, and mental pain by dissociating.

During the abreaction, *we* experienced severe body memories and a despondency that pulled *us* away from *our* deprogramming support people for days. The degree of hopelessness had *us* believing that *we* would never be safe from "them". On the first day following the memory download, *we* wept uncontrollably. For the first time in *our* deprogramming, *we* were consciously aware of experiencing re-fragmenting or splitting within *our* mind while still under the belief that it had actually occurred the previous night, and that *our* fragmenting was due to trauma inflicted in the here and now. After four days, *we* came to understand that *we* had instead had a full abreaction to an experience memory that had actually re-fragmented *us*. *Our* symptoms were so extreme and the visual memory so lucid that *we* believed *we* were there in the here and now, despite *our* younger appearance in the download. This is one of the dangers of attempting to deprogram on one's own. It would be when *we* finally allowed a member of *our* three- person support group back into *our* world on the fourth day—another recovering victim of *tmk*—that *we* discovered while talking with her by phone that this was a full abreaction and began to understand what an abreaction really was and the dangers of being alone during them.

Here, *we* want to include part of *our* journal entries from those days subsequent to the memory surfacing. These excerpts show how someone moving through the world under *total mind kontrol* can experience life.

> journal entry, november 1st
> ...at *our* last stop in town at the health food store, one of the employees had on an elaborate halloween costume...the twenty-something woman had gone to great lengths to recreate the depictions [of demons]...she was in black and red...a black satin cape with a hood...her face painted entirely in black and red face paint...horns protruding from the sides of her forehead...she was bagging groceries in the line in which *we* stood behind two other customers...*we* began to weep uncontrollably [as *we* looked at her], feeling as if *we* existed a million miles away from where *we* appeared to be...wondering who all of these humans existing around *us* were...*we* could feel no connection to them whatsoever...

Nine months later, *we* realized that the costume was that of the Sith from one of the recent *Star Wars* films. *We* saw a picture of this character in a magazine and recognized its similarity to *demons we* are familiar with.

In the above abreaction, *we* were so completely out of *our* body (dissociated) that *we* were unable to see *ourselves* as human. Also, red and black together have shown up in *our* programming memory downloads, associated with at least two different alters. This combination of colors was seen by some of *us* after being triggered in the first 15 minutes of the pilot episode of a network television show that *we* believe *without any doubt* to be a trigger for *trauma-based mind kontrol* slaves with kill programming. *We* are sure that this television show, along with many recently released movies, are associated with End-Time programming for *tmk* slaves. (See Book 1, Chapter 11, "The Forties", *My Own Worst Enemy*.)

> journal entry, november 2ⁿᵈ
> ...*our* low back seems locked in pain...sleep constantly interrupted... almost constant internal programs going off day and night...*we* see now that *we* are not supposed to recover for any use by "them"...something inside of *us* has changed since early a.m. of october 31st. who is coming out of that?...it is out of focus...*we* are finding it more and more difficult now to delineate groupings of days...it is all running together...an assault by *our* own memories...alters?...not wanting to be in *our* body...feeling a million miles away from everybody else...a state of limbo...

> journal entry, november 4ᵗʰ
> ...dealing with anorexic programming...nausea for last couple of days... *we* realized *we* were starving, like someone threw a light switch...it felt good to eat...*we* are on *our* way back...*we* hope.

8
More On-Task

The Perfect, Lethal Hostess

This memory download came during a period of ongoing downloads by *our* alters 24 hours a day. Preceding it, *we* were experiencing physical and emotional memories—pain in *our* body, emotional heaviness and deep sadness sometimes lasting for weeks.

We call the alter presenting to *us* in segments *the perfect hostess*. *We* have encountered her many times in a variety of on-tasks filled with extensive details, including faces. Her thoughts in her programmed mind are only those that assist her programmed on-task.

First, *we* are aware that she is responsible for several small groups of important people—at least people who believe they are important, though she realizes that they think more of themselves than others do. This recurring feeling of hers is initiated by the thoughts of another alter who is also present behind her during these experiences, apparently *waiting*.

[There have been several downloads and encounters with my alters in which one alter is hiding, so to speak, behind another alter. I have seen this in my third eye (mind's eye). In some cases it is an intentionally programmed issue as I suspect in this particular instance; an alter waiting to be triggered forward. At other times it has been something some of the rather devious alters had attempted to utilize in deep deprogramming against me. Remember, these dark alters are run by entities.]

We are in a large facility of some kind where these groups of important people are separated into various rooms. *Our* alter enters an expensively decorated room with rich, dark-stained wood walls and a dark rectangular wooden table at the center, the end of which faces the door through which *we* enter. Around the table are seated five men in their forties, one in his fifties, and two women in their twenties. One of the women has long blond hair and is dressed in black. *The perfect hostess* is aware that these women are mere ornaments for these men—lovers, nothing more—but must be treated with respect above and beyond what they deserve because of the men they are with, who are assholes but must be treated like dignitaries, her specialty. This was her understanding, yet the critique was not actually hers.

As *our* alter enters, everyone at the table looks up, the men frustrated at having been kept waiting. *The perfect hostess* holding *our* body is apologetic in her most disarming and charming way, and the men are calmed. A younger man at the far end of the table introduces the women to *us*, each of whom makes eye contact as she is introduced. The blonde is named Jennifer.

We would like to interject here that a recurring *see* and *feel* within memories is that *we* the alters are working with a capacity far beyond the five senses, yet this capacity is of restrictive use due to the parameters of the alter's program. *Our perfect hostess* alter is caught in a dichotomy: her ability to take in her surroundings and discern its value is extraordinary, and yet she is incapable of using this same information to reason out her own situation and reach the inescapable conclusion that she is in serious danger. In this particular situation, she knows exactly who these men and women are on a hierarchic level, but is not concerned with their three-dimensional existence except as it directly pertains to her on-task. She can walk into a room and immediately discern each individual's power status and know where and where not to tread based on the level of power present in any given individual. From this insight, every aspect of hosting them is determined. This is the very thing that makes her *the perfect hostess*.

The rest of her capacities branch out from this central ability of honing in on levels of power. She cannot think in terms of *entities* or *demons*, though that is precisely what she is "reading" in terms of power. *We* have *seen* her with both low-level *entities* and high-level *demons*, and her manner as well as her internal respect is drastically different. Her program is to get the on-task done and survive; for this, she is on extreme alert state inside while outwardly presenting a charming, cool, calm hostess. Many of *our* alters have an extraordinary capacity for discerning danger levels and maintain a perpetually heightened, alert state not necessarily equated with fear.

In this experience, *our hostess* is in a minimal state of stress because she herself is being run by *entities*—what *we* think of as internal handlers really running the programs but with the assistance of external handlers. *We* are very clear that *our* main handlers are the *entities* themselves. This alter's ability to "read" *entity* levels stems directly from the internal *demonic* handler deeply enhancing an ability *we* already have.

One of the noticeable differences in this memory was how out of program she was in presenting strong judgment about these people. She clearly *saw* and *felt* that they were "nobodies"—adolescent *entities* whose asses she could kick if allowed, and on some level wanted to but wouldn't because it was not allowed, i.e. it was not in her program to hurt or kill.

In the immediate aftermath of this experience download, *we* clearly saw another alter surfacing, one *we* were very familiar with, run and handled by Lilith: *she 29th*, a kill alter. *The perfect hostess* is also handled by Lilith. *We* know this because of the signature sexual energy used by *the perfect hostess* for success in her programmed on-tasks. Killing is not all that *she 29th* does, yet one of her signatures is to loathe those who think they are powerful when they are not—not in the way she understands power, at least. *She 29th*'s programming contains a pure hatred of anything less than power, which she refers to as "juice". To *our* understanding of *she 29th*, the only humans worthy of life are those possessed by high-level *demons*, though she would gladly kill them as well if her handler instructed her to, as she relishes absorbing their "juice" at their death.

From what *we* have been shown, *she 29th* does not think she is human, given how she loathes perceived *human* weakness. *She 29th* appears to be an alter that is a replica of her programmers and kontrollers. In fact, when she presents to *us*, her mannerisms and language are identical to those of *our* abusers, including their consistent, alternation between degradation and false love. She is therefore an internal programmer not only by *entity*, but also *in the alter* run by Lilith.

In many alter personalities, it appears that the *entity* is the whole negative source of evil energy, but with *she 29th* it is as though the alter is aligned with the programmers and *demons* who are really one and the same. This is what *we* have come to call "cult-loyal alters", of which there may be more inside of *us*. *She 29th* is a master at *seeing* and *feeling* individuals' "juice", a very accurate metaphor for life energy, including the ejaculate of the powerful upon whom she enjoys performing oral sex. *We* now understand that her hatred of humans is her programming that allows and justifies being able to engage in killing without remorse.

What became clear with this download was that *the perfect hostess* is attempting to co-exist with *she 29th*, maintaining her ever-charming essence while trying to keep *she 29th* from taking over. The reason *she 29th* is here at all is that she is part of the program at a later point—in other words, *she 29th* has been programmed to kill one of the men in the room, though we don't know which, a fragment not shown to *us*. *She 29th* does not willingly give *us* much information due to being cult-loyal.

[This would change for one request by me, and that was the construction of the colláge *The Story Behind the Story*, which relays the kill program to Dr. A. True Ott. A program that never took place thanks to God, the power of Love, and the deprogramming spirit.]

Eventually, *the perfect hostess* leaves the room and sends a couple of younger slaves, twins, in to "serve" the group. *We* choose not to go into the second part of this download at this time and will skip to the third segment.

Our on-task continued after *the perfect hostess* was switched to another alter. *We* are now in a smaller storage or utility room where a male is present. *We* believe he is a man, though to some of *us* the male *entities* can present as men—a much stronger presence. Whatever he is, he is present with *us* off to *our* right in the little room, though *we* do not see him as *we* would a three-dimensional person. *We* undo *our* pants and begin to masturbate.

Masturbation is a definitive program repeatedly downloaded by alters either to keep *us* in programming or to switch from one alter to another—that being the case here. *She 29th* began to come out. Together, the internal handler and male *entity* in the room ran the program necessary to switch *us*. *Remote handling*—particularly with switching sex and kill alters—took *us* some time to come to terms with. There were clearly many times a physical handler was present, and other times when *we* were, for all intents and purposes, alone.

[I would add here that remote technologies, actual physical technologies, have existed for many years regarding mind control. When I combine this knowledge with the proclamation of one of my alters during early deprogramming: "They are riding the technology into us," (us being *everyone*), I came to understand that there was a combination of remote technology and entity activity performing these switches as needed, *remotely* without any physical handler being necessary.]

This is where the conscious memory stops. *She 29th* does not tell *us* much; what *we* do understand is that *she 29th* was to end the life of one of the men in that room. She withholds everything not meant to get *us* back into the cult or to handle others for the cult, but gladly shares anything to confuse or distress *us*. *We* have been misled by her directions on several occasions since she first announced herself consciously to *us* in August 2008. By "cult", *we* mean the Network of government, military, intelligence, religions, secret societies, and corporate hierarchies.

Drive It In

These memories can be photographic upon presentation but void of specifics at the same time, due to *our* alter's programming to only be given the on-task necessities.

This memory came in two distinct parts—the first part being the programming, the second part being the programmed on-task that occurred in *our* younger years. In this instance, *we* are aware that the on-task presented by the alter is the programming for that on-task, even though sometimes the on-task has not yet taken place (like certain End-Time programming and kill programming), whereas most of the on-tasks that have been shown to *us* by *our* alters thus far have already taken place.

The first part is *we* are seated in a room with a table and a couple of chairs receiving "instructions" from men; different "instructions" are being given at different times in this room. *We* are in an altered state—a very non-emotional alter who knows these men as CIA—and the "instructions" are being given between separate events. Meaning, something is taking place in between the "instruction". At the time of this download, the main front alter was *consciously* unaware of the trauma necessary to the programming process to "lock it in", but in fact the "instructions" are being given between the traumas necessary to "locking it in".

The second part is the on-task, meaning what this alter did for at least part of the on-task. A high-level political event was occurring, a formal black tie event, and this alter's on-task was to "drive it in" in a particular vehicle. *We* are on a blacktop drive about a football field away from the estate. *Our* alter is dressed in black and white, yet what she is "driving in" is unclear, but *we* believe it is in the backseat and are fairly certain that the cargo is not a person. As to whether or not *we* drove to the front like the guests or continued to the back, *we* are unclear but suspect the latter.

We can still clearly *see* and *feel* the view of the very large, white estate with white Greco-Roman columns: the semi-circular entry up to the front of this large estate with its interior golden lights shining through the numerous windows as well as some exterior lights. The view at night is like a snapshot in detail. Several men and women in formal attire are entering while others exit vehicles near the entry where there is valet service. It looks like an individual's home.

This download was pivotal to understand internally how an alter only has the information necessary to her programming in the on-task. She can present to *us* but is incapable of giving what she does not have. *We* can *see* and *feel* her inability to ask why, what, where, who with any reasoning ability. The agenda beyond her part of the on-task is not even a question within her mind, nor is the end result.

Time Sensitive

This experience memory download came with much detail yet in fragments, in flashbacks. In the first part of the download, *we* are again aware that this alter was receiving training, instructions, and directions from what she knew to be CIA men. (Some of *our* alters are aware of being associated with men in the CIA.) She told *us* that the following on-task was performed by *us* with these CIA men in the location she showed to *us*, not solo.

We are in a large indoor space reminiscent of an airport, open with several escalators and a stairway before *us*, high ceilings going up several floors. Light colors predominate, double doors, tile floors, carpeted areas, people milling about with a sense of direction and purpose. *We* are going down a set of wide, carpeted stairs to the first floor. As *we* walk down, an escalator is coming up directly to *our* left. When *our* alter is just over halfway down the stairs, we lock eyes with a blond blue-eyed man maybe 30 years old getting on the escalator. The alter knows that once she reaches the bottom, she is to turn around and follow him. She chooses the escalator to the right of the one he is on. *We* are maybe fifteen feet behind him and though he does not turn around, this alter is aware that each of us seems to know who the other is.

Another fragment has this alter high up in what she says is the same building. It is different up there, lightly colored and the same carpeted hallway with double doors with bar handles, but much more closed in, with windows to *our* right. The area has the feel of an administrative zone, not public like down below. *We* are up quite high and alone now. *Our* alter tells *us* that *we* are entering places that *we* aren't supposed to. She is following "instructions," though this area is officially off limits to her. There seems to be no one around, yet *we* are clearly trying to not be seen by anyone. It seems to be midday outside.

The next fragment puts *us* back downstairs on what *we* know as the first floor, with people moving about, very public. As she walks on the highly polished tile floor, she is aware that the double doors with the long bar handles to *our* left are locked and she must find the right time to gain entry undetected. She *feels* a time schedule without being the least bit stressed about it. There is no fear, she is clearly on-task with a strong undercurrent of "time-sensitive".

This is most definitely an on-task that this alter performed in *our* past, associated with a "team" of other individuals, some of whom were associated with the CIA. The where, why, what, and who are not in *our* conscious mind.

Mutual Handling

The handler *we* refer to here is someone *we* have apparently had much contact with. *Our* association with him appears to span several decades, and he has more than one alter at his disposal. According to *our* alter downloads, his alters apparently personally use *alter 14*'s heavy sexual programming. *We* know who this handler is and follow his public lifestyle.

Alters can be used to handle other slaves, due to the *entities* running the alters making handling a mutual affair. In this particular case, *we* believe that *our* alter's apparent sexual encounters with this man reinforce his programming. (This is why you often see potential sexual partners sent in on an early deprogramming slave, to thwart and reinforce, if not reprogram.) *We see* him as a *tmk* slave created for public use within a very specific community. He appears to even have his very own alter within *us* who, due to her programming, is completely devoted to him.

She showed *us* the degree of her devotion after several months of her presenting to *us*. Because of *our* fear of her seeming blind devotion to this handler, *we* asked her to show *us* the details of *our* relationship or programming to him. Frighteningly, part of what she showed *us* was that without *any* resistance on her part she would allow him to kill her if he deemed it necessary.

This is really describing the programmed relationship between *our* alter's *entities* and *our* handler's *entities* facilitated by a three-dimensional and fourth-dimensional capability utilized within the programming process. *We* do not have the details regarding this programming practice, but *we* were seventeen years old when they were apparently "brought together" at an outdoor event. *Our* ongoing struggle to not return to this man via *our* alter is still overwhelming. *Our* "bond" with this man or his apparent *entity* is consistent with what has been shown to *us* repeatedly and systematically regarding *our* deep connection to him. (See Book 1, Chapter 2, "The Teen Years", *Brought Together*.)

The two different downloads here are *alter 14*'s apparent physical relationship with this individual, and the second is her *entity* relationship to this handler, as in the relationship between *our* alter's *entity* and his alter's *entity*. The *entities* are the actual handlers in both experiences, yet in the first the man is physically present and in the second he is not.

This download was preceded by a body memory including the standard fever, headache, both tissue and joint body aches, and in this case fear *we* call *fear gripping my heart* program, causing physical pain in *our* heart. At first, *we* were confused as to who of *our* alters was presenting. As it continued, *we* came to realize that there was more than one. *Alter 14* seemed to be the first, yet within her oral sexual encounter with this individual, he spoke words to her that triggered another alter to present as well.

After the download, *we* initially thought he'd made a mistake, but now believe that he was getting two alters at the same time: *alter 14* with heavy sexual programming, whom *we* believe this individual used for her particular sexual energy, including the kontrol she could exert effortlessly over *our* body; and the other alter being the one totally devoted to him, his alter alone.

[Alters co-existing within *our* conscious mind are now an ongoing state within *our* deep deprogramming. I do not know how this accessing was done during fully programmed use, but it came through as such very clearly.]

Alter 14 is waiting in a hotel room with only lace panties on. When she first began presenting to *us*, *we* realized that it was she who kept taking *us* to the store for lace panties. When *we see* an alter who is not very forthcoming with lace panties on, it is now a marker that she is present.

The man comes into the room and she is waiting for him. He looks at her without speaking, then begins taking his clothes off as she sits waiting for him to "instruct" her. *Our* sense was that he had just come from a meeting or lecture of some kind. He was dressed in a white button-down shirt, tie, and grey slacks. Once he is naked, he moves to a chair near the window, curtains open, next to which is a small round table. *We* see that *we* are many floors up. He looks at her a second time, then sits in the chair and says, "Come here" in a monotone voice devoid of emotion.

This individual has always been calm and has never spoken loudly nor forcefully to *us*. *We* believe that *our* alter's programming is such that there is no need. She is so well programmed that she obliges without any desire not to, it is what she does. In part, *we* all are programmed to please someone.

He is seated in the chair with his legs spread as she approaches. She crouches on her knees between his legs, awaiting his instructions, our *eyes locked*. He says one word to which she responds.

Many downloads shown to *us* by this alter as well as others require only the trigger word from this man while entrained by his eyes. *We* are clearly programmed to recognize his face and voice. *Eyes locked* is part of a trigger sequence involving code combinations repeatedly used by other handlers as well as on one-time occasions.

While stroking *our* head as this alter performs oral sex on him, he says to *us*, "Are you my girl?" thereby intentionally or otherwise pulling up the second alter (though *we* believe it is intentional). *We feel* the confusion in the two alters' minds as they perform oral sex on him in tandem.

We cannot stress enough the incredible difference *we see* and *feel* between the two alters. It is a struggle *inside, a physical pulling inside* as the two try to please him at the same time. He is getting the power, strength, sex, and kontrolled confidence of *alter 14*, while also getting the complete devotion, submission, innocence, and love "bind" of his own alter. *We* believe this is the desired effect he seeks. *We feel* the confusion in *our* mind during the download as he says, "Are you my girl?"

It is *our* understanding after so many experience memory downloads that it is not only codes and triggers that bring certain alters up and out,

but a visual recognition of the handler that assists in accessing *our* programming. This individual is a case in point. His face, physical presence,
and voice are triggers in conjunction with codes for some of *our* alters. *We*
are as certain as *we* can be that *we* were programmed *to* him so that he
could gain access when someone else could not. Is this in part what being
"brought together" meant? For *us*, it is the *demonic entity* within a *tmk* slave
that is the true handler.

This second download comes from *alter 14*, though *our* higher awareness also engages during the experience download as well, significantly
during the present while it is being experienced by *our* front alters.

Alter 14 is alone in a bedroom in someone's home. *We* are a younger
adult, maybe early twenties, though this is the age that *alter 14* always
presents. She is sitting on the end of the bed. A television screen on an
entertainment center is in front of her, maybe four feet off the left corner
of the bed against the wall. On the screen, *our* handler is addressing a
group of people; as mentioned above, he speaks publicly. *We* reach out and
put the television or monitor on pause, then roll back in one smooth, controlled motion onto *our* upper back and shoulders, pulling *our* feet straight
up with toes pointed to the ceiling, *our* arms straight out to *our* sides at
shoulder height to balance *our* weight. This alter has tremendous kontrol
of *our* body, so it is an amazing *feeling* when she is holding *our* body—
strong, knowing, every action with a tightness and grace to it. Slowly and
smoothly, she spreads *our* legs to the sides in a full split in the air. *Our* left
hand remains to the side on the bed for balance as she brings *our* right
hand in and under her lace panties, the only thing she is wearing, and
begins to touch *our* clitoris. Immediately, *our* body jerks as if hit with a
powerful, singular jolt of electricity.

At this moment inside the experience memory download, *we* are cognizant of a higher awareness now present *within the download* with *alter 14*.
We realize that a very powerful *entity* has just entered *us* through *our* vagina
and that the position *alter 14* assumed, followed by the act of touching *our*
clitoris, was the program that initiates and invites its entry. *We* can *see* and
feel this *entity* and its power on every level imaginable. It is very high level,
very powerful, and an apparent part-time resident of the individual who is
our handler. *We* call this *being* "Cain", among other names.

Immediately, *we* realize that *our* left hand is still outstretched on the
bed and *our* right hand still under *our* lace panties, and yet *we* are acutely
aware that there is a constant, steady pressure against *our* low back and

buttocks. *Our* higher awareness asks, *Who this is?* There is no other person in the room.

While still in this position, *we* relax *our* muscles and to *our* surprise and fear, remain in this position, supported from behind. *We* then pull both of *our* hands from their positions and reach behind *our* body to *our* lower back and buttocks region, *our* legs still up in the air. *We* clearly feel two forearms, *three-dimensional, physical reality forearms* moving quickly to tightly grasp *our* hands. Fear shoots through *our* body as *we* realize *we* are being restrained. *Our* higher awareness knows who this *entity* is, and his power, and is greatly concerned.

We try to vocalize the banishment of this *entity* in the here and now, but *our* teeth are tightly clenched, *our* tongue is impaired of free movement, and *our* throat is so tight *we* can hardly attempt a verbal banishment of this *entity*. *An entity is even attempting to access us while our alter is presenting this download in the here and now.* Once the *entity*'s grip is broken, *alter 14*—run by Lilith—reaches around to the front of *our* body and slips her right hand under the lace panties to again touch *our* clitoris—a classic example of how *our* alters are driven by *demonic entities*. *Our* higher awareness *sees* it all as *alter 14* presents the download.

We are still in constant struggle with them, even physically, as in this case, while in downloads during deep deprogramming. These *entities* are still within *us*, driving the alters. It is at this moment that *we* become aware that *we* are vocally calling out in a restricted voice the words of banishment in the here and now as *we* come out of this download, trembling with fear. It was very early morning darkness and *we* were aware of a *hum*, a vibration between *our* legs as well as within *our* womb. This is very common when these *entities* are present and active within *us*, especially those associated with *our* sex programming.

In 2011, long after this download, *we* are clearly aware that programming is being manipulated by both dimensional demons outside of *our* physical body and from within it, as well as having "inside" knowledge about remote programming via *black tech*. It is *our* contention that a past programming memory was being used in the *present* in an attempt to maintain the "programmed in" status of the affected alters to be used against this man.

[This vibration also occurs when microwave technologies are being used on me. **Directed Energy Weapons (DEWS)**—of which there is more than microwaves—can in some instances be detected by an individual without any devices needed to read the incoming frequencies. According to Richard Lighthouse of Targeted Justice (https://www.targetedjustice. com/), this can often be done just by using your hands to determine the direction it is coming from as well as feeling the pulse. I was clearly a crossover in the technologies being used over my decades of use. I contend as well that remote weapons were being used on me as early as the late 1970's. This however does not exclude the *entity* presence that in fact works through these technologies.]

This download and many others involving masturbation served as the catalyst helping *us* to understand how *our* alters are programmed to use masturbation to trigger certain alters to appear as well as to reinforce and maintain *our* programmed status. Another way to put it is to say that it maintains *our entity* handler's position within *us*.

In the days subsequent to this download, *we* began to realize that the *entities* were often the only handlers present in some of *our* on-tasks, and the only ones necessary. *We* began to look back over other downloads that *we* had written down and saw this pattern.

Training

This download begins with one of *our* kill alters accompanied by the alter who would show this fragment to *us* from her memory. *We* are standing in front of a cubicle, having just come down a hallway after stopping and looking into other cubicles along the hallway, all made up of concrete floors and walls about 7 or 8 feet tall without a ceiling, though there is a ceiling higher up in the structure surrounding the cubicle structures. Ambient light must be coming from high windows in the greater structure. The look and *feel* of this place is sparse, cold, and dead. Cubicle fronts are covered with curtains on rods. Inside the cubicle, it is like a shower eight or ten feet square with just a drain in the floor, no furniture.

Our kill alter is confused, in part due to two of *us* being briefly present. She is supposed to pick a cubicle to spend the night in, yet after opening the curtain, *we* are confused by the shower-like surroundings. So for the briefest of moments *we* are confused about where *we* are and why *we* are there: an apparent brief breakdown in programming.

Out of the corner of *our* eye, *we* see a young African-American woman walking around the corner as though she just exited a cubicle and was leaving in the direction from which *we* must have come in. *We* turn to look at her, but she does not look back at *us*. She is about *our* age (twenties). In this kill alter, *we* feel robotic, sober, and emotionless—common states for many of *our* alters. As *we* stand looking into the cubicle, *we* drop a small daypack on the floor. This part of the memory ends here with a despairing feeling.

Immediately following this download, this same kill alter would give *us* another experience memory from another time. (See the next section below.)

What *we* do know about the cubicles is that *we* were at a training facility on the outskirts of Tucson, Arizona as part of *our* kill programming, to be trained by the men *our* kill alter knows as CIA.

As of October 2010, *we* understand why the cubicle had a drain. The training had to do with the disposal of bodies by dismemberment. These downloads of alter memories have burdened *us* with extreme physical and emotional symptoms over the past fifteen years. The last 24 hours has been very difficult.

[We believe this episode is directly related to the "dark-skinned female body parts" relayed earlier under Book 1, Chapter 6, "Ritual Use, Ritual Death", *Human Flesh*. We believe the young female we saw in the hallway here was that victim, though without seeing her face straight on in the earlier episode, we can't be certain. Part of the reason is the location in the desert near Tucson. The previous location too was desert. However, the internal knowing says it was indeed the same young woman.]

Barrenness Inside and Out

This memory begins with *our* alter riding in the front seat of a van driven by a man. We are on a dirt road out in an open grassy, rolling area with lots of open horizon, sky, and no trees. There seems to be nothing for miles. It is daytime and we are returning from an on-task, headed to a small encampment of some kind in the near distance with a live-in travel trailer in front of which a blue tarp hangs to create a covered area. The man and *our* alter are silent. *Our* alter knows him, but *we* do not.

After we pull up and exit the van, the man lets a dog out of the trailer who begins to walk beside *our* alter as *we* walk out onto the open spongy

91

ground with light-colored protruding rocks sporadically spaced and varying in size. There are ground cover flowers spread about, blooming in clumps. *We* see yellow and purple small flowers. In the distance rain clouds accompany the rumbling of thunder. *We* go a ways, then turn back, knowing the rain will start any moment. There is nothing inside of this alter, no feeling but emptiness. She feels dead inside. There is no recognition of beauty in her surroundings, just a void inside; she is simply functioning. That is the end of the conscious download.

We understand that an on-task had just taken place and that the dead feel of this alter is directly due to that on-task, but *we* have no more details in *our* conscious mind.

[Years later we came to the conclusion that we were in the United Kingdom for this on-task. The following programming also seems to have taken place there. I have no conscious memory of ever being in the UK.]

"*Band on the Run*"

The following is what *we* retained after the download, but *we* could still *feel* the abundance of so much more. Sometimes the memory is so unbelievably palpable, just on the tip of consciousness. Other times, *we* consciously get more of the information but once again it is lost. It is so desperately frustrating.

We are in alter in *our* late teens, maybe 20. *We* are seated in the front seat of a parked car with a man in a gray suit who is seated on *our* right, the steering wheel in front of him. *We* understand it to be England. *Our* alter is looking out the passenger window at a well-manicured park with grass, sidewalks, shrubs, and trees. *We* are very close to the city, perhaps within it. A radio is playing Paul McCartney's 1973 song *Band on the Run*. *Our* alter says different lyrics in a monotone, sing-song voice, "…rent on the run…rent on the run…rent on the run…," three times as part of her programming, the man in the gray suit saying it with her. Homeless, her life is one of constant moving between on-tasks.

It is *our* understanding that this alter was to have her programming to stay "on the run" reinforced every time *we* hear the song. To this day, *we* have no sense of having roots anywhere, though *we* are attempting to dismantle this programming. In addition to the chorus, program reinforcement is in the rest of the song, too, some of which is so specific it is profound—references like "Stuck inside these four walls, sent inside forever," and "The first one said to the second one," all play unbelievably into *our* programming and *our* alter's consciousness, as you will see.

Music, Songs and Sound

Electric Programming to Forget

This fully conscious download in the early morning hours was preceded the previous night by a memory download by an alter with very explicit details of her experience. *We* remembered this detailed download very clearly in the early morning hours of darkness, three details in particular. *We* can no longer recall two of these details, due to what occurred while *we* lay there fully conscious, but do retain the detail of a vertical pupil eye of a *reptile*. This particular experience is one of several that have led *us* to recommit to utilizing *our* micro-cassette recorder immediately after, if not during, a memory download. Here is the sequence.

While lying in bed in the early morning darkness, three details were given to *us* by *our* alter. *Our* whole body jumped in pain with a jolt of electricity. One big blast. *We* realized that what had just occurred was important and recurring, so *we* reached for *our* bedside watch to mark the time; it was 1:33 a.m. Then *we* grabbed the micro-cassette recorder to record the electric jolt experience. That's how *we* lost two previous details as well as the alter who had been coexisting with *us*—completely gone in a *fully conscious* instant.

We understood that the blast of electricity (possibly programmed in reaction to surfacing information utilizing the body's naturally occurring electricity, or a remote tech wipe, so to speak), is to put away the alter who has the body in the usual programming usage (though in this case the one surfacing and giving us information was unapproved by our programmers/handlers), while the front alters return to the helm. *We* had memories of jolts before, yet being the front alter, *we* had no memories of what came previously; those memories belonged to others within *us* who had experienced them. *We* were shown that *our* alter has the details of programming and on-tasks until she is shocked and then she and her memories go back down inside of *us*, deep down, without any conscious knowledge on *our* part, the front alters. It was *stunning* to not only consciously witness with her, but to *see* and *feel* how well it works. *We* had full conscious memories present one moment, then the next they were gone—and *we* were consciously aware the entire time. It was so precise. *We* were being shown by several alters what occurs within programming during certain traumas and how it has worked on *us* so many times to put alters away and bring others up, sequestering the events and details with them.

Naturally, *we* had difficulty entering a state of rest after this, but eventually did. A wrinkly skinned *entity* remained present, despite pulling in Benevolence, a form of protection *we* use extensively in *our* deep deprogramming.

The one detail retained was a reptile eye from the memory download, yellow in color with a black vertical pupil, something *we* are quite familiar with, having seen the eyes many times. However, when *we* attempt to draw them, *we* can never capture the presence of evil that accompanies them, evil so palpable that *we* have yet to manage no fear at all as a response.

94

We believe *our* response is not only due to knowing who it is but also to its access and entry into *our* energy field and body, as well as its presence at torture programming sessions. Its non-physical *electric* presence alone is able to generate the energy of fear around and within *us*.

[Remote programming can occur with technology as well as being generated from the beings themselves. In deprogramming it became abundantly clear that the *entities/demons* ride the frequencies of the technology used by man, as well as frequencies not utilizing technology. They can use it or do it without the tech. More on this further on.]

95

9
Breakdowns, Reprogramming, Fragments

By *our* early twenties, *we* were having severe outward signs of program breakdown. *We* began experiencing self-mutilation programs at a
life-threatening level, severe alcohol and drug abuse, cutting *ourselves*,
attempting to break *our* bones, bulimia and anorexia, severe depression
accompanied by suicide attempts in an ever-spiraling self-destruction.
We now know these were all specific programs with specific alters, many
of whom *we* have consciously met and engaged. Many self-destruct programs are activated by *our* becoming consciously aware of what should not
be allowed to bleed into *our* front alter's consciousness. This is program
breakdown followed by built-in safety measures to alert *our* programmers,
kontrollers, and handlers that *we* were in need of reprogramming or *we*
would self-destruct.

During this time, *we* received two diagnoses of post-traumatic stress
disorder and bi-polar/manic-depressive disorder from two therapists
and wound up on lithium and anti-depressants for one and a half years.
Finally, *we* made the decision to stop taking them after the type of anti-
depressant was changed four times that *we* can recall because neither the
drugs nor lithium were working. Plus weekly therapy sessions were not
making *us* better, though it was there that *we* learned how to exist and
go on. *We* no longer recall a time in *our* life when *we* did not want *our*
lives to end.

Now, *we* see that *we* were being re-programmed for continued use and
kept in a continual disassociated state that allowed *our* programming and
alters to continue to function. It would not be until *our* late forties when
our deep deprogramming began that *we* were able to see that *we* were
rarely, if ever, in *our* body. *We* perpetually existed disconnected from it,
switching in and out of alters as desired by *our* kontrollers. "Out of body"
(dissociation) is a defense mechanism as a result of trauma and/or torture
and a variety of other triggers.

During these therapy sessions, the sexual abuse began to significantly resurface into *our* conscious mind. *Our* flashbacks and experience memory downloads became severe and self-mutilation and suicide were continuously running programs. At 23 or 24 years of age, *we* went to a Twelve Step-based treatment facility in Minnesota where *we* were also diagnosed as a sex addict (you think?) due to unstoppable sexual activity by *our* alters. *We* engaged with a man against all facility rules and were subsequently sent to an all-female halfway house where *we* continued to act out sexually due to programming, engaging sexually with a woman because of the lack of men.

Of course, all of this was the intricate foundation of *our* programming and multiplicity, but went unnoticed because of the indoctrination and programming of those in the mental health field. Had *we* even been strong enough to tell what was really going on, mental health professionals would not have believed *us*. *Therapists we encountered were part of a system designed to not assist intentionally designed tmk multiplicity slaves.*

[There are exceptions to this and for me one in particular. That being the first therapist we encountered working on a sliding scale for the county we lived in. He was the first person I felt safe with, to some degree, however, still with tremendous trust issues, yet found his compassion and sincere desire to assist life changing. For the first time I now knew there were people out there that cared and wanted to help.]

We had sex alters of all kinds and there was nowhere *we* could have been sent to avoid sexual activity; intentional design works well that way.

There was no help to be had within a mental health establishment with no understanding of multiple personality disorder, let alone the intentional total mind kontrol programming occurring within the religious, government, military, intelligence, corporate, and masonic sectors. Thankfully, *we* did not share all that was happening to *us* in these settings, which we believe saved *us* from being institutionalized or killed by *our* kontrollers.

The containment allowed their continued use of *us* for many years to come. By *our* mid- to late twenties, *our* anorexic and bulimic programming kicked into full gear as well. Many years later, it would become clear to *us* that the act of purging is a violent act *our* alter perpetrated on *us* to immediately dissociate *us*, especially when used as frequently as *the bulimic one* did to allow a different, totally dissociated alter to appear. *We* believe this was part of the reprogramming that took place during this time. *Our* programmer's recognized the need for a more powerful outlet for *our* rage.

Our twenties are a blur of fragments to *us*—prior to *our* deep deprogramming, anyway. *We* have fragments of experiences numbering in the hundreds but much difficulty determining the order of things, often switching years around in *our* front alter's inability to consciously remember the chronology. This has lessened, yet it still occurs. Often after discovering the correct order, it will fall out of order again, which is why *we* record *our* memories as soon as the experience surfaces. Programs are still running in *our* head that allow many of these details to be lost even after recovery by *our* front alters. This is occurring parallel to the ability of some alters to remember things as though they occurred yesterday.

Someone's Been Sleeping Around

98

Fragments

An example of the aforementioned combination of knowing and not knowing aptly describes *us* at 28-33 years of age. Twenty-eight years old marks the beginning of a barren area within *our* memory with many fragmented details—fragments as well as things *we* know from what *our* alters tell *us* without reliving it.

We remember starting an auto and boat detailing business around this time and having many lawyers, doctors, and well-to-do clients as regulars. *We* became successful in a very small, low-profile business. *We* also remember the man *we* were seeing and moved in with. *We* are as sure as *we* can be that he too was under some form of mind kontrol, yet whether the same "Network" as us and to what degree, *we* are uncertain. But the level of kontrol in *our* lives would suggest that he would have to be. Like *us*, he was having many paranormal experiences prior to *our* coming together and continuing for both of us while we were together.

It would be with him that *we* would have a very conscious **missing time** episode, meaning that he and *we* were both consciously aware of it at the time it occurred, having had previous time and space discrepancies, as well as ongoing episodes.

[With dissociation and total mind control, time—and even space—discrepancies exist when switching alters occurs. Additionally, this occurs when we encounter beings from other realms as well. There is more on this in Book 2 explaining what I experienced consciously in the process of switching alters.]

It was during these years that *we* encountered one of *our* most severe bulimic programs. *The bulimic one* predominated for months in *our* 28th year when *our* fear, paranoia, depression, and weight loss became visibly life threatening even to those around *us* who consciously understood nothing about *our* life. *Our* alters have told *us* that this was another time of heavy kill programming use and reprogramming.

We were not only reprogrammed (a term for extreme program reinforcement with possible additions), but a new aspect or method was introduced to *us* in 1990-1995. *Our* kill programming was *enhanced* or altered in some way, though *we* are currently unable to consciously determine exactly how.

[I have come to believe this has something to do with our clones as well as **eMKUltra** (Electromagnetic programming).]

Associations

When *we* have flashbacks of experiences from *our* late twenties and on, *we* get very foggy, though the fog eventually lifts, as it did regarding *our* 18-22 age. *We* remember "dating" wealthy men, though the front alters do not recall having sex with them. Other alters tell *us* that *we* did engage in sex, which can be very confusing and frightening at times. Unfortunately, *we* know that sex did occur, even how one of them sounds vocally in arousal. *We* remember specifics of the men, their faces and bodies, the way they smell, certain places *we* went with them, even being in their homes, their bedrooms, showering in their bathrooms.

With one much older man in his sixties, *we* have a very specific memory of coming back to his home on Clearwater Beach, Florida at night after being out somewhere with him (though I have no idea where we went). In the flashback, *we* are in a short black dress on his bed, face down, and he is on top of *us*. He says to *us* that *our* legs are so beautiful and strong, "Sleek and muscular, you are built like a race horse" as he spreads *our* legs and *we* feel the hardness of his penis pushing at *our* bottom. That is all *we* front alters remember. Alters in the frontline have sexual programming that the rest of *us* believe is there to appear normal to the outside world, but in terms of *tmk* use, it is clearly other sex alters more deeply imbedded who perform.

Our front alters have always believed that *we* did not sleep with him: someone else inside *us* did, as per the program accessed by the "race horse" trigger, with other triggers as well. (Single triggers are rare and would be dangerous if set off somewhere accidentally.) Some of these men knew each other; one had the entire fourth floor of a condo penthouse just a couple of doors up the beach from the 60 year-old man. Again, it was the same: *our* front alters did not have sex with him, but at least one of *us* did. *We* were in his bedroom and shower regularly. *We* remember his first name but not his last, and that he was in his late thirties, red-blond hair and blue-green eyes, fair skin that sunburned easily, wealthy and did not work. Fastidious. His inheritance came from Chicago through his father's alcohol business. Later, *we* would discover the business was mob all the way, Tampa Bay as well being notorious for mob connections. *We* also have a flashback of being with him out in a nice Italian restaurant near the beach and know exactly where this restaurant is, though *we* have never returned to it. *Our* use in *our* late teens and twenties in Florida involved the "Octopus", as it is often called in researching circles.

In conscious memory, we were involved with at least three different organized crime men during our teens and twenties.

Delta Blues

The song "Walking in Memphis" by Marc Cohn was released in 1991. *We* are uncertain what year *we* were programmed to this song for a particular kill of a person and his family, but believe it may have been in the late 1990's. (This entire program is broken down in Book 2 along with when and why we were programmed with this song.) When this programming was presented to *us* in a download, this song played nonstop in *our* head for four days, making *us* unable to function. *We* have since realized that *our* kill alter wants to play it over and over.

[This would occur shortly before we were to meet with the two men in Salt Lake City, Utah who would assist in our beginning deep deprogramming. It is no coincidence since we were programmed to act out a kill program involving one of the men and his family as we would discover in full later after meeting with him. I know this song was used to begin the trigger process before we would even meet.]

This has occurred with other songs used for programming. Until this download, *we* had never heard of Marc Cohn, nor did *we* know the title of the song but went to a local music store and relayed the lyrics to the owner, who recognized it immediately. *We* bought the cd and have since discovered extensive program reinforcement lyrics. *We* assume that the artist is innocent of any knowledge of this, as are so many used by these kontrollers.

Andrew Jackson Plantation

In the mid 1990s, *we* disappeared while on a trip to Tennessee with *our* mother while walking on the Andrew Jackson Plantation that *our* family lived near during *our* childhood. By "disappearance", *we* mean an actual disappearance from the physical view of those around *us*, though *we* were still there and observing from a surreal, altered state. During roughly twenty minutes to half an hour, *it appears we could not be seen in physical reality as witnessed by our attempts to be seen by those walking around us. We* do not claim to be able to explain this.

[The excerpt from the article below speaks to the drive for such technologies. Again, keep in mind black technologies versus above ground technologies. It is my contention that this "ability" that we experienced involved something more than physical technology alone.

> *"US Special Operations Command (SOCOM) is working on keeping the identity of commandos secret as they carry out missions."*
>
> *Research into using metamaterials to render objects invisible has attracted military attention from its inception, but although it has been ongoing for a number of years, no practical applications have yet been delivered.*
>
> *Back in 2008, the US Army Research Office and the National Science Foundation's Nano-Scale Science and Engineering Centre funded research at the University of California aimed at developing materials that could make people and objects invisible by redirecting light and other EM radiation around them. (www.army-technology.com, Hidden Threats —military cloaking technology, December 9th, 2011)]*

Missing Time

Our missing time with an aforementioned boyfriend in *our* late twenties occurred at his apartment where *we* also lived. *Our* memory was of a "black" man with black eyes coming through the bedroom doorway at the onset of missing time. *We* were terrified because *we* clearly understood he was there to rape *us*. More than an hour was instantly gone for *us*, as was true for *our* boyfriend, though both he and *we* were conscious of this at that time.

In recent years, *we* have encountered beings with this same cocoa-brown skin and black eyes, a being that did not look human to *us*; *we* just could not speak to what "he" really was, due to *our* no-talk programming and fear of not knowing how to talk of these things.

Starve and Purge

Our anorexic and bulimic programming was running full tilt during these years, a program that *we* have been shown time and again by *our* alters to be associated with *our* kill programming, as well as some of the most heinous aspects of *our* use by these *demon*-possessed men and women. Bulimic programming has provided a tremendous release valve for the immense rage that builds inside of *us*, allowing *us* to immediately dissociate at the first few purges and feel nothing. Anorexic programming allows us to feel in control. The hunger sensation being denied as well as being a distraction to focus on.

[This was explicitly experienced on one occasion before beginning deep deprogramming, in which the realization of the immense rage release was acknowledged. It literally felt as if I had been drugged when I lifted from the bulimic episode. It was that powerful and I recognized in that moment its purpose, though was unable to understand how I had arrived at the action in the first place.]

This program served many purposes, including release of rage from sexual abuse, trauma and torture, killing people, horrors such as cannibalism, and maintaining dissociation while *the bulimic one* accessed a cult loyal alter who could participate in terrible things. Through purging, *our* alters could maintain an ongoing, constant state of out-of-body dissociation, the optimal state for a *tmk* slave.

The Scientologists

At some point in our late twenties, *we* worked for a friend who received a contract to service a particular type of equipment at Scientology headquarters in the southeastern United States, an international destination for Scientologists from around the world. The job ran for approximately a month or more, and in addition to the memories of working in and on the equipment, *we* recall flashbacks of rooms we did not have clearance to be in, despite our crew being closely watched during our graveyard shift. *We* also recall being taken to the E-Meter room. My friend's contact person regarding the contract was a 12-14 year-old male dressed in Navy whites. *We* are now aware that the powerful *feel* of this boy and void of emotion emanating from him were from the *entity* inside him.

Batman

Batman was another programming theme used on *us*, both the series on television in youth and films later, even down to *our* auto and boat detailing truck that *we* used being the exact purple and green of the villain vehicles in one of the *Batman* movies (*Batman*, 1989). *We* would not realize this connection until 20 years later, when *our* deep deprogramming began in 2008. *We* now clearly understand that the truck was a neon sign to the **initiated** that would be given *our* access codes. For years, *we* drove around the tri-county area in Florida performing "services" for clients. *Our* front alters were always aware of the tremendous sexual energy flowing between *us* and some of *our* clients, but *we* couldn't understand why, as the sexual energy did not belong to the front alters. (See Book 1, Chapter 12, "Internal Programming", *Devotional Programming to Actor Christian Bale*.)

10
The Thirties: It All Starts to Unravel

In *our* early thirties, *our* programming began significantly breaking down. During these years, *we* went to the UFO community to seek help with debilitating memories of alien abduction. It was as if the "veil" was forever torn open to reveal a nightmarish journey through *our* lives that until then seemed to not be *our* own. *We* experienced terrible abreactions that *we* are certain re-fragmented *us,* thanks to *our* front alter's unawareness of who and what *we* were and to a personal support system headed by another *tmk* woman sent in to lock *us* down. As it all began to unravel, *we* were consciously struggling to stay alive.

Aliens, the "Female", and Reprogramming

In *our* early thirties, *we* picked up a book about alien encounters by a well-known author in the Ufology community, Budd Hopkins, the founder of the Intruder Foundation. This led to programming memory breakthroughs, after which *we* decided to write the Intruder Foundation to ask for assistance with *our* experience memories. A response came far more quickly than *we* had imagined, referring *us* to a UFO researcher and hypnotherapist who worked with people like *us.* This man introduced *our* front alters to the woman who would later appear in surfacing memories from *our* past whom *we* had encountered as the "female", though she was of course younger back then and the alter who had known her earlier was not one of *our* front alters. (See Chapter 2, The Teen Years, *"Female", Not a Woman.*)

When *we* first began to deprogram, *we* were still under almost full programming and were unable to see how unrealistic it was to believe that the *aliens* had presented a younger version of the "female" years ago and now was here to help *us* with *our* alien abduction memories. This woman befriended *us* and became in *our* mind an angel come to help *us* with *our* devastating alien abduction memories. She became *our* only friend, though for some reason *we* did not fully trust her.

It would not be until deep deprogramming in *our* late forties that *we* would realize she had evidently been sent in to evaluate *our* programming breakdown and reprogram *us*. Devastated for months by this realization, *we* could clearly see the programming language she had used on *us* in the Ufology setting—specific words and phrases, even concepts of methodology used by *our* programmers. It was blatant programming, but *our* front alters had no conscious understanding of it back then.

We also believe that she herself was having a program breakdown during the years she was reprogramming *us*. She may have been so far under programming herself that she was being unwittingly used, just as *we* have been by so many alters. But the bottom line was that after several years around her and the Ufology community, *we* were so close to a complete breakdown and suicide that *we* left Florida and headed west. Those around *us* had been very frightened and unwilling to listen to *our* experiences involving men in military uniforms torturing, drugging, and raping *us*, including invading the inside of *our* head. (Apparently a subject now being openly discussed in Ufology circles.)

During the subsequent years, *we* achieved a degree of anonymity that *we* had never known—or so *we* thought. *We* remained isolated, barely in touch with family or friends, and fell off the grid, so to speak. No car, no credit cards, no home, only temporary jobs, moving every few months—all in *our* front alter consciousness. *Our* programming was deteriorating, but freedom was not on the menu. Occasionally *we* could not hold it together and returned to family in Florida, then went off again, back out west. As *our* programming broke down, *we* sought out the familiarity of all that *we* had known, due to the extreme fear *we* were triggering by remembering. Constant moving around and returning "home" are significant parts of *our* programming. It is unfortunately very evident that *our* programming was still very much in use, as were *we*, by *our* kontrollers and handlers.

Nightly Giveaways

We began to have a very unusual behavior at night, a behavior not attributed to *our* front alters, given that *our* main front alter, whom *we* also refer to as the "host", not only does not have sexual feelings but actually has a repulsion to the human body and its imperfections as regards sexual acts, body fluids, etc. Upon close scrutiny, she finds men and women to be very ugly and cannot understand anyone wanting to engage in sex with what she sees. She does not vocalize this to those around her, knowing that others do not feel the same way and would view it as abnormal. So sexual arousal or thoughts must come from other alters, some of whom belong to the frontline system who take over without anyone being the wiser, even openly discussing sex and all its periphery subjects with quite the open mind.

During *our* heavy programming breakdown in *our* early thirties, *we* were consciously unaware of being a multiple personality, so it bewildered *us* when at night *we* began going through a series of activities before crawling into bed by *ourselves* that were obviously preparations for sex involving very particular acts of grooming, wearing certain lingerie of specific colors, etc. Everything had to be just so, and *our* main front alter was aware of *feeling* like someone else at these times, and that this someone else seemed in kontrol of *our* activities and sexual energy. (This was alter bleed-through where more than one alter was presenting with my front alter consciousness noticing.) *Our* front alter desperately tried to stop this behavior but could not, all the while unable to figure out who *we* were preparing to have sex with.

We are certain that *we* were being accessed for reprogramming at this time and were consciously aware of "someone" in *us* engaging sexually with men dressed in black fatigues who managed to somehow coerce *us* into performing fellatio on them while a black handgun was held at the side of *our* face for stimulation.

[For this particular sex alter, the gun was part of the trigger to illicit incredible sexual appetite. This was a rather common programming tactic used in models such as myself, referred to by one researcher as "gun fever".]

The most disturbing aspect of all of this was *our* seeming enthusiastic participation and pleasure involving complete submission and degradation. *We* now know that this behavior by this alter was a combination of being triggered in the here and now during reprogramming at night, and her memories from *our* past years of use. (See Book 1, Chapter 3, "18", *Torture, Programming, Guns and Reptiles*.) By *our* early thirties, *our* main front alter was *consciously* beginning to be aware of the actual presence of "someone else" co-existing with her in *our* body whose actions took kontrol over *our* body without her being able to understand or stop it. This behavior went on for several weeks straight with the presence of dark unmarked helicopters accompanying the encounters.

107

Indelible Images

Emanations of Light

We will discuss two occurrences here, one while *we* had no physical witness, the other with a boyfriend who *we* write about in the next entry. *We* were 35 or 36 years of age when both events occurred.

The first occurred while *we* were living in Florida, after the beginning of severe program breakdown and extensive *entity* encounters, as well as human male encounters within the three-dimensional realm. *We* awakened one night in *our* bed to a loud *Crack!* *We* opened *our* eyes and were raising *our* head from the pillow when *we* saw the last bit of concentric circles of light exiting the room through the cinderblock exterior wall of *our* bedroom. It was golden white and had clearly come from *us*. At that moment, *we* realized that the *Crack!* had come from within *our* head, not outside it. A fog was over *us*, time and movement were slower. *We* pondered this for a while in a calm, soft, peacefully surreal frame of mind while weeping—a common dissociated state for *us* after trauma or during abreactions.

The second emanation of light occurred with *our* boyfriend in his apartment in a town one town away from *ours*. *We* frequently stayed overnight with him. He was on top of *us* during sexual intercourse, so we were close, looking into one another's eyes, our movements being gentle in nature. The curtains were drawn so the room was almost completely dark with a little light from the parking area seeping in, allowing us to see one another slightly. *We* began to weep due to an overwhelming feeling of fullness in *our* heart, and that is when it occurred for the second time, though this time *we* saw it from start to finish, and so did he. After it exited the room, he and *we* had stopped moving and were looking at one another. *We* asked, "Did you see that?" to which he replied, "Yes, what was that? It came from you…" *We* told him it had happened before. *We* are still uncertain of the source.

[As brought into the narrative earlier, remote technologies have been in use for decades. It is my contention that they began using them on me as early as the late 1970s and early 1980s due to several different types of events suggesting such. Events I cannot explain in other terms. I am certain as of the 1990s they were being used extensively in my programming and accessing. I was in a crossover of old MKUltra techniques and the newer ones, such as eMKUltra. I have *consciously* experienced extensive eMKUltra technologies used on me in deep deprogramming. More on this later.]

Torture in Northern Georgia

The setting of this experience was a sparsely populated area at the time of *our* stay because the small community was mostly summer homes. *We* were brought there by the same boyfriend who witnessed the light emanation. However, he did not stay with *us* in Georgia because he was going on the road for two weeks to train as a truck driver.

The summer home belonged to a relative who used it seasonally. *We* did not see anyone else the whole two weeks. *We* were also almost completely broke. The whole time, *we* experienced *tremendous* fear, coming terribly close to losing the tiny grip on reality that *we* had.

The little chronology *we* have regarding events at this location is a blur with moments of precise clarity in the form of flashbacks and memory fragments that never left *our* conscious mind. Nights were terrifying. *We* clearly remember the first few days awakening with *our* mouth ripped about an eighth of an inch on both sides, so that when *we* tried to open *our* mouth, it cracked and bled. *Our* eyelids were covered in a scaly, red, itchy rash so sore that *we* tried to not scratch it. *Our* terror accompanying this the first few days was off the charts, though *we* couldn't *consciously* tell why at the time. *We* cried *ourselves* to sleep each night, afraid of the coming night, so scared that *we* physically trembled until drifting off in exhaustion.

We experienced the second most intense period of bulimia in *our* life during this time. *The bulimic one* predominated to deal with what was occurring. Later, by the time *our* boyfriend got back, he was stunned at *our* physical appearance and mental state of mind. *We* had had very limited phone contact with him and he apologized for not responding to *our* pleas for his return because of his job.

We remember awakening to a loud voice inside our head that said a biblical name starting with "E", but it left *our* conscious memory within minutes after awakening. The voice in *our* head in these instances is always loud in volume, but is clearly not a person shouting. It has occurred many times. Later, *we* asked *our* boyfriend who used to be in seminary school prior to *our* meeting him at a Mufon meeting to list biblical names starting with "E" to see if *we* could remember it. *We* never remembered the name.

This boyfriend had a curious past and heritage regarding paranormal experience, including a conscious sighting of Bigfoot that ended his faith in his Pentecostal religion. Also, it was his father who took him and *us* to the gun range his father regularly visited in Florida where *our* main front alter became conscious of *our* excellent marksmanship without being able to explain why to the heads turning at the range that day. Many of the men there offered to let *us* shoot their weapons, and *we* left there fully triggered into what *we* have come to call "gun fever". This activity triggered a violent, highly sexually charged alter that lived inside of *us*.

The two weeks in northern Georgia left *us* in a deep suicidal depression. *We* were used, traumatized, and raped, yet could not remember where or by whom. Ten years later in deep deprogramming, *we* recounted this experience to two men familiar with other *tmk* slave histories and learned that *we* may have been ritually abused by a shape-shifting reptile with a penis so large it ripped the sides of *our* mouth. (See Martin Cannon, "The Controllers: A New Hypothesis of Alien Abduction", *circa* 1990.) Mr. Cannon hit the nail on the head regarding certain aspects of mind kontrol. *Aliens* most certainly exist and people are being abducted. *We* know *we* were abducted and have a lifetime of personal experiences that allows *us* to see these *aliens* as none other than cross-dimensional *entities* of a purely malevolent nature.

[Obviously, there are other possible explanations for our mouth being "ripped". I will not go into that here as I imagine the reader can think of possibilities other than a "Reptilian". This does not discount the real presence of these reptilian beings. I can vouch for their existence as can much in our human history.]

We are often still amazed how *we* survived not only the torture over the years but also the terror that *we* lived in. Of course, that is how *we* became a *we*. *Our* heart still races while *we* write of this experience. *We* are uncertain if *we* survived because of the programming that resulted in multiplicity, a survival mechanism, or because of Benevolent, Unconditional, Creative Love. Or a strange combination of both?

Death at 39

At 34, *we* were shown by one of *our* alters that *we* were to be dead at 39. It is a clear memory *we* never forgot, one that did not slip from *our* conscious mind. *We* never understood why *we* were to die at 39, just that *we* would. *We* believe that the death programming was activated due to *our* programming beginning to severely break down, that it had been placed as a fail-safe program long ago, should it be needed.

We were in *our* bedroom in an apartment that *we* shared with an older woman in the first few years *our* programming really began to break into *our* conscious mind. *We* were walking across the bedroom during the daytime hours when, with no emotion and complete clarity, *we saw* and *felt* that *we* would die at 39. *We* even saw the number "39" in *our* head. *Our* response was calm, matter of fact, detached. *Our* programming was telling *us* this, *our* own alters.

While *our* programming was breaking down and *we* were still unaware of who and what *we* actually were, *we* were involved with the Ufology community, having gravitated to it to seek help as memories began surfacing. As *we* indicated earlier, this gravitation is part of a program in *us* that alerts *our* programmers, kontrollers, and handlers that *we* are in need of reprogramming. (*We* are speaking of *our* own experience and not necessarily of the whole Ufology community. *We* are also certain that the Ufology community is *heavily infiltrated* by *tmk* operatives, though there are also individuals attempting to find truth there, some aware of the disinformants, most not.)

A couple of the few surviving images from this time.

11
The Forties

We survived *our* death age due to a Benevolent experience, though to be fair and unbiased, *we* must admit that it was not the first time *we* were led to believe that Benevolence was acting in *our* life when in fact *demons* of tremendous deception were filling *us* with ecstasy. This is certainly possible, given how filled with deception, lies, confusion, and reversals of truth *our* lives have been. The love *we* have known from *our* tormentors is not the Love of Creation but a perversion of that Love—a pain-filled, binding prison designed in darkness, not in Divine Light, demanding submission and loyalty without question, a blind devotion through Luciferian programming.

[I would add to this Ahrimanic programming as well as Asuric programming. I have come to understand who some of these beings are. They are not abstract generalizations, rather they are individual beings of personality, abilities, etc. They have unique characteristics and aims for the world and humanity. I would discover that a tattoo I have on my right arm contains the symbol—according to Rudolph Steiner's providing this symbol in a lecture—of the being known as Sorat. This even explained an event I never understood before; a binding/wedding to Sorat. Rudolph Steiner's work has been and continues to be the only one to explain my lifetime of experiences in regards of the otherworldly beings I have encountered, often first hand, and no other. I would find my explanations and descriptions validated to some degree in his lectures and writings. I can also say with much gratitude that any and all binds and weddings can be made null and void with sincere understanding and actions taken in the name of Christ. It has taken much effort, discipline, study and dedication, continuously, to initiate myself into the *esoteric* side of Christianity. This is and continues to be my "salvation". I was involuntarily initiated into darkness, now I live and strive evermore into the Light.]

Simon

This experience took place in the Southwest desert in 2004. Much occurred in the first summer *we* were in the little town, more than *we* often care to remember.

Simon picked *us* up hitchhiking one day and *we* found *ourselves* thinking there was something dark and sexy about him, as well as closed off. He and *we* had previously briefly encountered one another through a mutual acquaintance, yet *we* spoke very little during the ride. Out of the corner of *our* eye from behind *our* sunglasses, *we* found *ourselves* glancing at his muscular legs and *feeling* a desire to put *our* mouth there. Clearly, this was not the desire of *our* main front alter, so the ride ended without incident and *we* soon forgot about him.

In relating encounters, *we* are relating—not one of *us* alone—so crossovers will occur: several alters' views of what *we* did, what he did, what was happening, as well as what the various parts of *us* were *feeling*.

The next time *we* encountered Simon, *we* were with two male friends, one being the mutual acquaintance Simon and *we* shared. This friend was engaging Simon outside the parked vehicle *we* were sitting in, standing at Simon's parked car to *our* right. *We* felt a surge of sexual energy in *us* and looked directly into Simon's eyes, who at that time was looking at *our* friend. *We* kept *our* gaze on him and within seconds he glanced at *us*, then quickly looked back at *us* due to what he saw in *our* eyes—what *we* now know to be *our* classic *entity*-driven, sex alter look. *Our* sex alters were up, as evidently were his. His quick return of *our* gaze told *us*, or rather *our entities* and alter, that the message was received. His look was filled with an intense lust, one that is quite common between *our entities* and the *entities* of another.

Most people have been made to believe that this is all perfectly natural. For *us*—meaning *our* alters and their lives—*we* assure the reader it is anything but natural. It is malevolent programming that is entity driven.

Our main front alter did not do this; she has no sexual feelings and is repulsed by the idea of human sex and all the fluids and imperfections coming in contact with another. It completely escapes her as to why people want to do this. It is instead another alter, and *our* main front alter had no idea what this other alter had set in motion, nor did she need to, as she would not be the one presenting if the opportunity arose.

We do not recall how much time passed before *we* saw him again—perhaps within a month or two in the same summer. *We* used to hitch rides, then walk to a hot mineral spring location on the Rio Grande, hike upriver to swim in the cold river, then sun on huge, smooth, lava rocks along the river's edge, doing this in the nude without anyone else being around.

As *we* approached the bottom of the gorge, *we* came upon the hot springs and Simon. He was wearing shorts, a straw hat, and sunglasses, and *we* immediately noticed that he was facing the direction from which *we* came, almost as if waiting for *us*, staring at *us*. *We* said hello without stopping and began *our* 15-minute hike upriver to a spot *we* had picked from above on the hike down. *We* loved swimming in the icy water and lounging on the big, hot, black, lava rocks. *We* were sunning with *our* eyes closed on a rock *we* had swum to on the opposite side of the river when *we* could *feel* that *we* were being watched. *We* turned *our* head toward the side of the gorge people hiked up and down, shaded *our* eyes with *our* hand, and immediately picked out Simon about five hundred feet up, facing *our* direction.

The probability that *we* zeroed in on him just by *our* sense of sight is almost nil. See the terrain and all the camouflage and you would understand that it was again *our entities* that zeroed in, not *me*.

We could not see his eyes, due to the distance and the fact that he had on sunglasses, yet *we emphatically* state that we *could* see his eyes *and still can*! But *feeling* him was the real pleasure, as all of *our* sexual senses rose up in that moment. After the sexual rush of *our* alters, *we* resumed sunbathing. A few moments later, *we* looked back at that spot and he was gone. Relieved, *our* main front alter believed *we* had been abstaining from sexual encounters for two years now and this was not something *we* intended to break. Enough was now breaking through to front alters to know something was amiss. Aware and not aware of several of *us* for many years, at least some of *us* felt no sex was taking place with *our* body, but unfortunately, unbeknownst to *us*, other alters were indeed being used sexually. The programmed masturbation locked in since infancy kept *our* alters and their *entities* gaining entry.

After more swimming and sunbathing, *we* packed up and headed back downriver, hoping to find someone at the springs who could give *us* a ride and *we* would not have to walk two miles out to the highway. By the time *we* reached the top of the gorge, an hour or two had passed since seeing Simon watching *us* from the trail. Up top, two vehicles were parked there—two chances for a ride out. About ten minutes into walking on, *we* heard a vehicle coming and turned to put out *our* thumb. To *our* surprise, it was Simon. *Our* first thought was one of curiosity: where had he come from?

115

His vehicle was not one of the ones parked above the hot springs. This was followed by a rush of anxiety as *we* knew *we* would be riding with him.

Our alters immediately began pushing up and out, vying for the front seat. In fact, more than one of *us* presented together as he pulled up and *we* got in. We were 42 years old and many alters had been consistently co-existing with the main front alter for years by now, yet *we* still had no idea that *we* were a multiple personality. *We* just could not come to terms with these other parts of *ourselves*.

Simon and *we* engaged in a brief conversation about recognizing each other, then he said he was going to the theatre to see a movie and asked if *we* would like to go with him. *We* declined. He then said he really did not care about that particular movie and perhaps he would go home and would *we* join him for a movie on his big screen? *Our* sex alters were going nuts inside *our* head and *our* body, and *we* were already getting wet between *our* legs due to their intentions. *We* could hear their responses in *our* head while the main front alter was saying aloud, "Thanks, *i* don't think so."

This was a raw *entity* lust for *us* and *we* knew that an encounter with him would be hard, raw, and aggressive, no gentleness, no caring, and that frightened many of *us*. What *we* now know is that his *entity* knew *we* would eventually come with him, due to *our entities*. Once *we* became conscious of *our* multiplicity, *we* came to understand how this happens and how it *feels*. Back then, *we* were still under full programming with no conscious knowledge of this and therefore no chance to stop it. The chatter of *our* alters was, and at times still is, very powerful. *Our* main front alter cannot remember how *we* accepted, but he dropped *us* where *we* were staying about a mile from his house and after some primping by *our* sex alters, *we* walked down. *We* did not bathe, which was intentional by one of *us*.

Once at his house, *we* casually talked on his couch while some of *us* knew what was coming. *We* can still see him sitting there, relaxed like a cat with a smirk on his face, his tail twitching in anticipation. He knew he had *us*. *We* were the canary and were his as *we* had been with *every* handler before him—only some of *us* did not know this. He offered *us* marijuana and *we* declined; he would smoke almost constantly for the next four days.

We felt the alter taking over when she said, "Can *i* take a bath?" To which he replied, "Sure," and got up to run the bath, light candles, add essential oils, pour *us* a glass of wine, supply a robe, and set a bottle of body oil out, this last requested by *our* alter. *Our* main front alter did not drink alcohol, yet thanks to *our* programming, others inside of *us* did.

He left *us* alone in the tub, coming in only once to see if *we* needed anything. By the time *we* exited the bathroom, music was on and he too was wearing only a robe with nothing on underneath. *We* remember being aroused by seeing the outline of his penis under the silky fabric. *We* also remember a rush of fear. By this time, several of *us* were presenting. This encounter would last for four terrible days.

Initially, the two of us sat on the couch and within minutes his tongue was down *our* throat when *we* heard her moan. *We felt* her take over and *our* aggression and lust burst out with her. It was the *feeling* of the switch in alters, then all goes blank. Then it becomes a fog of lust-filled, painful sex for four days, as if the distinction of days did not even exist, though they did due to *our* having to go to work on a couple of those days. *We* began to menstruate that first day and Simon's response was to perform oral sex on *us* with fervor, enjoying it immensely.

Our main front alter showed up now and again with disgust and repulsion and an overwhelming need to take a shower and wash it all off, leave and never return as *we* engaged sexually with him, *completely* entranced, *completely* lost. He made a batch of vegetable soup and salad each day since *we* were vegetarian, then it was raw intercourse again—a blur of painful, degrading sex with Simon in total kontrol, penetrating *us* brutally with her asking him to do it harder. He would bury his face between *our* legs and come up with *our* blood on his lips.

The entire encounter still makes *us* feel sick and sad. The dichotomy of all *our* programming rising up at the same time is still so energetically destructive within *us*, it is exhausting.

Simon was all of 28, *demon*-possessed, with the energy of both. *We* attempted not going back once *we* had to go to work. *We* were bruised, sore, exhausted, and *our* main front alter as well as others—mostly young child alters—begged *us* not to go back. But near the end of *our* workday, he would walk in the door. *We* can still see him. He was not beautiful, rather small in stature, yet when he came over to the chair in which *we* sat, squatted down before *us*, placed his hands on *our* thighs and gently spread *our* legs while his thick Romanian-accented voice lulled *us* back into *our* perverse programmed loyalty to him and the *entity* in him, *we* were completely entranced.

The hand on *our* inner thigh is a very specific part of triggering at least one or more of *our* sex alters, as has occurred in more than one memory download. (See Book 1, Chapter 4, "Killing", *Alpha and Omega: First and*

Last Solo.) In the case of Simon, some of *us* wanted him badly while others of *us* pleaded "No!" Some wanted him to hurt *us*, and he did. *We* remember saying, "No, *i* am too tired, *i* am too sore, *i* cannot come back with you tonight," to which he responded that he understood, that *we* should come back and there would be no sex, that he would take care of *me*. Then *we* were under him and he was pounding into *us*.

The pain by the fourth day was excruciating, yet she would always say "harder" because she was programmed to seek out pain and could sexually take so much of it. This was who he inadvertently accessed in *us*. There were clearly several sex alters surfacing. On the last morning, *we* were catching a bus to Denver, feeling disgusting. Simon was evidently done with *us* as the coldness emanating from him that morning was palpable. *Our* front alters felt like a whore and a shower would not wash it off. *We* could not figure out what had happened. Why had this awful person had so much of *us*? Even then, *we* could not remember all that occurred, yet *our* main front alter was repulsed and disgusted by *our* being a whore.

It did not end there, yet before *we* continue, here are some things *we* remember from *our* time with Simon during those four days.

After sex the first time, *we* asked him where his car had been when *we* came up from the hot springs. Why had *we* not seen it? He smiled slyly and said, "Right there." Then he looked at *us* and began telling *us* about the long line of witches he came from— that his family was from Romania and his grandmother, a gypsy, taught him many things. He revealed no details of how he had done it, yet *we* knew he had somehow cloaked himself and the vehicle from *our* view. There was no where for that vehicle to hide at the top of the hot springs trail.

He said he had had a very tough life. Simon was very self-serving and owned that with pride, definitely without any apologies. In his view, everybody was on their own. It would not be until 2009 during deep deprogramming that *we* would understand his traumatic youth and near-death events, and how he too was a multiple personality. *We* believe now he had alters but I had no ability to understand what was happening and why because *we* were unaware of *our* own multiplicity.

The house he took *us* to was in a very pricey area. Donald Rumsfeld, a senior white house official, had a home nearby and was apparently involved with *our* CIA programming and use at a distance in *our* teens and twenties in the late 70s and early 80s. This area was also home to a very famous movie star. Eventually, Simon would tell *us* that he lived there with his uncle who made Hollywood movies and was deeply involved in Hollywood, as was a significant part of *our* programming. Simon bragged about staying in a famous movie actress' home nearby, as well as in her New York City penthouse.

What occurred immediately after *we* went to Denver remained confusing and painful until the spring of 2008 when *we* talked openly about it with the two men *we* met and began *our* deep deprogramming with in Salt Lake City. In Denver, *we* immediately became very ill: a high fever, aching all over, severe bloating and pain in *our* abdomen. It was the weekend and *we* were frightened by *our* severe symptoms. After five days, *we* spoke to the friend *we* were visiting about the possibility of going to a hospital the next day if things did not change. That night, *we* were unable to sleep, due to the pain and severe bloating. *We* prayed for some rest and by morning the pain was inexplicably gone. Still feeling weak, *we* took it easy that day and the next day went for a walk in the woods where *we* sat quietly on a large boulder, trying to understand what had been happening to *us*. Who was Simon and why had *we* been crying since *we* left him? *We* were still incapable of discerning, still under full programming.

We will never forget what occurred next, fully conscious, programmed conscious. We *saw* and *felt our* solar plexus region rip open, as if the flesh burst from internal pressure, and a shaft of light continuously shot out into the air, covering an area the size of the Flower of Life tattoo that *we* have on *our* solar plexus, about three and a half inches in diameter. The force was so great that *we* cried out and began to weep. *We* could hear this light making a rushing sound due to its force. *We* felt incredible love and longing in *our* heart, an aching pain, and *we* were crying with deep sadness.

Within an hour or so, *we* began to write poem after poem about love and lust. Words are inadequate as to what *we* felt, what was happening, as if far too many of *us* were attempting all at once to express *ourselves*. *We* were confused about what had happened with Simon for whom *we* felt no love. All *we* felt from *our* time with Simon made *us* want to die, and yet that loathing mingled with a deep love longing.

We wept for weeks, now understanding that it was different alters up at the same time—those devoted to the *demons* that had sexually hurt *us* beside *our* main front alter who was disturbed and grieving—young alters abused long ago and again during *our* time with Simon. It was indeed as if part of *us* had died within that darkness and pain. What *we* felt now

119

was ecstatic as well as agonizing. *We* could not reconcile the darkness of Simon with *our* own, all culminating in ecstasy and pain.

The hole that ripped open in *our* solar plexus continued for weeks. *We* can still see it five years later, though now it is a memory shown to *us* by *our* alters. What *we* clearly know is that it was *entities* being born into this dimension. Simon's *demon* had filled *us* for four days through sex with *entities* and *demons* that were to be brought into this dimension through *us*, the vehicle. The front alters do not recall when the shaft of light stopped, though *we* recall weeping for weeks and continuing to try to write about what *we* felt, though never being able to get it right.

Some within *us* know what occurred here, others do not. *We* are sickened by this event each time it comes up, and it took *us* months to be willing to write it here. What *we* know is that *we* birthed an untold number of *entities* into the this dimension that day and the following weeks. *We* have come to loathe the tattoo and what they used it for.

We believe that Simon was not just your run-of-the-mill encounter, but that there was a purpose and plan to what the kontrollers wanted from our "union". Simon was sent to *us* and *we* were handled by him and his *entity*, entranced by an awful dark beauty that *our* programming told *us* *we* could not deny, and *we* obeyed as *we* always had. *Demonic entities* can do that and have done that for a very long time. *We* can also see from the fragments that *we* remember that Simon was very conscious at times of who and what he was, and enjoyed it. He was conscious of the malevolent darkness that he gave to, and felt entitled to the fruits it availed him of. He told *us* he would continue to take them.

We have been told since 2008 by *our* alters that this Flower of Life tattoo is part of *our* binding to the one *we* call Cain, who *we* believe was the *entity* driving Simon. (*Entities* are not the same as us, in that they can inhabit many at the same time. In addition, there are the offspring of these *entities*. One can have *the* Cain or one of his offspring. My personal encounters were with *the* Cain.) This tattoo was a beacon that told other *entities* and *demons* that *we* were owned by Cain. The light was associated with the light of the dark occult. Through *our* programmed alters, *we* gave Simon permission to rape *us* for those four days, to fill *us* with the seed of his Cain while he enjoyed *our* menstrual blood, a very desirable source of energy for these *entities*. The acts of sex that Simon and *we* engaged in left *us* physically ill and deeply emotionally depressed.

Another Disappearance

In 2006 or 2007, a well-respected acquaintance in a small village in which *we* worked reported (completely unsolicited) that she had witnessed *us* vibrating on several occasions as *we* sat outside our place of work when it was slow, as well as on one occasion *our* complete disappearance from physical view. This acquaintance had no knowledge of who and what *we* are, nor *our* previous experience on the Andrew Jackson Plantation. *Our* front alters were at a loss to explain it, yet *our* memory of it occurring in the mid-1990s was still in *our* conscious mind. This time there was a witness who with no prompting corroborated *our* knowledge of *our* alter's ability to do this. (See Book 1, Chapter 9, "Breakdowns, Reprogramming, and Fragments", *Andrew Jackson Plantation*.)

Stolen Trips

Some of *us* have crystal-clear memories of locations of programming and on-task use but until *our* deep deprogramming began did not understand how these things were possible. *We* have many fragmented memories of trips to places without the conscious understanding of why *we* went and what *we* did while there. Many of these trip fragments have now been explained to *us* by *our* alters, at least in part. Some trips involve disturbing fragments of *us* in alter in places *we* cannot name or find. Many are programming locations, literally named as such by other researchers of *tmk* programming.

We have returned to some of these cities and locations and found several of the places within the fragmented downloads. Here are some of the cities and locations *we* are aware of in *our* front alter consciousness at this time for both programming and/or use.

Atlantic City, NJ	Nashville, TN
Knoxville, TN	Memphis, TN
Knox Berry Farms, TN	Orlando, FL
Walt Disney World, FL	Cape Canaveral, FL
Miami, FL	Florida Keys
Tampa, FL	MacDill AFB, FL
Atlanta, GA	Northern Georgia
Las Vegas, NV	Laughlin, NV
Wall Street, New York	Europe, UK
Bahamas	Egypt
Hood River/Astoria, OR	Jordan

Washington State	Baja, Mexico
Mexico	Tucson, AZ
Death Valley, CA	Joshua Tree National
Albuquerque, NM	Monument CA
Santa Fe, NM	Taos, NM
Durango, CO	Denver, CO
Boulder, CO	Salt Lake City, UT
Moab, UT	Peru

Location, Location, Location

Cain's Bitch, Lily

There are two particular encounters with the *being we* call Cain that give a good overview of *our* life with him. Both encounters occurred with him

122

in his malevolent form while *we* were staying at a friend's home, and both occurred within a three-day period.

The first rape occurred one night while *we* were staying in the guest house near the main house where *our* friends live. The husband and daughter of *our* friend and a little boy they were watching for a friend for a few days and *we* had just returned from an evening movie. (*We* were giving *our* friend, the wife and mother, an evening off.) *We* had driven all of us in *our* current employer's van and pulled into the driveway about 9 p.m. and said goodnight. *We* went to the guest house while the others went into the main house. This family did not know who and what *we* are; only recently had *we* begun to even try to go there with *our* friend.

We had not left a light on, and because it was a rural area both the exterior and interior were dark. As soon as *we* entered the guest house, the hair on the back of *our* neck went up and *our* skin went to gooseflesh. It was pure fear, and *we* knew this *feeling*. Out of *our* left eye, *we* immediately saw the reptile form very close to *our* face.

At this point in *our* life, *we* had not yet realized that *we* are a multiple personality who is not consciously able to understand that, nor *our* programming as a *total mind kontrol* slave. However, *we* were frighteningly aware that *we* had been tortured and raped at the hands of men in military uniforms, and that *we* had had a lifetime of *alien* encounters, including this "dinosaur".

In this *conscious* encounter, *we* believed that *we* must be remembering this reptile from other encounters. (See Book 1, Chapter 3, "18", *Torture, Programming, Guns and Reptiles*.) *We* were not yet aware that he was currently present and going to rape *us*. *We* fought the desire to turn on all the lights and instead lit candles—without a doubt, *perfect programmed behavior!* Our experiences showed us that these *beings* do not like bright light, therefore *we* were only following *our* programming regarding his presence there, as well as the presence of *entities* and *demons* within *us* that do not like light. (Leaving the lights on all night was a real difficulty in the early days of deep deprogramming, given *our* alter's discomfort because of resident *entities* inside *us*.)

At the onset, *we* decided to journal about this, thinking it was a memory from *our* past. All the while, he is inches from *our* left eye, staring deeply and intently. *We* made some strong spearmint tea, hoping to countermand the restless night rapidly approaching because of *our* slowly growing fear. *We* had tried to fight *our* fears for months with absolutely no success, due to the fact that they were not only fears from the past but fears of the programming *still* occurring in the present.

We stayed up in the dimly lit room with him at *our* side for almost two hours, until *we* finally decided to lie down and attempt to rest. It was only a matter of minutes after lying down that the one *we* call Cain, the *being* in the form of a reptile (not his only form of presentation to us), began to crawl up and onto *us* in the total darkness, starting at *our* right foot and coming up *our* right leg, *our* legs already spread for him, completely unconscious to most of *us*. All *we* consciously knew at this point was that this *reptile* from *our* past was now here and going toward *our* vagina! Many of *our* previous encounters with him had been within other alters, so in *our* front alter consciousness, it was terrifying to realize he was here, now.

It felt as if a three-dimensional man were crawling on top of *us* with his very three-dimensional weight! Adrenaline rushed through *our* body and *tremendous* fear pushed a scream out of *us*, forming the word "No!" as *we* sat up with *our* arms striking at the air! *We* were swinging wildly just as he reached *our* vagina. Then his weight was gone, just like that.

Our heart pounded as blood flooded into *our* ears with a loud rushing noise. *We* began sobbing uncontrollably, saying over and over how *we* wanted it to stop. Others of *us* were present now, many who knew and feared him. It was the terror that *we* wanted to stop—the day and night unpredictable terror for which *we* had no explanation, the terror that kept *us* in an ongoing state of wishing *we* were dead. *We* were exhausted and scared, *our* heart beating in *our* ears as *we* finally told *ourselves* after several minutes that it was over and *we* should lie down and try again to rest.

And that is precisely when it started all over again with something or someone crawling up on top of *us*. Again, *we* screamed "No!" and sat up, desperately swinging, trying to make contact with something, someone, *anything* so *we* could keep some grasp on *our* sanity, something that would allow *us* to believe that *we* had even a slight grasp on sanity. And once again, he was on top of *us* no more.

Being a perfect, lifelong, programmed slave, *we* did not get up and turn on the lights. Instead, *we* cried *ourselves* into a rest state, but awakened in the early morning darkness with almost unbearable itching under *our* skin. Not until late morning did *we* awaken with *our* skin crawling and welts on the surface. The crawling and welts continued for two months, with new welts appearing every morning. The welts were large, often in clusters and itching unbearably, leaving scars if *we* were not careful. Each welt took about ten days to two weeks to run its course. *We* began to believe that something was being put into *us* by them, even that the men in military uniforms from other encounters might be putting nano-bots into *us*.

[Nanobots are now a common vernacular in the bio-sciences and bio-technology fields, however, that was not the case when I began speaking of them. It was foreign to all I attempted to engage and even made me sound ungrounded, which I was, but not for this reason. Thanks to the toxic onslaught of chemtrails and GMO foods, everyone has "nanobots" now, and many suffer with similar symptoms to what is expressed here: **Morgellons** is the most common name for it.]

Some of *us* would realize that Cain entered *us* that night through *our* vagina—returning to his *tmk* slave as he had many times before. *We* would not fully understand this until ten months later when *we* would tell *our* life experiences to the two men helping with *our* deep deprogramming in Salt Lake City. Being allowed to tell is crucial, particularly to those who know *we* are sane. *We* realized how insane all of this would sound to an uninitiated person, and that only someone living *our* life, or someone aware of the reality of all of this, would ever be able to hear, and up until the two men in Salt Lake City, *we* knew no one to tell.

On that first morning following the encounter with Cain, *we* had a disturbing cluster of welts on *our* back and *we* understood they were a result of Cain sodomizing *us*: three claw marks in a row. *We* were not aware enough, nor strong enough, to take a picture of the claw marks; *we* wish *we* had. *We* fully realized and accepted that these *reptile* encounters were not only something from *our* past but were a three-dimensional and cross-dimensional part of *our* life now. To explain it any further would have allowed the fragmented pieces of *our* lives to start to come together, and that *we* still did not know how to accomplish.

[A reminder: The *entities* are riding the technology frequencies. Everything, including humans, have frequencies. This is why the technologies are developing with such fervor; the influence of these *beings* behind the men and women at work.]

The second rape that *we* choose to recount here occurred at the same location three days after the first encounter while *we* were staying in the main house and *our* friends were out of town. *We* had known these people for several years and had a very close relationship with their dog, so communication between our minds was very common. (It was exceptional with this particular animal and many of the programming techniques presented thus far allow such "abilities" due to their severity. They are not only by-products, but actual aims of the programmers to serve their purposes.) It was much easier for *us* to communicate with her than with most people through verbal communication. The dog and *we* had no secrets; *our* secrets between *ourselves* were a result of *our* amnesic walls due to multiplicity. *We* had many people within us with whom this dog could communicate.

We did not like sleeping in the bedrooms in the main house because of the *entities* in them; *we* preferred the living room with its spacious high ceilings and open feel. *We* decided to allow the dog to sleep under the pull-out sofa *we* would rest on; she suffered from many anxieties of her own—perhaps due to *seeing* and *feeling* when *entities* were present—and was much more comfortable being near *us*, feeling an affinity to *our* understanding of *entities*, despite having *our* own.

So *we* put out the light and were lying awake in the dark when the *reptile* form of Cain appeared in *our* visual field. Immediately, the dog growled low from deep in her belly, and would continue until he was no longer in *our* visual field. *We* gently reassured the dog that *we* were okay and began what *we* refer to as "pibs" or "pulling in Benevolence", a powerful practice to get rid of a low-level *entity* presence and put up a shield of protection. Though *we* had not been able to rid *ourselves* of Cain completely, *we* continued to use it when *demons* were present.

We were unnerved by his appearance but not debilitated by fear, perhaps due to his return to *us* just three nights before. *We* drifted into *our* rest state, which was when he accessed *lily*, Cain's bitch, then appeared as a man, though *we* could still *feel* his undeniable *demonic* presence—no doubt the purpose of announcing himself before *we* moved into *our* rest. He said he was here to rape *us*. *We* would be sodomized, his favorite form of sexual assault. For *lily*, in all her programmed devotion to him, the pleasure is tremendous. The emotional and physical difficulty is for *us*, the others for whom this is a violent and degrading rape.

It was as though time was slowed down, the sodomy and all its sensations highly acute, the feelings of pure, raw, sexual pleasure for *lily* existing simultaneously with terror and disgust for the others in *us*. *We* could *see* and *feel* all the lucid details from *his* view behind us and *ours*, a common occurrence during sexual encounters with these *entities* and *demons*. *We* experienced a tremendous array of physical, emotional, and mental dichotomies all at once. *We* had not only all of the physical sensations but the conflicting thoughts that are both pleasure- and pain-oriented, creating much confusion and shame, which in turn keeps *us* dissociated—a torture that is a direct result of programmed multiple personalities. Cain is a master at this, and when he wants to cause *us* much pain he appears in a hideous malevolent dinosaur/reptile form. *We* could *feel, hear,* and *see* his lifelong message to *us*: "You are mine…"

When *we* came out of this encounter with *lily*'s pleasure still being so strong, *we* cried. This was a psychological and physical assault to reinforce Cain's hold on *us*, a bind that has dominated *our* life. It is difficult to break free or even understand that *we* can when so many different selves participate so willingly. It was not until *we* truly began to understand who those other parts were and why they seemed willing that *we* could even begin to attempt to fight back. Despite the intense programming, saying "No!" would become a reality, if only at times.

The welts continued to appear intermittently. *We* knew before they surfaced where they would surface. A few months later, *we* had a nighttime occurrence that had *us* believing that nano-bots had indeed been put inside of *us*.

Red Light District

The following experience is very common: something unusual occurs; *we* wake up, then feel perfectly comfortable falling back into rest immediately, though *we* feel anxiety or intense fear.

We were housesitting in the desert for a friend in which the large living room south wall was all windows. *We* always preferred sleeping on the sofa that ran the length of the windowed wall because *we* had a view of the outdoors and night sky removed from any man-made light pollution, which gave *us* a wide open feeling. It was as peaceful a place as any could be for *us*, despite the fact that *we* often underwent malevolent *alien* accessing when *we* stayed there. The home belonged to a former employer.

We were lying on the sofa on *our* left side facing the living room when *we* awakened and saw a swath of red light about a foot in diameter coming from above and behind *us* and shining into the living room. *We* turned to look out the window. The light was gone and the moon was out in a clear sky—at least that is how it looked to *us*. Something was missing, though. Moments? *We* felt very tired and fell back into rest.

An Alien Walks into a Gallery

This encounter occurred in the early spring of 2008 in the Southwest desert prior to meeting the two men in the Salt Lake City who would assist *our* deep deprogramming beginning in April 2008. As a matter of fact, it occurred within a couple of weeks of that trip and *we* are certain that it was by design. *We* were still consciously unaware of *our* multiplicity, yet very aware of a lifetime of *alien* encounters as well as *alien* and military abductions, including military mind access. This awareness ran parallel to *our* awareness of *our* many selves, though *we* could not explain them.

We had just returned from a UFO conference in Laughlin, Nevada where *we* had volunteered to work to cover the expense. *We* had gone in the hopes of finding someone who could help explain to *us* what had occurred and still was occurring, though *our* alters repeatedly warned *us* about the great risk of outing *ourselves*. *We* approached cautiously, never revealing what *we* remembered nor talking about the ongoing access that occurred at conferences. *We* observed and listened, reading people the way *we* had been trained.

At this particular conference, *we* met a man who would later be the connection to the two men who would assist in initiating *our* deep deprogramming. *We* were suspicious of him, thinking he had been sent to *us* as a government operative because of what *we* were remembering. Actually, *we* are absolutely certain he was sent as a potential handler, benefactor, and lover. In subsequent phone conversations, we openly discussed our mutual obsession with needing to get together "face to face" and how suspicious we both were of it. In *our* memory downloads, it turned out to not be the first time we had met, though neither of us were conscious of it at the time. *We* are not certain that he has conscious memories of this at all.

We also met a vendor who made sculptures of *alien beings*. According to her, she does not know much at all about the *beings* she sculpts, she just *sees* them and sculpts them. During one of *our* breaks while working at the conference, *we* walked through the vending room and were stopped dead in *our* tracks by a sculpted plaque displayed on her table. It was an uncanny depiction, at least in part, of an *alien being, humanoid,* and she had engraved "reptile hybrid" on it as well. She was sitting behind the table when *we* looked astonished and asked breathlessly, "Who is that?"

She invited *us* to sit with her behind the table and tell her about *our* encounter with that being at 18 years old. (See Book 1, Chapter 3, "18", *Binding Possession*.) *We* spoke to her of *our* deep obsessive love for him, sobbing to this stranger willing to listen and who knew of what *we* spoke. She said it was people like *us* who tell her who these beings are, though she has her own experiences with beings. She went on to tell *us* that she understood *our* feeling that *we* were kin to him, and that her military father told her at 30 years old that she is an *alien-human hybrid*. *We* sobbed uncontrollably in that room that day with her, knowing for so long that *we* too were not human—not in the way most people are.

[This is a tricky thing to relay. I am still certain that there was an **overshadowing** at the time of my conception. I no longer believe that I am not human and recognize, as mentioned previously, that there was a lot of programming to make me believe such. I have a soul and that soul is aligned with God and Christ and all that is intended for this world from the beings of light. However, the overshadowing offers potentials, the possibilities of access and programming become more successful, if I may say. Bloodline. This is still my understanding at this time, though I suspect I have only scratched the surface of these matters and that dark occult forces know this arena quite well.]

We bought the plaque and took it with *us*. In 28 years, it was the first time *we* had ever seen or heard of a partial likeness of the *alien we* had encountered at 18. But the part about *reptile hybrid* still frightened *us* and *we* needed to understand why. How was this *hybrid* connected to the *reptile* that had tortured *us* for so long? The evil one who owned *us*?

Just a week after *we* returned to New Mexico from the Nevada UFO conference and were working at an art gallery, *our* sole confidant regarding the extent of *our* memories regarding *aliens*, military mind access and programming would be visiting *us* at work when for all intents and purposes, an *alien-human hybrid* walked in.

[Obviously, I cannot explain this in any better terms, even today, however, if you had seen him and his behavior, you would understand this description.]

Most of *our* life, due to *our* programmed isolation, *we* had experienced many things without witnesses, which made it easy to justify that *we* were crazy. This friend admitted that at times she had doubts about certain things but knew it was as real, if not more so, as the world going on around us.

This very day, *we* were telling her about the conference, about meeting the man who would introduce *us* to the two men in the Salt Lake City area within the next two weeks. (He will remain anonymous due to *our* desire to protect him and *our* Love for him, feeling that he is not conscious of his own programming. He was to be part of a kill program in Salt Lake City which did not take place thanks to my awakening from programming. More on this in Book 2.)

We also told *our* friend at the gallery about meeting the woman who does the sculptures and what occurred with her. She asked if she could see the sculpted plaque, so *we* pulled it out of its hiding place as *we* were living at the gallery at that time so all of *our* things were with *us*. *We* were crying while showing and telling her about it, and shortly after pulling it out a customer came in, so *we* put it away in a basket in the corner with a cloth over it so *our* friend could look down into the basket while *we* assisted the customer.

Once the customer left, *we* returned to sit behind the counter with *our* friend leaning on the chest-high counter across from *us* as *we* continued to discuss the conference. Within minutes the front door opened and in walked a most unusual looking man. Both *our* friend and *we* turned to greet him. The door closed behind him and he scanned the gallery and made a comment *we* cannot recall. Neither of us took our eyes off of him. He then looked directly at *us*, not *our* friend, approached the counter and stood a foot from *our* friend while looking directly into *our* eyes until he left. It was as if she did not exist for him. He was no taller than *our* friend, five foot eight or ten, slight, fair skin with almost no pigment at all, big blue eyes, a head too big for his body.

The encounter was filled with small talk *we* cannot recall, except for him telling *us* when *we* asked that he was from Philadelphia, very proximate to New Jersey *our* birthplace and residence for the first few years of *our* life, also the birthplace of one of *our* alters, *rabbit*. As well, a place our mother used to frequent in her youth. (See Book 1, Chapter 1, "Shattering a Young Mind: The Early Years", *Rabbit*.)

We briefly glanced at *our* friend twice to see if she was seeing this. She was staring silently at him with her mouth hanging open, not even a foot away from him.

Witnesses to *our* life occurrences are rare. *Our* friend later verified that he and *we* were completely absorbed in one another as if no one else was there, *eyes locked. We* did not care what was being said between us because what *we felt* from him was exhilarating. Whoever he was, he was energizing *us* and it *felt* very good. *We* had no fear at all, just exhilaration and gratitude that a friend was there to witness it. *We* do not recall how long he remained, yet he and *we* did not stop speaking to one another for a moment: *eyes locked.* Just as suddenly as it began, it was over and he exited with a goodbye. Due to the high strangeness, *we* decided to wait and see how *our* friend perceived the encounter. Immediately, she turned to *us,* her mouth still hanging open, and said, "He looked exactly like the being on the plaque you just showed to me!" To which *we* replied with a smile, "Welcome to *my* world."

Of course, we talked more about it and *we* watched as she began to doubt that she had seen what she thought she had seen. *We* were not sure she was even aware of what was occurring, nor were *we* upset by it. It is quite common and part of why *we* think *we* do not exist in the way others seem to. She was still by far the most open-minded person *we* had come to know and *we* deeply appreciated all she allowed *us* to share, crazy or not.

We believe he was indeed some type of being residing in a physical body that resembles human, however, is not, at least not totally.

[I have heard the term "walk-ins" and perhaps that is what I witnessed. Whatever it was, the most important part of that day was that someone else was there to witness. A first for me. It gave me courage as now I was not so alone in it all. Perhaps "he" was someone sent to help by giving me a witness? I do not know.]

We have encountered throughout *our* life malevolent beings of purely evil intent, despite the ecstatic feelings they can and do induce to lock-in and kontrol. He was indeed energizing *us*—simply another term for reprogramming and program reinforcement?—while utilizing that energy.

What plagued *us* immediately after this encounter and for months after *we* began to talk of it was the desire to laugh almost uncontrollably while relaying the event—not because it was funny, but because it felt all too familiar as programming, as if *we* could not stop *ourselves* from

131

laughing, meaning that an alter driven by an *entity* was doing the laughing. The energy within *us* is the very reason that these malevolent *demonic entities* chose *us* for the very things they have used *us* for. *We* are bloodline.

Hard to believe? Yes. Does that make it untrue? No.

Salt Lake City: Deep Deprogramming Begins

In April of 2008, *we* met the two men who would assist *us* with *our* deep deprogramming, one of them becoming *our* lifeline through the first year and a half. Without him, *we* might not be here to tell what *we* know. In Book 2 of *Our Life Beyond MKULTRA* (found here further on), *we* will discuss in more detail the discovery of *our* many alters, including a more in-depth description of the process of breaking free of *our* programming and programmers, kontrollers, and handlers.

Our meeting with one of these men in particular was not by chance, nor solely of Benevolent design. *We* and he have spoken of this and verified independently that *we* were programmed to go to him by *our* kontrollers to kill his family, and him if necessary. This kill alter was to, *bring him to his knees*, in order to destroy his support. It is obvious to both *us* and him that they underestimated the power of Benevolence in his life and *ours*.

One of the first things that began to show up during deep deprogramming was the presentation of many different child sex alters who were able to take kontrol of *our* body because *we* had not yet reached a conscious enough understanding of who all were inside *us*, nor how extensive their programming was. *We* were deluged by alters needing to show and tell all they had had to endure and what it was they were programmed to do. Almost instantly it became a physical, emotional, mental, and spiritual 24-hour-a-day interaction with these young victims who are *us*. They had had to wait years to present what they knew to *our* front alter, given that *our* front alter consciousness had been too programmed to allow these young ones to come forward.

In truth, due to *our* front alter programming, others inside were not able to break free of their programming. First, others of *us* up front had to be able to *see* and *feel* to be able to assist in getting the help *we* would need to succeed. This is another intentional design of *tmk* programming.

During the numerous downloads presented by these terribly wounded young child alters, involving all kinds of deviant sexual acts preformed on adult men, there was also a very visual occurrence that repeated for the first several months. When *we* closed *our* eyes, *we* would see flashes of brilliant white light on the *inside* of *our* head. This light accompanied very physically painful downloads being presented by these young alters who had been repeatedly raped. *We* use the term "willingly" completely in the context of severe and extreme programming. These young alters are not to blame. *We* have forgiven them and continue to ask for their forgiveness, due to them having nowhere to go and no one to help them.

Some of the most painful body memories during this time—as well as still occurring—were in the anal canal, due to sodomy at a very young age. Sodomy was perpetrated on the physical and astral planes. The intentional use of sodomy in *total mind kontrol* programming prior to the age of three not only inflicts terrible trauma on a small person but accesses psychic abilities latent in bloodline slaves—apparently certain bloodlines being desirable, such children are chosen as slaves designed for use from infancy on. *We* would also discover that *we* were not the only ones experiencing these flashes of brilliant white light associated with sodomy.

[See "The Master Plan of the Illuminated Rothschilds" by Ron Patton, an interview with Marion Knox, a farmer, gospel singer, and counselor from Lebanon, Oregon—critical to understanding what is actually occurring within *tmk* programming and *why*. I find that often the *why* is not even acknowledged due to a more superficial understanding which usually pertains to the material realm alone.]

My Own Worst Enemy

During the first six months of *our* deep deprogramming, *we* were getting hit very hard, particularly during a two-week period when *we* were housesitting for an acquaintance. *We* were very suicidal and not yet strong enough to functionally handle all that was coming at *us*. Meltdowns were lasting for days at a time and *we* often felt *we* would not get through them and the lost time still occurring for *our* front alters.

To *our* complete amazement, on the television in this home *we* discovered that a new television show was going to be aired on NBC in October of 2008 about a "government agency-created, multiple personality assassin". In *My Own Worst Enemy*, the multiple personality assassin from the United States Army "volunteered" to have his mind intentionally split.

Needless to say, the premise of the show did not include all the *tmk* content or intention that *we* were becoming aware of.

A couple of minutes before 8 p.m. on the evening it debuted, *we* were sitting before the television in anticipation and fear. *We* already knew from *our* experiences in *tmk* that this show could not be an accident. *We* knew in *our* conscious mind who and what *we* were and did not believe that *we* were the only one. In fact, at this point in *our* deep deprogramming *we* had heard of other programmed killers, though *we* had not been in personal contact with any of them—at least not any who were deprogramming. *We* had already deprogrammed enough to know, without any doubt, that there was indeed End-Time programming in *us*, as *our* alter experience downloads had revealed, and it was not isolated only in *us*: there were others with End-Time programming.

The show started at 8 p.m. and *we* were already in trouble by the first commercial break. Initially, *we* believed that *My Own Worst Enemy* would be used as a disinformation tool. *We* still believe that, but wholeheartedly state that it was *much more* than that. The show was cancelled by December, not even finishing the season. *Our* contention is that its effect on kill-programmed slaves was far too powerful at this point in the End-Time program scenario. *We* believe it was designed as part of "**call back**" triggering and that its effect was greater on the slaves than the kontrollers were ready for.

Before the first commercial break, *we* were triggered by something in the show content or in the broadcasting frequencies, *we* are uncertain which. *We* tranced out while looking at the screen with an alter or alters triggered. *Our* front alters were aware of this occurring, yet were being pushed out by others in *us*. A time lapse occurred. *We* still do not know if what *we* saw was on the screen or in *our* mind, but clearly two (or more?) alters were co-conscious at this time.

We can see the television screen when *we* feel ourselves going off and switching alters, as though *we* were still looking at it but no longer *seeing* it. Something else came into focus with the aforementioned going out of focus behind it. *We* were now seeing a new screen overlaying the television screen, two separate screens, with the new screen looking graph-like in gray, black and red.

At the first commercial break, *we* got up, went in the bathroom, and induced vomiting because *the bulimic one* had been triggered to the surface. *We* remember this, and *we* do not; it is as though *we* witnessed it from afar. A pressure had built up inside *us* from deep within and the need to purge was overwhelming. *We* did not reason this out, *the bulimic one* just did it. *We* purged many times, though often a few purges will release *us*. This was not one of those times; there was obviously a need for a deep degree of dissociation.

As soon as *we* stood up from bending over the toilet, the phone rang. Immediately the front alters were more aware of what was happening, though not why. *We* exited the bathroom and answered the phone. It was the man helping *us* with *our* deep deprogramming. He had been watching the show at *our* suggestion and called *us* on the first commercial break. He kept *us* on the phone until almost 9 p.m. to distract *us* from watching the show because he thought it was too much of a trigger. *We* would later thank him for this, though *we* had alters who desperately wanted to see the show.

We *felt* so out of it when *we* began conversing with him, given that he called immediately after *our* bulimic programming. Fortunately, he had grown accustomed to dealing with *our* alters. Later, *we* realized that *we* were attempting to pull up alters to converse with him and switch out of *the bulimic one* and the highly dissociated alter that often follows *the bulimic one*. *We* could neither focus on what he was saying nor on what *we* wanted to say. *We* recall asking him to give *us* a minute or two to try to gather *ourselves*, explaining that *we* had just engaged in purging.

We were dissociated and at the same time aware of it—very bizarre for *us* to be cognizant of it as it occurred. *We* do not recall what *we* talked about, but do recall that the high-energy, fast-talking anorexic alter that *we* call *jacked* had surfaced, an alter who fronts for several others who wish to present. *We* tried to explain to him what *we* had *seen* and how highly agitated and filled with anxiety *we* were, with an overwhelming need to vomit.

Four days later, *we* were still housesitting and saw that an encore presentation of the pilot episode would be shown on a different channel at a different time. *We* watched the entire episode and lost time during it.

It must be difficult for a person who is not a trauma-based *total mind kontrol* slave to understand why *we* would watch the show after *our* experience with it the first time. *We* can only offer this: It is difficult not giving into programmed self-destructive behaviors that *our* other personalities live by. *We* are changing, but it is a slow, arduous process at best. Some of *our* other personalities are frighteningly strong in *us*. Our front alters and many of the child alters are often afraid of them.

135

We were also at a point in *our* deep deprogramming that revelations were often followed by allowing outside mediums to trigger *our* alters (like watching *My Own Worst Enemy*), though *we* do not recommend this to deprogramming *tmk* slaves. It is foolish and dangerous. The episode was deeply disturbing, and quite revealing, to *us* for the following reasons:

- The premise of the show is a government agency intentionally creating a multiple personality in a United States Army soldier—an alter personality existing alongside the original assassin alter over whom they have total kontrol. Even the so-called original personality (the assassin) behaves as reinforcement for kill personalities.
- The main character's daytime self or alter has complete amnesia about the existence of the assassin alter (who is supposedly the original personality).
- The assassin alter knows all about the daytime self or alter and even reports on the daytime alter to a handler, including what is wrong within his "system." Within *total mind kontrol* programming, this is known as a *reporting alter* and is designed to safeguard against any programming breakdown. *We* report on *ourselves*, thus turning *ourselves* back into the cult programmers.
- Programming is breaking down and the two alters are switching back and forth without the handler's kontrol.
- The assassin alter is an unemotional, detached, deceptive, systematic killer who consensually engages in sex with a female assassin for several hours, then kills her before she can kill him, knowing all along that this was her kontroller's plan for her to gain access to him. His daytime self alter is married and docile, as well as committed to his marriage.
- The assassin alter sleeps with the wife of the daytime self, then calls in to report that he is up and is not supposed to be. He is brought in for reprogramming and as they strap him into a chair and his mind is accessed, he fights against it because he is his daytime self alter and can't understand what is happening to him. At this point, *we* are triggered. What in particular did the actual triggering? *We* only remember that *we* could *feel* how similar the scene was to *our loop* programming going round and round inside *our* head.
- Quite possibly the most disturbing part of all was that during a commercial break later in the show, television viewers were invited to go

136

to the show's online website to find out more about the show and its characters. The ad said something along the lines of, "If you are like Edward [the main character], go to..." *We* cannot tell you exactly what was said verbatim, but *we* are certain that viewers resonating with the show were being invited to go to an online website. To *us*, this was *without any doubt* another way for real handlers and kontrollers to track the program status of real *total mind kontrol* slaves with kill programming who were watching the show. For weeks, *we* had an *unbelievable* desire to go to that website! *We* were truly *compelled*. Fortunately, *we* did not have internet access or *we* would absolutely have done so. Instead, *we* had time to think about the dangers of doing so.

This show and its website were ill-intentioned and related to End-Time programming call-backs. *We* still fight the desire to see this show and its subsequent episodes, but *our* current home is happily television-free. (See Fritz Springmeier's material on illuminati *total mind kontrol* slaves for specifics on End-Time programming. His comprehensive work is now dated, and his affiliations in question, but it is still a valuable tool for corroborating internal aspects. *We* do not agree with his views necessarily, yet his work assisted *us* when the time was right.)

Cain, Lilith, and Lucifer

From September 27th into the early morning hours of September 28th, 2008, beginning at 3:50 a.m. *we* encountered Cain, Lilith, and Lucifer. This encounter and program crossed the physical and astral worlds, with *our* physical world being manipulated. *We* marked the time *we* were being accessed by them because more often than not the time helped to decipher *our* programming.

Cain has claimed ownership of many of *our* alters throughout *our* programmed life. He presents whatever three or other dimensional form is necessary to deceive and illicit terror from *us*. Due to extensive sexual programming, *our* alters participate, despite the fact that rape seems to be his favorite form of abuse. He knows that *we* were so thoroughly programmed that he would be assured *our* alters would consistently succumb to his perfect seductions. His cruelty and arrogance are most sinister. Through *our* deep deprogramming, *we* began to realize that these sexual encounters served a much greater purpose than just kontrol over *us*; they allowed Cain and Lilith to achieve a union within *us*. *We* were used as a vessel for their unions.

We have alters who loathe and fear him and alters who love him—like alter *lily* who freely gives herself over to him in her programmed state for a perversion of Love. For some alters, it is the only form of love that *we* know. Even now, the love bind still mingles with repulsion and desire.

In deep deprogramming *we* came to recognize day after day, night after night, that programs were running almost continually. Keep in mind that what *we* were dealing with here were malevolent *beings* with extraordinary powers of deception, utilizing and manipulating this dimension and beyond to create whatever they deemed necessary to elude *us*.

We are in a car on a street in a neighborhood with a man and a woman, both fair-haired. The man is driving, the woman in the front passenger seat, and *we* are in the back on the passenger side. It is a dark older model four-door large sedan, late 1970s-early 1980s. In the middle of the road ahead, a round sewer lid is ajar and a large Caucasian flesh-toned snake is halfway in. As we approach, *we* say forcefully, "You have to run over the snake, you have to kill it, don't let it hide, it will come back, kill it before it gets inside, roll your windows up, it will get in if we don't kill it, it will find a way in and kill us!"

We run over it with all of the windows up, yet it is not dead. Like magic, it is in the car, just as *we* said. It is upright in the backseat with *us*. *We* struggle with it, knowing it is going to bite *us* in the face and kill *us*.

Snakes repeat in downloads of *the wild one*—part of the program to justify and elicit her kill programming. Like men's penises, the snake is flesh-toned. A significant part of triggering her kill programming was when an erect penis would appear during a sexual encounter. This pretty sexual teenager known as *the wild one* was programmed to kill during sexual encounters to save her own life. For her, sex was a life and death situation during which the snake (penis) being held at bay within her hands is going to bite her in the face (during the onset of oral sex) and kill her—a kill or be killed program, so she must kill first. This works if she is brought "out" during the act of fellatio.

In these downloads, *we feel* the strength of the snake moving toward *our* face despite holding it at bay with both hands. *We* also *feel the wild one*'s tremendous fear. What has not been presented consciously is the other codes to elicit the final kill *and* if she does it alone or another alter assists. The snake is still just a fragment of her programming.

[This scenario of a snake approaching my face to bite me and the accompanying fear of death has presented in the astral many times over during the years. Additionally, this snake is associated with the "reptiles" regarding the malevolent realm and its association to my programming. It is not strictly linked to *the wild one*.]

Next, *we* are in an open space with low grass. All seems gray, overcast, and dull in lifeless beiges and browns, without vibrancy, no sun, no color. Even the plants are beige and gray. This is a *feeling* as well as a visual appearance. A beautiful man is with *us*, young and lovely to look upon, his face, his body, his jet black hair. *We* want him, yet something is telling *us* to resist. He is strong in physique and seems to know how much *we* desire him. Like an animal, he displays himself with an air of innocence, but there is clearly cunning behind it. He is toying with *us*. *Our* alter is unable to get clear on this and hold onto it consciously.

[Clearly my higher Self was present during this episode in the astral during deep deprogramming. I was struggling with my awareness of what was taking place while Cain was attempting to reprogram/reinforce what was once present. This would occur nightly with painful frequency during deep deprogramming in the astral for the first and second year. With time, I was able to see enough patterns to begin to combat these efforts.]

We are trying to prepare food, soaking beans and seeds to make *living* food out of the lifelessness around *us*, trying to bring life out of this dullness. *We* are trying to make nourishing vegetarian food, but he is all around *us*, taunting *us* with his beauty and sexuality, with his twenty-something innocence, brushing against *us*, knowing and enjoying that *we* are having difficulty focusing on what *we* are doing. *We* desire him, but want to focus on what *we* are working with—the beige, gray sticks for plants, the dried beans and seeds *we* are trying to sprout to life.

All the while he is seducing *us*, a part of *us* knows there is danger here, but *what is it*? He changes from clothed and perfectly innocent to naked and fully seductive in an instant. *Our* mind is spinning with confusion as he brushes against *us* and *we feel* him reaching inside of *us*. He takes *our* breath away, he is the one *we* desire, the one *we* have *always* deeply, totally desired, and yet there is something, someone telling *us* to resist. (This is *lily* trying *desperately* to surface for him.) It is as if *we* had never known until now how he desired *us*. He tells *us* within *our* mind that it is to be a lifelong commitment and far beyond that, that he wants us to always be together, to marry, to wed. *We* understand that it is not to be an actual marriage but something different: *a union*. A *willing union* is what he seeks.

We continue toiling with *our* gray, colorless food as his innocence masks his deception *we* feel *ourselves* succumbing to. He is pulling at *us*, drawing *us* into him. *We feel* overwhelmed by the lack in the garden of pittance before *us*. For the briefest moment, *we* see beyond him to a vibrant color of green chard with red veins and call out, "There is young, tender green chard over there," its red veins and green brightness directly linked to Life. Yet Cain is attempting to influence this as human veins, human blood. But *we see* and *feel* this deeply; it is ultimately what this encounter is all about.

Our heart fills with hope; *we feel* it as a physical rush. Then just as quickly, he fills *our* view with his form, blocking out the hope, and *we* are lost in him once again, in *our* desire for him. *We* attempt to return *our* focus to creating nourishment by filling glass jars that contain the dried beans and seed with water to enliven the seemingly dead food. He is close behind *us* now, holding *our* hips in his hands, pulling *us* to his erect penis, *breathing* into *us*, pressing his whole body to *ours,* though both of us are clothed. His seduction is nothing short of bewitching perfection, and *our* programming and alters assure this, as well as who he really is.

We fumble with the jars, feeling *ourselves* slipping *into* him. When this occurs, *we* cease to exist. There is no longer any delineation between him and *us*. That is when *our* alter *lily*—Cain's bitch—comes out and fully takes over. *We* fight to stay with all that is good in *us*, to stay focused, but *we* fail. The jars spill and fall to the ground.

As they drop, *we feel* the darkness rise in *us*. It is *lily* filling *us* with her programmed, pure, raw desire for him as she reaches back with both of *our* hands and aggressively pulls him into *us*. Everything is lost, save him.

Our mind is filling with him as *we* feel his hard penis digging at *our* buttocks. He sighs, in the most coy, cunning way that says to *us*, "There you are, *lily*." *We* begin to grope through his clothing feeling his erection and more in lucid, explicit detail *we* will not share here.

Instantly, he is without clothes; he never takes them off or puts them on, they manage to be on one moment and off the next. His strong young body is mesmerizing, his skin so fair, his hair black, his penis erect and beautiful as he swirls around *us*, brushing his side, his thigh, his buttocks, his stomach, his penis against *us*. *We* are so filled with desire and *entranced* by his beauty and movements as he begins to "seal our union forever". He is what *lily* has always wanted.

Our descriptive narrative is an attempt to relay the *unbelievable power* of *our* programming and *the energy* that goes with it. In this encounter, *we* are fighting that energy to the best of *our* ability, but Cain wins out as he has so many times before. He tears at *our* soul and has the ability to affect *us* like no other due to *our* programming from infancy.

[The astral is the playground for these beings as they know the power available in that realm and their ability of working within it due to human consciousness' state while there. It is important for everyone to understand this, not just mind-controlled slaves. In the modern version, eMKUltra (see the Lexicon at the back of this book), the astral is being utilized against many across the world without their knowing anything about this. Understanding it from the entity perspective will assist in combating it. Understanding it from the technological standpoint is *crucial* now. The mind/spirit in the astral is the battlefield.]

Deep inside is the awareness of another, yet who? A good man, one *we* are trying to remember. *We* feel pangs of guilt because *we* cannot remember him. *We* are losing *our* ability to fight this dark one that Lilith craves so, this one that moves about in ways that no man can move. *We* are giving in, here and now, as he consummates our "union". All goes to the black void, right then and there.

[Lilith was the handler for many of our sex alters. As far as I can tell, she ran a whole system of alters. I came to realize some time later that the "good man" was not just man, but the Christ brought to earth long ago in the physical form, and the Christ who is once again here in the etheric realm. See Rudolph Steiner's works for more on this.]

Next, he is lying naked on a bed, resting in his perfect form, sprawled in all his naked glory for *us* to gaze upon from below, as *we* are below him

141

in every way, kneeling at the side of the bed, his hand hanging relaxed over the edge of the bed near *our* head. *We* are trying to wash blood off the edge of the bed near where his hand hangs. Running water pours into the pan. Fear and shame fill *us*, yet *we* cannot remember why. The light-colored sheets are tousled on the bed. Did *we* engage with him in that bed? Is that where the "union" that *we* cannot recall took place?

His soft, large penis is flaccid on his thigh, his eyes closed. He has no hair on his chest, nor in his pubic area, only black and lustrous on his head. In his presentations to *us* in humanoid form, he has no nipples or belly-button.

[This is a telling point of what we are dealing with here. In the "human" forms they often present, there is no sign of human birth and genuine form: lack of nipples and belly buttons.]

Why can we not remember? Where is the blood from? What is the source of the running water? In *our* head, *we* keep hearing a voice saying, "We must get this edge clean, we cannot allow his hand to brush against it." *Why? What is it? We* feel great anxiety over what has occurred, but are at a loss to speak of it or even remember it. *Why?*

We know there is something very ugly about this that *our* alter will not allow us to know due to its painfulness. Yet deep inside, *we* do know—*we* remember, and not. *We* are not strong enough yet in *our* conscious mind. During this download, *we see* and *feel* that something is very wrong, yet still feel the bond to him. The tearing at *our* parts is a familiar feeling, experienced time and time again—two or more parts struggling in *our* mind and soul. *We* are experiencing more than one alter—*lily, our* higher Self… and someone else?

Next, *we* are outside again in a field with large, old trees. It is twilight. Off to *our* left a hundred feet are his family, the women and children numbering about twenty. *We* do not see any men, yet *we feel* they are there. The women and children are walking a path illuminated by candles, some of them carrying candles in their hands. The woman at the front wearing a long white gown is his mother-lover Lilith. In appearance, she is older than he, her black hair heavily peppered in gray. *We* watch them walk. Seemingly, they ignore *our* presence, but *we* are keenly aware that they know *we* are here.

Next, *we* are indoors. He is close in front of *us* slightly to *our* right, looking intently and unwaveringly into *our* eyes: *eyes locked. We* watch as he changes into *our* ex-husband, which makes *us* very uneasy. *We* are not frightened, but know that *we* are being deceived.

To *our* left is Lilith, with the family beyond her. She too has that disarming intent stare, steady and domineering, an emotionless look containing no Love. It is clear to *us* that Lilith and the family believe *we* are not good enough for the one *we* call Cain. *Our* being deserving of this "union forever" with him is something *we* must prove. This is *our lily's* greatest desire: to be with him *always*, she *needs* to prove to them that she is worthy of eternal torture, deception, programming, and use without any Love whatsoever!

Whether approving or disapproving, Lilith must go along with whatever Cain decides, this is something *we* know. After Cain changes into *our* ex-husband, with *our* right hand, *we* press his solar plexus while we are *eyes locked* and begin to confront Lilith vocally about her and the family's judgment of *me*, *lily*. *We* speak aloud while they speak directly into *our* mind, not audibly.

We tell her that *we* should not be judged for not eating the flesh of humans—*why can't she allow us to not do so?* They ingest the blood and flesh of humans and have trained and programmed *us* to believe *we* must do the same. *Our* lack of that desire—a desire they relish—is of much concern to Lilith as regards *our* future "eternal union" with Cain. They are human-eating *demons*.

We are in an altered state as *lily* during this encounter and unable to grasp fully the great danger here to *our* human soul. They are attempting to get *us* to relinquish *our* soul once and for all. It is difficult to explain how normal all of this *feels* in *our* splintered mind, and yet all of *our* futures depend upon it. *Lily* really does not fully understand what she is being asked here, nor the impact it will have on *us*. She is no illusion, nor are they; *this is real in every sense of the word.*

[They attempt to do this in the astral when they are dealing with the strength of one who is not aligned with them. The programming won't work if their deceptions fail, and using deception is temporary, not a permanent soul-capturing success. To get one in full consciousness outside of the astral, to comply willingly, is their desire. This event presents the *secondary* action to procure alliance, yet it is not "everlasting". Mind control programming is all about deception, smoke and mirrors, hence why it never lasts, especially in those with strong Benevolent connections.]

Our other alters try to push through to her and warn her of the danger, but devoutly cult-loyal ritual alters are also present. *Lily* was created and raised in an atmosphere of incest and human sacrifice. This is no small matter. They derive much power from one who freely relinquishes the soul, especially a *total mind kontrol* slave's soul from a multi-generational blood-line. *We* cannot describe the depth of sadness *we* feel regarding encounters and downloads by alters who are completely deceived and devoted through program victimization to these sinister, treacherous *entities*.

Cain and Lilith are still looking at *us* without any compassion. Her eyes dark with color *and* intention, Lilith walks past *us* to make *us* turn slightly to follow her slow and precise movement and thus now see the room just beyond her. She is now on *our* right front and Cain on *our* left front, an open doorway between them.

The room seems old—a living room with things that *feel* like they have been gathered over much time. An old man is sitting in a wingback chair. He is looking at a fixed point in the room beyond *our* view.

When *our* eyes return to Lilith, she is still looking intently at *us* but with a small, narrow silver horn in her right hand, about a foot or foot and a half long, flared about two inches across at one end with a narrow tube curling and coming out into a narrow mouthpiece. Along its sides, the silver is etched in vine and flowers.

[This motif on the horn and the horn itself are important pieces of this occult process. The vine etching on silver would show up in another bind-ing ceremony, that one with a possible **Asuric** being I believe to have been Sorat. Silver was the medium again there. Both of these were "unions" regarding not only programming use, but soul/spirit capture attempts.]

She is holding it at the curl, raising it steadily and slowly toward *our* face, then gently blowing air through the horn at *our* open right eye—a soft, steady flow without any sound. She then drops it to her side and walks off while Cain in the form of *our* ex-husband stands motionless, staring intently at *us*, his form allowing *our* clear understanding that he has always been with *us*, always procuring *our* devotion.

We look back at the old man in the room and see about three feet thick from the ceiling down is filled with *thousands* of black flies. Sickened and stunned, *we see* and *feel* that this is *us*, the splintered, fractured mind of *us*. Collectively, the flies change into tan and brown moths but number less. *We* are speechless, understanding that the moths are *our* programmed splits—the black flies are all of the splits and fragments created by extensive trauma and torture while the moths are the ones they used, the programmed, collective us. *Our* heart aches as *we* turn *our* head towards Lilith who is still holding that unnerving, compassionless stare. The moths of "moth-er", Lilith. Our thoughts speak to her with deep sadness, *You did this, how could you? Why?* Then all is gone.

Our higher Self was present as well, attempting to influence the temptation of *our lily* alter. *We* do not judge *lily* for this; it is her very existence to be with him, and she gladly gives everything she is to him. She is programmed to respond to him willingly and in total submission. *We* present this for *us* and others like *us* out there to understand what is what and further our successful deprogramming.

The woman in the white gown with the dark eyes and gray-peppered black hair is clearly a presentation of Lilith. *We* believe she was presenting as a mother figure to sway *our* decision. She presented as mother-lover to Cain because most of those present, including many of *our* alters, are very familiar with incest. Of course, they were hoping *our* higher Self would not show up. And of course Cain shows up in the perfect, beautiful, human male form when deception and seduction are paramount. When he wishes to punish *us* and strike terror into *our* heart, he presents as a *demonic, dinosaur-looking reptile*. When he rapes *us*, he wants to display his ownership with degradation and make *us* feel the painful pleasure that *our* alter *lily*, or rather Lilith herself, feels while he hurts *us*. During these encounters, *we* hear in *our* head, *You are mine, and you like it*, as well as, *You are my bitch*. This is meant to arouse *our* alter and sicken *our* other alters. It is astounding how these *beings* are able to simultaneously activate terror and sexual arousal in *us* for various alters, though this is lessening greatly, thanks to deep deprogramming. These messages are typical of malevolent programming, no matter the beings or humans involved.

The old man in the room is understood to be Lucifer. It is poignant that at no time did he look upon *us*. There is a reason for this, but that information is not allowed to be presented to us. Her words are, "Look upon *us*."

[I believe that this information of what would have happened if Lucifer were to "look upon us" belongs to another realm of understanding. It was not so much that it was being withheld by an alter, but rather it falls into an occult category of not being allowed to be revealed.]

However, *we* feel much fear at the thought of it occurring and are thankful that he did not look upon *us* because something would have occurred if he had. It is still difficult to write about this. It took weeks before *we* would even confide in *our* deep deprogramming person what *we* knew about the black flies and moths. *Our* conscious mind had difficulty with it, and there were those within *us* who would not allow it to be spoken. It is quite common in *our* deprogramming to be consciously aware of something but incapable of speaking about it due to a restriction enforced by *our* alters, or more correctly by the *entities* handling and running these alters.

As *we* gazed into the Lucifer room that contained *our* mind splits and fragments three feet thick on the ceiling, *we* grasped from Lilith who was staring at *us*, *Do you understand?* The degree of sadness in *our* heart was immeasurable at this moment, *even* in alter. The clear message during this encounter, as well as hundreds of others, is that *we* are one of them and have *always* been one of them in ways not written of here, and no one will ever Love *us*. It is reinforced in more ways than *we* could ever write, even if *we* continued to write for the rest of *our* days on Earth. It is the message reinforced in everything they do and don't do. *We* have believed for all *our* life that *we* were born of evil and that *our* desires and deeds reflect that day after day, week after week, year after year. This is programming at its best and worst, yet there is more.

We have always known that *we* are responsible for killing others since *our* late teens and early twenties. *We* have anguished over it and yet been unable to explain how. *We* were aware of numerous terrible sexual acts with men whom *we* could not put faces on, let alone names. This is all part of *our* programming and bloodline legacy.

In this encounter, *we* were being told that all of *us* are eternally trapped in that room with Lucifer. If *we* were to believe that through and through, *we* would relinquish *our* soul to them, give up hope, and allow *ourselves* to be completely immersed within the darkness and no longer be aware of the pain *we* feel over being so evil in the presence of Benevolence. What they offer *us* is a complete letting go of all hope of redemption or forgiveness. In this they convince that the longing to be good will no longer plague one. They are banking on *our* inability to tap into *our* pure Benevolent Self due to their programming. It was to be the final damnation and they would have *us* believe that *we* would find solace within it.

Cain's presentation as *our* ex-husband was another way to grind in the fact that he has always been with *us*, the one *we* wanted, the one to whom *we* wittingly or not gave all of *our* devotion. *Our* ex-husband represented all the men whose forms he resided in or kontrolled from afar. The elaborate seduction was to deceive *us* into allowing Cain and Lilith to use *our* body as a vessel for their union. It is a coerced, programmed relinquish, and those who have experienced it through the depths of *tmk* will know of what *we* speak. *We* front alters do not pretend to fully understand this, yet *we* will share what *we* know. As long as *our* higher Self is in charge, they cannot enter *us* to engage in this union; *they must get us to relinquish to them.*

We have *always* known that there are spiritual laws in this universe that all must abide by. Cain was accessing *lily*, and once done, *we* were pushed out and he and Lilith were in and uniting in the way they do. What *we* know is that there is *power* within this use of *our* body, but aside from the obvious, we don't understand what else takes place. These seductions by Cain are more numerous than *we* can relate here, yet on many occasions involving Lilith, it all goes blank at the moment of the sexual act, the *union* of Cain and Lilith. This became quite clear in deep deprogramming. While they engage in *our* body, *we* are pushed out, which is why *we* don't experience the act of sex in many (though not all) of *our* sexual encounters with him. At times, *we* experience the sexual act and energy with him, but are not consciously aware of Lilith's presence. It is all about who of *us* are present—which alters are up and running. Some occasions are about something else—another purpose for Cain not always clear to *us* consciously. In other words, more than one agenda in this encounter: the use of *our* body while once and for all attempting to get *us* to willingly relinquish *our* soul. The bliss of eternal, carnal pleasure is the lure, yet the truth is *eternal torture, programming, and use devoid of all that is human and Divine.*

On the day following this all-night encounter, several things occurred to drive the point home. The first was two long distance phone calls from family members under *tmk*—one in the morning from a brother who offered his home for *us* to return to, expressing his love and how much all of them missed *us*. The second call a few hours later was from *our* mother who, completely unconsciously, had been calling long distance with program triggers for months from the same town. They were both following their programming to get *us* back into the same "family" that had just worked *us* over all night.

[My family was not SRA in the sense most think of, yet they were mind controlled and others had access that performed such deeds in which I was involved. I see my family as victims, and in some instances perpetrators out of that victimization, as I became.]

But the scariest occurrence of all was Cain's three-dimensional effect upon *our* surroundings to make sure that *we* remained aware of his reach over *our* life.

When *we* began *our* deep deprogramming, *we* purchased a micro-cassette recorder due to the 24/7 memories and so much nocturnal activity with *entities* and programs. Either *we* were unable to write fast enough or in a situation in which *we* could not write. Memories flourished at night and early a.m., so *we* would grab the micro-cassette and record. When alters went back deep down inside, detailed memories often went with them.

That morning *we* recorded the all-night encounter in detail, then got out of bed to make *our* tea, came back to the recorder, rewound it a little, hit play, heard *our* voice loud and clear, stopped it, gathered *our* writing materials, went back to fix *our* tea, and were back and ready to write in less than five minutes. Again, *we* picked up the recorder, rewound for about a minute, and hit play. But this time the distorted, deep, and inaudible sound that came out of the recorder sent chills down *our* spine. *We* continued to rewind, thinking it was the batteries, then went forward, awaiting something understandable but it never appeared. *We* replaced the batteries to no avail.

We sought the important recording of a full abreaction days before to a program access phone call during which part way through *our* higher Self had the wherewithal to use the recorder, but it too was nowhere to be found. Completely gone. *We* had replayed it a couple of days after recording it and it had been fine, just like *our* recording only minutes before. In *our* head *we* heard, *I am still here with you, I can do what I like, anytime, anywhere.* Fear arose in *us*. Cain had taken *our* recordings and destroyed them (with a little help from remote technologies?) After fear, *we* became angry, but more importantly, *determined*. With pen in hand, *we* spent the next two hours writing out what had occurred that night before and in the early a.m. hours in more detail than *we* had recorded on the recorder. *We* were tired of being frightened and tormented.

This occurrence with the micro-cassette and distorted tape is an example of the layered *entity* and *demon* energies of the many minds *we* have that are able to affect objects in the three- dimensional world—the *demons* that drive alters in *our* mind, given that a programmed *tmk* slave is made up of many, many minds.

The day's final frightening occurrence presented by these *entities* occurred at work at 1:45 p.m. A customer walked into the art gallery in which *we* worked, lived, and slept on the floor. After a brief conversation, the person walked up to the counter, looked *us* in the eye, and announced that she had an alter ego named Lily. *We* were speechless, barely containing *our* shock. She and her husband innocently explained how this was indeed the case, not knowing the import of what they were doing or why they were entering this gallery and telling *us*, etc. *We* marked the time.

Surreal, but the reality of *our* life as a *tmk* slave. In that regard, it is not the least bit unusual but normal, frequent, and systematic.

[Many would see this as willing gang-stalking. I can say that this particular couple was completely unaware of the true meaning behind what they were doing. To me, they clearly looked more like they were being tapped from afar, remotely, and sent to reinforce what had taken place for me, another slave, that morning. I see them as mind controlled subjects, not willing participants. There is a difference between the two.]

Relinquishing

Many things preceded this almost fatal event. Aside from a lifetime of trauma, abuse, programming, and use, on the 4th of October *we* had dealt with extensive co-existent sex alters and kill alters with *our* front alters. On the 5th *we* contended with Lilith, Cain, and Lucifer in the black flies and moths encounter described previously, denoting *our* tremendously splintered mind—something *we* front alters were now painfully aware of. On the night of the 5th was Cain's seduction in his hideous black-eyed *demon* form, followed by his appearance in human form.

In the following encounter, Cain stayed present and visible to *us* from before bedtime until morning, revealing the more hideous *reptile* presentation in the beginning and at the end to remind *us* of his power to seduce *our* alters programmed to him, no matter how disgusting he was to *our* front alters. His ongoing expression of ownership of *us* is part of *our* daily psychological torture.

On the morning of October 6th, a friend who clearly had a crush on us would call to say he needed a ride somewhere because his vehicle had broken down. Gladly, *we* agreed to help. It was not until *we* hung up that a rush of fear hit. Very early in the day, *we* knew *we* were in trouble. It would just be one of many, many days during which *we* would have to hang on while all hell broke loose. That is what the first year of deep deprogramming repeatedly meant for *us*. All the way there, *we* did *our* pibs and pulled in Benevolence, but when *we* arrived, several triggers were waiting for *us*, including Led Zeppelin playing rather loudly when *we* walked into his home.

[This particular group and their music was used to program us to another individual for a kill program. More on that in Book 2.]

This friend did not seem to have any conscious knowledge of who he was nor his role with *us*. After several delays, he attempted to touch *us* as he had on other occasions, a palpable desire coming from him and felt by *us*. *We* had no conscious, sexual relationship with this person, though at times the sexual energy between us (due to the *entities*) was apparent to *our* front alters. *We* pulled away and did not allow him to touch *us*. Neither of us said anything, yet both of us were aware of *our* response. This interaction and another in the week previous allowed *us* to begin to recognize his role with *us:* entity to entity reinforcement.

[I would like to state that this can be done with *anyone*. The person I was referring to here was not MKUltra, but just someone with entity attachments that influence his life. *Anyone*. Like the couple who came into the gallery where I worked to announce her alter Lily.]

Later in the day, *we* sought out his presence but do not recall why, then admonished *ourselves* for doing so. *We* later realized that someone in *us* was just following their programming.

By early evening of October 6th, *we* were in a state of high distress with *our* entities working *us* over terribly—co-existing with several alters and hearing things in *our* head designed to isolate *us* and provoke extreme programmed rage. While this was occurring, *we* had moments of clarity, but *our* alters' strength was very powerful; it is not as simple as consciously exerting *our* will. Several messages in particular really got to *us*, such as why *we* give so much concern for the welfare of humans. *Is it no wonder the demons see humans as a pathetic food source? We* left several long distance distress calls to one of *our* deprogramming people, but he was not available. Later, he said that *our* alters expressed "detached from pathetic humanity" views on his voicemails.

By 9 p.m., *we* were lying on top of *our* sleeping bag on the floor of the art gallery, curled up in the fetal position on *our* left side, no longer crying as *we* had for hours but filled with programmed rage turned inward, completely disillusioned, lost, and alone. Yet alone is the one thing *we* never really were, what with *entity*-driven alters always internally and externally present. It was in the world around *us*, the "world of man", that *we* felt completely lost, alone, and insane.

Our heart physically hurt. *We* could *feel* the other parts of *us* taking over. *We* kept trying to hang onto *our* front alter's consciousness as it slipped in and out of *our* head, growing more and more faint as other voices grew stronger. *We* were "relinquishing", though someone, something inside was barely hanging on, still there. *We* knew parts of *us* were giving in mentally, emotionally, and spiritually. *We* were worn out. Then a moment was upon *us*; all that remained was whether or not *we* would let go completely. *We* had already relinquished consciously to a degree that *we* felt *we* had not done before, not within *our* deep deprogramming, not while being consciously aware of it. *We* lay there aware that the concerted attack *we* had been under for weeks, months, and years had left *us* too vulnerable. It all felt so monumental, so all encompassing, as if there would only be them and *us* forever—constant program messages running in *us* day and night for the rest of *our* life. Deep deprogramming had made *us* front alters consciously aware of these things a little at a time.

To the *entities*, it was all a game, one they enjoyed and seemed to have all of eternity to play. All that *we* had been programmed to believe lay before *us*, thanks to *our* deep deprogramming. Within *our* programmed walls in *our* altered state, *we* struggle to free *ourselves* from their deeply embedded grip. Programming is reality for *our* alters, as real as any life being lived. *Our* connection was with them, not with the "world of man" going on around *us*, the world in which *we* felt no real connection to anything or anyone, the world *we* came to perfectly mimic through *our* alters, what *we* were to appear to be per *our* programs.

In that moment on top of the sleeping bag, so small, curled up like a little girl, unable to cry anymore, *we* heard a voice in *our* head say, *Call him and it will all stop.* The temptation was a physical, emotional, and spiritual ache for release from pain. *Our* heart and soul felt so unbelievably tired that *our* collective parts were considering giving *ourselves* to them in all of their terror, and seeing this as a respite. *We* knew all too well exactly who "he" was: Cain.

Yet in all of *our* combined misery, someone else spoke, saying calmly and with much intensity, *If you call him to us, we will be lost to them forever.* *We* knew this to be true. Though *we* were programmed, *we* were still by all means "conscious". This was not taking place in the astral, this was awake, this was traumatically awake. It was the voice of *our* higher Self *we* clearly know. Despite all they had done to *us* from birth, all that *we* had done to do their bidding as a programmed *total mind kontrol* slave, *we* still couldn't give up *our* soul. Without a full, conscious "relinquishing" of *our* soul, they would never really own *us*. They had used smoke and mirrors, and now they wanted *us* to choose to be theirs for all of eternity. This is the great spiritual law: Lucifer, Ahriman and the Asuras, the masters of deception, can *use* someone through deception, but can only own someone by their choice. *We* had unconsciously split under ongoing trauma and torture in order to survive *our* trauma-based *total mind kontrol* programming. Rather than die, we had fragmented in *our* mind, a most primal, *unconscious* reaction.

But now *we* knew that if *we* called to Cain, it would mean the removal of all thoughts of good and Benevolence and *we* would commit to all that *we* have had to endure, and this time it would be forever! This is their ultimate deception: that it will feel good and alleviate the pain by removing any memory of Goodness, when the truth is it will be more carnal, raw, and ugly than *we* are able to describe. As a *tmk* slave, *we* struggle constantly during deep deprogramming over being redeemed by Divine Goodness that is active in *our* true Self, *our* human soul.

In their name and under programming, they form a perverse bond that is the antithesis of Love, though they use words like "belong", "family", and "love" to mirror to *us* Love's reversal—what *we* may not have with humans, due to *our* being part of malevolence. They coat it with the sugar of physical pleasure that is brief and never enough to cover the stench of eternal ugliness.

The higher Self who warned *us* is the strongest part of *us*, though difficult to reach through all of the programming. It is a part of that Benevolent Light that they fragmented in *us* so that they could use *us* as they did. They shattered, programmed and used *us*, enabling the *entities* to drive the alters. The very reason they chose *us* is related directly to *our* Benevolent Spirit.

We listened and did not call upon Cain to take *us* away from the on-going pain. Instead, *we* lay there consciously not protecting *ourselves* in *our* complete exhaustion and despair. *We* did not call upon Cain, nor did *we* call in Benevolent protection. *We* lay there released to it all and will never forget how it felt. *We* lay knowing they were near, *seeing* and *feeling* several of them showing themselves in that darkened room. Within minutes of 9 p.m., all became a blur of *demons* and alters.

Our accessing began with a powerful hit of sexual arousal that had been completely non-existent minutes before during *our* deep despair—an easy way into *us* due to the extremes and depths of *our* sexual programming through systematic sexual abuse and torture. In *our* mind appeared many men in whom *entities* and *demons* lived, along with other *beings* that *we* did not know on a conscious level. It was a free-for-all *we* would pay for later, one after another in degrading and violent sexual acts accompanied by terrible messages. All of this took place in the astral.

We marked the time at precisely 12:34 a.m., due to the recurring *flipping snapshots* program associated with *our* End-Time programming which involves a circle and direct associations with *Batman* programming. (12:34 works to reinforce the programming, whether a.m. or p.m.) The front alters do not retain what these rapidly flipping snapshots are pictures of, but an alter associated with the End-Time programming knows. *Our* head hurts during and after this program runs, the snapshots flipping at a rate of about one every second sometimes faster to bypass my conscious mind, and running from ten or fifteen seconds to several minutes. The longer the duration, the more painful the distress in *our* head.

Our vulnerability was utilized in many ways during this "relinquishing". In the morning, *we* heard in *our* head the most hideous sound of an inhuman scream that marked the time 5:14 a.m., another recurring sequence of numbers and morning awakenings in running programs. *We* would come to consciously understand from this encounter what it is they seek from *us*, a trauma-based, multigenerational bloodline human.

Here are excerpts from *our* journal entry on October 7th:

> *...we gave ourselves to them...it caved in...to them it is nothing...curled up on our left side in the fetal position like a little girl...*[Fritz Springmeier's writings indicate that assuming this position during extreme torture is a sign that the child is giving up their will to live.]
>
> *...we relinquished our protection in a state of losing faith...so disillusioned...the foundation of our choices...[how] unbelievably tired our heart*

153

felt...[finally] no crying...something released inside...a powerful part within us that sees the respite of giving ourselves to them...we do not believe there is peace, we are not that foolish, we see it as carnal pleasure, brief, then an ending of the struggle between light and dark within, there is no love there, only worship and serving of a pure evil...we would be entirely evil, all goodness...pushed out of us...a perverse rest in being evil, without having to fight them...

The following refers to the encounter under "Cain, Lilith, and Lucifer":

...'Relinquish' means forever lost in the death realm...for us [it means] eternally in that room with 'lucifer,' eternally bound to the pure evil we saw in that room with all of our parts...they would like us to believe we are already there...they present to us that we are family, already one of them...they prey on our...isolation, loneliness...created and enforced by our programming by them...our use as a 'kill model,' especially that, has in itself created an overwhelmingly complete sense of separation from...man, woman and child...in the deepest parts of...we are not human...that is what we felt last night...a 'killer'...more like them...what human will have us when they really know who and what we are? that is their game with us...

Our insights the next day were profound, but *we* were also painfully aware of the ground *we* had lost by not summoning protection. However, to date *we* have neither given up nor allowed ourselves that level of relinquishment again and never will. *We* came to know even more how precarious the ground upon which *we* stand is. Though *our* faith in Benevolence as *our* only salvation from them was stretched to the breaking point, it did not break. *Our* separation from the "world of man" is fueled by judgment and fear of *us*, a reality *we* experience over and over, year after year, and contributing to reinforcing the programmed message, *You have nowhere to go, no one [human] loves you, you belong with us.*

12
Internal Programming

These are downloads of internal programs going off from within *our* systems. Some are alters interacting with other alters within the programming, often showing *our* internal structures while one in particular is *our* mind being split.

Lily and the Others

We are in an open and spacious room with twenty to thirty alters present, all women with various faces and hair colors. This is part of how at least one of *our* systems is designed—rooms and buildings containing alters seated in front of and facing one of *us* in a tiered fashion as if seated on bleachers—almost as if they are facing a speaker, but it is just one of *us*. A black, old-fashioned telephone between *us* and the alters begins to ring. *We* answer it and it is *lily*. (Telephones have been long used to access alters in *tmk* programming.) *Lily* sounds hysterical, speaking quickly and fearfully. *We* say to her, "*Lily*, calm down, catch your breath, tell *me* what happened."

At this point, a couple of the alters come down and stand near *us* with concern and support. *Lily* says she is being pursued by *demons*; she can *see* and *feel* them, making a direct reference to Satan himself while talking of many other *demons* without naming them. *We* feel deep concern for her, knowing *we* must get to her to help her, but cannot, which severely distresses *us*. *Our* contact with *lily* at this point in deep deprogramming is minimal—she has remained elusive and distant and *we* desperately want to talk with her.

Next, *we* are no longer on the telephone, but have a pair of scissors in *our* hand and are attempting to cut off *our* hair, pulling it to the back of *our* head with one hand and holding the scissors in the other. But the hair *we* are holding does not feel like *our* own; *we see* and *feel* it as Lilith's hair, black and gray, thick and wiry. *We* cannot cut it so one of *our* alters comes to try and help *us*, but she can't either. What is clear to *us* about Lilith's hair being on *our* head is that *lily* is showing *us* how bound to Lilith *we* are. She is part of *us* and *we* are part of her, as in *DNA linked.*

[Human hair often is an attachment point for entities. In other words, they live in the hair of accessed individuals. This is not a theory, but something many in the occult know. I know of a woman programmed and utilized by the Mormons who in a witnessed ceremony cut her long hair short and threw the cut locks into a fire. All present witnessed the light energy of the entities escaping that fire. This also gives a bit of precedent to some famous female figures, clearly programmed individuals, who cut off their hair while exhibiting signs of a breakdown. My opinion is this was not just defiance, but a deeply spiritual act of attempted escape.]

Our conscious programming download ends after eventually involving many alters coming forward, so many that except for *lily we* are uncertain of their identities. *We* are grateful for the appearance of this deep alter, despite her being directly pursued by "Satan". Per her programming, she is very loyal to Cain in particular, though unaware of this programming, as is the case with so many of *our* alters.

[Unlike some religious forms of Christianity, the esoteric form of Christianity recognizes in the forces of light and dark separate beings. My experiences present Lucifer, Ahriman (Satan) and Sorat (a leader of sorts to the Asuras?) as the main players, with an assortment of beings I have not been able to identify who have made appearances. My experiences with the dark ones was clearly delineated in this way, though without the names at the time. My interaction and understanding of those assisting humanity include Christ, the Archangels and Angels, as well as several other categories of beings according to Dr. Steiner. In Rudolf Steiner's works you can find these separations and explanations of the various hierarchies of beings. Steiner refers to the "gods", plural. *Lily's* download showed the separation of Satan and Lucifer as an example. She feared Satan taking her from Cain who is affiliated with Lucifer, in my experiences.]

From *our* journal following this download:

...we feel very sad today, our heart aches, we feel/felt helpless, unable to help her, she is still out of reach. we are deeply disturbed by her connection

*to 'Satan', we want to understand in our conscious mind, yet we do not…
even though we can feel it in our body, we ache all over and feel a low grade
fever rising…*

Downloads come during deep deprogramming at a mind-bending
rate. After relaying this particular download to one of *our* deep deprogramming team, *we* asked him to tell *our* front alters about "Satan," of
whom *we* do not have much, if any, conscious knowledge.

[My front alters had none of the occult knowledge, at least when early deprogramming was taking place. Not so these days since much of what was
once hidden deep within has surfaced. Additionally, we found much validation as well as continuing to find truths in the study of Anthroposophia
(Anthroposophy).]

What does "Satan" mean? It has been made infinitely clear to *our* front
alters that every detail *our* alters present in a download means something.
There are no unimportant details, particularly when *lily* comes up from the
deepest part of *us* to tell something and going against all of her programming to do so. This is so rare that *we* instinctively knew that the direct
reference to Satan was very important. *We* also asked why there were references to Satan *and* Lucifer from *our* alters. What is the difference between
the two? *Our* front alters do not know consciously and have a programmed
difficulty understanding. *We* could *see* and *feel lily* trying to tell *us* that she
feared being taken from Cain to whom she is faithfully devoted. Clearly,
she was breaking her programming to tell *us* even this much.

Two Bodies, Same Person

This download occurred during a particularly heavy time of downloads.
They often occur in overwhelming waves. This day *we* left *our* job early
due to physical symptoms of cellular memories—split-brain headaches,
fever, body pain in tissues and joints as well as *fear gripping my heart*
programming.

First, *we* had a download of *alter 14*, a kill alter with heavy sexual
programming performing oral sex on her apparent handler in a hotel room
at his one-word trigger (in addition to this alter's recognition of his face).
This alter being used sexually by this particular person was very confusing
to *us*. *We* then had a download from this same *alter 14* being handled by

"*25*" shown to *us* during this download for the first time. The handling in this download repeated over and over throughout the night.

There are two of *us* young adults, mirror images of one another yet clearly two different personalities with definitive energy signature differences. Different people. *Alter 14* awaits "*25*" in a motel room. *Alter 14* is clearly a kill alter aware that she is waiting for "*25*" to come. "*25*" seems to be a handler in this scenario, coming to talk to *alter 14* to keep her in kill mode. They stand *face to face* in the motel room, "*25*" talking to *alter 14*, her instructions are to *maintain alter 14 in kill mode*. *Alter 14* is to remain in the room waiting in kill mode. *We* cannot hear what "*25*" said to *alter 14* that "maintains" her in kill mode; *we* who were conscious in this download were not told. Whatever it is, it works. "*25*" leaves only to return what seems like hours later to again talk to *alter 14* to maintain kill mode.

Two clearly distinct personalities, visual mirror images of one another. We saw the numbers 14 and 25 clearly and consistently. *We* also understood that *alter 14* was accessed and "maintained" by "*25*" though *we* do not fully understand it or how it works. Do they work in tandem? *Alter 14* was aware of "*25*" and what she was doing, just as "*25*" knew *alter 14*, yet *alter 14* seemed to have that "ask no questions" consciousness while "*25*" seemed to be the handler.

During the download, *we* looked at the time on *our* watch and were aware that two different times were being "seen". The actual time was four twenty-something a.m., but *we* could not clearly see the time while also *seeing* 4:33. Moments later, *we* realized two parts of *us* were *seeing* two different times, one the present time, the other the time from the original experience. Also within the download, *we* were experiencing the body memory that began earlier in the day—fever, split-brain headache, body pain, and *fear gripping my heart* program, the last being a self-destruct program.

[As shared previously, downloads often show up around the same date or time, even the same time of year, as the original experience. Hence in this case showing up within minutes of the original experience time and being shown that in the present. This made quite an impression on me. Further discoveries I have made about "25" in deep deprogramming have *completely* changed what I understand her to be. There is more on that, much more, in Book 2.]

Pursuing a Kill Alter

This download came in three segments, a common occurrence with experience downloads. The alters show *us* experiences from various points within their lives, at first appearing random, but scrutiny reveals they never are. This segment was the first of the internal system download in which the kill alter introduced herself consciously and visually to *us*. [I had not been aware of her prior.]

We are walking toward a five-by-five wooden platform 40-50 feet up in the air. As *we* approach, *we* see a mirror image of *us* on the platform, both of *us* young adults. She climbs down a wooden ladder attached to the side of the platform. Neither of *us* is hurrying; *we* both move steadily, calmly. However, *we* are aware that *we* are pursuing her. As *we* step onto the platform, she is still descending the ladder. She and *we* look into each other's eyes long enough for *us* to know that she is one of *us* and has no emotions at all. Her energy signature told *us* she was a kill alter. Without speaking audibly, she says, *You cannot get that close*, meaning she is a deep alter and that is why *we* will not be allowed to catch her unless she decides to let *us*. She disappears below the platform as *we* near the ladder. *We* climb down and when *we* reach the bottom, she is nowhere in sight. We stand on a wooden platform like the one above, only this one is next to a fast flowing river maybe twenty feet across. We step from the platform on one side of the river bank into short, soft, green grass, turning to look for her. She has disappeared.

[The river bank is reminiscent of Alice's journey in *Through the Looking Glass*. During part of Alice's journey, at several points, she must cross a "brook" to move to the next "rank". This is intriguing when one understands that this story line, as well as the subsequent *Alice in Wonderland*, is prominent in early generation MKUltra programming.]

Her programming dictates that she will always be out of *our* reach. *We* were pursuing her inside of one of *our* systems, a journey through one of *our* internal systems in which *we* saw her because she surfaced enough to allow *us* to do so. This tells *us* that she has reason to come up, as in she *saw* something occurring within the system with others of *us* in deep deprogramming that told her it might be desirable to surface. *We* suspect that she witnessed *us* interacting with others in her group telling her it was okay, or she was somehow forced up by the revelations of other presenting alters. *We* are uncertain why she appeared to *us*, but reluctance and unwillingness are not always one and the same.

The second segment of the download will be skipped here, though it is her information as well; it is not necessary here.

The third segment occurred immediately after the second and has had a disturbing effect on *us*. *We* were shown the words, "HURT THEM, KILL THEM" in large white block letters running from bottom left to upper right inside *our* head, "HURT THEM" in front and partially on top of "KILL THEM", as if coming out of "HURT THEM". The reason for the in depth description here is that *we* clearly understood that this alter was to see the "HURT THEM" while being triggered by "KILL THEM" on another level.

We are uncertain what to call this alter. She is the same one that was on the ladder in the first segment, but with her limited appearance, she has left *us* uncertain as to her identity. The energy signatures are strong and distinct, but alters are often adept at keeping *us* from naming them unless they permit it. As *we* deprogram further, it becomes more common for other alters who surface to tell on these secretive alters and force an appearance to help *us* acknowledge their existence. *We* know that this alter is a kill alter and believe her to be one of possibly four that *we* are now consciously aware of.

This is a typical example of internal programming: bizarre, frightening, and endlessly disturbing while deeply informative. *We* are grateful it is being consciously revealed to *us* as *we* attempt to break free of *our* programming. *We* must experience and remember what *our* alters experienced in programming and on-task in order to understand *our* systems, and it is only at their discretion, in their time. *Our* responsibility is to provide as safe and non-judgmental an atmosphere as possible so that they will continue to come forward. This is not as easy as it at first may sound. *We* have to *see* and *feel* what they present in many cases for the first time, and that is an ongoing struggle. *We* must fully *see* and *feel* with them what they experienced, their *feelings* or lack thereof, and in the more extreme programmed behaviors, it is very painful for the rest of *us*.

When they present, they are usually breaking programming, though unfortunately this is not always true, given that many alters come forward to present per their deception programming to ensure that *we* and anyone trying to help *us* deprogram are disinformed. Deception programming appears to be very complex and extensive and *we* are diligently working *our* way through it as it appears.

We often know the alter's fear level of death or disappearing—the same thing to them—but not their specific programmed penalty for breaking programming. Often, they are not aware that they are part of a system of alters, which in and of itself keeps them from interacting with any of *us*. *Our* main front alter was not the only one who thought that she was just a *me*, despite others' presentations throughout *our* life. It has taken a year of deep deprogramming for *us* to realize that the continued cycles of doubt are mostly, yet not exclusively, from the front alters—a doubt repetitively cycling within the frontline system. With continued deep deprogramming, *we* will have to face it eventually once and for all—at least that is what *we* believe and hope.

We also know that there are alters much deeper in the systems who also have very singular views of who they are. Some alters know there are others, yet their programming runs independent of acknowledging the rest of *us*, or they are not aware that there are any others of *us* at all. There are many who recognize that they are not alone, with some even programmed to interact with or run other alters as a handler. It is an elaborate set of systems that involves many keys, codes and triggers, as well as screen programs to prevent dismantlement. *We* are still in the process of discovering *our* own systems, and the extent of deception programming makes *us* feel that *we* have only begun to scratch the surface of its structuring.

Devotional Programming to Actor Christian Bale

This experience memory had *us* initially thinking that *we* had interacted with this particular movie actor, but *we* have come to understand that *we* were programmed *to* him. Whether or not he was physically present during the programming experience, *we* are uncertain. It may not seem possible that a person could not know that, yet *we* can assure you that in *our* case, *our* programmer's skills are still quite astounding to *us*. They are masterful at what they do.

Upon researching Christian Bale's life, *we* discovered that he started in movies as a child. It is *our* strong suspicion that he is a *tmk* victim as well. He is twelve years younger than *us*, so *our* programming to him occurred when he was in his twenties and *we* in *our* thirties.

The part of this programming experience *we* have in *our* conscious mind is this: *We* are working out in a health club, a seemingly repetitive setting for programming. Bale is there to work out as well, yet neither of us is doing so at the onset of the experience. We are standing on a light-blue, tight weave carpeted area sunken about six inches below the surrounding floor in a crescent shape with metal railings on either side. [This small crescent shape area seems to have no functional purpose that I can discern in any normal sense anyway.] *We* are facing him, engaged in talking about him moving away. *We* remain cool on the exterior but feel a pain in *our* heart because *we* must be in contact with him. *We* ask him if *we* can remain in touch and he replies, "Yes." (*Our* need to see him, to stay in touch, is *our* programmed motivation to see every movie he stars in.) *We* are relieved and yet disheartened by his impending departure, due to the programmed sexual relationship between us. At that point, a sexual act occurs between us, yet this memory is lost to *us*: the programming may have been to make *our* alter believe in the sexual relationship, a necessity for other programs, whether Bale was personally present or not.

The most disturbing aspect of the whole experience is the three or four "Round Tables" (Freemasonic symbol?) of observers framing us: the same gray and white-haired men dressed in dark suits who have appeared within many downloads, some balding, some wearing glasses, almost always sitting quietly at Round Tables while intently observing *us*. *We* exercise caution, looking out of the corner of *our* eye, not directly nor too often or long at the observers, as they unnerve *us*. The entire time *we* interact with Bale, *we* are aware of these men and at a loss as to why they are there observing *us* with such quiet intensity. Bale seems oblivious to their presence. Are they observers on the *exterior* or *interior* of *our* mind? Three-dimensional observers, or observers in *our* mind and part of *our* internal system?

We have also suspected these observers to be members of the Church of the Latter Day Saints authorities due to the gray and white-haired men and women present during End-Time programming that took place at the LDS Conference Center in Salt Lake City, Utah that involved one of *our* kill alters. (See Book 1, Chapter 4, "Killing", *Alpha and Omega: First and Last Solo.*)

We have a programmed compulsion to see Bale in *Batman* movies because they represent a modern version of a story *we* were programmed with beginning in *our* youth. Since *Batman Begins* (2005), *we* have compulsively watched every film from previous decades with various actors playing Batman, even asking *our* local video store when the DVD of *Batman Begins* would be out so *we* could buy it and watch it as much as *we* liked. Once it came out on DVD and *we* owned it, *we* had to negotiate with *our* alter to not continue buying the film (much like J.D. Salinger's *Catcher in the Rye* that Mark David Chapman and the Mel Gibson character in the film *Conspiracy Theory* had to buy over and over). Fortunately, *we* had begun deep deprogramming by then and were able to talk *our* alter out of buying copy after copy.

When *we* found out that Bale would star in the 2008 sequel *The Dark Knight*, *we* waited for months for its release and went the second day it arrived (only because *we* had to work on the first day). *We* were so triggered by the film that kill alters surfaced during and afterwards, then *we* received immediate downloads about the storyline being associated with End-Time programming within.

Like so many films, these are not innocuous pieces of harmless entertainment but serious mind kontrol venues designed and utilized by programmers and kontrollers to trigger and reinforce *tmk* slave programming. *We* are certain of this and will not go into all of the details of the film's effects on *us*. What is certain is that several of the characters in the film are representative of alters—Gotham City being Salt Lake City, etc. The most important conscious understanding *we* have is that in *our* End-Time programming, *we* are to assist in creating chaos, one program being to deliver something (bio-weapons?) for the direct purpose of protecting Gotham/Salt Lake City for the malevolent ones who own it, and their agenda, furthering it at *our* programmers' bidding. Batman protects while the Joker creates chaos. These two characters, as well as others like Two-Face, are *reinforcement* to alters within at least one of *our* systems.

We suspect that more than one End-Time program has been installed. *Tmk* slaves worldwide are being triggered and recalled (see **Call Back Programming** in the Lexicon) by these films. The fact that Bale's second *Batman* film *The Dark Knight* was one of the highest grossing films worldwide that year sends shivers up *our* spine. *We* live in a world that most people never even suspect exists, yet that world is very real and powerful, its seeming conspiratorial innocuousness being part of the power these mind kontrollers wield. How do you fight an enemy you are not even aware of, let alone unwilling to hear about?

Various researchers are aware that the *Batman* storyline is programming—a corroboration that occurs over and over as *our* deep deprogramming progresses. Every time *we* found something that *we* had recorded from *our* alter's experience of downloads from another *tmk* slave or researcher's writings, it helped to loosen the grip of *our* programming and fueled *our* ability to further deprogram.

In 2009, Bale starred as John Connor in *Terminator Salvation*. Naturally, *we* went to see the film and some of *us* were triggered, given that it is about many things that are non-fictional. With enough research into long-standing documentation on the subject of *total mind kontrol (tmk)* programming, the reader may be able to imagine "fiction" as the delivery system for truth. Not only does *Terminator Salvation* double as global programming reinforcement and triggering for *tmk* slaves with kill programming, but it deals with the very real subjects of artificial intelligence (AI) and the creation of cyborgs, man- and woman-machines, using covert technology to cross human genetics with all sorts of other DNA sources. This is very real and no longer just science fiction. (For history on this, read *The Last Circle*, a baseline for investigations into such topics as **artificial intelligence** and how it relates to the PROMIS software distributed by the company named *Oracle*. Remember *The Matrix Trilogy*?)

Rife with Hollywood extremes, *Terminator Salvation* is a powerful tool for reinforcing messages to programmers' slaves. That w*e* are one of them through and through for all time, *our* very insides designed by them and solely owned by them. *We* wept out of a deep connection and resonance with Sam Worthington's character the cyborg Marcus Wright, the most powerful scene for *us* being Wright hung in chains and finally realizing the implications of not being fully human. This is the world of *tmk* programming. This *Terminator* film is about End-Time programming and involves many, many *tmk* slaves.

Splitting

This experience memory came as the second part of a two-part download. Though the first is a very significant experience memory, *we* have chosen not to write it here. What *we* know is that the alter who shared these two pieces of memory is the same alter—not a kill alter but someone who is youthful and innocent, despite her programming. This memory is another of the memories that *we* suspect may take much time to assimilate, if *we* ever really do. With this one, like other memories of this nature, despite their extreme difficulty, *we* are grateful they are being brought to *us* by *our* alters so integration takes place amongst *us*, integration being a conscious collective of parts living together in a productive, healthy manner, hurting no one, including any of *us*, while helping to bring awareness to the atrocities still taking place *daily* in *tmk* programming.

No Place Like Hollywood

During this download, *we* are in total darkness in *our* head when suddenly images made of light begin to appear inside. Some *we* cannot put into words, some *we* can. *We* recall a hand made of light appearing and then fading. *We* recall a head and face made of light, then fading. Many things appeared in *our* head, parts of things, fragments, all in the darkness, all made of light. *We* were very frightened as the images appeared and faded and a terror and pain built inside, a pain *we* could and could not *feel*.

Then an extreme white light appeared, brilliant and accompanied by severe pain somewhere inside, though *we* don't know where. *We* began to

165

scream as it went brilliant white before and inside *us*. It was unbearable and yet during the download *we* could not *feel* it because it belonged to someone else within *us*. This alter was showing us her experience of splitting under torture. Then *we* split, *our* mind fragmented. This download left *us* screaming from a primal place. The depth of sadness is too difficult for words. Alters were being created as *our* mind shattered. This was torture for the sake of shattering *our* mind. When *we see* and *feel* this experience, it is as if everything just stops and time is suspended. Nothing can reach *us*, *we* are away, removed, undetected, invisible, partial.

After this download, the desire to die, to take *our* own life, was severe as *our* suicide programming ran and ran.

13
Where the Alters and Systems Live

Living in these systems—if you can call it living—is what *our* consciousness has worked at. This section studies the fragmented, conscious pieces of the combination of systems and alters that *we* know of so far, thanks to *our* deep deprogramming.

The Alters

The following list represents alters *we* know to be present within *us*, at least well enough to list at this time. It has been therapeutic to name them, and it is *our* hope that other slaves may be able to recognize some of these alters in themselves, if only by nature or specific programming.

It was also very powerful in *our* healing, after coming to know many of those present in *us*, to discover that other slaves have documented similar alters in themselves. *We* found it validating as well as of assistance in breaking down *our* isolation programming a little bit. Often, alters come into a conscious presentation over and over for months, and in some cases even for years. Through *our* whole life, they have been coming up and taking over the body to present, and yet *our* front alters were not conscious of who and what they were, despite being aware of some of them in some aspect or another.

Now *we* define this process in two ways: one, coming forward without conscious recognition, and two, coming with conscious recognition by *our* front alters. The first is full switches of personalities without conscious recognition, the second conscious co-existence. Integration to *us* is the conscious knowledge that *we* are a *we*, someone with distinct multiple personalities, and then engaging with *our* alters on a conscious level. This is a simple, rather rudimentary explanation, yet accurate in its most basic form for *us*.

The accepted integration method for multiplicity in the mental health community leaves much to be desired as far as *our total mind kontrol* programming is concerned, though *we* are sure there are many well-intentioned mental health professionals out there. For *us*, the *core* is not the front alter—not even close. The core is deeply hidden from *us*. *We* believe that *we* have only *once* consciously encountered *our* core or someone representing her thus far in deep deprogramming.

Alters present to *us* consciously, but often *we* are unable to *see* and *feel* them clearly enough to name or list them until they present in a way that is more clear. Many want to be known yet remain elusive with varying reasons valid only within the parameters of their programming. It is very clear to *us* that *we* have alters who are still fully programmed and able to be accessed as long as that programming remains hidden from the rest of *us*. *We* are diligently working to change this. It has also become clear that possibly some of the alters participating in *our* deep deprogramming were created by *us* as opposed to the extremely large number apparently designed by *our* programmers. As of October 2010, *we feel* the ratio of conscious, co-existing alters has shifted in that the few alters *we* created—apparently allowed by *our* programmers to remain—are now far out-numbered by alters they designed. Mostly young child alters appear to no longer be run by the *entities* or their programming. *We* view this as being very positive in relation to healing.

Most of the programmers' deep alters are still following programming contrary to *our* deprogramming, but not all. The most dangerous ones are cult loyal, and some of these are still hidden from *us* (at least in part). *We* are able to sense them as if from a distance, a *see* and *feel* as if they are hidden just beyond a wall obscuring their particular programming. Their existence is palpable in that it involves downloads that show bits and pieces of programming, but not enough to dismantle. *We* believe someone, or several, are trying to tell.

- *The core*: *Our* original self that has never developed emotionally, physically, or mentally. *We* do not believe that *we* will integrate and return to this core that has never developed. *We* feel, based on *our* personal deprogramming thus far, that this concept can prevent programmed multiples like *us* from ever reaching a deep enough understanding of their own systems and alters that they become empowered enough to not only break their programming but sustain the empowerment to live a life outside its reach. Attempts to re-access *us* have not ceased, contrary to what most of those around *us* say about how this is all supposed to work.

- *The infant:* Part of *our* original self.
- *Rabbit:* A three-year-old animal alter created by extreme torture, trauma, and sexual abuse.
- *Currently unnamed child sex alters and fragments:* Uncertain of how many…though numerous in deprogramming presentation.
- *The rage alters:* Used to disassociate and distance *us* from the truth of *our* lives and situation, as well as to isolate *us* from others; also facilitated a kontrolled release of lethal rage due to years of abuse, trauma, and torture.
- *The flying alter:* Since childhood, *we* are certain that the "others" taught *us* how to "fly" *in* the physical body. (Obviously, astral programing alters: child alters in this case.)
- *The breathe under water alter:* Since eight years old, *we* have consciously known that *we* can breathe underwater due to this alter. (An alter exposed to drowning torture to facilitate psychic abilities as well as splitting to create new **clean slates.**)
- *The disappearing alter:* Not sure when this alter was designed, but *we* have experienced this alter's ability in the everyday here and now, though cannot explain how this ability is achieved.
- *Nancy, the cheerleader alter:* Programmed at eight years old, second grade, to seduce older men in her gold and black cheerleading costume with black, patent leather boots while seductively singing Nancy Sinatra's, "These Boots are Made for Walking".
- *The wild one alter:* A loose and wild teenage alter *we* know to be a kill alter disguised by an emotional immaturity that can be mistakenly perceived by her targets as innocence. She has psychopathic characteristics, appearing as *two distinct personalities* in one alter. A naive sexually promiscuous teenager who once triggered into her "kill" program is lethal without rational thinking.
- *The whispering child alter:* Speaking softly, she has presented many times, trying to hide. She *feels* like she is about age six or seven years old.
- *The screaming alter:* She screams always and constantly inside of *us* for all of *us* so *we* don't have to; this allows the proper functioning of other alters.
- *The thief alter:* This alter has been with *us* since adolescence, created either by *us* or by *our* programmers. She steals with no remorse, is quite good at it, giving *us* a perverse sense of control in an out-of-kontrol

life. Also perpetuates "shame and guilt" program reinforcement to others in *us*.

• *Lily, Cain's bitch:* Called up time and time again for Cain's use, she is cult loyal in a very victimized way.

• *The run alter:* This alter takes *us* into hiding and safety, away from others around *us*, as in not insiders, particularly to motels and hotels per motel and hotel programming after on-tasks. This alter has been triggered out inadvertently and extensively during deep deprogramming.

• *The workout alter:* An alter who is very disciplined and consistent in working out despite any mental, physical, emotional and/or spiritual issues that may arise for other alters during programming and on-tasks. Used to keep *us* disassociated from pain, rage, and memory as well as in physical shape, she keeps a potent degree of disassociation.

• *The one who takes severe sexual pain alter:* She is the one who can take being brutalized sexually and keep taking it. She is used by sadists. *We* are uncertain if she and *the stage alter* are one and the same.

• *The stage alter:* Raped with penises and objects (including a wooden cross) on a stage before an emotionless audience, she has limited contact with *us* and *we* don't know much about her though *we* suspect she may be *the one who takes severe sexual pain*. [As of October 2010, *we* have been given information that another *tmk* slave has reported that she too was raped with a crucifix, a tactic utilized by some programmers for ritual and programming.]

• *The adult woman who sexually abuses little boys alter:* *We* awoke one morning with her holding *our* body. In other downloads, she is teaching very young boys about the pleasurable feelings of their penis. *We* have held her at bay due to what *we* have to encounter with her presence, so little is known about her at this time. Definitely cult loyal.

• *The perfect hostess alter:* She is attractive to men, amenable, strong, clever, intelligent, flexible, with strong sexual overtones, lies perfectly, and can handle anyone from any walk of life. She is lethal as she can and has fronted for kill alters. Hosting for kontrollers is conscious for her, though they only tell her what she needs to know to perform within her programming: cult loyal but not trusted with too much information. She can read the power level of the *entity/being* "running" a person near her—i.e. the *demonic* hierarchy level—which serves her programmed on-task successes.

- *She 29th:* The most cult loyal consciously known to *us* so far—lethal, raw, hard, cynical, prone to rage, with kontrolled sarcastic, aggressive sexual energy toward elites and the ability to immediately identify *entity* hierarchy level, calling it "power" or "juice". She enjoys inflicting pain, be it emotional, mental, or physical, is very cunning and intelligent, and programmed to hate and kill humans of any age and gender due to not believing she is human. She has kill programming to "Fuck them and kill them", this being her programmed justification: "If they are too fucking stupid to know better, they deserve to die." In her mind, her successful seduction proves their unworthiness to live. *I* suspect that her strong cult loyalty is programmed to thwart any deprogramming: she presented consciously to *us* within the first four months of deep deprogramming, talking to *us* like *our* programmers would, possibly even being one of them inside *us* who was programmed to surface early as a significant part of "deception" programming. She clearly does not want *us* to succeed at deprogramming. In her case, it is difficult to distinguish the *entity* handler from the alter split off to be used by *our* programmers. *We* have come to suspect she is so bonded with the *entity* that extraction seems impossible, so for now complete containment is being utilized.
- *Alter 14:* To an extent *we* find difficult to express, she is lethal, kontrolled, extra-perceptive beyond the five senses with highly attuned physical kontrol over *our* body when she is holding it. She has heavy sexual programming and is apparently used sexually by at least one of *our* apparent handlers for his own personal gratification. She is aloof, calm, detached from emotions, though not entirely emotionless. This alter has the ability to crush the windpipe with her right hand.
- *The kill alter that we pursued within our system:* We know almost nothing about her at this time, nor are *we* able to even name her, though she *feels* almost entirely emotionless.
- *"25":* Part or all of her duties include maintaining kill mode on *alter14*. [When you get into book 2, you will find a much different explanation of this "alter". It is not appropriate here due to context being necessary to reveal what is and isn't as regards her.]
- *The soft one:* Attractive, charming, demure, with an innocent sexuality; has a very powerful effect on those around *us* when present in her innocent way.
- *Greer's girl:* She is totally devoted to the apparent handler of the same name; brought together with him at 17. Even after becoming

171

conscious of who and what this man is to *us*—his suspected *tmk* programming, *our* own tmk programming to him, etc.—the false love and bond to him is so consuming that *we* often experience a physical ache. Their bond is one of the strongest internal bonds *we* still have, *we* believe associated with *our* Cain programming. This alter's devotional programming was used during *our* early deep deprogramming in an attempt to bring *us* back into programming or possibly death ("going home").

- *The crystal alters*: They number in the hundreds, parts of the crystal structure system within. They are adult sex alters, some full personalities, most others fragments utilized for specific on-tasks. This is still in discovery. [I suspect that many in the structure are not even programmed, but rather clean slates.]
- *The anorexic one alter*: Used to disassociate *us* in a variety of situations and maintain dissociation for extended periods.
- *The bulimic one alter*: Robotic, empty, "purges" to accomplish one of several program goals, leads to *the completely dissociated alter* and is utilized for a powerful release of rage necessary to keep us functioning.
- *The completely disassociated alter*: She appears after *the bulimic one*.
- *The one with the raspy voice alter*: Part of *our* frontline system, she appears when *our* main front alter enters exhaustion, allowing *our* detachment while maintaining communication with those around *us*. She *feels* like a buffer of sorts between the main front alter and the totally disassociated alter that appears after *the bulimic one*, serving as a middle ground and keeping *us* functional in the "world of man".
- *Jacked*: This high energy, fast-talking anorexic that does not need to eat (different from the "anorexic one") has very high energy and downloads with lots of pacing due to having to get information out or it may explode! It talks fast and cannot stop until it is all out. It is like a conduit presenting information from within for several other alters. It does not appear to have a gender.
- *The protector alter*: Part of *our* frontline system, she comes in when the front alters cannot handle the emotional pain anymore. She observes everything and makes judgments without emotion, neither engages nor talks much, yet functions for survival as a highly attuned observer who is not well suited for public interaction.
- *The adult dancer alter*: A teenager, she presented consciously while performing in a very uninhibited, raunchy manner for a group of men to

the Grand Funk Railroad singing "We're an American Band".

- *The occult alter*: She calls in the "Mothers of darkness". She seldom presents to *us*, which makes *us* suspect that she and the adult woman alter who sexually abuses little boys may be from the same "group" of alters. She took kontrol of *our* body in deep deprogramming to a very frightening and powerful degree, with the rest of *us* fully conscious.
- *The front alters known as the front line system*: They are designed to present to the world around *us* a well-rounded, highly functioning "individual," no matter what *our* other alters are exposed to at the hands of *our* kontrollers.
- *The "host" or main front alter*: The first line of defense, part of the frontline system, she is a conduit of sorts for many others to present through. She was programmed to be unaware of *our* MPD, including the alters in the frontline system who know about her. [See https://stillnessinthestorm.com/2018/12/illuminati-insider-chapter-thirteen-shell-programming-internal-councils-human-experimentation-function-codes/.]
- *The perfect employee alter*: She is very strong, gregarious, humorous, quick-witted, intelligent, observant, and dedicated to *our* work, whatever it may be at any given time. She is part of *our* frontline system presenting to the outside world.
- *The self-inflicting pain alter*: One of several alters who inflicts pain upon *us*, this one can utilize many low-level painful experiences to allow consistent, ongoing dissociation.
- *The cutting alter*: Cuts *us* to dissociate when serious measures are required. (Likely part of a small group associated with the alter listed above.)
- *The bone breaking alter*: Attempts to break *our* bones to dissociate when a profound degree of dissociation is required. (Likely part of a group associated with the two alters listed above.)
- *The suicide alter, "eat a bullet" program*: Self-explanatory, she was programmed long ago for future need. It would have taken place in April 2008 at the end of an on-task kill that was averted by deep deprogramming. It was to give credibility to the "stalker" explanation for the kill so that no sincere investigation would follow.
- *The suicide alter, "stop my heart" program*: She can stop *our* heart at will to provide no need for investigation afterward. [It is likely that the

173

self-inflicting pain alters and suicide alters all belong to a group, but I am uncertain.]

- *Adam: We* are uncertain about him as he does not present like the others. He may have been shown to *us* as of June 2009, or he may be an "insider" heavily involved in *our* programming, as he knows *us* very well. *We* continue to *feel* him so deeply within that *we* often feel that he may be one of *our* kill alters. This is very much still in discovery.

- *The holding pattern alter:* The alter between other alters when *we* are to think, do, and say nothing. A waiting alter very observant visually and auditorily, with no apparent emotions or sense of self.

- *Jack:* A male alter, he is in 12-step programs, about fifty years old, tan, shoulder-length blond-white hair, loves the tropics, and wears big black sunglasses and a pale yellow button-down, short-sleeved bowling shirt along with plaid shorts. He presented only once to try and stop *us* from a particular action in January 2009. (As of May 2012, *we* believe "Jack" is a disembodied human spirit that briefly gained entry at an extremely vulnerable time in *our* early deep deprogramming.)

- *The organizer alter:* She is an obsessive-compulsive organizer, distracting other alters from the pain of moving forward into experience memory downloads. Part of the frontline system.

- *The denial alters:* These alters fight attempts to deprogram and are found in *our* frontline system as well as in deeper alters.

- *Our higher Self:* This part continues to assist *us* in what appears to be truly Benevolent ways, encouraging *our* survival with words of Unconditional Love and empowerment like "Stay alive". For years now, *we* believe this to be the truest part of *us*. What *we* do know is that Benevolent, Unconditional, Creative Love is the very reason *we* survived and still survive, despite many attempts to end *our* life.

The Systems

This section, as with many, is still very much in discovery. Thus far, *we* are certain of how at least two systems are set up in *us*, but *we* do not consciously understand how they relate to one another. *We* believe there is a third system, but very difficult to access. Is it possible that they are all parts of one another?

- *Rooms and buildings:* Alters—often in groups, sometimes alone—are repeatedly found in "rooms" and behind "doors", accessed by "stairways", "ladders", even "rivers" that evoke a deep-felt connection in *us*. But are these "rivers" actually part of this particular system? *We* have found both human and nonhuman alters in these "rooms".

- *The crystal structure*: This structure has the most potent effect on *us* because it is one of the most beautiful and terrible things *we* have experienced thus far in deep deprogramming. Downloads are not in the least two-dimensional—far from it. They have *palpable, physical, spiritual "life"* to them. *We* can *see* and *feel ourselves* as the very parts of this crystal structure that contain alters numbering in the hundreds, each being a multi-faceted crystal making up the living crystal structure. It glistens with life and even moves as if in an occasional breeze, leaving a powerful feeling in *us*, a longing, a reverence, a desire to just look upon it, despite its parallel terrible nature due to what it is: a living, breathing system of *our* alters doing the bidding of programmers—in this case *our* sex programming as adult alters. [As mentioned previously, I believe that these alters are not all programmed, yet were there if needed.]

   It is *our* understanding that most of this system is still intact on every level, but not fully. *Our* view from below through an opening indicated missing crystals, with the remaining ones in a state of stasis, awaiting being needed and called up. This structure is a sphere with crystal pieces interlocking with perfect precision and a small space between for movement. *We* could *see* and *feel ourselves* here, *our* many parts, many fragments and full personalities. It is truly beautiful and terrible for *us* all at once.

- *Galaxy*: *We* are still very uncertain about this even being a system, believing it is possibly more about certain programs relating to *our alien* programming as opposed to a system. Very little has been revealed, yet what has been revealed in part is from very palpable, living, conscious downloads from many years ago, long before *our* deep deprogramming began. Memories that have been with *us* on a conscious level for many years involve a vast open darkness filled with lights, a palpable, living darkness beyond three dimensions. This has also shown up heavily in the colláge work created by many of *us*.

[I have come to understand that this "Galaxy" has been and continues to be my connection to the Cosmic Intelligence that sustains me and all of humanity, not a system at all. I have had spontaneous access to this throughout my life as a renewal and infusion without the conscious understanding of it until deep deprogramming could shift my conscious state. If you recall, many of the tortures were designed to give me insight into other realms, or perhaps better stated access to the spiritual world as would be seen by an initiate. It has been a respite amidst the programming and destruction attempted on me. It has been the support and reinforcement of the Light side present all along. It has been a Light in the dark...]

[As of 2022 I can say with great gratitude and joy that none of these alters have control over me. My part in that was courage, diligence and making it the number one priority which often sidelined other behaviors and desires in my so called "everyday life." This is a *must* in my opinion, and the inability to choose this is also, in my opinion, the reason a total mind controlled victim is not able to gain control or any significant level of freedom and integration. The main thrust of my recovery of my true self is most certainly due in part to the spiritual help I have received and continue to receive. One must commit completely to this path and work for it, as well as ask for that Benevolent assistance.]

14
Running Interference

These programs are all seemingly designed and implemented to keep *us* in varying states of dissociation and the truth of who and what *we* are out of reach. The power of these programs still frightens *us*. It is only with much time and commitment, and most assuredly the power of Benevolence alive within *us*, that *we* are not completely at their mercy any longer.

We want to *emphatically* state that *we* do not consider *ourselves* cured, whole, or free. What *we* do *see* and *feel* is that *we* are no longer being completely run by high-level people or malevolent *beings* but are learning to deal with the other personalities in *us* so that they too are no longer running to these programs. *We* continue to battle the programming and *entities*. A more wholesome recovery may be possible, but *our* current deep deprogramming process and the ever present danger in believing *we* are finally free constitutes *our* journey through it all, not a dissertation on how it ought to be. *We* are not *entity*-free, but a large degree of forward movement has occurred, and in some cases is significant. A partial list of *our* interference programming:

- *Fog*: *We see* it inside *our* head. It facilitates loss of memory, particularly during a surfacing memory and leads to confusion.
- *Walls of water*: *We* hear it and *see* it inside of *our* head as it "washes away pain".
- *Obsessive-compulsive organizing*: This allows distraction from acknowledging alter presence and affects the many of *us* that can be in *our* head at once.
- *Obsessive-compulsive cleaning*: Temporarily alleviates *feeling* of "filth" inside, due to sexual use and kill use, particularly specific on-tasks of the latter.
- *Agoraphobia*: Occurs when too much starts to surface at once and *we* are totally debilitated.

- *Stealing*: Gives a certain young alter a sense of control over her life.
- *Excessive watching of programming and program-reinforcement shows and movies*: Shows and movies that *we* were specifically programmed to, as well as those that reinforce *our* programming.
- *Listening to programming and program-reinforcement music*: Both music that *we* were specifically programmed to, and music that reinforces *our* programming.
- *"Run"*: Leave now, pack up or don't pack up, just get out, get away, fueled by intense anxiety and paranoia. Most downloads have involved *us* going to motels/hotels per that program.
- *"Cut"*: This is done with a razor to dissociate *us*.
- *Bone breaking*: This is *us* perpetrating this upon *us*; profound disassociation the intent.
- *Severe headaches, "split-brain headaches"*: This surfaces with experience memories and alters, often accompanied by intense body pain, fever, chills and vomiting, as well as extreme fear and panic, and can appear instantaneously.
- *Intense body pain*: Found in *our* tissues and joints, even *our* skin. *We* call it "cellular" memory.
- *Fevers*: Usually low-grade alternating with high, accompanied by cold and hot spots, with hot on the inside. During these, it *feels* like *we* could breathe fire while chilled on the outside of *our* body. (The above two—as well as other symptoms we have followed and patterned out in deep deprogramming—are likely associated with remote eMKUltra technologies. See **Directed Energy Weapons (DEWs)** in the Lexicon.)
- *Bulimia*: Conscious purging that provides the act of violence to "self", keeping *us* dissociated and *our* alters easily accessed. *Tremendous* rage release.
- *Anorexia*: Designed to starve *us* and keep *us* dissociated.
- *Masturbation*: Keeps *us* disassociated, plus used to switch alters during solo on-tasks. Additionally, it thwarts *our* deep deprogramming and allows *entities* ongoing access to *our* sexual energy, a very powerful kontrol mechanism.
- *Repetitive "loop" programming*: A cyclical program that can run for hours. This is programming reinforcement at its best, or worst.
- *Numbers and number sequences*: Used to trigger alters in combination with other triggers used at the same time, usually sequences of at

least three, as well as and reinforce programs (each time the number is seen, the program is reinforced without conscious knowledge). "13", "18", "22", "222", "33", "333", "1234," "514"…larger sequences exist.

- *"Flipping snapshots" program*: Associated with End-Time programming: a circle and "12:34" as well as flipping pictures.
- *"There is nowhere you can hide that we can't find you and kill you"* (See Book 1, Chapter 2, "The Teen Years", *Nowhere to Hide*.)
- *Crazy*: Maintains *our* programmed status, allowing others to maintain disbelief as well.
- *Doubt*: Maintains ongoing programmed status.
- *Internal entities*: Programmers, kontrollers, and handlers.
- *External entities*: Same as above.
- *Excessive physical activity*: A powerful distraction or dissociation, depending on extent and potential pain level.
- *"Alien abduction"*: Feeds the "crazy" programming and works as screen memories, which are *very real, not an imagining,* with malevolent dimensional *beings* engaged as well as human programmers, kontrollers, and handlers.
- *Isolation*: Creates and maintains an ongoing loneliness, still present within *our* deep deprogramming due to others' inability to hear, let alone accept, who and what *we* are, as well as *our* valid fear of allowing an intended handler or kontroller into *our* lives. Reinforces programming to "trust no one".
- *"No talk" programming*: Tell no one anything!
- *"Remember to Forget" programming*: Self-explanatory and is triggered by certain cues.
- *Threats*: Originate from both internal and external *entities* and those sent in the three-dimensional world around *us*. These can be sent direct, as in face to face, or occulted from others view, yet clear to *us* utilizing **twilight language/symbology**.
- *Deception programming*: Presented by alters, reinforced by external disinformation.
- *Extreme fear and panic*: Maintains programming states.
- *Guilt and shame*: Maintains programming and shifts blame from perpetrators.
- *Suicide*: Facilitates disposal of malfunctioning slave while discrediting the slave in the process.

- *Death/murder*: Specifically at the hand of kontrollers or handlers, this can be done quickly or over years. A researcher we know refers to it as "rotter status" (not *our* term). This is often when a victim is sold off for other uses, such as remote technology experimentation or to a member of the Network for use and disposal. The various levels of usage (and sale) are rather numerous, so a victim can be sold more than once in this regard. Experimentation, prostitution, etc.

Next Level, End-Time

15
Programming: Codes, Triggers, and Reinforcements

These are parts of *our* programming that *we* have discovered within and without *us*, given that *our* programmers have designed programs that are constantly reinforced by the world around *us*. The power of these triggers causes sadness and fear in *us* as their effect on *our* alters can be overwhelming. While at times evoking anxiety that escalates into panic, they can also reinforce and calm because they are designed to keep *us* in programmed mode.

The following are in no particular order and do not comprise a complete list. It is impossible to cover all of the triggers, and many of *our* codes are not consciously evident to *us* at this time.

- *Touch*: Specific touch locations as well as certain movements such as a circular hand movement on *our* buttocks will bring out a young child sex alter. Another touch involves a hand on *our* inner left thigh (requiring at least two other triggers to be effective) to summon a sex alter.
- *Pain*: Inflicted by others as well as *our* own programmed alters. (*We* have alters who are programmed to seek out pain.)
- *Violence*: Programming breakdown during deep deprogramming can trigger violent alters as well as viewing violence in films to appease these alters so *we* can function. *We* refer to this as "low-dosing".
- *Blood*
- *Butterflies*
- *Horses and unicorns*
- *Gems and crystals*: Pink, green, blue, clear, purple, black, and more. In some cases they represent alters, as far as *we* can tell.
- *Barbie dolls*
- *Stuffed animals*
- *Nursery rhymes*

- *Sexual abuse and sexual acts*
- *Penis*
- *Colors*
- *Clothing*
- *Mirrors*: Used by *entities* to access *us*, they appear to be portals for malevolent ones.
- *Symbols*: Delta triangle, circle, Flower of Life, Infinity/Möbius strip, Japanese symbol for Chaos (this one is more than just the Chaos symbol, it is associated with Sorat as well), symbol of Cain, Eye of Horus, Fleur-de-lis, six-pointed star, etc.
- *Trigger words and phrases*: Far too many to list here, some used once and others ongoing.
- *Guns*: Particularly a .45 and 9mm.
- *Reptiles, demons, aliens, entities...and more than listed here*:
    Hybrid reptiles (humanoid-looking but clearly not human)
    Full blood reptiles (that look like a dinosaur)
    Alien grays
    Nephilim (humanoids with brown rough skin and black eyes)
    Large black male silhouette
    Fuchsia silhouette
    Double-headed fox (One head on top of the other)
    Snakes
    Komodo dragons
    African lions
    American mountain lions
    Black-eyed humanoid with long, gray hair
    Blue-eyed, humanoid female with long stringy blond hair
    A man with solid black eyes, fair skin, no body hair except a head full of black hair, a perfect physique with black tattoos on his torso and arms reminiscent of black snakes. This is one of the forms the one *we* call Cain takes.
- *Vertical pupil eye, black eyes*: Reptile eyes *and* cat eyes, as well as solid black eyes.
- *Specific foods*: McDonald's french fries, Chef Boyardee beef ravioli, and more.
- *Telephone calls*: Someone else on the other end of the line.
- *Recorded telephone messages*: Pre-recorded messages generated by a person dialing it, initiating it via computer, or generated by an AI computer.

- *Tones*: Sent via telephone or independently. By telephone, they are rapid and high-pitched in a sequence, elsewhere they have been single and varied. On one occasion, they came through a motel room wall in which *we* were staying for several days during deep deprogramming. They have also been sent while out in nature (eMKUltra).
- *Tattoos*: Very particular types and more so in certain locations on the body.
- *Specific people*: Individuals *we* are programmed to (Examples being Dr. Steven Greer, Danny Glover, Christian Bale, and Dr. A. True Ott).
- *Musicians and music*: Musicians and music *we* were programmed with: Led Zeppelin, Kiss, Perry Como's "Moon River", Nancy Sinatra's "These Boots Were Made for Walkin'", Marc Cohn's "Walking in Memphis", Paul McCartney's "Band on the Run". There is *endless* program reinforcement music.
- *Movies and television shows*: *I Dream of Jeannie*, *Batman*, Disney films including *20,000 Leagues Under the Sea*, *Bambi*, *Jungle Book*; Charlie Chaplin's *Button, Button, Who's Got the Button*, which is also a game found in *Alice in Wonderland*, a major programming storyline. Reinforcement includes but is not limited to *The Bourne* films, *My Own Worst Enemy*, *Dollhouse*, and *Harry Potter*. (Note: Hollywood is not for entertainment. It was and is designed for programming. This goes for the music industry as well. Until one realizes what it is humanity is dealing with here, the concept of total mind kontrol programming will remain elusive to the conscious mind.)
- *Actors*: Two we are currently conscious of: Danny Glover, a lifelong activist *we* were programmed to as part of a kill team; Christian Bale, to whom *we* were programmed to go and see his films for triggering and reinforcement of *our* programming.
- *Internal clocks*: Programs triggered by internal clocks (often nocturnal) involves *entity* handlers.
- *Electroshock*: Used during programming and to reinforce programming; additionally to sequester alters and their memories.
- *Drugs*: Used during programming and rituals, as well as during the heavy programming and use years of alters.
- *Lights and flashing lights*: Repeatedly triggered *us* into alters when *we* were exposed to them, even in deep deprogramming, which is when we came to understand it by co-existing with those triggered.
- *Health clubs, fitness centers, and gyms*: Located in *our* town as well as

183

around the country to pull *us* in. Used as screen memories during programming to keep *us* from knowing *our* real location as well as possible Network work out facilities for their people and their slaves.

- *Motels and hotels*: *We* were programmed to go to these for use and programming as well as after an on-task. To this day, *we* still struggle deeply with programming to *move into* a motel for a few months' stay. (As of 2012, *we* still desire this, but it is manageable.) (This has been presented in more than one Bourne film where the mind-controlled "asset" awaits orders in a hotel/motel room.)

16
Early Deep Deprogramming Diary Entries

I have included these few entries as a sample of the ups and downs, the ins and outs, of early deprogramming. Looking back, it is a wonder to me that I survived the process, a process that the programmers believe few will.

June 9, 2009. We awoke with deep sadness, not wanting to get out of bed ever again, but a tremendous amount of energy is running through *us*, despite what *we* deal with day in and day out. *Our* energy is seemingly endless at times, yet *we* also feel a deep exhaustion inside that never abates. At work, *our perfect employee alter* is viewed as an endless bundle of energy, and even that is changing as *our* deprogramming continues. *We* have come to understand that this energy and the way people are drawn to it is a result of having so many inside *us*.

For the first time in *our* collective consciousness, it makes sense that the mind is energy and *we* have many minds creating lots of energy. *We* can run on very little rest, often for days, and remain high-functioning and productive, eventually crashing briefly or longer, depending on the severity of experience memory downloads. Then, *we* start up again. *We* don't think *we* sleep the way a non-multiple personality does, considering certain alters never sleep. Someone inside *us* is always awake, which is why *we* refer to sleep as rest for *our* body as opposed to *our* mind.

July 21, 2009. It is *our* hope to focus even more on aspects of the deprogramming process. Staying true to *our* original intention to present *our* process as it truly is, *we* have had a very difficult time recently. Just over a week ago, *our* main front alter had a full abreaction to the understanding of *our* personal relationship to the ones *we* call Cain, Lilith and Lucifer. It occurred late on the 12th and early morning of the 13th of July—not a coincidental number. *We* have not recovered from this and are still unable to *feel* any connection to anything around *us*, except within the context of high functioning. *We* feel as if something was lost a week ago—possibly *our* main front alter? *We* are awaiting her return. It is still unclear to *us* exactly what has occurred, but *we* are trying to remain vigilant, despite being unnerved by having discontinued contact with *our* support group. *We* believe this to be temporary, though *we* are also encountering self-destruct programming every day and are again negotiating amongst *ourselves*.

August 10, 2009. We are again in contact with one of *our* support people and have begun to grasp consciously what has been occurring in recent months. *We* will continue *our* deep deprogramming, it being *our* continued hope that writing about *our* experiences will assist other *tmk* slaves with their deprogramming.

December 21, 2009. The holidays are too close for comfort. This is not a time of celebration for *us*, but a time to get through. *Our* memories of the holidays and what they have held still haunt *us*.

Reaching out to present this information in a safe, anonymous public format will not be easy, if it is allowed to occur at all. The party that *we* attempted to reach out to did not respond, and *we* received a threat in town shortly after doing so. This is not the first threat or attempt to silence *us*. But *we* are not deterred and hope to tell what *we* know in a way that may assist in making a difference to the future of all of us.

January 13, our core's birthday. The first in many years that *we* are attempting to do a very low-key personal celebration. Due to *our* experiences in years past with programmers, kontrollers, and handlers, this day, like many holidays, has not in the least been a time of celebration for *us*. It is *our* second birth date cycle since beginning *our* deep deprogramming. 2009 was filled with an experience memory download by one of *our* teen alters presenting extreme trauma and sexual abuse from *our* 13, 14, and 17 teen birthdays, after which *we* re-fragmented.

Experience memory downloads often have a re-fragmenting effect, no matter what *we* do. It is *our* hope that this will change with time and the strengthening of *our* collective selves working together. So far, this birthday has brought something quite different. At first, the following concerned *us* until *we* realized that it made perfect sense.

Immediately upon awakening on the morning of January 9th, *we* saw that something had been moved in *our* room. *We* were startled because *we* had no conscious memory of moving it. *We* subsequently realized with anxiety that *we* had done a full switch between alters and that an alter had set the scene in *our* room for *our* awakening that morning. For months, *we* had assured *ourselves* that full switches were no longer occurring, neither writing about it nor talking about it with *our* support people in an attempt to not face it or its implications.

On the morning of the 11th, it happened again: another stuffed animal had been placed in a different spot for *us* to see upon awakening. *We* could no longer deny it, nor the implication of *what* was moved—a stuffed animal, something used by *our* father in *our* youth to assist in switching alters.

While journaling in the late morning about these two occurrences, *we* decided *we* needed to voicemail a long distance support person. While doing so, the alter who had done these acts appeared to *us* within, stopping *us* mid-sentence: an adolescent, young teen alter consciously presenting to *us* for the first time. She did not name herself and remains somewhat elusive, as many of *our* alters do upon first conscious presentations, but her interactions have helped *us* piece together various fragments that have been in *our* conscious mind for some time that we couldn't understand, including *our* father's ongoing gifts of stuffed animals with the code word *Fontainebleau* (the name given by my father to a very large stuffed blue dog he gifted me) throughout childhood, adolescent, and teen sexual abuse and programming.

On the 12th of January, at this young alter's urging, *we* learned of The Fontainebleau hotel in Miami, Florida directly associated with the Network and where *we* may have been used in the 1970s and 1980s. More of *our* past abuse and use was revealed and thus assisted *our* deprogramming.

The point is this: Instead of abreacting at the knowledge of full switches still occurring, *we* chose to continue to stay aware and alert to these presentations of the teen alter instead of putting energy into fearing unconscious switches. *We* came to the realization that the alters *we* do not know about consciously—and in almost two years of deep deprogramming, *we* now know that there are many of these—would still have *entity* handlers running them. Hence, full switches are not only possible but probable. Until these alters present to *us*—those parts of *us* that split off from *us* in the first place—*we* will not have the ability, with their assistance, to remove the *entity* from each alter so they can become part of the conscious collective of *us*.

Thus this birthday experience was a success rather than a setback. After all, simply not being aware of something does not make it not so. (If only it was that way!) It is *our* contention that being unaware of an enemy allows it to continue to perpetrate its malevolence and thwart disarming it. *Our* awakening is and continues to be through the knowledge that *our* alters bring to *our* conscious collective selves. [The truth is that I did not need to have every alter present to me to coalesce into a whole person. More on this further along.]

March 4, 2010. We have taken the initiative to anonymously present *our* lives as *we* have experienced them online in the realm of alternative radio through a show called *The Story Behind the Story* hosted by Dr. A. True Ott under the alias of "liz". (As of October 2010, Dr. A. True Ott is now on *www.themicroeffect.com*.) Exposure is very frightening, but it is still *our* contention that time is of the essence for all of humanity as well as for *our* collective of selves.

The triggering that occurs as a result of each show is strong, due to internal self-destruct programs of dissociation, doubt, flooding, anorexia, bulimia, and rage alters co-existing with *our* front alters, with full switching. The greatest struggle, however, is with *our* suicide programs. *We* pull in Benevolent energies ("pibs"), but it takes several days to regain temporary relief. It is *our* responsibility as a multiple personality recovering from trauma-based, *total mind kontrol* programming. It may very well be a slave undergoing deprogramming who brings pieces of the truth to light to a public ready to hear it.

May 2010. We are very aware that deep alters are still under the active programming of the *beings* that run them. Others of *us* are working to dismantle those programs. Some of these alters have End-Time programming ready to be activated, one of whom is to be activated with details involving three men who are also *tmk* slaves, two of whom *we* have identified and the third *we* believe *we* have identified. Two of these slaves live in the town to which *we* moved just over a year ago—part of the reason *we* are moving quickly toward going public, despite risking *our* anonymity and possibly *our* ability to support *ourselves*, given the possible misunderstandings of those in *our* immediate community. This is a very real fear of *ours*.

October 29, 2010. Some of *our* deeper alters have been surfacing more frequently in recent months. This is a blessing as well as deeply difficult to experience. These alters are presenting more details of experiences that others of *us* have been aware of "at a distance", so to speak, fearful of these details surfacing, even keeping them a bay, yet knowing them to be necessary to *our* healing. *Our* need to know, at least in part, demands that *we* know what happened to *us* so *we* can face these experiences as well as what *we* were made to do under programming. *We* are only as strong as *our* personal healing, and it will last only with conscious knowledge and Benevolent, Unconditional, Creative Love in *our* heart, soul, and spirit/mind. *We* do not seek someone to fix *us* nor save *us* but continue to heal *ourselves* with the Unconditional Love that is offered on high. With this, the more *we* consciously understand about *our* programming and use, the stronger *we* are in dealing with every attempt at accessing or harming *us* still being perpetrated by *our* programmers, kontrollers, and handlers, third-dimensionally and otherwise.

We give thanks everyday for *our* survival and ability to participate in a productive life. *We* have even begun to be able to pray regularly for others, now that *we* can *see* beyond daily torment by *our* kontrollers.

This malevolent kontrol is not relegated only to the life of *total mind kontrolled* slaves. It is the agenda of *our* programmers to kontrol global society. *We* are just one of many slaves prepared with individualized, extreme, ongoing programming while global society is being processed on a mass scale, society at large being subject to mind kontrol as well. We are all engaged in a parallel struggle to free ourselves from the grip of the very same malevolence, *we* being but a micro-level example of what is being perpetrated on a macro-level.

Here is the good news. If one wants to take their Divinely gifted power into their own hands and stop these malevolent ones once and for all, they can. In *our* experience, it is necessary to do this not once, not twice, but continuously to protect *ourselves*, asking for the protection of all Life with the highest intention.

The ultimate reason for *our* survival and ability to progress more and more into this truth each day, despite an ongoing onslaught by *our* own past experience memories held by *our* alters, as well as continued attempts by malevolence to thwart that process, is acknowledging truth and Unconditional Love. Of this *we* are *certain.*

Hence, it is *our* contention that this must also be the solution on a

189

macro-level. In *our* personal experiences throughout *our* life, as well as currently in *our* own deep deprogramming, malevolence cannot abide in the presence of Benevolent, Unconditional, Creative Love. Truth being the greatest act of Love, means any act out of truth is based in Love. This is not a theory for *us*. It has proven itself to be true time and time again, hundreds of times over. *We* are not always consciously aware enough to utilize this, nor strong enough to choose it, yet when *we* are, it works. Each time it works, the opportunities *we* are consciously aware enough to utilize increase. Strength is gained.

We know *we* are not completely free, but *we* have attained a degree of self-awareness and commitment that allows *us* to continue on this path not only for *us* but with the hope that *our* writings or radio presentations will reach deep into another programmed slave to touch the truth of who and what they are.

We will continue to actively seek a deeper understanding of Benevolent truth and Love each day, tempered with the reality that *we* have been programmed and used for all *our* life—not to diminish the possibilities, but to maintain a preparedness for what still occurs within *our* mind and from without.

[This is not to be mistaken for being a doormat. Truth and Love, as intended, can be fierce! This is warrior speak, not acquiescing under the false influences of malevolence that lull humanity into an apathetic, disempowered state.]

Lucifer, Ahriman, and the Asuras: A Global Empire

17
Epilogue: Our Keys to True Freedom
April 2010

This epilogue is directed toward those who wish to assist *total mind kon-trolled* slaves attempting to deprogram. *Our* ability to manage *our* lives as a multiple has in some ways become less difficult. Sometimes, the message *we* wish to relay is so very clear and uncomplicated, but as with *our* internal pro-gramming, moving through *our* message feels like *we* are walking through a minefield. *We* suspect those like *us* will understand what *we* mean.

Many in the world offer healing, salvation, and wholeness to multiples like *us*, but the value of such offerings to a newly deprogramming *tmk* slave like *us* is highly questionable, even suspect. *We* wish that what we have stated thus far in *Our Life Beyond MKUltra* were not so, yet it is so, no matter how often *we* try to tell *ourselves* it is not. Add to this *our* wish that the journey through deprogramming be safe, but this seems to have no basis in fact, at least not in *our* estimation at this time.

It has been *our* hope to present an overview of *our* particular *total mind kontrol* slave experiences under the almost complete kontrol of *our* pro-grammers, handlers, and kontrollers, as well as to offer a view into *our* attempt to deprogram—*without a therapist* but with a deprogramming support group of three—by respecting *our* collective of alters so they will communicate with one another.

We chose not to seek out a therapist because *we* have very little trust in the mental health field's capability regarding multiplicity and trauma-based *total mind kontrol*, not to mention that some members of the mental health community work in the programming Network. *Our* knowledge of who and what *we* are unfortunately brought with it a con-tinued need for isolation for early deep deprogramming. This is not a recommendation; *we* are just telling readers about some of *our* choices and why *we* chose them.

Prior to meeting the two men in Salt Lake City who have assisted *our* beginning deep deprogramming, more than one handler was sent to pull *us* back in for reprogramming. *Our* extensive sexual programming would be the easiest way for *our* kontrollers to access *us*, though *we* have not engaged in sexual relations with anyone, at least *consciously*, since *our* encounter with Simon. (See Book 1, Chapter 11, "The Forties", *Simon*.) There is, however, a continued use of *our* sexual energy beyond the third dimension very much affecting *us* three dimensionally. *We* were told many times and in many ways throughout *our* life, *You belong to us.*

One of the most difficult aspects of *our* deprogramming has been having so many child and adult sex alters repeatedly presenting their programming to *us*. Though difficult to explain, in some cases they are no longer being driven by the *entities* but trying to feel what they have always felt. To them, *entity*-free space feels like a void and they are temporarily lost, so they take over the body until satisfied that *we* know and accept them without judgment. In a couple of instances, they have engaged in their particular programmed behavior in a frantic manner, desperate to get back to the source of energy they always knew, despite the malevolence of the source.

Deep deprogramming has relieved some of the intensity of these alters, but their struggle has made it evident that the amount of time and energy put into designing *us* as a *tmk* slave was extensive. For almost two years *we* have repeatedly struggled with those within regarding whether or not *we* should "go home" to *our* family (as they call themselves) by allowing one of their handlers—human or entity—to take *us* back; or if *we* should allow one of *our* suicide alters to take over the body and end it all. Should *we* continue to fight *our* way out of their hold on *us* day by day? The latter, fortunately, has repeatedly won out, but not without setbacks.

Alters still driven by *entities* speak loudly about *us* relinquishing the body once and for all, but somehow along the way through connecting with Unconditional Love, abstinence from sex, and the revelations of others within *us*, *we* have attained a degree of communication and cooperation within *our* systems of alters that is working, if only at times.

Most of the world is not ready to know the role malevolent dimensional *beings* currently rule in this third dimension through lies and deception, but *we* believe in the struggle to regain humanity's rightful place on a peaceful, Love-filled planet, despite the fact that the world for *us* seems like one huge trigger, given how *our* programming was designed for 24/7

193

reinforcement. As *we* deprogram, *we* are at least able to recognize some of these triggers, either during the triggering or some time after, and dismantle the programs to some degree. *Our* success is due to the communication *we* are developing within *our* systems of alters, though *we* are still uncertain as to how many alters and systems *we* have and may never know consciously.

[As deep deprogramming progressed, I realized through experience that not every alter within every system needed naming, nor did I have to encounter every on task or programming session to become whole. The beauty came in the realization that through much learning, diligence, and compassion, along side of prayer and courage, I was to find my true Self and release the hold malevolence had on me and those within me. I am now a person who has recovered herself with the assistance and guidance of powers beyond this physical realm alone, while being a strong participant in that process. True seeking did indeed allow me to find.]

We are a collective of selves with many alters consciously present and aware of one another. *We* felt some relief when *we* recently read that a programmed *tmk* slave will appear more like a multiple in deep deprogramming than ever before. (*We* thank Svali, an ex-illuminati programmer, for providing this information online. Now available in book format: *Svali Speaks—Breaking free of cult programming*, 2016.) Reading this saved *us* from despair.

We agree with Fritz Springmeier: what a *tmk* victim needs for healing is a physically present support system to guarantee the time and safety necessary. *We* cannot stress enough the value of *safety* for the deep deprogramming process. The one thing *we* have never experienced in *our* life is the feeling of safety. But these simple conditions are exactly what is unavailable to most *tmk* slaves. Such supportive conditions might protect the energy necessary for the continued programming onslaught from within and without.

Differentiating between what the key to true freedom is for *us* and what many well-intentioned others would have *us* believe it is has led *us* to be sure of one thing: partaking of instantaneous "healings" could lead to *our* demise. Every day, the journey through deep deprogramming is one of life and death with danger on all sides from both internal and external forces.

We return to the trust issue. Many who have approached *us* during the first two years of deep deprogramming have been malevolent in nature (or programmed as such unbeknownst to them. We forgive those who know not what they do.) Distinguishing between those of truly Benevolent intentions and those influenced, wittingly or unwittingly, by the malevolent ones, has been and is exceedingly difficult. Many are unwittingly used by malevolent forces, and others aware of their malevolent affiliations. This can get very complicated, but becomes easier to discern over time if one is committed to deep deprogramming, which *we* define as not giving *our* lives over to a kontroller or handler, wittingly or unwittingly, while learning from *our* alter downloads…with lots of prayer!

Many who have no conscious knowledge of what a *tmk* slave must go through to deprogram—including slaves whose programming is just beginning to break down—do not realize how difficult it is to deprogram within a deprogramming community that is heavily infiltrated by malevolent kontrollers and handlers. Many do not want to hear this, understandably, and *our* intent is not to cause disharmony, only to write it as *we* experience it.

In *our* earliest years of programming bleed-through, *we* more than once experienced "helping" individuals who *we* would find out more than a decade later had been sent to assist in reprograming *us*. Thus, *we* continued to be used by them for years to come. Other deprogramming slaves have reported this as well.

But the biggest mistake *we* could have made was to believe that *we* could not be accessed once deep deprogramming began. Only with constancy of effort and time have *we* been able to *affect the hold programs have on us*, and it is still *our* intention to take that understanding to a whole new level.

These are the things *we* know. First, at the very core of *our* being, *we* are and always will be a beautiful child of Benevolent Creation. *We* were neither born evil nor completely owned by evil but were in the hands of "sin"—cut off from Benevolent, Unconditional, Creative Love and God—due to an overshadowing kontrol since the womb by programmers, malevolent ones who are the very force behind every aspect of negativity here in the world. Whether the programmers had a hand in *our* conception or access to malevolent technology, it is *our* contention that *our* bloodline prior to *our* birth led to *our* use by them. The "black," esoteric tech, as *we* refer to it, has been used for longer than most individuals believe humanity has existed on earth.

Second, the only *true* Power that exists is Benevolent, Unconditional, Creative Love. Most humans practice *conditional* love, but Unconditional Love knows no conditions, none. It exists within every human being, a gift, a birthright, a Life Force for those with a human soul. It knows neither judgment nor separation, nor does it feel any desire to value the life of one human over another. The human limitations in the world for which all of humanity is falsely blamed, are the signs of malevolence. The only true Power of Unconditional Love has been hidden deeply from humanity by a well-honed, masterful deception designed and implemented over eons by these malevolent ones. This understanding is out of reach for most individuals' consciousness. To love one as more worthy of Life than another is purely a concept of the dark forces influencing it.

Third, the malevolent ones' most masterful design includes numerous alternatives to filling the void created by the deep masking, and thus loss, of conscious understanding of the very truest nature of humanity as it is unconditionally intended to be. The malevolent ones know more about us than we do about ourselves, particularly that to maintain a position of perceived kontrol over humanity, the deception must be unwittingly or wittingly acceptable. In other words, humanity must remain almost completely unaware of the void being offered instead of Unconditional Love. Those who sense the void usually switch from one false alternative to another (ingenious religious designs) in an attempt to fill it.

There is indeed God, but it is that purest Benevolent, Unconditional, Creative Love that lives in and is the very Creator of all things, all Life. Malevolence cannot Create, ever; it can only destroy. In fact, the earmark of malevolence is destruction. If *any* act involves *any* taking away, *any* destruction of *any* Life, you can be assured that malevolence is overseeing it, subtly or overtly.

Unconditional Love knows nothing of destruction; the two cannot *ever* abide together in the same heartbeat. In the presence of Benevolent, Unconditional, Creative Love, the *perceived* power of malevolence cannot abide. Malevolence's deception that it is a power, that it has power, is simply non-existent. It is coercion, cunning and intelligence, but devoid of truth and Love.

Make no mistake: any forsaking of Life by man has its foundation in malevolent doctrine, no matter what claim of goodness is behind it.

We have parts who know that all of these actions and programmed thoughts go against all that is good, all that is the true Love. Even the care-taking of some alters by other alters is based in programming, not in Unconditional Love, and was for survival and could eventually become a hindrance that could threaten the very life these alters claimed to protect. *We* knew that with conditional love, the internal power struggle will forever remain, *our* Spirit separated, and that the malevolent ones and *our* programming would always have kontrol.

This is not the illusion of "unity" touted by the programmers, kontrollers, and handlers as a "global village" of organizations and corporate structures run by malevolent ones. The United Nations and its affiliate tentacles is anything but Benevolent! But do not take *our* word for it. Do the research, follow the money *all the way*. If it is not immediately apparent, remember that it is designed to be hidden.

Stay with it and you will find direct associations between the malevolent ones and their minions. This is not for the faint of heart or those wishing to sustain ignorant bliss, which *we* assure you will not last much longer anyway.

BOOK 2

First Edition Introduction, 2013

*"You go home, some wave their hats, some turn their backs, it's all the same,
none of them know where you've been, it's all the same..."*

— *Spartan*, Dir. by David Mamet, 2004

Due to the nature and complexity of *our* life as a *total mind kontrolled* slave, *we* strongly suggest that readers first avail themselves of *Book 1*. Without its information, this work may seem inadequate as an introduction to the subject of *total mind kontrol (tmk)* programming as *we* have known it. Books 1 and 2 work together to relay *our* history as chronologically as *we* can manage, as well as the deep deprogramming process as *we* experienced it.

By the summer of 2011, *we* became reasonably comfortable with the conscious existence of the many *us* within and made a real effort to begin referring to *ourselves* as *i*. *We* have experienced this before, but always from *our* front alter's consciousness without the full understanding of who and what the many of *us* were. Due to still switching between *i* and *we*—depending on *our* intention—*i* have chosen to write Book 2 predominantly as *we* for consistency if nothing else, despite the fact that within the deprogramming community, speaking as a "we" may seem inappropriate when it comes to being whole. It does, however, seem very appropriate to the many parts of *us* and is a very valuable part of *our* healing process as well as crucial for grasping fully on a conscious level who and what *we* are. "I" may never consciously meet all of *us*, but at least *we* need not be subjected to the abuse and use of *our* programmers. To own *our* truth aloud has been very healing. Besides, both professionally and otherwise, there is still much misunderstanding of multiplicity (MPD) and its relation to *total mind kontrol* programming. So please forgive the plurals and italics and other eccentricities in *our* writing. It is very important for it to be acceptable to refer to *ourselves* in the plural because for the whole of *our* life, *we* were programmed to never believe *we* could break free.

In *our* early deep deprogramming, a combination of programming and fear kept *us* from being able and willing to share information due to *our* desire to be as certain about it as *we* could while maintaining credibility in *our* dealings with those *we* have been fortunate enough to work with.

Though *we* cannot vouch for much of the information found online, it is *our* hope that readers will familiarize themselves with some of the vast amount of material now available on mind control programs like MKUltra. Put key words into a search engine and prepare to develop your discernment. Do not be fooled: just because something goes beyond one's personal experience and current public knowledge of what is possible does not relegate it to the trash bin. Readers need to keep an open mind, due to the "national security" nature of mind control and how the public has been indoctrinated to perceive the subject as too surreal to be true. If one sincerely wants to understand what has been and is currently occurring, it is readily available, but it takes courage, desire, determination, and effort to find the truth and stay with it.

What is written here—at least the general methods and sources of those methods—will one day be public knowledge. *We* believe that people incapable of accepting the reality of *tmk* programming at its most basic—who accuse victims and first-hand witnesses of having a penchant for science fiction and fantasy—do so as disinformation agents or out of a lack of research into the backroom "black tech" associated with various government, military, intelligence, religious, and corporate organizations.

For over a decade before deep deprogramming began in April 2008, *we* attempted to deprogram on *our* own due to *our* inability to find the assistance *we* needed, all the while living under programming and being accessed daily: an impossible situation. *Our* programming continuously bled through in fragments. *I*, the front alter, knew something was and had been terribly wrong for the whole of *my* life, and this was what encouraged *me* to continue to seek help, despite the improbability of finding it. In April 2008, at 46 years of age, *we* found the necessary assistance.

It is the goal of Book 2 to relay the continuing process of discovery and understanding of *our* lives as a *total mind kontrolled (tmk)* slave as *we* undergo deep deprogramming, including the severe challenges that go with the process. Each word carries a significant part of who and what *we* are regarding what was done to *us*, why it was done, how *we* were used, and what that means for the deprogramming process. At last, *we* have gained the courage to write about *our* life in a way that requires courage. *We* no longer hold back, despite the skepticism or danger that may follow.

Even after more than five years of deep deprogramming, *we* still do not consider *ourselves* to be free from all programming, nor from the influence of *entities* and *beings* as *we* know them.

They continue to access certain alters and trigger certain programs. In addition to what *we* refer to as *entities* and *beings*, a very real attack continues through mind kontrol "black tech", validated by sources inside the world where "black tech" arose from esoteric, occult sciences and is being used. It is *our* contention that the evil known to *us* and "black tech" work together, and that the former is the true designer of the latter.

We classify *our* current status as managing *our* alters and choosing to live a life as "i" supported by *we* to the best of *our* ability on any given day. *Our* life today is, thankfully, nothing like it was even two years ago. *We* work each day on *our* personal understanding of *our* wholeness while attempting to record the process for others like *us* who are attempting to break free of their programming. Hopefully, understanding what *we* have gone through will help their process and offer a better chance of surviving it.

Due to the nature of *our* design, *we* were to self-destruct through numerous programs installed years ago and be triggered into running as *we* began to awaken from *our* programming. No retirement party, only the struggle for sovereignty without total destruction.

Malevolence stems from a very dark force that works in a very real, tangible way through humans and never stops trying to use up *our* life energy. External and obvious violence is no longer needed for murder, unless necessary to send a message. Their ability to kontrol from within the mind facilitates murder that cannot be proven as such. Their goal for *us* is to die a slow death while discrediting *ourselves* through a "suicide" that will be anything but suicide.

The disturbing nature of the material is unavoidable; it is the nature of bloodline ritual abuse trauma-based *total mind kontrol* programming. Where possible, *we* will avoid going into detail if it is not necessary for revealing *our* process to those who must face a similar process, as well as to those attempting to assist them. Due to the presence of so many alters, *our* process can be difficult and surreal.

The degree and scope of what *we* reveal may rock the foundations of previously held belief systems, but *we* hope *Our Life Beyond MKUltra* will also benefit those attempting to educate themselves as to what lies at the core of world government, military and intelligence agencies, religion, and corporate structures.

We cannot cover all aspects of *our* programming in even two reasonably sized books. *We* have attempted a cross section of *our* history as a *tmk* slave, why *we* became such, and *our* use by *our* programmers, kontrollers, and handlers. Chapter 9, "Tools for the Recovery of Our Splits", is an overview of methods *we* have utilized and continue to utilize in deprogramming.

As for other recovered slaves who have put out their stories, it is not *our* desire to comment on their writings beyond thanking them. Anyone who is fortunate enough to break free to any degree and recover lost parts of themselves is truly fortunate, no matter how that process occurs. Far more slaves never have the opportunity to break free and end up dying while still fully programmed. *We* struggle with this, especially given that *we* are one of the more fortunate. It has been and continues to be a process to not feel guilty in light of the many who have died as a result of *our* survival.

To those who feel trapped and alone, you are not, by any stretch of the imagination!

It is also *our* intention to bring forward some of the truths about what *we see* currently happening in the world around *us* and the more than significant role *our* programmers, kontrollers, and handlers are playing in its design and implementation, including the motive that is more often than not frightening and triggering to *us*. In *our* estimation, most people have absolutely no idea what has been at work around them in their lives and on the world stage for an amazingly long time. The awakening that is necessary and crucial for this reality to be *seen* is both spiritual and intellectual. Seeing with clarity is a daunting task fraught with difficult emotions that must be faced. Truth is not easy; hence the ability of the malevolent ones to maintain the lie. Truth can also be devastatingly frightening, albeit liberating. In *our* opinion, seeking truth is the greatest act of Love due to it leading to wholeness and understanding. Without truth, we live a lie.

The amount of handling, kontrolling, and containment that *we* personally have witnessed within the deprogramming and "conspiracy theory" communities is truly astonishing. *We* are extremely grateful to those who have offered sincere support; they know who they are. For the many thousands still trying to find a sincerely safe place to start, they can fall prey to the despair that fuels the programmers and what they have been doing for so long. Because of this, *we* will no longer allow others to dictate what is what regarding what *we see* and *feel our* experiences to be, nor *our* interpretations of what is and is not going on around *us*. *We* spent more than four decades being told that what *we* knew was happening was not happening, which to a degree continues to happen because of a lack of willingness to hear those who have a part of this terrible story.

Throughout Book 2, you will find more colláges created by the many of *us* to give voice to those inside who in many cases still wish to remain anonymous. The power of these creations is truly amazing in revelation and healing; the messages found are still bringing understanding to *me*, the front alter, as well as *my* highest Self.

We have changed the names of certain persons who are victims of *total mind kontrol* programming as they were not given a conscious choice to start with. In most cases, they are mentioned because they were sent in as potential kontrollers or handlers. In cases of surveillance and threats, as well as failed attempts to "put us down", *we* were not able to get their names.

1
Updates

Since Book 1, *we* who are consciously attempting to break *our* programming now understand some things more clearly, having gained more insight into what was formerly presented to certain parts of *us* on a conscious level, fragmented memories now *seen* as pieces of a larger puzzle and thus providing greater understanding as to how *our* programming and use worked over the years. *We* still receive downloads, yet thankfully not 24/7. Just as *our* internal mind is dismantling a little at a time the separation created through trauma-based programming, hundreds of fragments are beginning to fit together. The experience of internal healing is allowing the missing time of external experiences to fall into a sequence of events: *our* life. Prior to this, years were literally missing.

She Has a Name

In Book 1, *we* listed the alters *we* were conscious of at the time, their characteristics and abilities, and gave examples of situations in which they functioned for *our* programmers, kontrollers, and handlers. (See Book 1, Chapter 13, "Where the Alters and Systems Live".)

In the early morning hours of April 11, 2011, unable to sleep, *we* pulled out one of *our* colláge books and began going over some of the pages. *We* do this every few months, often seeing information placed there by some of *us* without others of *us* knowing why. With time, *our* front alter's understanding can grow deeper in context not because of new information but because of *our* conscious mind's willingness and ability to finally put the pieces together. This is why recording everything that *we* can from downloads without censoring is so valuable. Time and again, downloaded pieces come together and make perfect sense. The fragments are usually astoundingly clear in detail and only need to be *seen* and *felt*.

In this particular case, the name of one of *our* alters had been there all along, never forgotten, and *we* just needed to *see* the name placed twice within a particular colláge to remember the alter's name, an alter with extra-ordinary abilities. Previous to this, *we* knew her as the 8-year-old *breathe underwater alter* with the name "esmeralda" pertaining to *our* personal history, though *we* had not been able to *see* that the two were actually one. *Esmeralda* is the name of the *breathe underwater alter* programmed in part with the film *20,000 Leagues Under the Sea* and the earlier use of *The Incredible Mr. Limpet*, as well as the later use at 12 years old of *The Day of the Dolphin*. Disney World in Orlando, Florida was used extensively to reinforce *our* programming after *our* family's move to Florida in 1970.

[Disney World in Orlando, Florida had a *20,000 Leagues Under the Sea* attraction from 1971 through 1994. Obviously, by 1994 it was no longer needed for programming/reinforcing programming as methods and narratives change with time.]

We have reason to believe that Dr. John Lilly's government-funded research was associated with the programming of *esmeralda*, particularly her ability to breathe underwater. The ability may sound outlandish, but *we* assure the reader it is indeed real *programming*. An inside source through a person *we* have worked with in deprogramming has received information that there is indeed an *alien/demonic* that breathes water. *We* have never internally disputed *our* alter's ability to do this. As previously written, this ability came about in part through forced drowning. (See Book 1, Chapter 1, "Shattering a Young Mind: The Early Years", and Chapter 2, "The Teen Years".)

This alter was used as a weapon to gain underwater access and cover distance without being seen. Knowing that someone inside was able to do this has never left *our* conscious mind.

[As previously mentioned in Book 1, I now believe that the drowning was utilized for creating psychic abilities (out of the everyday consciousness perception)—which I clearly have had over the years—and to also enhance our ability—through entity participation—to hold my breath for extended periods of time. I did experience rather exceptional abilities in regards to swimming for long distances and lengths of time, even moving into an altered (*esmeralda*) state at a point during. This was something I recall even practiced in a small kidney-shaped pool at our family home in

Florida during my teen years. I remember the sensation triggered that led to knowing "I could swim forever."]

Water

We're an American Band

Our alter *the adult dancer* revealed her programming to the song *We're An American Band* by Grand Funk Railroad, and how the program has much more to it than just a raunchy, sexual dance performed for men's pleasure. *The adult dancer* was designed in America and has numerous sex alter programs that can be accessed with the proper codes. The lyrics of the song in the programmed introductory dance are telling the initiated that this alter is only one of a "band" of sex alters with programs to be accessed, that via this alter, *we* are a veritable "party" within the one body.

> *We're comin' to your town*
> *We'll help you party it down*
> *We're an American band...*

The adult dancer alter is specifically designed and programmed for group gatherings. This also showed up partially in one of the colláges that *we* made back in the winter of 2009 entitled *Music, Songs, and Sound.* (See Book 1.)

22

The number 22 shows up in various memories. In Book 1 under Chapter 3, "18" is a subsection entitled *Torture, Programming, Guns and Reptiles.* Some of the more profound internal images from that programming session were a Delta triangle made of blue light and the numbers 18 and 22. *We* were 18 years old during this particular torture/programming experience, and 18 was when *our* heaviest use years in kill programming began, including *our* on-tasks in a solo capacity. At 18, *our* kill alters began to kill without a handler physically present at the actual kill. (See Book 1, Chapter 4, "Killing", *Alpha and Omega: First and Last Solo.*)

Eighteen is a coming-of-age time, but for *us our* coming of age had grave effects on *our* physical, emotional, mental, and spiritual status as a functioning *tmk* slave. *We* do not believe that 18 years old was the age of the original fragmentation of all of the personality splits for kill programming; much had been done earlier. *Our* deterioration was imminent, due to how abhorrent *our* kill programming was to the most basic element of *our* human soul.

There is much *we* do not consciously understand about what occurred that night, but *we* do know that the internal grid structure held full personalities and fragments of kill alters—all part of *our* kill program system. Twenty-two clean slates were subsequently utilized as either full personalities or fragments, or left to float in anonymity without being programmed. The grid formation inside a Delta triangle was made of blue light, blue being significant to *our* color programming, especially kill programming. Two reverse "S" curves off the two bottom corners of the triangle represented the "serpents" ultimately in kontrol of this design that night. (The "S" curves have more significance that *we* have yet to fully understand, including the use of reversals and mirror images in programming alters.) Inside the triangle, the grid had 22 lines running vertically, but *we* cannot consciously access the number of horizontal lines, yet *we* believe the amount would result in 22 squares inside the triangle (as is seen in the collàge that reflects this memory on the cover of this edition). This particular geometric structure had everything to do with the kill alters designed that night. In this torture and programming session, more splits were designed, but the session had more to do with internal structuring.

Recently, *we* came across references to the number 22 in the book *The Hermetic Code* by researcher Michael Hayes, who states that the number 22 is repetitive in religion and human biology and a "sacred" number. According to Hayes, 22 has a relationship to DNA and the harmonics of the human body on a cellular level. He even mentions a "grid" associated with the numbers recurring in harmonics at the base of all creation. The Hebrew alphabet has 22 letters, the Major Arcana (greater secrets) or trump cards of the tarot deck, etc., which is interesting when one understands what is really occurring with a bloodline *tmk* slave during programming, what it is the programmers are attempting to achieve ultimately, and what it is they are really working with in bloodline slaves.

Reinforcing Omega

In Book 1, *we* wrote about *our* first programmed solo on-task kill and programming for that alter's last kill, including the end of *us*. (See Chapter 4, "Killing", *Alpha and Omega: First and Last Solo*.) What has become clear is that when *our* alter is being programmed for *Omega* in the Church of the Latter Day Saints Conference Center in Salt Lake City and sees the bright red cursive writing lit up in a neon cinema sign, it was being used as program reinforcement for the *Omega* program involving Batman, specifically regarding being programmed to the actor Christian Bale who plays Batman in the trilogy *Batman Begins* (2005), *The Dark Knight* (2008), and *The Dark Knight Rises* (2012).

Prior to any knowledge of the third film to come out in the summer of 2012, *our* extremely frantic and intense download following a triggering event in January 2011 regarding *our* End-Time programming involved "The dark lord is rising…now in Salt Lake City", known to *us* as Gotham City via programming. Then on July 20, 2012 at the premier of *The Dark Knight Rises* in the Century "Cinema" in Aurora, Colorado, a 27-year-old man claiming to be the Joker allegedly shot and killed 12 and injured 58. That he was programmed is obvious to *us*, the proof being amazingly evident in the news reports shortly after.

[This terrible psy-op gave even more credence to the cursive, red neon "Cinema" sign in my programming session appearing as it would on a marquee. Was I supposed to be the one used as a patsy in this MKUltra murder contract? Was my awakening and deprogramming what thwarted that?]

    I described how observers or *Watchers* were present. There is a direct link between *our Omega* program, the LDS Church Conference Center and Watchers, Christian Bale and Batman. Batman programming began in the mid-1960s for *us* via television.

[There will more on this later in this book, including my going on radio and speaking about this type of programming and the triggering we had from the first two films in this series, *prior* to the James Holmes shooting.]

    It is also clear that *the wild one* alter was used during the *Alpha* segment of this particular program (and possibly other alters). Additionally evident that during the *Omega* segment there were at least two alters—a kill alter that was not *the wild one*, and what *we* believe to be a ritual alter known to *us* as *the ritual occult alter*. *We* are pretty sure that more than one alter is used for rituals, though *we* have not consciously engaged them in any rational manner in deep deprogramming. Needless to say, they are very uncooperative. Even *she 29th* is very well versed in ritual killing. In this download, *our* alter's energy signature and personality are removed from emotions, and she is more fearless than *the wild one* whose psychosis is motivated by emotion. Once in the garden on top of the LDS Conference Center, *the ritual occult alter* feels very different from the others. She has dark occult knowledge much like *she 29th*, but in a different way.

    The next entry regards the same download and *ritual occult alter*.

The Serpent in the Garden of Eden

One of the most important alter downloads for *us* is described in Book 1, Chapter 4, "Killing", *Alpha and Omega: First and Last Solo*. Part of the reason is that it was a profound download at a critical time in *our* deprogramming. It helped to confirm *our* willingness to go to Salt Lake City, Utah in April 2008, despite fears that *we* should not do so because it was dangerous. But *we* also knew *we* would find some of the locations in the download in Salt Lake.

We found much more than that.

Since this 2008 download, *we* have come across some very interesting information regarding the mythology surrounding ancient archetypes, specifically Lilith and the snake that often represents her in various old texts. In *our* alter's download while *we* are in the garden at the LDS Conference Center in Salt Lake City, *we* encounter a large, Caucasian-colored snake covered in thick mucus slowly making its way along a sidewalk when one of the female Watchers approaches *us*. As *we* stand nearby watching the snake, she lifts her foot as if to crush its head, at which point *we* stop her, saying, "No, it is life."

The undeniable sexual inference here—the flesh-colored snake covered in thick mucus—is directly associated with the many erect, ejaculating penises that *we* encountered throughout *our* use both during rituals and on-task. It is apparent that one of *our* programmed specialties was satisfying males orally. In this particular download, *we* can *see* and *feel* that there is much more to the snake in the garden—known by some ex-LDS insiders as Cain's garden—as well as who in *us* made the comment about life: *lily*, part of Lilith's entourage. Through various alters, *i* have access to some of Lilith's knowledge, frightening as it may be at times.

Recently, *we* found direct references to historic language that explained to *our* front alters what others of *us* clearly knew from programming and use. Many of *our* alters have provided profound historical information that those of *us* living on a more day to day conscious level find bizarre until corroborated. Corroboration helps make sense of *our* downloads and gives *us* greater conscious understanding of *our* perpetrators' methods and madness. In other words, intellectual understanding is a vital part of deprogramming.

For example, *our* connection to Lilith is from *our* programmers' use of demonology on *us*. In *Cloak of the Illuminati: Stargate Secrets of the Anunnaki*, written by William Henry, are references to Aramaic and Arabic meanings of various mistranslated words of old. In chapter 8, he writes about the Babylonian icons showing "the great goddess attended by her serpent, offering man the food of immortality, the manna." Further on, he writes of the "golden light of heaven being guarded by a serpent or dragon (Draco)." The "golden light of heaven" is monatomic gold, known in other terms as "Starfire". (See Book 1, Chapter 6, "Ritual Use, Ritual Death", as well as, *The Dragon Bloodline: The Secret History of an Ancient Bloodline*, Nicholas de Vere.) According to Henry, in the Gnostic texts it is stated that this "serpent is the goddess herself."

Furthermore he writes, "the Aramaic pun identifying Eve, the teacher, and the serpent…mother of all…to instruct….Eve's name in Arabic a perfect combination of the concepts of 'life'…with the name of the serpent." In *Human Race Get Off Your Knees: The Lion Sleeps No More*, David Icke refers to the Arabic name of Eve as being synonymous with "life" and "snake".

Though it is abundantly clear that most of *our* numerous perpetrators were male, females were clearly involved too, especially in programming rituals and reprogramming. Those *we* encountered were directly involved in *our* child, teen, and adult years. Gray-haired females were present during *our* programming inside the LDS Conference Center and during a ritual following the programming in what *we* know as Cain's garden on top of the Conference Center in the early to mid-2000's. Most of the public focus is on the males, and rightfully so; they are numerous and wield a lot of kontrol. But they are front men for the real power, meaning *occult* power. In this arena you will find women at the top.

[There is much more within mind control technologies regarding snakes. I have come to understand, with collaboration with another MKUltra victim, that the Transhumanist agenda—much of which is being "next level" implemented during the COVID psy-op—regards syn-bio. (See Elana Freeland's book *Geoengineered Transhumanism: How the Environment Has Been Weaponized by Chemicals, Electromagnetics, & Nanotechnology for Synthetic Biology,* 2021 to understand "syn-bio" or Synthetic Biology.]

One of *our* most frightening and powerless moments during *our* first year of deep deprogramming came early one morning in Arroyo Seco, New Mexico, when one of *our* darkest *ritual occult* alters surfaced and took complete kontrol of *our* vocal cords and—most frightening—*our* thoughts. *We* fought her by repeatedly attempting to pull in Benevolence, but her words kept coming out of *our* mouth with *us* fully conscious and aware. As *we* attempted to wrest control, all *we* could do was keep *our* mouth closed so her words would not come out, fighting within *our* mind to call upon *our* Benevolent Self to rectify the situation while she called upon "the mothers of darkness"—not fathers, because the real occult power lies in the female, and this is who you will find sitting on the throne of occult power, not the male.

Who do the males use in sex rituals to bring in the *demonic* power? Females. Who do the males use to birth *demons* and *entities* into this third dimensional realm? Females.

When calling upon "darkness", who is called? *Mothers.*

The men, present as observers, silently watching *our* programming and alter's performance in any given programming scenario; the women observing and engaging *us* during programming scenarios, asking *our* alters questions that gave even them the impression that these women were testing *us* while *our* alters' limited, programmed consciousness restrictions thwarted their ability to figure out who they were and why they were present. Males kontrol as patriarchs, but females have the power within them.

However, there is a very real, high-level male *demonic being* who sits and presides, but not alone. He cannot do it without Lilith. In the occult ritual realm, the female cannot be left out. Without her, there is no power. And yet in certain ways, she is subject to male kontrol. A relationship exists here that both males and females recognize and honor at higher levels.

A "female/woman" was a significant part of *our* teen programming who was again sent in during *our* early to mid-thirties when *our* programming was beginning to break down. *We* did not know her in *our* front alters; other alters told *us* who she was. She figured out all that *we* were remembering and assisted in reprogramming *us*. She was of a particular bloodline and connected to Siemens, a military defense contractor. *Our* attachment to her, based on the need to find out as much as *we* could, allowed her reprogramming to succeed, the result being *our* continued use for more than a decade, during which *we* were not yet strong enough to break free. *I* clearly recall the eerie way she stared at *me* to this day, and doubt she consciously knew who she was or what she was doing. I also use the term "**containment**" in such instances.

Those who wish to replace god worship with goddess worship apparently have no idea who it is they are turning to, which is precisely how the malevolent ones want it. The goddess currently attempting to replace the patriarchal god goes by many names, one of which is Lilith, she whose ability to charm with beauty and strength goes unparalleled in the malevolent realm.

211

[She is not to be confused with Sophia: "The content of consciousness, the soul attitude and experience that make a person a full-fledged human being...the consciousness of one's humanity." https://anthroposophy.org/may-5th-sophia-community-circle/.]

An Unholy Trio

In Book 1, Chapter 11 "The Forties", the section titled *Cain, Lilith, and Lucifer* refers to an experience whose significance is ongoing. This encounter was about maintaining their access to *us* and keeping *us* in the fold while attempting to get *us* to consciously "relinquish" *our* soul.

It has become obvious to *us* that some of *us* within know quite a bit about occult terms and practices. Particulars show up in *our* downloads that *our* front alters know nothing about. It may take months, even years, before meanings become consciously clear, such as the silver horn that Lilith used just before *we* were able to *see* Lucifer, or rather a human-looking representation of him, while *our* fragmented parts flew above him, trapped on the ceiling. The answer to this mystery came from another *tmk* slave and was validated by a researcher who said that similar "horns" have been used throughout occult antiquity to summon Lucifer or malevolence. There it was.

During *our* encounter, Lilith slowly raised the silver horn to *our* right eye while gently blowing into it, allowing *us* to *see our* fragmented mind in the room just beyond her in which Lucifer sat. The horn was utilized to reveal Lucifer accompanied by *our* parts. *We* think that the air being blown over *our* right eye is connected to the right eye of Horus, in part due to the fact that since the late 1990s *we* have worn a silver ring acquired in Egypt that is the right eye of Horus. It is one of the program items *we* have attempted to rid *ourselves* of without success. In early deep deprogramming, *we* gave it to someone to keep and have since requested that it be returned and now wear it often. (*We* work on things a little at a time and have to prioritize.) Suffice it to say that there is a direct link between the right eye of Horus and the All-Seeing Eye of Freemasonry.

[The ring was removed and gotten rid of years ago along with many things that no longer call to me.]

Used to Take Out Theirs

Downloads have suggested that *our* kill alters were utilized to take out some of their own Network members, unwitting and witting alike, rather than innocent bystanders. Children were either killed in our presence or by *us* as victims of this Network and *our* demonized alters. Not an easy thing to come to terms with...

Members of this Network must abide by many rules, regardless of whether the member was involuntarily recruited or not. Even slaves who consciously choose to ally themselves with these malevolent ones enter under a plethora of lies and deceit. In many cases, the penalty for breaking the rules may be death; *we* know this due to alter downloads in which it is apparent the target is privy to at least some inside information. In these instances, *our* presence before the actual kill was not feared or unexpected, and in some cases interaction with *our* alter or alters was occurring. What *our* kill alter was sent there to do is obviously not known to the target, yet it is clear that they were expecting a sex slave or knew *us* in some other capacity from within this Network. On occasion, the kill is done in such a fashion as to send a message to those in the know, namely, *If you step out of line, we will kill you.*

It is difficult to convey *our* depth of understanding regarding killing their own being a significant part of *our* kill alter's on-tasks. The number of kills by *our* kill alters combined is difficult for *us* to accept, the majority being targets they deemed unfit for future service for one reason or another. Suffice it to say that *our* combined solo and team kills present an unrest in *our* heart and soul that *we* are uncertain can ever be forgiven. *We* never consciously chose to be this, ever. Yet *we* have to find a way to live with what *our* alters have done while under *total mind kontrol* programming, knowing that *our* most primal choice to survive eventually resulted in *us* killing.

In truth, all who are under *total mind kontrol* programming are victims, so the question is when does someone become witting?—a question that has no straightforward answer when it comes to *total mind kontrol* programming. This evil Network employs a labyrinth of programming, precise science, and ancient malevolent knowledge to convolute minds born into terror and horror and rebuild them to perform unspeakable acts with neither conscious awareness nor remorse.

How does one determine who is who, victim or victimizer, when most of those working for them have also been tortured and split? *We* have met

213

some who have lucid moments until their denial programming takes them over again, much as occurred for *us* throughout *our* life. When a *tmk* slave has programmers, kontrollers, and handlers keeping them programmed all of the time, making conscious choices is near impossible. For *us*, this is a very gray area. Once programming begins to break down significantly enough for a slave (high-level or not) to consciously see it as such, and at that point they are unwilling to take steps to face the truth, then this becomes a choice, does it not?

Of course, choosing will undoubtedly be the most difficult thing a *total mind kontrolled* slave has ever done, bar none. Not only will the slave have to break free from their own programming and internal and external programmers, kontrollers, and handlers amidst numerous programs designed to thwart such from happening, but they will have to do so amidst an indoctrinated, disinformed, misinformed, slumbering human populace who at best will barely tolerate what a deprogramming slave will reveal, let alone be able to acknowledge its truth and validity. People who are willing and able to sincerely assist in this process do exist, but it may take years of patience and fortitude to find them. It can be done with the assistance of Benevolent, Unconditional Love, of that *we* can assure you.

S&M and the Lawyer

In January 2011, one of *our* kill alters revealed another memory fragment as part of a memory that surfaced years before. (See Book 1, Chapter 5, "20: More Sex and Killing", *The Island and Shiny Purple*.)

It is difficult at the very least and devastating at the worst to experience what *our* alters have had to live through, what they were programmed to do and ultimately did, but *we* also are grateful for *our* willingness and ability to face what has come into *our* conscious mind in the best way *we* know how and are capable of at the time of these presentations. This has been and continues to be an integral part of *our* deep deprogramming and healing.

Dealing with kill alters and their programs always fits into the category of the unthinkable. One of the most difficult and recurring emotions that *we* struggle with is guilt encased in shame fed with the knowledge that *we* survived at the expense of others. Not only did people die around *us* at the hands of others, but many died at the hands of some of *our* alters. Intellectually, *we* understand that *we* were under *total mind kontrol* programming and that the devastating and destructive nature of the events is why *our* multiplicity came about in the first place, but *we* continue to struggle deeply with what was done by the alters that share *our* body.

On the night of January 9, 2011, *we* felt the presence of one of *our* alters wanting to present to the rest of *us*. *We* cyclically have profound downloads around *our* core's January birthday. Thanks to deprogramming, *our* ability to manage such alters has become rather adept. In the two or three days prior to this download, *we* had been experiencing a somber adult alter with well-hidden, underlying rage. To alleviate spiritual, mental, emotional and physical symptoms and continue dismantling programs, *we* decided to allow her energy to come forward and reveal what it was that she had been attempting to show *us* for these few days. We *felt* strong enough to deal with her presentation of memories.

We were not prepared for what occurred. *We* can *see* and *feel* that this alter had heavy sexual programming, but there was also more to her, much more. At first *we* thought it to be a sex alter, though *we* would be startled and sickened when the sexual encounter being presented to *us* turned into a kill.

This alter was talking in a very erotic, sexual manner to a man with dark hair underneath *us* in bed. *We* were engaging in vaginal intercourse with *our* alter in kontrol, due to the fact that he was tied by the wrists to the headboard. *We* were leaning over him, *our* mouth close to his left ear, verbally arousing him, the alter telling him that she was going to kill him, which seemed to arouse him more. At this, those of *us* witnessing this for the first time were confused. Why would an alter admit to a target that she was going to kill him? At that moment, *we* got *our* answer. The man had willingly engaged in the sexual encounter and was doing so for this alter's programmed skills associated with restricting air flow to the brain during orgasm to heighten the orgasm. This is what the alter shared with *me* in *our* head: S&M sex programming that the man wanted—his taste. (Erotic asphyxiation.)

At this point in the encounter, *we* sat up straight while still engaging in intercourse, reaching with both hands to place pressure on his neck with *our* thumbs, pressing firmly on either side of his windpipe while leaning *our* weight into *our* arms to restrict air flow. As he began to orgasm, *we* began to *feel* our alter's rising excitement, her breath and heart rate quickening. *We* quickly realized that she was fully intending to kill him. *Our* heart rate and breath were not the only changes *we* felt. To *our* heart-wrenching dismay, *our* kill alter began to get very sexually aroused

215

as the man beneath *us* began to fight for air. The look on his face quickly changed from excitement to terror as he too realized she was not going to release her grip.

Inside *us*, the darkest, most malevolent physical feeling arose from deep down. It crept up and consumed *us* as several of *us* lived what she had done long ago. Her dark pleasure was sickening and frightening as *we* endured her programming and even *our* body reaching orgasm while strangling the life out of the man who'd been a target all along. This kill alter was not only performing her on-task kill; the malevolent energy handling her—running her program—was energizing itself directly from the very life force of this target. The *entity* placed inside *us* during programming clearly gets off on the deaths of targets. *We* know this *entity* very well as "Lilith", and she is the interior programmer and handler of more than one of *our* alters. *We* would go so far as to say that "Lilith"—hideous, compassionless, and purely evil—has overseen many, many of *our* alters.

We were physically, emotionally, and spiritually sickened by this kill alter download. After time had passed, some of *us* asked other alters to tell *us* what had occurred here, what it was all about, what she had done, why she does what she does? It is despairing enough to experience these events, but it is even more so when *we* front alters don't understand the programming so *we* can dismantle it. Engaging *our* alters on a limited basis is a significant part of *our* deprogramming. This is what we *saw* and *felt*, what *we* were shown and told.

The following is taken directly from *our* journal entry the following morning, January 10th. It is presented here just as it was written there.

> "…'she' is 'used' as a set-up to actually 'kill' at orgasm, the male 'targets' orgasm…'used' against those who want 's&m' style sex…the set-up had the 'target' believing it would be a 'mock death' at orgasm while 'she' restricted their oxygen by 'mock strangulation', yet it was not 'mock death', it was real! 'her programmed rage' saw to it…this 'alter uses strangulation' (and 'knives') to 'kill'…it does not seem to be 'she 29th' ('juice')… 'we' suspect 'alter 14' or 'the kill alter that we pursued through our system', the latter 'we' know very little about…this 'alter' from last (nights) download…(has the) 'crush windpipe' ability…and obviously heavy 'sexual programming' as a 'kill alter', both of which fit…'alter 14' strangulation…both hands…on top of the male 'target' during climax…with him in restraints…assured success…"

At first, *we* were confused by the who and when of this original experience, but it is now clear. This was not *our* first solo on-task kill at 18 years old, a sexual encounter turned into an on-task kill. The kill alter up and running in part of that download was *the wild one* whose programming is very different when it comes to kills. At the onset of the casino download at 18, the target had gray-to-white hair; in this kill download in January, the target was younger with dark hair, and the kill alter was definitely not *the wild one*.

Our alter clarified when and where this had taken place. In Book 1, *we* wrote about being on an island with two men—one a lawyer—and being triggered to go to his room for a sexual encounter during which he died. This download was that kill.

It has also become abundantly clear that sex and killing often went together in *our* programming and on-tasks. Some of *our* kill alters have sex programming as part of their personality, while others are often fronted by sex alters before the kill alter presents. The methods and abilities of each alter and distinctions between them clarify with time. Their reluctance to clarify takes a while to understand. Given that memory fragments number in the hundreds, it is impossible for *our* front alters to hold all of this in *our* conscious mind all at once, not to mention *our* own programming playing tricks on *us*, especially by *our* deception alters—despite the *entities* that used to run them being gone, at least from inside of *us*. Apparently, this is a significant part of *our* design and continues to be effective in obscuring deprogramming.

This on-task was indeed a case in which *we* were taking out one of theirs who evidently broke their rules.

A. True Program

The following program and its origins, as well as its connections to recent historic events, are almost unthinkable. It took three years from the time it was first presented to *our* conscious front alters, many downloads by several alters, and abundant external information before *we* came to accept what was all too clear.

We call this "A. True" program because the name of the individual it refers to is Dr. A. True Ott, who, along with his family, was to be a *she 29th* target. What *our* programmers, kontrollers, and handlers did not recognize is that *we* were not only being directed by them, but were also being assisted by *our* higher Self interacting with powers beyond this world as of

April 2008. (See Book 1, Chapter 11, "The Forties", *Salt Lake City: Deep Deprogramming Begins.*)

The many specifics in this program are far too vast to be included here. *Our* intent is to provide the reader with an overview. *Our* journal entries going back into 2007, prior to meeting Dr. A. True Ott in April 2008, indicate that *our* alter's information regarding this particular program was surfacing due to *our* programming breaking down. Over the same period, several handlers and kontrollers attempted to access *us* to reinforce this program (as well as other programs) and eventually trigger it in full. In other words, the stage was being set in 2007 by whoever wanted some of the Ott family to die.

Some things never get any easier to talk or write about, no matter how much time passes. Because of *our* somewhat consistent interaction with Dr. Ott during *our* deep deprogramming, *we* have been able to receive an unusual degree of corroboration from him and his sources independent of *our* own revelations. This is rare and *we* are grateful for the opportunity for such corroboration, despite the difficulty in facing this program and the apparent reach of the handlers involved.

As deep deprogramming continued, the corroboration revealed connections both past and present that frightened *us* deeply and in some instances shocked *our* front alters—connections even running into *our* current town of residence and a handler sent in to monitor and interact with *us* within two weeks of *our* arrival in January 2009.

With this program there is no easy place to start, due to the information at times overwhelming *us*. *We* have spent years piecing together the fragmented memories, much corroborated by Dr. Ott's independent experiences and shared months later. (From April to December 2008, *we* had no contact with Dr. Ott but continued to work with the man Dr. Ott introduced *us* to in April of that year.)

At this time, *we* believe that the original program to kill Dr. Ott's family and him if deemed necessary, was placed in *us* in either 1998 or 1999. *We* remember driving alone around that time from Florida to Las Vegas, Nevada and Salt Lake City, Utah. There are only flashbacks of arriving in both locations. In Vegas, it was night and *we* went to a run-down motel. *We* believe the kill programming had to do with Dr. Ott being privy to information regarding the assassination of President John F. Kennedy in 1963. (Unfortunately, the subsequent murder of John F. Kennedy, Jr. also played a part in *our* Dr. Ott programming.)

To *our* front alter's dismay, it appears it was Dr. Ott's association with what is known as the Gemstone File, particularly #5, that led to *our* being programmed to kill his family in front of him and then him if he did not comply with the wishes of *our* programmers. This need for compliance was to be shared with Dr. Ott during the ritual kill of his family at his home by the purely evil alter known to us as *she 29th*. In addition, there were periphery issues about Dr. Ott's work as well that were more motivation for them wanting to *bring him to his knees*, yet *we* cannot speak specifically to those as *our* programming appears to center around Gemstone File #5. What *we* can say is that as of the 1990s, the Mormon Church did not like Dr. Ott very much.

Our front alters have no knowledge of ever having heard of or meeting Dr. Ott prior to March 2008 when his name was brought to *us* by a man sent to "contain" as well as assist in the set-up of the program for the Otts. Dr. Ott became *our* immediate and total focus at the mention of his name by this person over the phone until *we* drove to Salt Lake City less than a week later with this man acting as *our* handler as he introduced us. *I* had never heard him on radio or elsewhere. *Our* obsession with him came from *our* alter being programmed to him and his family and upon *our* mention of "military abduction" on the phone to this potential handler—who is also MKUltra. His and our relationship is another story entirely.

The 1991 song "Walking in Memphis" by Marc Cohn was one of the tools used in *our* programming. Particular phrases and words worked as codes and reinforced the program each time *we* heard the song, even in the years after. Alters were programmed without the conscious knowledge of *our* front alters until the programming bled through. When *we* eventually brought this particular piece of information to Dr. Ott during deep deprogramming, it was very poignant for him as well. Unbeknownst to *our* front alters, he had researched and named this particular artist and song publicly as programming music years before we met in April 2008. The very song that was used to program *us* to him and his family! The song was presented to *us* from inside by *our* alters shortly after *our* "face-to-face" meeting with Dr. Ott in April 2008 because *our* alters recognized him. Think about this. The music he outed was used in *our* program against him. It gets stranger…

Walking in Memphis was not the only music used to trigger *she 29th*. Led Zeppelin's music was used extensively during the few days in April 2008 in the Salt Lake area to get her "juices" flowing, especially *When the*

219

Levee Breaks. The particular *feel* when *she 29ᵗʰ* is present is not at all pleasant because she is filled with rage, hatred, and cunning, and is highly sexual in a very kontrolled, deceptive manner. She is a frighteningly powerful alter.

[See *A. True Program* collàge at the end of this segment. It may be helpful to view it along with this written piece as it may assist the reader to better understand what this program was really all about, as well as the levels from which it had to be run.]

According to Dr. Ott, he received a file from a client back in the mid-1990s and was instructed to hold the file and forward it to a particular address in the event of the man's death. Dr. Ott did not read this file until years later while going through some of his papers after the man had passed away.

[2022: An update on the below original update in brackets. I do not know why Dr. Ott's work is no longer available, but it will be missed. He did *phenomenal* work in the area of mind control and beyond. The article listed below, as well as others I had at one time referenced in these books, is no longer available. With the level of censorship over the recent years it should really be no surprise. Even our history is being scrubbed. I did however find some of the information regarding this issue by John Hankey on *The Fedora Chronicles Forbidden Library*. Mr. Hankey was in contact with Dr. Ott at some point in an attempt to bring this information out. This would lead to a reactivation of my programming to this family in the late 2000s. The link to that article is provided below.]

[2012: Before going any further, please go to the November 2010 archives at *www.atrueott.com* and read "Remember November 22, 1963: The Assassination of JFK". This was a very convoluted series of programmed events reaching back many decades; the number 22 was particularly poignant in *our* kill programming reaching back at least to 1980.]

The *A. True Program* was being called up in the months preceding April 2008. *We* had been put through a series of programmed alter behaviors to get *us* ready to meet with *our* potential handler. All the program circumstances were aligned, including obsessive journaling about Dr. Ott (initiated by *our* handler's mention of his name over the phone) to provide a "lone nut" explanation for his impending possible murder, namely a woman with stalking tendencies. In early March, this potential handler met with *us*, himself an MPD MKUltra slave (still currently under programming, as far as *we* know). *We* could *see* and *feel* that something was very wrong with all of this and had been for a long time, but *we* could not consciously get at *why* we felt it so strongly.

In addition, *we* had been journaling since the previous year regarding another individual *we* had been programmed to in an apparent kill program many years prior. The program of that kill would arise in *our* front alter's conscious mind and replay for several months during deep deprogramming. These two kill programs were similar, though this is not the time to go into it in any detail. Suffice it to say that the journaling was reflective of *our* programmed-in excessive memories and *feelings* of obsession regarding that target. During the later part of 2007, *we* were lucid regarding these entries, especially *our* concern about having feelings for a man *we* consciously did not know, as would be the case in 2008 regarding Dr. Ott.

During the first 48 hours of *our* meeting with Dr. Ott, *we* made such comments as, "I don't want to do this…something is going to happen…" Dr. Ott and the other man present can verify *our* distress and emotion as *we* consciously began pulling together pieces of *our* history while sharing the information with them. Of course, getting help with *our* memories was the cover story for meeting with them and why *our* kontrollers and handlers had allowed it in the first place. But for several of *us*, *we* were sincerely trying to get help, despite *our* dark alters working *us* over very hard per their programming to make sure *we* performed *our* on-task kill. The arrogance of *our* programmers and kontrollers allowed them to believe that between *our* programming and the activities of *our* handler, this on-task was a sure thing. *We* shudder to recall all that was occurring to kontrol the outcome. How *we* and the Otts actually survived this without *our* alter performing the kill can only be explained by Benevolence, that of *our* higher Self's will as well as Dr. Ott being a man of faith and prayer.

We clearly recall the programmed rage of *she 29th* surfacing over and over and her repeated attempts to take kontrol during *our* drives each day to meet with Dr. Ott and the other man. *We* were indeed getting real help, but it was only the beginning and *we* were still under heavy programming.

By day two, *we* spoke with these two men about *our* skill with a handgun, despite *our* front alters' hatred and fear of guns. *Our* potential handler was present for the meetings in the first five days (his front alter persona was to help MKUltra victims get assistance—particularly women) and the information being revealed had a visible effect on him. Of import to *us* was that on occasion during these meetings, *our* handler and the other man would leave the room and *we* would have a minute alone with Dr. Ott. On these few occasions, *we* found *ourselves* saying things that did not make sense to *our* front alters, such as, "*I* was sure you were going to recognize me."

While all of this was occurring, Dr. Ott's wife was apparently distressed by *our* presence in their home on the first day and continued meetings at their office. It was causing tension between them. On one occasion, Dr. Ott apologized for *our* not being able to stay at their home in a guest bedroom due to *our* financial situation, a direct result of Mrs. Ott's distress. *We* told him, "Leave her be, she is just trying to protect her family," *our feeling* being that she should indeed be afraid of *us*. During a solo moment in his office, he shared that Mrs. Ott asked a very poignant question the night before after being told that one of the main ways in which *we* were used was as a killer: "How do you know she wasn't sent here to kill you?" to which he replied, "I don't."

It would not be until December 2008 that *we* would learn of Mrs. Ott's level of distress during that week in April, brought to *us* by their mutual friend who, when *we* told her of the program within *us* to kill Dr. Ott's family, was visibly stunned. She confided she had received many worried phone calls from Mrs. Ott. The incidents and implications are far too numerous to list here. Like *our* mind, the information was fragmented among all who were present. *We* remember *crystal clear* knowing things that certain alters and their programs would not allow *us* to speak of.

As *our* deep deprogramming continued, it became clear that *we* had access to things in *our* mind that *we* were forbidden to speak of. When *we* tried to talk about certain things, *our* throat constricted, information would not come out, and the presence of someone else was *felt*. Eventually, *we* came to consciously better understand this program and were able to override and dismantle it.

By the fifth day of *our* stay in the Salt Lake area, it became clear that *we* needed to leave the home in which *we* were staying with *our* potential handler. Some of *our* front alters were conscious that *we* were being accessed, triggered, and reinforced every day and night, though at this time we couldn't figure out all the specifics. *We* were living in programmed terror and high anxiety with alters taking over and those of *us* in conscious awareness with only fragments bleeding through.

Strange events occurred that fifth day in downtown Salt Lake City. The handler, the other man *we* were working with introduced to us by Dr. Ott, and *we* had gone to video some of the places in and around Temple Square *we* had been during *our* programming and use. At the end of the tour, a threatening surveillance occurred while the two of us stood on the sidewalk waiting for the handler to pick us up just outside one of the gates to Mormon/LDS Temple Square. When he picked us up, we told him about the surveillance and it really shook him up. He knew danger was present, and it was apparent to the other man and *us* that it had taken him far too long to get his vehicle. However, he had no *conscious* idea that the threatening surveillance would occur, as his tremendous fear after hearing about it showed.

[His delay was a programmed response intended to allow timing for the viewing of the threat shown to myself and the other man with me as we stood outside the gate to the Temple Square.]

During those five days in his home and during the activities we shared, both of us were repeatedly accessed day and night. For *us*, it included physical penetration of *our* vagina—by whom, *i* honestly cannot say. It was evident to *our* front alters that *our* handler/victim was fighting with his own programming. On the last night, several men were in the house. Both he and *we* in our front alters knew they were coming before they actually came. *I* remember this as if it occurred yesterday. It was so surreal, watching it happen as it was happening. He was on high alert after returning from Temple Square and hearing of the surveillance, as were *we*, and *we* tried to speak of them coming, *we* could *see* and *feel* it just after midnight with the neighbor's dog barking for some time. Time was starting to slow down, how it *feels* right before a switch of personality when *i* am conscious enough to *see* it coming. When *we* spoke with authority and calmness to *our* handler/victim about what was happening—he was also in an highly agitated state by this time—he just stood looking at *us*, trance-like, no response, not the usual response for his front alter who would be more likely to go outside with a weapon to see if someone was out there and chase them off. Instead, he stood frozen in program mode, and *we* knew they were coming and it was too late. We were speaking to him calmly, repeatedly using his name to try and call him out of his trance, to no avail. *We* can still *see* and *feel* this in *our* mind's eye. Both he and *we* were going to switch personalities. *It was happening and there was nothing i could do about it!*

We finally left his house after this episode, and upon awakening the next morning with the clear knowledge *we* had been penetrated in *our* vagina, and then after an almost lethal drive to Wendover, Utah, 111 miles away, wound up in a motel in downtown Salt Lake City to continue *our* work with Dr. Ott and the other man. While driving alone at 65 miles per hour on a highway west of Salt Lake City on *our* way to Wendover to see if there was a familiar casino of *our* use years ago, *we* were wide awake with adrenaline one moment, falling asleep at the wheel the next. It was that drastic, as if someone kept throwing a light switch, coming to at the sound of an 18-wheeler's horn, jerking the wheel, coming out of it, struggling to keep *our* eyes open. This area has no shoulder, just deep sand along the roadside.

This near-death event was strange and terribly frightening. *We* were aware that *we* had recently passed Dugway Proving Grounds. It would not be until *we* were in the motel in downtown Salt Lake City later that day, relaying what had happened on the phone to the other man *we* were working with, that *we* would learn that other mind-kontrolled women had reported such instantaneous sleep. By leaving the handler's house without having performed the on-task as programmed, *we* had been hit with a sleep program while driving at 65 miles per hour. *We* also wonder about Dugway Proving Grounds having something to do with it. *We* have since read other slaves' reports of sleep programming. In this instance, it was intended to be a murder program. *We* were never meant to leave the potential handler or Salt Lake City—not alive, anyway.

During the meetings following *our* move to the Salt Lake City motel, *we* described what *we* had witnessed with the handler/victim. Dr. Ott and the other man were not surprised by *our* insights that later led to memories of *our* history with this *tmk* slave. Too in-depth to go into here.

Though *we* would require much more deprogramming, this was the first time in 46 years that *we* told parts of *our* bizarre story and not only did they not think *we* were crazy but they had heard similar stories before and worked with others like *us*. *Our* downloads began occurring nonstop day and night, as if some of *our* alters were feeling a degree of safety that someone was sincerely listening and hearing *us*. Even some of *our* front alters—programmed never to believe what repeatedly showed up *our* whole life in so many ways—were now listening, though it was very difficult, it was undeniable.

After a few days, the three of us were in the middle of profound work when without any notice, Dr. Ott was nowhere to be found; neither the other man nor *we* could reach him to set up that day's meeting. Despite his absence, the other man and *we* continued. On three occasions two days apart, two different dark male individuals approached *us*, once trying to gain access to *our* motel room at 2 a.m., another in broad daylight when the man *we* were working with was present. Angered by all that we had to put up with, *we* confronted the man in the parking lot of our motel, *fiercely* I might add. At this point, some of our kill alters still had the ability to share consciousness. The huge fierce looking man left as I stood before him shouting at him, close and in his face. I will never forget the tranced look in his eyes as he stood, massive, muscular arms folded in front of him, as he turned and walked to his supposedly non-running car in the motel parking lot (part of his excuse to be there) and drove away.

When finances forced *us* to head back to Taos, New Mexico, a couple on a motorcycle followed *our* every move. We even tested them and they proved their mission was watching to make sure I was going back to Taos. The surveillance continued in Taos; potential handlers appeared but *we* did not take the bait: some of *us* were far too awake.

Ongoing events are recorded in journals, on micro-cassette tapes, videos, and DVDs, copies of which are in the hands of others. On one occasion, a man and woman followed *us* to make sure *we* had an "accident" while running a mountain trail through rocky, rough terrain to release the rage and fear plaguing *us*, a plan *we* thwarted with the assistance of either *Beings* on high or a profoundly tuned-in intuition that was common (or remote handlers trying to protect us?), urging *us* mid-run to turn and leave the trail immediately. I would see this Delta-trained man and woman (presenting as a "couple") and realize they had passed by my car three times before I had headed up the trail, only to find their car parked in such a fashion as to thwart my being able to pull out fast when I ran down. The eye-to-eye connection made briefly told me what I knew all to well; it's a *takes one to know one* when eyes meet.

For the next couple of weeks, everything sank in on a conscious level like never before for *our* front alter. *We* retreated from encouraging acquaintances or friends to be around *us* because *we* feared for their safety.

Our front alters were becoming consciously aware of who *we* were dealing with and their sinister nature. To this day, *i* get goose bumps when *i* remember that day on the trail.

[I have no doubt who that man and woman were: highly trained covert operators warned that if the plan did not play out as needed, *be careful, she still has enough programming to cause you harm and difficulty.*]

It enhanced *our* commitment to deprogramming. Sobering fear can do that.

Our extensive, consistent, and painfully detailed alter downloads of the *A. True Program*, coupled with Dr. Ott's relationship to information regarding the assassinations of John F. Kennedy and John, Jr. with his wife and her sister, culminated in August 2008 when *she 29th* attempted to take *us* back to Salt Lake City to *finish it.* Even in 2009 and 2010, when *we* moved to *our* current location in Moab, Utah, *we* were approached by one of two handlers awaiting *our* arrival. Over the course of two weeks in September-October of 2009, this handler repeatedly switched alters and alluded to his possible role in the Kennedy assassination in 1963 while threatening *us* with rape and murder and the lack of assistance *we* would get from local law enforcement due to corruption. He named his "connection" to the Kennedy family: his handler, a prominent doctor closely connected to the Kennedys. His alter's belief was that he had been picked to be an assassin by the doctor who had repeatedly expressed his hatred for the Kennedys.

[*We* followed up on this doctor's alleged connections to the Kennedy's and prefer not to name him. This potential handler was also a lifelong sharpshooter, including winning at many gun competitions, and continuing to do so during *our* time in his acquaintance. I believe he was not actually at the fateful Dallas execution, but had difficulty in the programming—a possible mental breakdown—and he was thus excluded. That he was part of this programming is not at all in question to me as I witnessed him in the 2000s.]

What became frighteningly apparent by late summer-early fall 2009 was that *our* programming to Dr. Ott's family and this handler was directly associated with Dr. Ott's work regarding the Gemstone File #5 he had in his possession as early as the mid-1990s, and that having this potential handler appear in 2009-2010 was a result of the same connections. This absolutely stunned *our* front alters. *Our* programming in the late 1990s was a result of an event from 1963! (Dr. A. True Ott has not had this file for many years now and is not a threat in exposing this information.)

The following chronology is what *we* know to be true thus far. Some of the details have been left out due to *our* need to keep certain identities hidden—in particular, details associated with handlers in the town *we* currently reside in, one of whom is a supervisor in law enforcement.[This is no longer an issue for me and has not been for some years now.]

- Due to previous CIA programming in *our* teen and young adult years, *we* have connections with George H. W. Bush and some of his associates.
- *We* have connections with the highest levels of the Mormon/LDS Church hierarchy, including alter memories of Thomas Monson and Dallin Oaks.
- On numerous occasions, *we* were used by *our* programmers and kontrollers to kill members of their Network for one reason or another, reasons never revealed to my alters.
- Dr. Ott's "excommunication" from the Mormon/LDS Church occurred after he questioned the validity of Church history and revelations of who and what they really are: Lucifer/Lilith worshippers.
- Dr. Ott began discussing the Gemstone File #5 in his possession with the editor of John Kennedy, Jr.'s *George* magazine in the summer of 1998. *The editor sought him out*, not the other way around. This was unrelated to the file he held, or at least that is how it was told. (Was this coincidence? I personally know far too much to believe in that luxury for the uninitiated. Divine guidance intended?)
- Dr. Ott received a phone call from John Kennedy, Jr. in early July 1999 during which John, Jr. enthusiastically revealed that he was moving forward to prove George H.W. Bush's complicity in the assassination of his father, plus exposing others in the conspiracy. According to Dr. Ott, John, Jr. stated that a grand jury was being convened.

John, Jr. was killed *just two weeks* after Dr. Ott received the call announcing his plans. The murder halted Dr. Ott's desire to expose Gemstone File #5 to anyone else due to obvious risks to his family and himself. By this time the file was in the possession of *George Magazine* to my knowledge.

- We were programmed to Dr. Ott and family in 1998 or 1999 to perform a ritual kill in his home.
- By the middle of 2007, Dr. Ott was again discussing the Gemstone File with John Hankey, who wrote "The Reason JFK Jr. Was Murdered", September 12, 2007. https://thefedorachronicles.com/library/jfk-jr-murdered-john-hankey.html
- By the middle of 2007, *we* had been triggered to return to the UFO community with *our* memories. Alters begged *us* not to return, repeatedly telling *us* that *we* were outing *ourselves*, *our* every move was being watched, that return would be dangerous, etc. *We* attended the conferences with a guarded, newly emerging conscious awareness. However, when potential handlers appeared, *we* were still unable to fully comprehend who they were, but did know that they were not to be trusted, the word "operatives" coming into *my* consciousness.
- By February-March 2008 at a IUFOC conference, *we* met the potential handler (under programming himself) who would take *us* to Dr. Ott in April. From the moment *we* met this handler *face to face*, he unwittingly offered *us* numerous triggers and "hooks" and a plethora of peripheral activity to ensure *we* would go to Salt Lake City.

[This is classic access protocol. Potential handlers are sent in with just enough information and coded speak to hook the one looking for answers and assistance. It would occur in my early deep deprogramming many times over with various operatives (including MKUltras). Even after much awareness and time passing, it still can occur...and it is powerful. However, with this particular individual it was more powerful as I would over time recognize my alter relationships with him ran back years.]

- By the April 5-6 weekend, *we* were in extensive long distance phone contact with the potential handler after meeting him at the IUFOC Conference in Laughlin, Nevada, revealing to him *our* torture and mind access by military, to which he responded with Dr. Ott's name, *stressing with emotion*, "You have to meet with him..." over and over. Immediately, Dr. Ott became *our* total focus, *our* belief being that he would recognize *us*, that *we* needed to meet him and only him. The handler mentioned other people to meet in the Salt Lake City area, but *we* wanted only Dr. Ott. On this same weekend, *we* began hearing voices (remote electromagnetic mind control technologies) in the home in which *we* were staying in Arroyo Seco, New Mexico. In addition, *we* were receiving access phone calls on the landline there.

Out of the blue (color programming play on words) on Monday the 7th, *we* packed up and drove to Roswell, New Mexico for one night and exposed *ourselves* to the same program trigger *we* had exposed *ourselves* to during the latter part of the previous year while attempting to find help within the UFO community. This particular program trigger has to do with Dr. Steven Greer to whom *we* were programmed, including an apparent kill program with bizarre similarities to the *A. True Program*, though not including Dr. Greer's family.

[The similarities lie in the obsession with each, programmed-in sexual relationship narrative, and false "evidence" in my journals after kill follow through of a "stalker" mentality.]

In one of the April meetings with Dr. Ott, *we* would speak very emotionally about Dr. Greer, Dr. Ott having been told by someone in California that, "You and Dr. Greer must meet and talk." *We* are certain that this was part of *our* programming to both Drs. Greer and Ott, though *we* cannot speak to who the person in California was.

[It seems to me that this would add another tie-in for me being the stalker/killer. The fact that they would have met.]

The similarities in *our* kill programs to each of these men, particularly regarding the way *we felt* about them, ran very deep. (See Chapter 2, "The Teen Years", *Brought Together* and Chapter 8 "More On-Task", *Mutual Handling*. Book 2 presents a much clearer understanding of how *we* were made to believe that *we* knew Dr. Greer intimately.)

- Upon experiencing the trigger on April 7, *we* left Roswell the next day and set out to meet with the handler in a town near Salt Lake City, even calling him from southern New Mexico to announce *our* coming. Initially, he was flustered and attempted to delay *our* arrival by a couple of days.
- A partial memory of being in a motel somewhere along the way to Salt Lake and talking on the phone in the evening with the handler.
- According to a conversation with Dr. Ott eight months later, approximately one week before *our* initial arrival in Salt Lake City in April, this

same handler paid Dr. Ott a visit. They knew one another, but this visit was unannounced and involved the handler showing up in Dr. Ott's office parking lot, calling him by cell phone and asking him to come down, then showing Dr. Ott two newly acquired guns in his trunk, a rifle and a pistol. Just before the handler indicated he was leaving, he pointed to the pistol and said, "This one has your name on it." Dr. Ott was a marksman and thought the handler was offering the gun to him, which he declined by stating he had no need for the gun, to which the handler replied, "That's not what I meant," then abruptly left.

Our *A. True Program* called for a 9mm to be provided by the handler, the weapon *she 29th* repeatedly spoke of using in the ritual kill. When *we* revealed this to Dr. Ott, he asked a mutual friend of his and the handler's if the handler owned a 9mm. An affirmative was stated.

- Heavy access during *our* five-day stay at the handler's house: programming music, sexual encounters in alter (rape no matter how one looks at it), meeting with men in alter for instructions, internal programs being triggered and running all night (as well as an apparent astral programming session in the house setting). *We* are not accusing this handler/victim of rape; *we* do not consciously know who it was but attribute it to the night the male "posse" came into the home of this handler as we were both switching alters.

[This in part took place due to the potential handler calling the "posse" after the Temple Square incident reported earlier when myself, the handler and the other man I was working with went to Temple Square. This is known as a **reporting alter**, and most trauma-based program victims have them.]

- When *we* left the handler's house after five days—inadvertently revealing to *our* programmers that *we* were breaking programming—a concerted effort to threaten and kill *us* was initiated.
- In December 2008, Dr. Ott said that approximately one week after *we* arrived in the Salt Lake City area in April 2008, he received a phone call from a long-time source in Washington, D.C.— a man with very high-level connections (including the Intelligence Community whom *we* have since engaged on the phone)—warning that Ott's family was in danger. "You have two visitors…your family is in danger…" This was why Dr. Ott very wisely decided to leave town for a bit with his family without notifying *us* or the other man *we* were working with.

- Ongoing access of *us* after Salt Lake City, with internal programming running day and night.
- On August 28, 2008, just four months later, *she 29th* announced that she was coming forward as a witness, and by August "29th" she was consciously co-existing with *us*, presenting as an ally, albeit a very manipulative one. Prior to this, her presence was palpable yet unidentified. For months, she tried to deceive *us* into returning to Salt Lake City and the various ways *we* could acquire a 9mm before or after *our* arrival there, one method being to return to the handler's house to trigger his programming to assist *us*. Naturally, this would have involved sex. When deception was not working, she used force, and on more than one occasion she was able to kontrol *our* body and mind to a frightening degree (remote technologies?). While in Taos, *we* found a sawed-off shotgun left for *us* by another unwittingly-influenced person. Those of *us* awake enough enlisted a young woman *we* were confiding in to get rid of it and not tell *us* what she did with it. That month, *she 29th* repeatedly presented to *us* in explicitly painful detail the ritual kill that would last at least a couple of hours in the home of Dr. Ott. (This technique of repeatedly forcing a slave to internally perform a kill prior to the actual kill, per programming, has since been corroborated by an inside source as one of their methods. This was not the only kill program in which repetition was utilized.)

  Our struggles back then with *she 29th* are still some of the most potent and frightening to date. *We* warned the other man *we* were working with in Salt Lake City of these daily struggles by phone, telling him that if he could not reach *us* or knew *we* were headed that way, to notify Dr. Ott immediately.
- By December 2008, *we* were again in contact with Dr. Ott and heading to Salt Lake City while managing *she 29th*. Once in Salt Lake, *she 29th* attempted to gain an "audience" with Dr. Ott by claiming she only wanted to speak to him. *We* were now in control and did not allow it and were going to tell him about the *A. True Program*, suspecting that he already knew, and wanting him to know they may send others. During this meeting, *we* assured him that it would not be *us* who would do this, *ever*.
- Dr. Ott was able to corroborate *our* insights, even about events that occurred before *our* arrival back in April 2008. At this time, neither he

nor *we* knew about the Kennedy associations, at least not in regard to *our* programming to him.

- *We* left Salt Lake City—the city that sickens *us*—and went to Moab, Utah to find a place to stay and work. *We* feared returning to Taos, New Mexico, due to many terrible memories, including an apparent escape from an underground facility with terrible implications as well as recent attempts on *our* life. Financially broke, *we* could not go far. After arriving in Moab, *we* realized that *we* had been programmed to go there. No matter where *we* went, *our* programming was being accessed.

- Within two weeks of *our* arrival in January 2009, one of two handlers began a casual *face to face* approach, repeatedly engaging *us* in a public building. Immediately, *we* red flagged him but were still desperate for information about *our* situation and history. Never did *we* approach or encourage him, but *we* did listen intently and ask questions when *we* could.

- In September and October of 2009—subsequent to reaching out to two people online with information regarding a public person *we* know to be mind kontrolled—the handler threatened us. According to a source who will go unnamed, the two people *we* attempted to reach out to online are intelligence operatives posing as valid members of the conspiracy community. "I have a dossier on them," the source said.

- Within an hour of the threat's delivery, *we* came *face to face* with a law enforcement officer who was also closely monitoring *us* but not interacting with *us*. This was *my* first *face to face* encounter with this officer. These two encounters back to back worked: *i* was frightened.

- During two weeks in September and October 2009, the sharp-shooting Kennedy-associated handlers' alters presented revelations to *us* that were key to recognizing what the reference to "gems" in Dr. Ott's Gemstone File #5 meant to *us*, knowing *we* have "gem" alters.

- *We* had known for some time that at the end of the programmed on-task ritual kill of Dr. Ott's family, he too was to be killed if he did not comply with *our* programmer's wishes, after which *we* would be killed by a suicide alter waiting in the background, an alter *we* had consciously met while she was hiding behind *she 29th*. This suicide alter was programmed to take *us* to a motel for *our eat a bullet* program (one of *our* suicide programs), after which *our* journal entries about Dr. A. True Ott and Dr. Greer would be discovered and *we* would be labeled a stalker and crazed lone assassin, as has repeatedly been programmed into the public mind by media broadcasts about many other *total mind kontrolled* slaves with kill programming. [Lee Harvey Oswald (not the actual killer but a patsy), Sirhan Sirhan, James Earl Ray, Mark David Chapman, etc.]

- In April 2008, one week after *our* arrival and just shy of a week after *our* first meeting with Dr. Ott, the alleged D.C. source Mel Laney—close to intelligence circles, with a high-level Mormon/ LDS Church history—warned Dr. Ott of impending danger. By then, *our* programmers, kontrollers, and handlers were aware that *we* were probably not going to complete the program to kill neither Ott nor his family, due to having left the handler. *Our* programming was bleeding through far too much to follow through. But wasn't the call's actual purpose to appear as a warning and build trust between Dr. Ott and Laney? What is clear is that the lag time suited the programmers, not Dr. Ott since I had already left the situation.

In recent years, we have warned Dr. Ott that they are coming for him. Mrs. Ott was involved in a near fatal car accident, her recovery slow and long but successful. The man driving the vehicle that hit hers at high speed was associated with Hill Air Force Base in the Layton, Utah area north of Salt Lake City. According to Dr. Ott, after the "accident" a letter arrived when Mrs. Ott was there and Dr. Ott was not, intimating that the "accident" was intended—an intentional "hit" attempt on Mrs. Ott. The objective? Obviously to *bring Dr. Ott to his knees*, just as *she 29th* had been programmed to do.

Greer

Throughout *our* deprogramming, *we* have struggled with the truth per *our* programming regarding Drs. A. True Ott and Steven Greer. At times, *we* felt that *we* knew both intimately, but especially Dr. Steven Greer. In fact, as with the actor Christian Bale in Book 1 (see Chapter 12, "Internal Programming", *Devotional Programming to Actor Christian Bale*), we still question whether or not *we* had intimate interaction with him. What has come to light is that it is much more likely that it was programming to make *us* believe *we* knew him to further their agenda regarding *our* kill program, as with Dr. Ott.

The similarities regarding *our* programming to both of these men are stunning, especially the *feelings* that were programmed in. *Our* personal

233

contact with Dr. Ott during *our* deprogramming was considerable, whereas *our face to face* encounter with Dr. Greer in Denver, Colorado occurred after he gave a speech. In both programs *we* have repeatedly witnessed kill as well as *alter-nating* love/hate emotions toward each, up close and at a distance. Sometimes, these emotions came out of nowhere and were debilitating, such as awakening in a rage and wanting to kill them.

A. True Program

The recurring link between these two men around *our* programming to them has greatly lessened and become very manageable (dismantled), though anger and desire can and do still *alter-nate* on the surface. *We*

234

have explicit memories of sexual interaction with each, but consciously realize that these are programmed-in memories to provide a basis and/or motivation/justification for killing them as well as to support *our* journal writings that could later be used by law enforcement to dispose of *us* in the Department of Justice system. (Corrupt all the way!)

Memories of *us* with Greer have been extensive and emotionally charged, but the programmed memories of a sexual relationship with Dr. Ott only showed up as the full revelation of *our* kill programming to him was being revealed. This leads *us* to believe that they were put in as *we* revealed the kill program fully to *our* conscious mind (*entities* and remote technologies), the hope being that it would assist in overriding the revelations and allow *us* to complete the intended on-task. This occurred during summer and fall 2008 when *we* were being worked over extensively to *finish it*. *We* were programmed to believe that *we* loved these men, with hate being *alter-nated* in as well for kill justification.

When programming assassins in *total mind kontrol* programming, the slave is made to repeat the kill program as it is to occur over and over again. This occurred for *us* in both the case of Drs. Ott and Greer and how they made *our* alter personality believe the relationship was real. The levels of hatred and love *we* experienced is difficult to express in words. With Greer, *our* incredible need to be with him, to find him, was most certainly that of an irrational stalker mentality. During the expression of these longings, *we* repeatedly heard that *we* were "going home". *Greer's girl* believed she was "going home" to him, though it was crystal clear that *alter 14* was the one programmed to kill him. What saved *us* (and perhaps him) was a parallel conscious awareness of the irrational and bizarre nature of these *feelings* in light of *our* also *seeing* and *feeling* that *we* had never actually met him. *We* front alters were awake enough to *see* great danger revolving around all of this. As stated to *our* confidante regarding why *we* dared not go to see him speak in a nearby town in the summer of 2008, "*I* am afraid someone wants *me* to go."

There are only a few possible location connections in Greer's and *our* past. Prior to the start of Greer's presentation in Denver in 2009, one of Greer's bodyguards zeroed in on *us* in the 5th row of the audience. At one point it felt like a stare down. Moments later, this same bodyguard whispered into the ear of another man in the small group surrounding Greer, who then walked to the end of *our* aisle and remained standing there. *Our* vacillation between love and hate during this time was astounding! Perhaps the bodyguard could sense the *Greer's girl* energy and *alter 14*.

When *we* saw Greer after his talk, he attempted to avoid eye contact and abruptly dismissed *us* when *we* asked him a question regarding his speech. *We* view him as another victim of mind kontrol—a *takes one to know one* perspective. Programming for obsession and the appearance of an ongoing relationship to an individual is apparently the *modus operandi* of these malevolent programmers.

We do not believe that *our* kill program to Greer was intentionally triggered in 2009; it was the pressure of the existing program coming into *our* conscious mind that caused the distress and danger. *We* were "going home", going back to them, *our* programmers, kontrollers, and handlers. To some of *us*, it felt incredibly alluring.

Alter Memories

Symptoms experienced as a result of programming and consciously during deep deprogramming involve all of *our* states: spiritual, mental, emotional, and physical. Early on, emotional meltdowns involving tears and outbursts as alters surfaced resulted in physical symptoms including fever, severe headache, nausea, vomiting, body pain, chills accompanied by shakes, profuse sweating often accompanied by the intense smell of an organic body chemical release—the smell of fear—and light sensitivity. In addition, there is always the sense that it is coming before *we* are able and willing to allow the full download to surface.

But what *we* want to address here is the shaking that occurred as a result of resistance—a programmed resistance of an alter trying to take the body against the wishes of those who were now collectively assisting *our* deep deprogramming. The alters, after all, were programmed in, and it became infinitely clear that programmed information was part of *no talk* programming. However, *deception* programming such as screen memories were allowed.

The alters assisting deep deprogramming had already broken programming and were for the most part living outside of it, though not completely—not all of them. The shaking (as well the other symptoms) had gone on for many years prior to deep deprogramming; it just became more frequent and pronounced to *our* conscious mind. As *we* came to understand that *our* alter wanted kontrol, *we* were able to decrease the shakes during certain downloads. Like the other symptoms, the shakes did not completely disappear, but with clear insight and continued deep deprogramming they have lessened greatly.

2
Continuing Revelations

Three years into deep deprogramming has brought a relatively new life that *we* are managing. *We* make choices based on what *we* deem appropriate and desirable. *We* trust a couple of people, which means more than you can imagine. *We* have some truths, something too few people are willing to pay for, despite the fact that it may cost them far more in the future.

Some time ago, *we* were asked what *we* wanted most. *Our* answer was safety and peace. To feel safe and peaceful in this world is a real feat and it can only be accomplished through truth, and that comes through Love. To *us*, facing truth is an act of Love of one's self and others and is of the most powerful kind. Truth allows *us* to make informed choices with the knowledge that *we* are really doing the best *we* can. Singly, *we* cannot change all that needs changing, but *we* can affect it with truth as an ally. Living a lie is the saddest thing in any world to *us*, and doing so as a victim is the worst oppression *we* know. Given the choice, who would not choose truth? There is a difference between the manifest reality of what is and the perception of what is believed to be. They are very different indeed.

As *our* dearest friend says, truth can handle investigation, lies cannot. *We* are learning this by discovering who has traumatized, programmed, and used *us*, what *we* have been, what *we* have done, and the Unconditional Love within *us* that will affect all of that. As well, what is being done to the global populace. Drastic measures are indeed required for *us* and for all.

This next section is devoted to the many downloads presented to *our* conscious mind prior to writing Book 1 but not included due to length and/or personal difficulty in writing about these things. Because they have become a significant part of *our* understanding of *our* programming and use as well as *our* greater insight into their meaning, *we* include them here. *We* continue to refer to the malevolent beings as *entities, demons, aliens,* and *beings* interchangeably, including terms like "full-blood", hybrid, and *reptile* as well as *our* experiences with the *cats*, among other things.

The challenge of language is that when we say *demon* or *cat*, another person's mental picture may not fit *ours*, which *we* believe was by programming design. What *we* attempt to describe are experiences and *beings* that most people have no conscious interaction with. *We* do not wish to mislead, yet at the same time *we* desire to remain true to what *we* have experienced, not what someone else thinks *we* have experienced. We are all involved in this story, no matter who is telling it. What does not change for *us* in *tmk* and its periphery is that whoever these *entities* are, wherever they come from, they are malevolent and have been a visible, tangible, real force in *our* life.

The Minions

El

We cannot say for certain when or how this programmed-in view came about, but *we* are haunted by how at least one of *our* alters views a member of the Rothschild family, the one known as Evelyn de Rothschild (born August 29, 1931). *We* have information about *our* apparent relationship to this man, but not enough for public disclosure.

We will, however, share *our* alter's view of him. To her, he is a god-like figure; thus the title *El*, an ancient name for God. Evelyn de Rothschild was one of several figures to show up in two different colláges about *our* programmers and users. In the *Warlords, Guns, and Money* colláge in Book 1, he is accompanied by David René Rothschild (born December 15, 1942) with the words "see to it that it produces offspring", as well as "old money, new money, dirty sex", "the insiders", and "secret sex"—all specifically around Evelyn, a name closely associated to *us* and *our* family, patriarchal and matriarchal. David René has the words "beta" and "high quality" near his picture. In addition, Evelyn has the numbers "13" and "14"—a direct reference to *our* age—while David René has "15". To the left of both men are pictures of two sexualized women, both faceless, one with exaggerated lips—one of the ways *we see ourselves* to have been sexually used by *our* programmers. In *Faces of Them*, Evelyn de Rothschild shows up with "El" and the word "dragon," a god-like *reptile* revealing that parts of *us see* him as something other than a man.

Offspring

This is a difficult topic for *us*, so it will be brief. *We* have children *we* know nothing about. *We* never brought any to term, aside from the *entity* deliverance through the Flower of Life tattoo (see Book 1, Chapter 11, "The Forties", *Simon*), but know they are eight human/**overshadowed** hybrids. One is not 3-dimensional, but belongs to the one *we* call Cain. *We* did not incubate the children in *our* womb for long, due to *our* use; someone or something else did that. These pregnancies occurred before 18 years of age, the beginning of *our* heavy use years. Is it obvious who the fathers were? *I* cannot say for sure...

Pilots, Airplanes, and Helicopters

One of the consistent presentations by *our* alters involves terms associated with flying. *We* are not referring to *our* flying alter, but to flying as in aviation. *We* have numerous downloads regarding the presence of helicopters, airplanes, and pilots being present throughout the years of *our* on-task use—all fragmented but also very precise and clear. At least one of *our* programmers was a pilot, though *we* cannot tell who.

In the early 1980s, one of *our* alters met a young pilot at a remote air strip in central Florida and flew with him in a small private plane that day and into the night to at least four other local airports, some private, some public. This alter memory, fragmented as it is, has never left *our* conscious mind; *we* just tucked it away as unexplainable. In recent years, *we* have discovered several of the locations *we* were taken to, including Tampa International Airport.

We can still clearly *see* the remote airstrip with a small shed-like building in Pasco County where *we* met the pilot. *We* recall the young-looking male pilot wearing glasses, some of the inside of the cockpit, the view of the day sky and later the night sky, as well as a particular runway during one of the take-offs at Peter O. Knight Airport on Davis Island. In the fragmented memory of Tampa International Airport, *we* recall the visual approach to a certain hangar away from the commercial planes. In the recalled fragments of conversation with this young pilot, both on the phone before our meeting and during this encounter, the words remembered intimate that *we* were to have a "job" with his "company".

Most of the hours of this encounter are still missing from *our* conscious mind. *We* have no recollection of returning to *our* boyfriend's car which *we* drove to the remote airstrip, nor if that was even *our* point of return. (This boyfriend was a member of a family closely involved with *our* family through *our* father.) *Our* sense is that this encounter went on for more than a day and a night and that *we* were not returned to that remote airstrip.

During these same years, one of *our* handlers was a helicopter pilot responsible for his and *our* many trips to the Bahamas, a location of some of *our* heavy use, especially sex and kill programming. *We* recall on at least two occasions being in two different types of helicopters with him—one a bubble-front doorless type and being out over the Gulf of Mexico, the other flown by a pilot and co-pilot, the "Cadillac of helicopters", he told *us* upon take-off. *We* recall leaving a very expensive restaurant on Sanibel Island in Florida one night with this handler and going to an airport and boarding what *we* believe was a commercial flight to the Bahamas, though *i* have no memory of getting on a commercial flight, yet *i* do have memories of being in the Bahamas.

Part of this handler binding *us* to him involved gifting *us* with an expensive round bracelet made of gold. A single *circle of gold* shows up repeatedly in *our* program triggers and reinforcements, though *our* understanding of the specific purpose in each instance still escapes *me*. Despite this, *we* are painfully aware that these two intertwined triggers work well. In this instance, *we* can recall the deep *feeling* inside *us* upon receiving this particular piece of jewelry from him while sitting in his DeLorean car.

We noticed aviation terms in certain programs associated with *our* on-task use, particularly *our* kill programming. One in the *A. True Program* relates to the lyrics "And I boarded the plane/Touched down in the land of the Delta Blues" in the song *Walking in Memphis*, by Marc Cohn. *We* have memories of *our* mother and *us* standing on the tarmac of a then-small airport in Largo, Florida (now St. Pete-Clearwater International Airport (PIE)) awaiting the arrival of men coming in on a private jet. This was the early1980s. This too never left *our* conscious mind. It is brief and lucid, and *we* can still *feel* the heat of the Florida sun.

While researching high-level females hidden within these secret networks and what they were doing in some of *our* downloads, the Guild of Air Pilots and Air Navigators (GAPAN) came up as being linked to these females. Because of *our* connections to Rothschild organizations and British intelligence agencies, the GAPAN connection struck *us* as profoundly true. This particular guild has been a Livery Company in the City of London since 1956. Another link showed up with Northrop Grumman, a military contractor corporation the guild is affiliated with. Northrop Grumman shows up in *our* colláge work and *we* associate *our* connection with them to be through DARPA (Defense Advanced Research Projects Agency), quite possibly the most evil agency on earth.

Solo Kills, Team Kills

This part of *our* history has been shown in bits and pieces over many years, some of the bits having never left front alter consciousness due to some of the deeds, physical evidence, and memory having bled into *our* conscious mind at the time of the original event. Other bits came years later when the strength of who *we* really are on a soul level disrupted *our* programming enough to begin extracting *ourselves* from it.

Through numerous fragmented downloads, it is apparent that *we* not only killed solo but with other slaves in tandem, as a team—the intention of at least one of *our* End-Time programs: that one or more of *our* alters would participate with a small team made up of three, possibly four males and *us*. *We* believe *we* know who two of those men are and suspect the identity of the third. Sometimes, the team may have had a fourth man.

We do not know what *our* team was specifically programmed to do, but *we* do know that one of the men who was to access one of *our* alters by engaging in sex with *us* was in a supervisory position of law enforcement; sex was to be his first access so he could continue into *us* more deeply with other keys to bring up another alter for team utilization. *We* know who he is and have broken all ties to him, most significantly on a spiritual level, as well as another local man who was to be used on the team. As far as *we* know, the other man is now living elsewhere, having left *our* location less than two months after *our* spiritual disconnect from him. He would inform me that he was going back to Maryland, I suspect due to his programming breaking down—as I witnessed it—he is likely being "retired" at 70+ years of age.

To *our* knowledge, *we* never engaged sexually with the law enforcement officer due to breaking through *our* programming. However, the desire to do so for one of *us* was apparent to *our* conscious mind and even affected *our* body physically for about a year and a half every time *we* encountered him. He too was aware of this energy, though *we* have no reason to suspect that he is aware of his own programming. Despite his kind greetings when *we* encounter him, we consider him to be dangerous. It gets real creepy when you know of another's alters and yet continue to meet with the fronts. This officer is a "sleeper" who we believe has thus far been used minimally so as to save him for the End-Time agenda. As with others *we* have been programmed with, *we* would occasionally have a strong repulsive feeling when *we* encountered him, the opposite of programmed-in desire. This repulsion has shown up with every single handler and/or kontroller *we* have encountered, due to other parts being aware and predominating over the part that is programmed to or with that person. The dichotomy of these emotions is profound and can occur almost simultaneously.

[In 2022 while spending a winter back in Moab, Utah, after noticing several years ago when I still lived there that he was no longer on the police force (and having this validated by his unwitting mother who often entered a business in which I worked), I saw him in the local grocery store.

242

The rush of adrenaline I experienced surprised me. I never realized just how physically big of a man he was and I felt some anxiety.]

We believe that this particular team program was to take place, at least in part, around the Salt Lake City area but include Moab. *We* have found some of the programming locations in the last three years. Due to some of what *we* found in those locations as well as certain programming well established inside of *us*, color apparently plays a significant role in this program. Color programming goes far beyond affecting only *our* team; color and at least one of the locations *we* discovered are meant to affect many teams regarding at least one of their End-Time programs.

Additionally, *our* program involves being on a river with the aforementioned men—not an actual river but a part of *our* programming on the inside of *us*. This internal river is related to accessing one of *our* End-Time programs. By going down this river, *we* move into the program. *We* believe the man who was to engage *us* sexually was to be the one who would take *us* "down the river" by utilizing codes to access another alter once *we* were accessed sexually. This is where the fourth man shows up, possibly *our* male alter, but *we* cannot grasp it consciously. It is as though sometimes he is there and sometimes not—very frustrating. Nor have *we* discovered the codes. *We* can still *see* and *feel* this internal river and *us* on it with these men in *our* mind. *We* cannot *see* two of the men's faces well enough to recognize; they remain just out of view in the background.

During this last year, *we* were able to witness the two handlers and *us* in the same room together at the local gym, gyms being part of *our* programming and *we* strongly suspect theirs as well. *We* were engaged in a conversation with one of these men—the sharpshooter—in *our* front alter when the other one appeared. Despite the obvious risks, *we* engaged this man when he approached, due to *our* deep desire to know more about *us*. *We* remained calm and observant, but it was beyond bizarre. The law enforcement officer greeted *us* as he walked by, but the man speaking to *us* only glanced at him, having told *us* on numerous occasions that they hate each other. He related numerous stories of police corruption, including rape and murder. Local law enforcement had harassed him, including this particular officer, and claimed that FBI protection had to be sent by his high-level kontroller/handler in Colorado, a very successful public figure who took over as kontroller of this man after the death of his handler who was once associated with the Kennedys (as

243

explained in *A. True Program* above). During *our* conversations, he would switch personalities.

The energy *we* felt in those moments in the gym that day was electrifying. This is the part of programming that is often misunderstood: the energy of malevolence.

In addition to the above End-Time program team, there were several kills in which one or more of *us* worked with other slaves.

To *our* conscious knowledge, it has always been a male counterpart. *We* know the identity of one of these men and it is *our* understanding that *we* worked with him numerous times and had an ongoing sexual relationship with him—his alter and *our* alter—for years. This is important to maintaining both his and *our* alter programming; in fact, it is how it works in part.

Mutual handling is a common and necessary aspect of *total mind kontrol* programming, and everybody gets handled. *We* have been used to reinforce the programming of those who have handled *us*, and *i* have even witnessed that it still occurs with *us* on occasion, despite *my* conscious awareness. In *our* team on-tasks, it worked as a *loop* of programming moving through all involved, like a circuit.

[I was told by someone that our team kills outnumber solo kills more than two to one. I do not know if this is true.]

Unsanctioned Encounter of Another Slave

This particular memory is included to show how the process of partial memory and piecing things together can sometimes work for *us* over time. The process entails profound, lucid memory downloads to front alters memories regarding a male victim/slave in 1980-1982. *We* fronts never forgot our encounter with him, but there seems to have been more than that.

The sequence of events is often difficult to hold onto consciously so that lucid pieces of memory often fall within a range of years for *our* conscious mind. This is due to the effect programming has on *our* sense of time, or rather *our* inability to recognize and maintain the sequence of events over years.

The man in this event had the earmarks and behaviors of a *tmk* slave. The circumstances of his death are suspicious, as well as *our* currently unexplainable memory of him immediately after his death telling a very different story than that told to *our* front alters within the weeks shortly after his death. For now, *we* have only part of the event in conscious memory.

We remember quite well from *our* youth that *we* were desired by men. *We* do not consider *ourselves* exceptionally pretty, but *our* attractiveness was profoundly apparent, thanks to the programming and *entities* placed within during programming. In addition, *we* were fit, strong, tan, blond, and young—an irresistible hook, line and sinker when dealing with others who also had *entities* within, covering any and all who were looking to engage sexually with a *total mind kontrolled* slave. Even unwittingly, truly healthy people are not going to solicit such encounters with a fully programmed slave, though they might want to claim so. People are frequently unaware of what draws them to someone, but regarding someone who has been tortured, traumatized, raped, and programmed as a sex slave and a killer, it is difficult to deny that an energetic desire would signify that *both* parties were *entity-* compromised, would it not? *We* are talking about a slave still under full programming.

Memory presentation by *our* alters, combined with parts of the events that remained consciously present with other alters, is the particular process *we* refer to here. *We* want to use this particular example because there has always been conscious memory present of this person and some of his actions, as well as the seemingly ridiculous explanation given to *our* front alters regarding his death.

The man in question first approached *us* on a causeway in Florida one afternoon when *we* were 18-20 years old. *We* were getting some sun in a bikini when he drove up in his black Corvette, got out, and engaged *us*. There was something wrong about him that unnerved *us*. When *we* realized he was not going to leave, *we* packed up and excused *ourselves*. On other occasions on the same causeway, he continued to approach *us* frequently enough to cause *us* to change locations and keep an eye out for him. Then one day he showed up at *our* condo where *we* were living with *our* mother but were then alone. It frightened *us* that he had followed *us* home. He knocked at the door. *Our* front alters were terrified by then, so *we* hid and hoped he would not try the unlocked door handle. *I* can still *see* that door knob!

Shortly after, *we* told *our* father and a man for whom *our* father and *we* worked. They were partners in business, but it was obvious that this man had some power over *our* father, though *i* never knew what in particular.

245

This man and his family were a significant part of my life, hence wondering what their possible role was, witting or otherwise, regarding *tmk*. *Our* extensive involvement with the daughter and one of the sons raised that flag; she even went to Mexico with *us* on one occasion.

A couple of weeks after reporting the encounters with this frightening man to *our* father and his partner, *our* father's partner told *us* in the office where *we* worked too that the man was dead. *Our* first involuntary response was relief. When *we* asked how he knew and what had happened, he told *us* that he had known the man for some time. This did not make sense to *us*. Why was he telling *us* this now? Given that we all lived in a large, highly populated, tri-county area, how could he have known the now dead man? He briefly explained their association through someone else, then told *us* that the man in his late thirties had apparently "died in his sleep…he lay down to take a nap and suffocated to death…" He had had a serious car accident years before, which may have been why he "died in his sleep by suffocation". *I* recall my dad's partner telling *me* he "died of tonsillitis".

We clearly recall doubting what *we* were being told. Even back then under programming, *we* never trusted anything *our* father or his partner told *us*. They were both pathological liars. *We* can remember thinking how odd it was that this occurred after *we* reported the man to them, without any way to identify him to them. Yet now he was known by *our* father's partner and died a strange death. And to top it all off, *we* can *see* the man lying in bed on his back on top of white sheets, dead. How can *we see* this? Were *we* there? Was he murdered? Were *we* involved with this man in alter? At that age, at that time in *our* life while under *our* heaviest use, would it be difficult to believe? Stalked by another slave? Was there a familiarity of *me* to him? Is that why he persisted?

We know how this feels: to know someone because of associations in different alters. How is it *we* can *see* him lying in his bed, dead? *Our* front alters do not know. Why did *our* father's partner wait to tell *us* that he knew him? And how did he know who he was, that he was the guy who followed *us* home? *We* don't recall ever knowing his name, but perhaps *we* did.

It is another fragmented memory that cannot be concluded, yet a part of *us* thinks that this encounter with him, the "stalking", may have been program bleed-through. Additionally, *we* feel that the outcome—what *we* were told and was sealed into *our* own programming—felt like a threat to *us*, a warning to stay in line. Years later, *we* still have feelings of fear and repulsion toward the man in question, even in memory, and no remorse about what did or did not happen to him. These feelings come from deep inside of *us*. He frightened, repulsed, and enraged someone within *us*. *We* sincerely believe it possible that this man's advances towards *us* got him killed.

The Price of Loyalty for Bloodline Families

We often find *ourselves* wanting to restate the difficulty in *our* deep deprogramming of facing what *we* must face to become empowered enough to live *our* own life without kontrols. This is because such difficulties cannot be overstated and are unthinkable for most people, as they should be. But in the world *we* come from these difficulties are necessities and even considered "elevating" in that they are a way for malevolence to fracture souls. There is nothing "elevating" about any of this. To Benevolent human nature, it is abhorrent, not illuminating.

What occurs in this malevolent world always has purpose and is not random, though often going unnoticed by the uninitiated. Deeds demanded of members serve the purpose of binding their souls to Lucifer, Ahriman, and/or Asuras. Each ceremony or ritual, whether blatantly cruel or masked as a blessed religious rite, carries a dark purpose not only for witting participants, but for the unwitting too, many of which can be found in mainstream religion's houses of worship. Deceit and subversion go hand in hand when the ultimate play is to completely kontrol the human soul.

[It is my contention that the pervasive infiltration of religions, institutions, agencies, organizations, corporations, military, intelligence, governments, charities and more is global and mind bending in its scope.]

We have been told that a human being cannot become fully witting without fracturing the mind and thus the soul, that one's humanity cannot survive the heinous acts demanded by this Network without fracturing, which is why it is employed. *Our* experiences of mind and soul splitting point to the truth of this. Through fracturing the human mind and soul, malevolence can gain kontrol. A truly whole person could not withstand what is required of trauma-based *total mind kontrol* programming. What many among the initiated fail to realize is that the *alien/demon/entity/being* enters through both trauma-based *total mind kontrol* and the more high-tech version of mind kontrol: eMKUltra. Trauma is the key in both. *They are riding the technology into all of us.* What is being designed now is still loaded with trauma and torture, and more so for the black high-tech variety these days. (See under Resources *Project: Soul Catcher, Volume Two: Secrets of Cyber and Cybernetic Warfare Revealed,* and *The Matrix Deciphered* by Robert Duncan for details on covert technology.)

Our haunted mother told *us* of bizarre nightmarish encounters during each of our births: me and my two brothers. During the birth of my eldest brother, the first child, she was told "there was another". With each of our births, this nightmarish "dream" told her how many more were to come, and also how many had been. She was unable to face it fully, nor explain her terrifying memories due, we believe, to her multiplicity that sequesters memories and allows secrets to be kept and witting members and unwitting *tmk* slaves kept functional. Was this first child taken from the womb? Did it ever make it into this world? Did it die during programming? *Our* mother either cannot or will not say.

Our first-born cousin Kelly (Brice Taylor and Cathy O'Brien, MKUltras, both named their daughters "Kelly") on *our* mother's side also died after briefly coming into this world. The hushed mystery around her death occurred while *our* aunt and uncle lived in Puerto Rico with *my* uncle working in the Navy at a top-secret base tracking Russian submarines. During these same years, he reported to me—after I shared some of my strange memories with him in the 1990s—a significant UFO event that occurred on that base back in 1965.

So two other high-level slaves had daughters named Kelly and were programmed in the decade prior to *ours*. Apparently both of their daughters were programmed as well.

Sacrifices occur under varied circumstances: for a ritual in a specific place at a specific time, for a planned gathering, or as a very well planned "accident". It may take place privately in the home or on the world stage for other members to witness. In most cases, a sacrifice on the world stage—individually and *en masse* ritual scale—goes unnoticed time and time again by a slumbering, indoctrinated, mind-kontrolled public. Make no mistake: this is no theory. Hundreds if not thousands of individuals have witnessed it over and over while the uninitiated refuse to face what is hidden in plain sight for one reason or another. The huge conspiracy frightens the uninitiated so deeply that when they get anywhere near it, it is as if they enter a dream state. Knowledge of such evil comes only if one has a truly spiritual awakening, whereas false spiritual awakenings allow the veil to remain in place. For those who have awakened to this terrible truth and actively continue to register it in their lives, it is *seen* with further revelations of truth.

Escape and Retrieval Teams

We arrived in the Taos area in either 2003 or 2004 and spent the better part of five years working in a small gallery and sleeping on the floor when *we* did not have a house to stay in. *We* took various trips *we* recall only fragments of around the West and Southwest and spent much of *our* time in a small village called Arroyo Seco and other small enclaves near it like Arroyo Hondo a handful of miles west. By the time *we* arrived in Utah, *we* had been moving around the United States and working "under the table", trying to hide from them and unable to tell anyone exactly who "they" were.

The following incident occurred in the mid-2000s during *our* stay at a friend's who was the caretaker at a beautiful home out on one of the high mesas between Arroyo Seco and Arroyo Hondo. We covered for her while she was away. The narrow, winding, country road leading to the home was known as Hondo-Seco Road and the views for miles in all directions were spectacular, including a distant view of Taos Ski Valley and the Sangre de Christo Mountains. During *our* first stay there, *we* had an "*alien* abduction" experience.

When you understand *our* programming more deeply, you may understand why *we* often returned to places where frightening events occurred—events that occurred no matter where *we* went while *we* were incapable of consciously breaking *our* programming. This was *our* life. At the time, it did not seem to matter where *we* went nor what *we* did. This mindset is very real while fully programmed, and still occasionally occurs.

Our conscious memory of the abduction incident is brief but vivid, as in *see* and *feel*. In the night, *we* have the sensation of a small gray *alien being* rolling *us* up and off the bed with his hands, but instead of falling towards the floor, *we* ascend. The next morning while sitting with *our* tea—distraught, anxious, exhausted—*our* front alters recalled the moment in an adrenaline-driven flashback. As with many downloads, the parts *we* were shown were just that: parts, fragmented memories in segments, depending on the alter doing the presenting and if there was more than one alter present during the original occurrence, as well as who is willing to come forward with their memories. In this particularly vivid, frightening memory, we believe that more than one alter was presenting.

We are running full out down Hondo-Seco Road at night. The ambient light of the moon in the desert means very good night vision. *We* are naked, barefoot, and running eastbound as fast and hard as *we* can down the narrow blacktop section of winding country road. *We* had just escaped from an underground area that *we* had been taken to that night, traveling underground in alter for two miles before winding up on Hondo-Seco in a dead run. *We* are being stalked by a large "mountain lion" in the sage field to *our* right, a *cat* that will rip *us* apart if it catches *us*. A huge, brilliant conical light shines up from the mountain valley in the distance and widens as it ascends. It is extremely bright and high.

Exiting the valley from within the conical light is a helicopter banking in *our* direction. This alter knows it is coming to retrieve *us*. She also knows that it is 18 miles "as the crow flies" to the Taos Ski Valley and that the helicopter is a dark military helicopter with an armed retrieval team in it. *Our* alter wishes that the *cat* would just get it over with and end this life she can't escape from. She tells *us* that this helicopter did indeed find *us* and return *us* to the facility, an abduction that had everything to do with *our* End-Time programming, parts of *our* human soul and parts of *us*, as did *our* trips to Salt Lake City during these same years. In this encounter, the facility extended all the way to outer Taos, underground.

We believe this event had to do with maintaining *our* general programming and use, due to significant breakdowns occurring by then. "Enhancements" to *our* programming have taken place in several such underground facilities. *Our* trip in 1989 across the United States also involved being taken to underground facilities, particularly in New Mexico. *We* have been in at least four different locations underground and suspect several more, including a facility associated with Sandia Labs in Albuquerque and Los Alamos National Laboratory not far from Espanola (perhaps the same facility?), an incredibly dark town. Though *we* know of a vast underground in Salt Lake City, *we* cannot state with any certainty that *we* have been there. That *we* can *see* in our mind's eye the extensive underground below Salt Lake City radiating out from Temple Square is undeniable.

Our memories of Salt Lake City are of being programmed and used on-task above ground in various buildings, including official Mormon/

LDS as well as others. Programming trips to Salt Lake City in the mid 2000s involved a facility for training and programming, yet all *we* have in conscious memory is walking through an empty concrete room towards an open doorway through which the sun is shining. *We* do not see the outside of this Salt Lake facility, which is stark concrete with low ceilings, no windows or doors, just openings. The outdoor area *we* are heading to is walled in concrete, walls at least 12 feet high designed to keep those inside undetected as well as unable to escape. The outdoor area has the feel of being below ground level, though obviously not very deep. The only things in the room *we* are walking through are a couple of metal folding chairs and two other slaves, both male. Needle marks are on the arm of one of the males, and the other *we* know to be an ex-convict. One is Caucasian, the other African-American; one of them is openly homosexual. This encounter is all about kill programming, as is the certainty that it is in the Salt Lake City area.

Another underground facility was in Florida, despite the water table. *We* know of one other person who claims underground access points in Florida. Another we suspect is Oak Ridge National Laboratory in Tennessee. *We* have been there, yet are uncertain if it was above or below ground. In at least one of these facilities, *we* saw some type of genetics program. Years ago while in alter and led by a man holding *our* left arm, *we* were taken through a room of cages in which were various unnatural creatures, things that ought not to be.

Other underground facilities and access points are in Laughlin, Nevada, Moab, Utah, Joshua Tree National Monument, California, and Denver, Colorado, to name a few. *We see* and *feel* these to be both third-dimensional and beyond third-dimensional access points—Sandia in Albuquerque being third-dimensional, Moab being a portal beyond the third dimension. After all, the multi-dimensionality of much of *our* world cannot be denied, whether one grasps it consciously or not, can it? Including human DNA.

Overshadowing

"Hybrid human" is perhaps the most politically incorrect topic in the deprogramming community, or anywhere for that matter. It can be talked about in theory, even as a real, tangible possibility in some DARPA lab hidden somewhere, but when bringing it into a very real context

251

one-on-one in the here and now, responses are incredulous looks, laughter, or utter silence.

We understand the difficulty, given that there is little context available on *total mind kontrol* programming. For the initiated, however, it is an absolute must to come to terms with "hybridization" in order to understand what many high-level bloodline slaves have been caught in for decades. Overshadowing. Enhancement. Tweaking chromosomes. [And as of 2022, openly brought to the public at large.]

We edit and re-edit this section out of fear of publicly stating things. *Our* intention is to write without censoring, but it has proven to be more challenging than originally expected. It is important to write *our* experiences as *we* remember them and understand them, regardless of how acceptable they are to the uninitiated and initiated alike, given that this book's main purpose is to assist other slaves awakening from their programming who need to know what that looks, sounds, and feels like while it is happening. There is no Hollywood movie glamour here. It is horrific! So *we* are going to add back in what *we* have repeatedly wanted to edit out and by doing so release more of the programming that keeps *us* hidden and silent.

Hollywood takes its ideas from mind kontrol programming and not the other way around, embellishing them to create absurdity to further indoctrinate and mind kontrol an unwitting public. This belongs to the "hidden in plain sight" methodology.

The hybridization—enhancement—we speak of is neither new nor difficult for programmers; it is used for many high-level bloodline *total mind kontrolled* slaves. Programmers have performed this level of hybridization—or overshadowing—at the highest levels for decades with the black tech available in this age, but hybridization itself goes back eons. Programmers must work within the constraints of each civilization. They can manipulate black tech to suit their needs but must also use calculated caution to not destroy civilization by overloading it too quickly.

[Tweaking chromosomes is common practice in the above ground biosciences of today. I can assure you its practice has existed in the black tech for decades, if not longer. Attempting to add in DNA/genetic code of certain animals has also been long practiced. This supplies abilities beyond the human realm alone, as does tweaking chromosomes.]

There are reasons for this particular area of enhancement, specifically regarding *total mind kontrol* programming. It is a fact that hybrid *total mind kontrolled* slavery will directly or indirectly affect the lives of everyone in the future. In other words, mind kontrol is not an issue for only a few. The "ghost in the machine" is here and evolving in evil and unthinkable ways while being presented as something beneficial.

(See *Madness in the Fast Lane* under Resources at the back of the book for an example of *enhanced total mind kontrolled*, whose alters were attempting to follow programming and met with resistance.)

Two must-reads for the uninitiated and initiated alike on the malevolent black tech in use for some time are Tom and Nita Horn's book *Forbidden Gates: How Genetics, Robotics, Artificial Intelligence, Synthetic Biology, Nanotechnology and Human Enhancement Herald the Dawn of Techno-Dimensional Spiritual Warfare* (2011), and *Project: Soul Catcher, Volume Two: Secrets of Cyber and Cybernetic Warfare Revealed* (2010) by Robert Duncan and The Mind Hacking Strategy Group. *Soul Catcher* validates and corroborates the mind tech that programmers, kontrollers, and handlers are using, including specific names, words, and terms for what *we* have memories of. *Forbidden Gates* is well documented and of a spiritual nature, *Soul Catcher* comes from an almost purely scientific, hands-on, insider position. Both are extremely valuable. Even now, more than three years into deep deprogramming, their corroboration has an amazing effect on *our* conscious understanding of *our* programming. (However, needless to say *we* do not agree with the *Soul Catcher* conclusion that program scripts are the *origins* of spiritual programming.)

It has long been *our* contention that these two camps—the spiritual and the scientific—must come together for any of us to have a real chance at freedom. Half the picture isn't enough; the big picture is necessary because of how the malevolent ones utilize disinformation and indoctrination to divide those of us who know only half the story. They are not concerned with the amount of information a person has, only if that information leads to a large enough number of people coming together to actively attain freedom from their methods.

As long as there are differing camps, we remain divided. If we can come together and really *hear* one another, not just listen, we can discover the truths we each have, weed out deception, and build a bigger picture. We need only remember who the real enemy is, though at times discerning *where* that enemy is can be daunting.

We were designed in the early 1960s and consider *ourselves* to be an old model, though with eMKUltra enhancements. During the last year,

253

we had face-to-face contact with one of *our* handlers who is now almost 70 years old but in better shape than most 50 year olds, still in use, and a marksman to be contended with. He is clearly a *total mind kontrolled* slave with multiple personalities.

Think about what is currently underway 70 years after his programming. In addition to *tmk* programming, the level of enhancement currently underway blows the minds of damn near everyone *we* know. Whether or not the most recent "hybrid" models can break free of programming without destroying themselves, *we* cannot say; certainly, ongoing programming attacks do not cease in deprogramming for any of us. Then considering the current extremes of black tech being utilized, and the ease with which programmers can near or far destroy a human being, it begs the question, can anyone totally break free of this? *We* continue to experience attacks.

Few accept how many are currently being designed and programmed, which is unfortunate for all of humanity and leaves slaves alone to ask, *When do we become more them than human?* Think about it. Those who refuse to consider *entities* and DNA enhancement leave it for others to grapple with alone when truly this should be a *human* question.

For those slaves used solely for sex, aging will determine the end of their use, though aging becomes unnaturally slow under programming. High-level bloodline slaves are not used solely for anything. The malevolent programmers *we* know use slaves for a lifetime with that lifetime being extended as long as possible in the interest of the programmers. When you are truly no longer useful, then you will be killed one way or another, quickly or slowly.

[What I have come to understand is that an aging slave can be sold off to others, those further down on the Network "food-chain", to be used in other terrible ways. A still-attractive slave can be used in drug-induced prostitution or further experimentation—experimentation being clearly some of what I have experienced in deprogramming—due to being more expendable now. I found this to be the case with me as I experienced what seems to be more evolved technologies utilized on me, at least for periods of time. These often ranged from two to three months, then that would cease only to find another one start up within the weeks following. I have thus formulated that we get sold off possibly on the Dark Web and may be sold several times over as we are slowly degraded and possibly killed, often inadvertently. In other words, if experimenting on us leads to death, it no longer really matters as information is gained. I have found this ceased for the most part for me and I attribute this to my Spiritual Science (Anthroposophy) path, though I am not invincible by any means. I am reminded on rare occasion by remote technologies that they think they have power, but they do not.]

That many die in youth is also true, and the numbers are sickeningly staggering. Many slaves are designed for death or sacrifice, bless their souls. Yes, they design some slaves to be expendable at an incredibly young age.

In the end all slaves are expendable, no matter how high up they go. These *beings* are not limited to this dimension and do not die when the human host does; hence the use of multi-generational bloodlines.

For *us*, long-term use shifted with time, though killing was still active into *our* forties and stopped then only because of *our* deprogramming. There is no freedom for *us*, only extrication from ongoing use while managing *our* alters and trying to survive that process. [Sovereignty in mind and soul is possible, this I now know beyond any doubt.]

Our concern now is that *we* not be used in a public spectacle as part of a disinformation campaign while appearing to be deprogramming, which is part of the reason *we* have kept a low public profile while attempting to check and re-check everything to the best of *our* ability.

Programming involves methods and *beings* that go beyond the everyday perceptions. Any who think they are not in unknown territory when working within the deceptive world of *total mind kontrol* programming are kidding themselves.

Below is *our* journal entry from April 1, 2011, explaining in depth some of *our* understanding from a strictly personal perspective regarding "hybridization". *We* decided not to remove all of the quotation marks nor attempt to capitalize as is expected in these journal entries. This is how *we* preferred to write, and it is how all of *our* books looked prior to editing.

> "... 'we' suspected it was the 'demons' inhabiting 'us', those 'we' were trying to extricate ('ourselves' from). 'we'...were unable to fully (understand) the reasons behind it due to 'our' own fragile state and youth in 'our' deep deprogramming...(sequestered memories) come into 'our' conscious mind guided by the Benevolence known to 'us' as Unconditional, (Creative) Love... 'we' intentionally, sincerely pray for this (Benevolence to) assist 'us' and guide 'us', daily...(in the first couple of years of "our" deep deprogramming) 'meltdowns' were frequent and debilitating and 'death' would have been easy to 'trigger'..."

as was repeatedly attempted in numerous ways.

> *"...too much too soon could...have (ended "our" life). as 'our' deep depro-*
> *gramming progressed, the lifelong 'knowing' that 'we' are 'hybrid, that 'we'*
> *are, as 'they' (repeatedly) told 'us', 'one of us...' that 'we' are, 'a female, not a*
> *woman...', that 'we' are 'kin' and that 'we' come from, 'the red place...', that*
> *'we' are, 'a star child...',*

No matter who is behind the programming and genetic experiments, contrary to what many Transhumanists want people to believe, this is not desirable. It is of a purely malevolent and evil design and intention, and is currently being done in the blackest of programs and projects.

[And has always intended to be brought to the global populace. This has already begun as it is done in levels and layers of an agenda lasting many, many years.]

During *our* years of programming and use, *we* witnessed aspects of it. For *us* front alters—programmed to be more rational and logical—it is difficult to accept as well, but remains a consistent knowing.

Nephilim, aliens, demons and *angels*—many questions still arise about humanity's origins. The *beings we* have encountered vary. We group them under *demons, aliens, entities, beings* and others, and they are most definitely malevolent, of purely anti-human intentions. *We* base this conclusion on *our* direct experiences with them. *We* do not have Benevolent *alien* experiences; therefore, *we* leave those encounters to someone who sincerely may. *We* do indeed believe that Benevolent life forms exist elsewhere in the universe and the spirit realm—within the third dimension and beyond—but cannot say, in *our* almost 50 years, that *we* have ever personally encountered such manifestations interacting with *us* in any human or humanoid form.

[I can now say that Benevolent beings not only exist, but are indeed available to support and assist humanity, not only on a personal level, but as a whole. I have witnessed things that assisted my survival in this process of deprogramming. I did not visually see beings, but rather had encounters in which I was warned and allowed to escape an impending attempt to harm me. I visually witnessed on one occasion the freezing of all action by two men who came to harm me. I was allowed to escape those sent to do me harm—possibly even take my life—on more than one occasion during deep deprogramming. Additionally, during my recognition of what had taken place on one of those days and why, I experienced a safe, loving presence in the room with me afterwards.]

What *we* have encountered repeatedly is protection by a Force *we* refer to as Benevolent, Unconditional, Creative Love—unchanging, non-dualistic, non-contemplative, pure. It is *our* definitive personal experience that the manifesting human and humanoid forms we have encountered are malevolent deceptions attempting to mime Benevolent presentations for programming purposes.

The majority misunderstands that evil does not always present in a dark, mean, and cruel fashion, and it makes sense that it is much easier to lull someone into submission with false love and pleasurable, carnal feelings. These *beings* present as false gods and false representatives of such gods. True Benevolent, Unconditional, Creative Love is unchanging. The very Force of Creation and Life. It is all around us, always there, waiting to be wholly accepted. The dark ones cannot abide in it. The feeling of Benevolent, Unconditional Love is not like the so-called "good feelings" presented by malevolence. The difference lies in their energy signatures.

It is *our* contention that some of these *do not originate here*, though they have staked a claim as such.

[I refer here to what is known in Anthroposophy as the Asuras, and personally to a being known as Sorat who I believe to be associated with the Asuras.]

We will not try to speak to what else may or may not be out there, dimensionally or otherwise, but will stick to what is based on the experiences of *our* alters and *our* higher Self. *Our* personal interactions with these *beings* can be called *alien* and *demonic*.

We personally know both enhanced and non-enhanced slaves, and *see* others out there who fit each category. Demonology is utilized in *total mind kontrol* programming in both cases because the *demonic entity* runs and handles the alters designed in internal systems by the programmers. Demonic possession can and often does change the appearance of a human who is program-possessed by it. The demonic can and does affect the third dimension, profoundly in some cases.

257

The true physics of this third-dimensional realm is other than most think. If a person could personally witness a switch between alters while the slave was under full programming, one would *see* and *feel* things that would change everything they thought they ever knew to be true. The energy in the space around the occurrence changes powerfully and can be detected by those able to *see* and *feel* it. Most people are just not paying attention, thanks to mass programming and dumbing down.

[I recommend Russ Dizdar's material for more on this. He was a man—now deceased—who personally experienced the switching of alters in mind-controlled slaves and witnessed physical changes that accompanied them.]

Thanks to synthetic biology in use along with the demonic, it is a real cauldron of evil unfolding around us. Occulted tech and esoteric practices combined are being utilized to design *tmk* slaves.

Malevolent ones deceive masterfully, presenting alternatives for those beginning to awaken with such masterful deception that the awakening person often has no idea that they are simply entering another lie designed by the very same malevolent ones. It is the equivalent of walking through a minefield, and the only relief *we* have found is to focus *our* conscious intent on truth and Love while doing the necessary work. Consistently exercising this protection clears *our* mind so *we* can *see* the truth.

Thanks to deprogramming, it is now apparent to *our* conscious front alters that the average person does not share the abilities *we* have developed or experienced throughout *our* life as a programmed MPD slave. *We* have even found Benevolent uses for some of them, while others will remain forever off limits. Many of these "senses" are not exclusive to *tmk* slaves, such as the ability to *see* and discern between Benevolence and malevolence. Far too many people are paying homage to these malevolent ones and don't know they are. This matters and will continue to matter for each of us. Blind good intentions will not stop humanity's enslavement, and the malevolent know this better than anyone.

We have encountered large predatory *cats* like mountain lions. Like the *cats*, the *reptiles we* have encountered also have vertical pupils.

Another *being we* understand as a Nephilim often presents with cocoa-brown skin and pupil-less black eyes. When *we* were 18 years old in Florida (see Book 1, Chapter 3, "18", *Binding Possession*), *we* had a defining "kin union" with an *alien* humanoid with tanned skin, his eyes amber and cat-like (vertical pupils). We were *kin* from "the red place", and his effect on *us* was the most profound to date—a love connection that became such an obsession in *our* conscious front alter state that *we* tried to capture him in numerous drawings and poems. *We* even sculpted parts of *our* body in the gyms over the years to resemble his.

Why is it so easy for humans to perceive *alien* encounters and *alien* abductions as Benevolent? Never once has there been an encounter with an *alien being* during which *we* were asked if *we* agreed to or approved of what was taking place. Never once! This is exactly how *total mind kontrol* malevolent programmers work.

Additionally, *we* have encountered a being hundreds of years old with translucent white-gray skin, whose knowledge is extensive and ancient. The one *we* encountered in the mid-1990s was 700 years old, which means he would have been born around 1295 in Earth linear time.

The *beings, aliens, demons, entities* and others *we* have encountered have presented numerous forms in the earthly dimension and outside of it as well. *We* have been taken outside of this dimension as well as used within it—out of body, as has also often occurred, dissociation and existing in an out of body state having been the norm for *us*, given that it allows for continued programmed use with relative ease. They have utilized *us* to bring *demonic entities* into this dimension through *our* body. (See Book 1, Chapter 11, "The Forties", *Simon*.)

[When one understands the nature of the entities and that they are riding frequencies, it is not a far fetched idea of how they come to enter this realm of existence. Some of them are from this earthly realm, though not necessarily incarnated in physical form, though desiring to be. Others are from outside of it yet wish to gain entry. Think of the state of even the above ground technology these days. Having a look at quantum physics will give an idea, however, even that is very incomplete in its current conscious understanding. I recommend one look into such things as CERN (and there are many other hadron colliders/particle accelerators around the globe), HAARP (many other phased array antennas around the globe as well, including very small ones in 5G phones), Sentient World Simulation (SWS), D-WAVE Computers, Artificial Intelligence, Synthetic Biology, etc.]

They use distinct abilities in *our* various alters as well as certain "senses" in *our* physical being that originate from something other than *our* human biology. *We* have clearly been used outside the body as well on what most people would call a psychic level, though that term does not feel quite correct.

[I believe this is due to the concept that arises in the mind of an individual when one says "psychic". It is not complete in conscious understanding as with so many concepts in this world of ours.]

Some of these abilities will remain forever as potentials, as they are only possible in *our* experience with a full *demonic entity* possession. Suffice to say, *we* will never attempt to find out, as doing so invites malevolent energy. The struggle to remain in a state free of their use has been far too difficult to do anything so foolish as inviting it in. *No slave should ever be asked to perform; if you are asked, watch out for who is asking.*

What these *alien* presences are that allows them to be placed in *us* to run *our* alters and programs is still unexplained, except for concepts found in demonology and Anthroposophy regarding a malevolent presence combined with almost unimaginable esoteric technology.

Our abilities crossed with malevolent *entity* possession under full programming involved human and animal encounters, and even encounters with others like *us*. In the following descriptions, *we* will keep the identities of other involved individuals hidden. It is not *our* place to "out" or endanger anyone. Some may read this and know it is them *we* speak of. To them, *we* would like to say that *we* mean you no harm and only hope that *our* inclusion of any incidents involving you here will only assist you in your pursuit of truth. Whatever the circumstances, *we* only hold Love in *our* heart for you.

Breathing Underwater

This is a continuation of Book 1, Chapter 1, "Shattering a Young Mind: The Early Years", *Breathing Underwater*.

Though *we* have never seen this ability in operation, some of *us* have always known it to be true, given that it is a perceived ability belonging to one of *us*. *Our* front alters had great difficulty with it, due to their more rational programming. *We* only began to speak of it after beginning to trust the two men *we* were working with in deprogramming. Through one of them, *we* eventually found a corroborative witness to this ability—not a scientific explanation, but validation from another who through research has been exposed to the surreal world *we* came from for many years. *Our* reasoning tells *us* that if it is a possibility for *us* under "black" circumstances, it is happening for others like *us*.

Breathing underwater involves both an esoteric and a technological perspective. The long-time ability to design human-*alien* hybrids crossed with malevolent *entities* (*aliens*) creates alters able to breathe water. *We* have more than one memory over the course of many years that shows *us* in alter clearly breathing under water without any gear. In both memories, *we* are training in pools, submerged, and breathing in the water.

[I cannot say to this day that this has not been achieved. Obviously, it sounds incredulous, even to me (at times). And yet, I still intuit that something has been achieved. Knowing how long the infamous "they" have been moving towards it with well-funded science as well as understanding from a first person perspective what the entity influence is that desires to take humanity down the wrong evolutionary path and how this actually is achieved through various individuals over the centuries, I remain both a believer and a skeptic.]

In one memory, *we* are not alone in a very large, deep pool. This memory has a military *feel* to it, as in *we* are training with a military faction in a very kontrolled scientific setting. As already written about in Chapter 1, "Updates," under *She Has a Name*, this ability allowed *us* to be used as a weapon to gain access to locations by covering distance underwater without being seen. In one of *our* memories from *our* adolescence, the water in the pool seems slightly thicker than normal; in another memory from around the same age, it does not and *we* are submerged in a small tank in a white room and being told, *Stop holding your breath*, hearing the words telepathically while viewing two men above *us* looking down at me through inches of water over *our* head.

Finally during *our* late teen, early adult years, the water is again normal and *we* are submerged in a very deep training pool.

First came Marvel comics, then Hollywood films like *X-Men* that for years have been presenting human heroes with exceptional "enhanced" (or non-human) abilities. *We* have been going to them and then downloading to *our* support people how these films profoundly trigger *us* and provide program reinforcements. If this is occurring to *us*, it is occurring to many slaves still under programming around the globe. (See Appendix A, "Enter-Entrainment" as Triggers and Reinforcement.)

Do we really know all there is to know about the possibilities of the world in which we live? Do we grasp all there is to understand about multi-dimensionality? And do we have even the slightest idea where the level of technology is in the black/covert arena? *We* think not. (See Appendix B, The Feasibility of Liquid Breathing in Man, 1969.)

Extra-Ordinary Skill Set

This extra-ordinary skill belongs to at least one of *our* alters known to *us* as *alter 14*. In Book 2, Chapter 1, "Updates", *S&M and the Lawyer*, *we* cite her as one of two possible alters responsible for killing a lawyer with whom *our* alter was engaging in S&M sex. *We* are still not able to state definitively who this alter is, due to this being the first time that *we* encountered this degree of raw sexual rage possibly associated with *alter 14*. That she is powerful and precise and can kill with her hands is not in question. The killing written about above had much more to it within that rage. Another possible, and even likely, candidate is *the kill alter that we pursued within our system*, a nameless kill alter that *we* know very little about though she is clearly a cool, calm killer similar to *alter 14*. *We* repeatedly have to encounter these alters to really come to know them, given that downloads are fragmented, plus they are reluctant to reveal things. Uncertainties abound regarding what *we* know and don't know about *our* alters, especially the deeper ones.

For some time now, *we* have known that *alter 14* has at least once utilized a very particular skill to kill. Some time back, a download revealed her attempt to kill a man in a parking lot at night utilizing this skill. The man was one of two men trying to abduct a woman whose identity *we* did not know but understood to be a *tmk* slave. *Our* alter had met with two men in an office earlier that same day not far from the parking lot to be "instructed" (programmed) regarding the impending abduction. *We* do not know if *our* alter was specifically instructed to kill the man or to stop the abduction using any means necessary. It is very possible it was a training exercise in which *alter 14*'s abilities were being tested and that an expendable man was indeed killed by her during the exercise, as intended. That he tried very hard to survive is quite clear to *us*. (See Book 1, Chapter 4, "Killing", *Alter 14's Right Hand Grip*.)

Due to the actual kill taking place, *we* originally believed that it must have been an on-task. On more than one occasion, *we* recall specifics about kill alters being "instructed" (programmed) before on-task kills. Regardless of it being an exercise or an on-task, the skill of *alter 14* is beyond *our* human front alter strength or ability. *Alter 14* is not completely emotionless, but does not feel very often or deeply, which is part of the reason *we* are avoiding drawing a conclusion about the identity of the alter in the *S&M and the Lawyer* experience.

Alter skills with knives has not shown up before as well. It *feels* like this skill might also belong to *the kill alter that we pursued within our system*—an empty alter capable of things requiring little or no feelings whatsoever. *We* even strongly suspect that she was the one who received training in the facility on the outskirts of Tucson, Arizona, a training involving body disposal, specifically dismemberment.

[This technique of discerning and recording who shows up doing what is very valuable in deprogramming. It can be the deciding factor in ultimately being able to dismantle programming by coming to understand who is who, and who is doing what and who is showing me what, where, and when. The alter's revelations play a vital role in this and my ability to relieve them of their duty, so to speak. This cannot be stressed enough. It is my opinion that most of them want this, to be set free. Even those who have been so called "allied" with the dark side. I find they are ultimately just a part of me and want out, despite their reluctance and often even disruption to that effort.]

"Star Child"

This encounter in the 1990s has all the surreal content that *we* became accustomed to throughout *our* life. It reminds *us* of the *being* that walked into the gallery in which *we* worked in Arroyo Seco, New Mexico in 2008, only weeks before *we* met the two men in Salt Lake City and began *our* deep deprogramming. The only difference is that visually this male looked completely human in the encounter we are about to relay. (See Book 1, Chapter 11, "The Forties", *An Alien Walks into a Gallery*.)

We grew up in the Tampa Bay area in Florida. *Our* programming had begun to break down and *we* had nowhere to go and no one to talk to except kontrollers and handlers sent in to lock down *our* programming, so *we* talked amongst *ourselves*, a habit that basically **reprogrammed** *us* to continue working for them as usual.

On hot summer days, *we* walked miles around *our* town and often 12 to 15 miles into the next town along the Gulf Coast. Being near moving water calmed *us* and was used by them internally within *our* systems to "wash away pain", (*Walls of water* program.) People couldn't understand why *we* walked in the heat and humidity. For *us*, it was a strange combination of driven punishment and staying tough and strong, given that remaining dissociated at all times was an important part of *our* programming. Walking also assisted in escaping the self-mutilation pain *we* experienced as part of *our* programming to forget acts performed on *us* by others. The Gulf Coast provided plenty of moving waterfront and natural beauty, so *we* would walk for miles close to the water as a way of soothing all that consumed *our* mind and body, most of it just out of conscious reach.

On this day *we* were in much internal distress and had pleaded to any goodness that might be out there for an answer to the question of who *we* were, what *we* were, what had been happening to *us* and why. *We* begged for a response and stated with all sincerity that *we* could not make it through another night. Times like these were not uncommon for *us*, particularly when fragments were making their way into *our* conscious mind.

About 20 to 30 minutes later, *we* were sitting on a bench along the seawall at the water's edge among the palm trees along a rather busy, two lane road when *we* glimpsed out of the corner of *our* left eye a man approaching on the winding sidewalk running in front of *us*. Still about 20 feet away, he was looking directly at *us*. No one else was in sight. He had driven over the curb, pulled his car up onto the grass, and parked. Our eyes met when he was all of 10 or 12 feet away. He seemed average in every way, other than his focused stare.

He said, "You are a star child."

Before any thought occurred for *our* front alters, *we* heard someone within reply out loud, "Yes." As soon as the word came out of *our* mouth, *our* front alters asked in *our* head, *Who said that?*

We think he then stood before *us*, but it gets very foggy at this point. An inconsequential and brief conversation took place, his eyes locked onto *ours*. Then the memory again becomes crystal clear, even photographic, as he turned and walked back to his vehicle. *We* fully expected him to just disappear from physical view and so watched and waited for him to do so.

It was so surreal. *We* could *see* and *feel* that he was not of this world running on around *us*, unlike everything else around *us*. He was like *us*. He got in his vehicle, waited for a break in traffic, backed over the curb and onto the road, did a u-turn, and headed back in the direction he had come from. *Our* eyes never left his vehicle.

In *our* programmed consciousness, *we* could not tell exactly who or what he was. Now, of course, *we* ask *ourselves*, was he a handler sent in due to *our* negative state of mind, come to keep *us* functional? This encounter was not the only of its kind, and typical in that *we* were almost always alone and without witnesses, due to *our* isolated state, programmed to be alone most of the time. Events like these reinforced *our* isolation even more.

[*Clearly*, this man was sent in to access another alter to reinforce and shore up what was bothering our "system" of alters. The *eyes-locked* combined with *You are a star child* accessed the appropriate alter so he could stand before me and repair, then this information went back down inside of me when he put that alter away, hence my not being able to "remember" what took place while he stood before me. My begging for assistance in a sort of prayer is what brought him to me. This tactic is classic *modus operandi* for the handlers. Sending someone in with codes to shore things up is on-going and simple. Much of this, of course, now is done in the eMKUltra style, remotely.]

One of *our* fears had been that those around *us* would see that something is very wrong with *our* life. After all, no one believed *us* when *we* tried to talk about it, so *we* hid as much as *we* could. *We* desperately needed help, but the truth *we* told kept that help away. *We* had long realized the people around *us* were not experiencing things in the same way. To *us*, they seemed to be asleep. *We* had been told directly and indirectly for *our* whole life that what *we* were experiencing did not exist, that people would never believe *us* and *we* would be "put away" somewhere, as *we* believe *our* great aunt was; she was gone one day and *we* never really got an explanation about where she went or what happened to her.

Even though the programmers lie, they could not have been more right about this. No one believed *us*. Instead, they felt sorry for *us* in *our* pain and struggle with what little *we* attempted to share. Eventually, *we* learned to not even try to talk about it, just to survive it.

The Ancient Ones

During the mid-1990s in Clearwater, Florida, *we* were having significant program breakdowns, what acquaintances later confided seemed like a nervous breakdown, a convenient mental health diagnosis that allows everyday explanations to cover what is really occurring. At the time, *we* were renting a room from a wonderfully tough, legally blind, psychic older woman whose past had made her into a straight shooter when it came to matters needing to be said. *We* liked her a lot and appreciated her candor; few had the courage her years and experience had given her. *We* did not confide many details of *our* life, but she was still able to validate *our* abductions and paranormal experiences without words. This empowered *us* as much as *we* could be empowered while undergoing heavy access, abuse, and torture (including rape). Most of the time, *we* were so out of *our* body, *our* feet hardly touched the ground—severely dissociated due to terror, yet conscious enough to realize *we* were waking up. The most difficult part was being unable to talk about it because of *our* programming and the limitations of how far into it *we* could go before that glazed, distant look came into people's eyes.

This particular *alien* abduction (astral programming session) occurred in the early morning hours. *Our* bedroom had a private entry and two cinderblock exterior walls. At the onset of the experience, *we* got out of bed in alter, walked through the apartment, exited through the front door, crossed through the screened-in patio, and wound up standing in the small courtyard. This alter was *waiting*. Years later, *i* asked her what she was waiting for and she replied, *I don't know, just waiting*. The rest of this memory is fragmented, but lucid in fragments.

The next visual *we* have is shrubs below to *our* right moving downward, as was *our* building. Next, *we* are standing inside something and looking at a 700-year-old *being* with light skin in the most beautiful robe *we* have ever seen; sparkling with gold and silver threads, and other colors as well. The long shiny robe drew *us* in, remaining in *our* mind even now (due to *our* color programming?) The taffeta-like fabric covered his arms and most of his hands, the bony fingers protruding. The robe's collar stood tall so that only the *being's* head showed, as if *we* can and cannot *see* him. Clearly, *we* were not meant to remember him, and yet *we* do as if out of the corner of *our* eye. He was not a *gray*, of that *we* are certain. Whoever he was, he was powerful and important. This *we* could sense in every way.

Our head began to hurt because the *being* was downloading important information into *our* brain that *we* would understand at a later time. While this was occurring, *we* felt a warm sensation in the palms of both hands, but *we* could not turn to look at *our* hands because *we* were paralyzed. *We* were also aware of small someones on either side of *us*, each holding one of *our* hands.

Next, *we* were coming into *our* bedroom through the east-facing cinderblock wall. This alter was consciously *seeing* what was going on but terrified by it. *Our* horizontal body was coming into the room sideways, *our* left side entering first through the wall. *Our* bed was positioned against the cinderblock wall so they only had to lower *us* into it. I believe this to have been an astral body programming session.

During *our* return through the cinderblock wall, *our* alter saw that *our* arms were on backwards, as if they had been taken off at the shoulder, spun around, and reattached at the deltoid muscle. Telepathically, she screamed to the small *gray being* assisting *our* return, *My arms are on backwards, you can't leave me like this!* By the time *we* were in bed and the covers were up over *us*, the small *gray being* still present at the bedside, *our* alter saw that *our* arms were attached properly and currently on top of the covers. *We* looked at the *being's* big black eyes, then all went blank.

[Nightly astral programming sessions were common with these beings who played a significant role in such. The lucidity of this experience made it seem like something so much more, such as my physical body coming through the cinderblock wall. Do not get me wrong, I would not be surprised in the least if it really had. I have no doubt whatsoever that covert technologies have indeed arrived at *physical teleportation* via work on **quantum teleportation.** There is more personal experience to back up my claim. See *Disappearing* written further on.]

The direct brain download in this experience has occurred before and after. On at least one occasion, *we* remained fully conscious while co-existing with *our* alter as she walked *us* to *our* bed, laid *us* down, and allowed the process to occur fully awake. *We* could *see* and *feel* the information being directly downloaded just as if *we* had been plugged into hardware. *Our* eyes were closed but fluttered due to the downloading and *our* brain began to hurt—a discomfort rather than pain. Afterward, *we* were consciously aware that there was more in *our* head than before the process. It is *felt,* yet the specific content was not available to *me.*

267

Strange Encounters

We can still *see* and *feel* this experience and its onset that occurred in the mid-2000's. *We* had not yet begun deep deprogramming, but *our* alters and their memories had been profoundly coming forward for years. *We* were visiting *our* family in Florida and feeling unwell (due to the usual accessing, use, and download symptoms) and went to the local health food store with our mother. By the cold dairy section, *we* noticed a dark-skinned woman coming in *our* direction. As *we* made brief eye contact, *we* read that she was not going to just pass *us* but did not consciously know that yet. She continued past *us* and *we* did not turn around. However, *we saw* and *felt* her stop and turn to look back at *us*, then decide to approach *us*. *We* still did not turn around but could *see* it all occurring.

[In such a dissociated state this is very possible. I was hurting deeply and this allowed part of me to be on the outside and *visually* witness the woman's action despite my physical stance of having my back to her.]

Hesitant, she came up beside *us* and said gently, "Excuse me, I don't know what you have, but I need some of whatever it is…Would you mind if I just stood here for a moment?" *We* replied that it was okay, so she gingerly grasped *our* hand, looked into *our* eyes, and relaxed. She was obviously perplexed by it all, but seemed to feel better after 20 or 30 seconds. She then thanked *us* and moved on.

Such circumstances are not new, though we never really derive comfort from them, perhaps due to not fully understanding what people get, especially when *we* are feeling unwell. What is at work must be the tremendous energy running through *us* while under full programming with *demonic* energy present. Multiplicity by its very nature has an abundance of energy not found in a single personality. The mind is very much about energy, and many minds in one body means more energy. The intentional separation design of multiplicity is not born out of Benevolence; it is an effect of malevolent efforts.

When it comes to trauma-based, *total mind kontrol* programming, the *entities* running the alters have a palpable energy that often goes unnoticed on a conscious level. This is visible in *our* interactions even today, particularly when what *we* refer to as the *we* part of *us* is stronger in *our* day-to-day life than the *i*.

We do not attribute this solely to malevolence, though it is true that in *our* past malevolence predominated and continues to affect *us* in degrees. Some of this energy may be attributed to *our* strength in Benevolence as well, though at this time *we* are not comfortable discussing that. Some of *our* personalities—the parts of *us* that were split off—seem to have settled back in while others are still working at it, and yet others of *us* appear to have no intentions of doing so. In the latter, *we* cannot deny the direct malevolent influence involved.

This energy is more visible and available to be *seen* and *felt* by those who have developed the ability to do so. To *us*, there is a clear difference between the Benevolent and malevolent aspects of *us*. Just because something "feels good" does not mean it is Benevolence. This is a misconception, *we* assure you. Malevolent ones are very adept at making humans feel good. *We* are well versed in malevolence's deceptive good feelings as perpetrated upon *us*. True Benevolent-based feelings have a very pure, Unconditional quality to them and they are unmistakable (and consciously more so as *we* continue to deprogram). Malevolence has its own signature and a phenomenal capacity for tapping into someone's feel good needs and deceiving them. After all, they designed most feel good phenomena in human society.

[It is possible this too was someone sent in to shore us up again during repercussions of programming and use. However, I truly believe this encounter was not that. Even today, I still recall this lucidly and not only believe this woman was picking up on the vast energy flowing though me, but others did so as well. Similar encounters would occur elsewhere, under different circumstances. They had very different feel to them than the one in the "Star Child" encounter written previously.]

Dimensional Rape

One of the most disturbing examples of this occurred in Arroyo Seco, New Mexico in mid to late 2000. (See Book 1, Chapter 11, "The Forties", *Cain's Bitch, Lily*.) Two different rapes by Cain occurred within days of one another, both crossovers between this dimension and beyond.

What did not make it into Book 1 was a rape in Tucson, Arizona. Between 2005 and 2010, *we* were compelled to drive to Tucson for visits, always camping out on the west side beyond Gates Pass. (Talk about making accessing easy.) *We* also slipped into Saguaro National Monument at the east side of Tucson to spend the night in the open desert air. Not coincidentally, *we* usually went when few people, if any, were there: off season, isolation being their ally. *We* loved and feared it at the same time and yet continued to do it under *our* programming. *Our* time in Tucson was intermittent over many decades because it is a main location for programming and program reinforcement. A facility somewhere on the outskirts of Tucson is used by intelligence agencies for programming *tmk* slaves. *We* have memories of the interior of the facility, but do not know its exact location.

On one of those camping out occasions, *we* came to while being held down by a male *entity* and being energetically raped. The malevolence that held *us* down on the large rock formation took the form of a black silhouette in the shape of a human man, yet it spoke in the plural. One of the things it telepathically said to *us* as it began to rape *us* was, *We know what you want.* In body, *we* were paralyzed while fully conscious in mind and emotion. The sexual energy of the *being* was undeniable, just as they wanted it to be. The experience was degrading and terrifying.

During these "visits" to Tucson outskirts, many strange things occurred, including being buzzed up close and personal by military helicopters in full daytime consciousness. One night, *we* came to in *the bulimic one* alter in the campground restroom while a helicopter hovered so close overhead that the cinderblock restroom shook. On another occasion, a helicopter even broke formation to buzz *us* in daylight. *I* could *feel* that they were fucking with *me*, but could not figure out why. UFO incidents at night were also profound. (For more on *our* earlier training at this Tucson facility, and use, see Book 1, Chapter 8, "More On-Task", *Training*.)

Us, Luna and Cain

This experience is an example of *our* ability to communicate with animals, domestic as well as animals in the wild. *Our* communication with the following domestic animal and her ability to interact and perceive with *us* in both third-dimension and beyond experiences in real time cannot be overemphasized. *We* are no master of such things, but this has always been— spontaneous and random, but repetitive.

We were housesitting in Arroyo Seco in the summer of 2008. Visitations in a *reptile* form by the *being we* call Cain had become commonplace for *our* front alters, many encounters in full waking consciousness, all of which ensured an ongoing struggle with shame and guilt, fear and confusion. (He would access the alters while *our* front alters co-existed consciously.) Sodomy rapes were his favorite, reinforcing a lifelong message that *we* were not only powerless to stop it but owned by Cain per programming. Physical traces were left behind, including three claw marks on *our* back from one sodomizing visit. (See Book 1, Chapter 11, "The Forties", *Cain's Bitch, Lily.*)

It was late at night and *we* were resting on a pullout sofa bed in the large living room with high ceilings. *We* preferred resting there due to the overwhelming sense of entities present in the bedrooms. In the living room, *we* felt less claustrophobic. This also allowed the very sensitive dog Luna to sleep close to *us* under the pullout sofa. She too preferred being close; like *us*, she had many fears and anxieties. *Our* communication was telepathic and our relationship easy and comfortable. *We* received specific responses and clear concepts from Luna who could perceive and experience beyond this dimension occurrences right along with *us*.

On this particular night, Luna experienced and acknowledged Cain's presence, which was extremely significant for *us*, given *our* painful isolation among people. Luna crawled under the sofa once *we* turned out the light. She preferred to be there, as if she felt safer under there. Almost immediately, Cain appeared in his dinosaur-like form in *our* visual field to the left (as usual)—the form he took when he really wanted to punish *us*. Many times, he presented a more human form when he wanted to trigger a certain alter's programming. On this night however, it was to be psychological punishment.

As soon as he appeared in *our* visual field, Luna began a low growl from under the bed. *We* spoke in reassuring tones aloud to Luna to reassure her that he would not harm her, that it was all right, *we* would handle this, etc. Her growling lasted until Cain disappeared from *our* conscious visual field—in other words, once *our* alter *lily* took *our* body and he sodomized *us*. This was rape in every way, but due to *lily*'s programmed participation, *we* experience relentless guilt and shame.

[One of the fascinating aspects of this type of rape is the degree of sensation, including the profound visual presented, even from the perpetrator's perspective. I will not try to explain further, as it would seem pornographic, however, the experiential perspective is from more than

271

one person/being at a time. It is also very up close, rather than at a distance, visually. Explicit comes to mind.]

This Kind of Love

Disappearing

On two occasions, *we* were consciously aware of physically disappearing within the three-dimensional realm. Both events occurred within a decade of each other. (For the first, see Book 1, Chapter 9, "Breakdowns, Reprogramming, Fragments", *Andrew Jackson Plantation*; the second is under Chapter 11, "The Forties", *Another Disappearance*.)

In 1994 or 1995 on the Andrew Jackson Plantation in Tennessee, *our* front alters were aware that everyday humans around *us* could no longer see *us*. *We* were at the end of an unusual trip to Tennessee and North Carolina with *our* mother who was not conscious in her front alters that the trip was an attempt to halt the programming breakdown that had begun. We had flown to Tennessee, rented a car, and for reasons unclear at this time, had then driven back and forth across the state to certain locations, often more than once, for a week or more. Aside from the incident at the Andrew Jackson Plantation and segments of the following hours on the airplane flight back to Florida, *we* have only fragmented memories of the trip.

A series of strange events occurred on the plantation before the actual time of the disappearance. *We* were aware that something was occurring that *our* front alters could not explain. Even *our* mother could see this, but as usual shied away from what frightened her. *We*, on the other hand, lived in a high anxiety state, always attempting to get at what was occurring but unable to do so.

By the time we entered the main house of the plantation on the self-guided tour, *we* were paying attention. *Our* tour headset did not work, so *we* were not wearing one like everyone around *us*. The rooms in the house were sealed off with Plexiglass doors to prevent entry and yet allow a clear view. At the front entry and scattered about, attendants were dressed in period garb to open and close doors and keep an eye on things.

At the onset of what *we* can only refer to as a dimensional shift, *we* were standing still in a line of people behind *our* mother. We were all awaiting entry down a hallway where the bedrooms were. It came on very quickly, so quickly in fact that *we* barely had time to notify *our* mother that *we* had to leave immediately. Energetically, everything began to change around *us*. *We* could *see* that *our* field of vision was closing in as if shrinking on the periphery. All was becoming black, concentrically closing in on *our* field of view. *We* did not consciously know what was occurring and suspected that *we* were going to pass out. What else could it be?

We tapped *our* mother on the shoulder and when she turned around to look at *us*, *we* could only manage to hold *our* finger up and say, "*I* have to go now!" The "okay" look on her face told *us* that she could *see* something that told her not to ask questions and that *we* needed to leave. Briskly, *we* headed toward the front door already opened by a staff member, feeling *we* might not make it as the blackness was closing in so quickly. The female staff member was holding the front door open for *us* when everything changed.

273

It was as though *we* had burst forth from the house into another realm. It was still the same place and still the present, but it was somehow different. *We* felt different, and the *feel* of what was occurring around *us* was different, as though everything had slowed and shifted. Everything looked the same, but energetically it definitely was not—as though *our* vision were crystal clear and sounds were clarified, more intensely brilliant. *We* had somehow slowed down and all was more in focus. *We* were very calm, very aware, and somehow separate and removed from everything around *us*, as though no longer a part of it, only observing from the outside while in a body in it. This may sound like dissociation, but what was occurring was far more than that. *We* had indeed switched conscious states, but the truest part of me was present. Everything around *us* was as it had been, it was just *us* who seemed to have slowed down and shifted into something else.

Once out the front door, *we* turned back to look at the house, trying to figure out what was happening to *us*. As *we* stood looking, people filed by *us* to enter the home. No one was looking at *us*, even though *we* were so close to them. *We* stood looking into the eyes of the passing people, waiting for some acknowledgement, particularly in light of the fact that *we* were looking them directly in the eye. They did not even glance at *us*. *We* decided to add movement and began slowly walking down the path against the flow of people while staring at each person coming along. Not one glance. The nagging feeling that *we* were not visible sank in. *We* stopped and stood there, watching them file past inches from *us*.

We were there in *our* body, of that *we* were certain. It is just that *we* could not be "seen." *We* did not know how but *we* had shifted out of the spacetime they were in. In hindsight, *we* wish *we* had attempted to reach out and touch someone, but *we* did not think like that then. *We* believe that *we* were still very much present but not visible for some reason. Somehow spacetime for *us* changed.

We do not know exactly how long this went on in linear time, but estimate it to have been about 20 to 30 minutes before *we* were "seen" again. *We* went back into the home, down the small hallway to the bedrooms.

[At this point in this event, I looked into one of the bedrooms, the one on my left, and had a visual come into view while doing so. It was of me in a different body with the man of the plantation. I was undressing for him. We were lovers and I was an African American woman. Another

274

"memory" surfaced while gazing into the small shed area outside the back of the house that was too plexiglassed off.]

I exited out the back of the house to meet up with *our* mother about an hour later. Several other "paranormal" events occurred before meeting *our* mother, but most important is the debilitating headache that started within two hours of the disappearance, a headache so unbearable that by the time the airplane landed in Florida, *we* considered calling for a wheel chair to get off the plane. Of course, headaches are common for *us*, due to *our* alters either taking kontrol of *our* mind and body or attempting to do so while experiencing programming and on-task memories. Currently, they often precede and/or follow surfacing memories. In this case, *we* are certain the headache resulted from the event involving disappearing.

[More accurately, this was changing states of consciousness and having access to another realm, temporarily. This was also in part *desired* by my programmers due to the awakened abilities that assisted what they wanted to use me for in certain situations. It also makes perfect sense to me that they may not be able to control such in every instance. They are not gods though they think of themselves as such. I have had many, many spontaneous episodes of psychic and paranormal ability over the years and this makes perfect sense when one considers what has been done over a lifetime and the potential openings within the mind as a result of this.]

The ability to disappear—what most call "paranormal"—was utilized by *our* programmers, kontrollers, and handlers. Today, quantum physics is expanding the idea of "paranormal". Under the right circumstances—such as being under full programming and *entity*-possessed—disappearing can be accomplished by manipulating the natural laws of quantum physics.

From a very early age, *we* were programmed in *our* alters to be able to perform extra-ordinary things to the programmed commands of those who understand such things—not three-dimensional *beings* but *beings* that can enter and extensively affect the third dimension. Once accomplished, it is normal, not "paranormal".

The second experience of *our* front alters occurred in the small artist village of Arroyo Seco, New Mexico in the mid-2000's. An unsolicited

275

acquaintance reported that she had seen us vibrating prior to disappearing from view, after which *we* returned.

We worked and stayed in a small art gallery for four years, coming and going often on a somewhat seasonal basis. Diagonally across the two-lane country road was another gallery whose proprietor *we* were acquainted with—an intelligent, educated, respected member of this small community and successful business owner.

One day, while talking of spiritual matters and her knowledge of Noetic Sciences, she abruptly announced that she had seen *us* sitting very still out in front of the gallery on the bench as *we* often did. She said *we* had been wearing sunglasses and were vibrating, after which *we* disappeared and shortly reappeared in the same exact position. She was certain of what she had seen but could not explain it. *We* had never told her about *us* (nor have *we* since). Due to *our* previous experience in Tennessee a decade earlier, *we* knew it was somehow true.

[Within the targeted individuals community (organized gang-stalking/ directed energy weapons attacks), it is somewhat common knowledge that intruders can be cloaked and appear to be "invisible" while being physically heard and felt in the room. See: "Spectral invisibility cloaking renders objects unseen by shifting the frequencies of light that interact with an object." https://www.techtimes.com/articles/231425/20180630/ new-cloaking-technology-makes-real-life-invisibility-cloaks-possible. htm]

Earth-Shaking

This series of tremors over a period of ten days is also surreal, at least to those who do not experience such things. Due to the vast number of potential witnesses, it also deeply challenged *our* front alters' consciousness. With all *we* have seen, felt, experienced, and been able to do that at times defies the laws of the world around *us*, *we* can only conclude that there must be stages or levels to *seeing* and knowing, and as one passes through those stages, sensitivities are gained. However, if one is designed from the beginning to have those sensitivities and is then programmed by torturous means to further "enhance" those sensitivities, it stands to reason that such people would experience the "paranormal" as normal in that it occurs consistently, frequently, and ongoing.

In March 2008—a month before meeting the two men in Salt Lake City who would assist *our* beginning deep deprogramming—*we* were attending a UFO convention and staying at a hotel in Laughlin, Nevada. *We* had gone to the convention in search of assistance in extricating *ourselves* from the malevolent programming, but attempting to do so under great discretion and caution.

The most profound tremors took place in a room with approximately 100+ people listening intently to Jim Sparks, a self-proclaimed *alien* abductee from Florida who as of 2008 was living in Las Vegas. *We* were sitting a few rows back from the front alongside a new acquaintance who was also a speaker. All of a sudden, *we* began to shake so violently in *our* chair that *we* believed *we* might fall out of it. We looked around the room: everyone was calmly seated, intent upon the speaker, their eyes riveted, enthralled with the presentation.

No one else was looking around, concerned about the source of the violent shaking. *We* asked Joe next to us, "What is that?" He looked perplexed, saying with his look and body language, "What was what?" Several small tremors followed, at which *we* again looked about. No one was the least aware of what *we* could feel.

More than one tremor of great intensity occurred while *we* were in bed in *our* hotel room on subsequent days.

Several days later, two people engaged *us* in conversation and announced that they too had felt the shaking on more than one occasion. One is a publicly, self-proclaimed "hybrid", the other a *tmk* slave who exhibits extensive programmed characteristics as well as alter personalities. *We* read their sincerity, and they were able to describe in detail what *we* felt.

Why the three of us? Was it due to our degree of overshadowing at conception? Did more people feel it? Was it an individualized black tech attack? Was this something perceived due to being *enhanced?* But to that *we* have to ask, *How many anomalies must accumulate before people begin to sincerely consider things not yet considered?*

It was not the first time *we* had experienced such sensations, and it was most definitely not the last time *we* would consciously do so.

3
Living With *Our* Alters and Their Memory Downloads

The very nature of deep deprogramming entails disturbing downloads of *total mind kontrol* programming, plus constant discussion of what is coming into *our* front alters' consciousness as well as the way it is coming forward, making the entire terrible process very exhausting for *us* and for those active in *our* support system. The first year *we* were dealing with so many alters and attempting desperately to manage them, but from then on *we* slowly began concentrating on how to not overload those around *us*.

A significant part of *our* programming was specifically designed to keep *us* under programming, and the amount of programming put in to facilitate this is astounding. It is not the natural inclination of a human soul to live under lies and deception, and it takes much energy to do so—hence the extensive, extreme programming.

The design and use of so many alters is part of the methodology. *Our* front alter system was never supposed to become aware to any significant degree of *our* multiplicity, and especially not to explain its true nature. Despite significant alter bleed-through, *we* in the front were programmed to rationalize to such a degree that it would be absurd to the average person. Yet, to a heavily programmed slave, it is just another normal part of life. *Our* alters had been presenting various things to the rest of *us* off and on for all *our* life, but *we* were still so heavily programmed, kontrolled, and handled that *we* did not have a chance to gain enough conscious time outside of programming to start to put the pieces together. A long list of programs and alters in *us* is specifically designed to deny the truth of *our* situation. *We* still struggle with this, despite all *we* know. It doesn't just stop, though now *we* are able to *see* and *feel* it as it occurs and therefore manage certain aspects.

As the years progressed, so did the program bleed-through—hence *our* ability to recognize truth, if only in fragmented pieces. When *we* began to seriously *see* and *feel* the many parts of *us* and know at different times the various personalities pushing up—often several at a time—it became very empowering to be able to understand that *we* are a "we", an "us", and have been since early childhood. *Our* front alters had always referred to *us* as "i" and "me" per their well-designed and systematically reinforced programming involving trauma, torture, ritual abuse, horrification, and demonology. When *we* were allowed to *see* and *feel* the many of *us*, it became an important and empowering choice to be able to consciously acknowledge the presence of all of *us*—not only for the parts of *us* who were working so hard to break out, but also for the many who had been unacknowledged for the whole of their existence by the rest of *us* and those around *us*. This became a significant part of *our* deep deprogramming, part of *our* healing, and *we* knew this despite others' inability to understand it.

The depth of *our* appreciation for *our* support group is difficult to express in words. If it had not been for their Loving, *we* may not have survived deep deprogramming. It was crucial to *our* deprogramming to allow the various personalities to come forward to show *us* and tell *us* about their lives for both the deprogramming and the healing of all of *us*. Deprogramming is an ongoing process for *us* as a multiple rather than an event.

Another crucial aspect is that the "i" and "we" run more deeply than solely a programmed-in-alter issue. A consciousness belongs to "me", the human essence, and a consciousness belongs to the "we", the other essence born of *entity* design despite *entity* banishment through Benevolent, Unconditional Love and consistent, daily practice. Some of the knowledge belongs to the *alien* manipulators, not to the Benevolent *me*. Intellectually, *we* understand things about humans that *we* cannot *feel* or desire the way humans around *us* do. With the assistance of *our* Higher self, *we* understand that the "i" and "we" will never completely go away, due to those co-existing physically in this body. *We see* it as multi-dimensional.

Though *we* relate to many life stories written by other *tmk* slaves, *we* hold a somewhat different view of the wholeness or integration issue: that of becoming a somewhat integrated multiple who can function reasonably well within the world around *us*. For *us*, the issue of "me" and "we" never goes away, though *I* am more and more becoming comfortable with speaking in the "i" and feeling what that means for *us*, due in part to having neither met nor engaged all of *our* parts, nor do *we* expect to do so, given their numbers. Encountering to integrate each one is not necessary for *our* healing as *we* understand it. *We* used to envy slaves who seemed to have attained this wholeness. Now *we* are grateful for their ability to do so because whoever breaks free by whatever means contributes to others' attempts to do so.

[I have clearly become "I" with the techniques I utilized for deprogramming. This was a combination of understanding through study as well as a daily spiritual practice in initiating myself into the Light side of Christian esoteric practice. This is based in Anthroposophy for me, the Spiritual Science that resonated so deeply with what I had experienced and with many of the beings I encountered. I am a lifetime student now and continue to learn.]

Anatomy of a Meltdown

Another side to this is that some of *our* alters have access to knowledge that *we* in front alter consciousness do not. Besides downloads, *we* have found corroborative evidence in historical records as well as research documents from recent decades. *We* cannot verify others' research, but *we* have ample evidence that some of *our* alters have an extensive knowledge base due to their direct and intimate long-term associations with these malevolent ones.

It is also abundantly clear that alter parts of *me*, once released from the program's hold due to the removal of *entities*, still interact with *me* out of a consciousness associated with a lifetime of programming. Their frame of reference does not change overnight; it is a learning process that can take years. Ultimately, *we* suspect, they will always contain aspects of programming though are not in any way in kontrol of *us*.

First and foremost, this is a profoundly spiritual issue for *me*, not academic. Many of *our* original parts split off long ago are no longer locked into programming; they have been released back to *us* through deep deprogramming and are still *me*, fragments of *me*. *Our* humanness is what allows *us* to deprogram, despite *our* body's confusion.

4
Us and Current Events

Our programmers intended that *we* would be used up and not allowed to walk away or ever be released. Becoming useless—too awake to be re-programmed for continued use—generally means a young death, but *our* death at an early age was bypassed for reprogramming. Still, *we* have had to deal with attempts at both a quick death and a slow death for some time now. Programming inserted long ago, combined with current black tech, can assist a quick death and facilitate a slow death.

Right from the start, slaves are designed for different purposes. Designing then requires much time, effort and a lot of money. *Our* design was well thought out and intended to be lifelong and for a long life, unless irreparable malfunctioning of *our* programming occurred. *We* will address the circumstances of *our* use and draw conclusions about those who used *us*.

As recently as the mid-2000s—*our* early forties—we were in for a programming tune-up as part of an End-Time program related to places and events in and around Salt Lake City. This is only one of several such programs in *us* and pertains to all high-level (meaning slaves whose access is granted to power people) slaves with functioning programming, the operative word being "functioning".

Given that *we* have not consciously encountered all of *our* alters, how could *we* possibly state that *we* no longer have any functioning programming? This is one of the most dangerous presumptions within the deprogramming community. Some alters in *us* are designed to present a whole, integrated, stable person when that is not the case. *We* know: *we* have glimpsed what still shows up from within *us*. This has been one of the most difficult areas to talk about, even within *our* support system. *Our* ability to discern between a part that is the part of *us* that was split off long ago and no longer being handled, and a part that is still run by malevolence, is becoming more honed with each passing day. *Our* ability to *see* and *feel* this in others is also quite adept at times, often despite their own denial.

282

Below are some examples of how *we see* and *feel* the world around *us*, namely current events. What *we* refer to here is truly *seen* and *felt* by *us* as if a part of *us*—not separate, not something else, but a palpable part of *us* in a way that can evoke tremendous emotion due to what *we* are. These things *we see* and *feel* are profound and difficult and often severely affect *our* ability to function in *our* everyday role. Depending on the event and its association to a part or parts of *us*, this experience can last for minutes, hours, days, weeks, or more. The need that *our* part or parts have to understand what is contained in any particular *seeing* and *feeling* can affect the duration of *our* need to present it. Due to the emotional nature of some of the more personal associations of what *we* witness, it may take months for what *we saw* and *felt* to be evidenced to others in a more rational, perceivable way. Sometimes it never is.

Jon Huntsman, Mormon Manchurian Candidate, and The New Jerusalem

On the evening of January 2, 2011, what was shared by a friend in a voice mail triggered several of *us* to download through *jacked*, a conduit alter who allows others within to present information, usually very emotionally. *We* experience such downloads as meltdowns that are emotional and mental releases. Due to the number of alters and the information held by them, managed releases are significant to *our* healing.

Deep deprogramming entails experiencing a barrage of physical reactions as well as emotional responses before, during, and after downloads. Recognizing them makes it possible on a conscious level to *see* and *feel* them while the downloads are happening, not just after the fact. The positive aspect of this process is that some of *us* can observe and often discern what is happening to others of *us* while it is happening. This is one of the benefits of alters co-existing consciously—basically, *our* multiplicity.

The trigger on January 2nd was that Jon Huntsman, Jr., while still Ambassador to China, had made an off-hand remark about running for President.[1] At the voice mail's mention of Huntsman, a rush of adrenaline surged through *us* as fear made its way to the surface. The name Huntsman resonated strongly for someone in *us*, raising her fear and triggering an

1 Huntsman's mother is Karen Haight Huntsman, daughter of LDS Church apostle David B. Haight, and his father is billionaire businessman and philanthropist Jon Huntsman, Sr. of the Huntsman Corporation. Through his father, Huntsman, Jr. is the great-great-great-grandson of early LDS Church leader Parley P. Pratt. – *Wikipedia*

emotionally charged download of information regarding a malevolent event happening at that time in Salt Lake City: information from the alter's past due to events occurring in the now. An alter apparently knew Jon Huntsman, Sr., a prominent member of the LDS Church and father of Huntsman, Jr.

What occurs during such memories can be so intense that the download process needs to be presented to several sources to alleviate the pressure in mind and body experienced from within. The process is numerous presentations of information in several formats. One or more alters needs to release experiences and information pertaining to certain events, including programming not yet dismantled—all of which means it happens in a way that is rarely orderly and neat. What *we* attempt to do is record the information presented as well as relay it to individuals *we* have taken into *our* confidence. *We* are helped in *our* deprogramming process, they are helped with information from an insider.

Huntsman ran deep into the past as well as into designs for the future by the programmers, kontrollers, and handlers—namely End-Time programming. *Our* apparent personal connection to Jon Huntsman, Sr. may have begun in the early 1980s when he was a Mormon/LDS Stake President. *We* were taken to a meeting of LDS presidents numbering a hundred plus—possibly Stake Presidents—and introduced to them as a "new team member" of the "company" by a person many years later we recognized as Thomas Monson, the current LDS Church President. (See Book 1, Chapter 3, "18", *The Mormons*.) (Thomas S. Monson was the 16th President of The Church of The Latter-day Saints from 2008-2018, when he passed away.)

The download regarding Huntsman dealt with the current status of their agenda. Even though there was only a casual mention by Huntsman, Jr. of the possibility of a future run for the United States Presidency, *our* alters heard something quite different. *We* include excerpts from some of the emails *we* wrote during the following days and weeks subsequent to emotional phone downloads of fear placed to trusted friends and researchers. By February, *our* alters were satisfied that they had been heard. (At times, some plead to be heard and understood.) For *us*, the Huntsman experience was a combination of alters needing to be heard and a clear message that *we* knew things about what these events signified—that a great danger was rising—and showed *our* alters where the programmers were in their scheduled End-Time program, which was terrifying for *us*

284

due to *our* own End-Time programming. The Mormons were going for the White House and the name Huntsman was directly related to it. At least one of *our* alters was terrified of these current events due to how evil she perceived him to be. The download was emphatic and emotional. This journal entry is left as it appears in *our* journal.

> *"...'the dark lord is rising", right now, in salt lake city, utah, from under temple square...the 'world of man' has absolutely no idea that it is occurring!"*

She proclaimed that it would not be the Vatican that would birth "the dark lord" or anti-Christ; it would be the Mormon Church while all eyes were elsewhere. Huntsman, Jr. had to be seen for who he was—the heir to Huntsman, Sr. Huntsman, Jr. had been "groomed" (programmed) for this his whole life, and it had everything to do with the rise of "the dark lord" in downtown Salt Lake City. It wasn't about Huntsman, Jr. being "the dark lord" so much as signifying the agenda's progression, which to *us* meant that now *the dark lord was rising. We* could even *see* it coming from under Temple Square.

Some of those around *us* felt strongly that Mitt Romney would be the Mormon U.S. Presidential candidate, not Huntsman, Jr. What *we* did know was that the name Huntsman and the rising darkness were directly related to the Mormons going for the White House, and it was now, and Huntsman would be associated with that administration coup. These events were associated with the End-Time program and terrified *us*, but *we* were unable to state *our* reasons in a rational manner because of *our* alter's emotionally charged delivery.

[This would have implicated that something was initiated as of 2012 when he announced the possibility of a presidential run. Deep State codes are hidden in plain sight, as this one was. I cannot claim to know the specifics of what was initiated, but I know beyond doubt that this announcement was the initiation of it. This is a tactic utilized by the Network to inform Network members. This was regarding End-Times programming, which indeed has come to be triggered in a variety of ways from my perspective.]

Despite this, those in whom *we* confide knew that *our* alters' emotional distress had valid origins, that the emotions associated with these downloads were a part of the process, and had learned not to dismiss *our* words as simply emotional distress. They had seen *our* alter downloads so many times that they knew to listen and wait. More often than not, *we* were on target, at least in part, and with a little time, research would prove the validity. They already knew the relationship between the Mormon/LDS hierarchy and *tmk* programming, so when Jon Huntsman, Jr. left his post as Ambassador to China, followed by actions that unofficially announced his possible run for the United States Presidency, they saw in part what some of *us saw.*

- *(As of July 2011, it is apparent that Mitt Romney is destined to run for the White House in the 2012 election. "Our seeing and feeling" that John Huntsman, Jr.'s association to this runs so deep has not changed, not in the least. That he is somehow directly associated with the dark lord rising in Salt Lake City, currently, has not gone away despite the public appearance of Mitt being the Mormon's man for the White House. The depth of "evil" within the Mormon Church at the highest levels is very closely associated with Jon Huntsman, Sr.)*
- *(As of later July 2011, it appears that Jon Huntsman, Jr. is indeed going into the Presidential run. He is a "shell" that is being used by them with his foremost kontroller and handler being his very powerful, dark father. He is the Manchurian Candidate extraordinaire. This move by them is signaling to us and our programming that "the dark lord is rising in Salt Lake City, now". Mark our words, the Mormon Church in Salt Lake City, Utah is the New Jerusalem for these "evil" ones. These events are clearly triggering some of our programming. Our colláge "The Manchurian Candidates" is about this.)*

[For my Alter, the "New Jerusalem" was an inversion via programming of the genuine New Jerusalem as written in Revelations. Inversions are common in programming.]

- *(On August 12ᵗʰ, 2011, we would discover that there is another film in the* Batman *series planned for release in the summer of 2012. The title alone works as a trigger on us due to our programming. It is titled,* The Dark Knight Rises. *Please refer again to the above quotes from us back in January 2011 regarding Jon Huntsman and the Mormon/LDS plans for the future. Also recall that we have written extensively about one of our End-Time programs involving Batman, Salt Lake City, the Mormon/LDS Church, and that the name Huntsman triggers information regarding such, even bringing on an "abreaction", and we quote, "the dark lord is rising in Salt Lake City". Replace "knight" with "lord" in the next programming film in the Batman series due out the summer 2012, and you have "The Dark Lord Rises". Remember, for us, "Gotham City" is Salt Lake City in this particular programming. Programmers can make "Gotham" be any city U.S.A.! This is not about the Presidency, it is about what this move by them triggers in us and signifies about their progress in attaining their End-Time agenda.)*

The Manchurian Candidate

Raymond Davis, Lahore, Pakistan

We worked hard to keep these skewed bits of truth mixed with untruth at bay the first two years of deep deprogramming while trying desperately to find some semblance of breathing room. By *our* third year, *we* began exploring current events, due mostly to *seeing* and *feeling* that our End-Time programming was still too potentially active and not dismantled to the degree *we* deem necessary.

When the news broke about the US diplomat shooting two men in Pakistan, it struck a profoundly sad cord. *We* read the account of the shooting in the streets of Lahore and wept. The Pakistan tale was one among many such triggers bringing up information from those of *us* adept at *seeing, feeling,* and understanding the motives and operational methods of those *we* had come to know intimately over a lifetime. Externally, they are men and women associated with government, military, intelligence, religion, and corporate organizations; internally, they are the *entities* placed in *us,* many of which ran these men and women in the Network.

It is ironic that what they did to *us* to make *us* more useful could now be used against them through personal recovery and monitoring events in the world. Now, *we* could witness where they are in their plans to subvert the few freedoms that humanity still has. Monitoring events is an emotional process because of the triggers in the media that lead to alter downloads. *Our* downloads can stretch far beyond the scope of information in the initial trigger, given that it is a matter of *seeing* into what is said and what is not with knowledge *we* have because of *our* exposure to these malevolent *entities* for so long and in such an intimate way. In some ways, their knowledge became *our* knowledge, which in turn became a way to assist *our* deep deprogramming as well as researchers seeking to more fully understand what *we* are uncovering.

The events in Lahore were so familiar to some of *us* that it brought tears, but it was also due to the media mixing what would confuse the average observer with what was there to be *seen. Our see* and *feel* regarding the Lahore incident is as a set-up, not an accidental screw-up. Upon hearing audio on the internet of Davis being interrogated by local Pakistani policemen, it was immediately clear that he was a cool, calm intelligence operative and not a "diplomat". This was as much due to how he sounded as to what he said. There was no fear. The eye witness accounts reveal an execution, not a robbery gone wrong. Davis is ex-Special Forces. These guys are military mind-kontrolled. *We* have met some and they have relayed what can only be described as traumatic mind kontrol programming memories.

The entire incident fueled unrest between the United States and Pakistan, another leg of the war agenda in the region as well as to reinforce the false belief that a Global Union (United Nations) backed by a Global

Police Force (United Nations Police) is necessary, which basically already exists. The unity being offered up is anything but. Do the research, follow the decisions and the funds. Look into the shadows beyond what is dished up as news; *see* who is there.

We doubt Davis had all of the details from the start and are sure he figured some of it out shortly after, to his dismay. All slaves get used up, witting and unwitting alike.

Jared Lee Loughner, Tucson, Arizona

On the server's homepage, *we* saw a photo of Jared Lee Loughner with a caption. What lived in *us* for so long leapt out of the computer monitor into *our* entity-programmed mind. His "crazed lone gunmen" attack matched parts of *our* programming. The article that questioned the "lone gunmen" disinformation quickly disappeared. (Unfortunately, *we* did not pay much attention to the source to be able to recover it.)

When a person truly comes to understand how programmed assassins work, details and signs become obvious in news stories *flooding* the public—overwhelming media with stories filled with misinformation, disinformation and dissemination while floating just enough truth to secure belief. With this technique, the viewer or reader can be taken down whatever path the programmers deem appropriate. In this way, the truth is obscured and lost in seas of *flooding*, just as in *our* early deprogramming, *we* were *flooded* in an attempt to overload *us*. It worked repeatedly to slow *our* process and ultimately stop it. In the public realm, it works to obfuscate and confuse until Joe Public gives up and caves to what he is told.

The Loughner case was one of those stories. One must then look not only at the mainstream story put out by the kontrolled media outlets but beyond them, and not only at other articles but at the history of the persons involved. The public is so indoctrinated that they generally do not look beyond the superficial details of "a crazed, lone assassin"—the wet dream of the programmers, kontrollers, and handlers that *we* know.

Jared Lee Loughner is a *total mind kontrolled* slave sent to take lives in Tucson, Arizona and come out of it looking like a crazed, lone gunman on a killing spree with no one of consequence the wiser. To them, he is as disposable as we all are, eventually. *We* have a repetitive history of programming, trauma, and training directly related to the military and CIA in Tucson. Others report the same. The University of Arizona in Tucson

289

is part of the mind kontrol Network, and the Loughner name is very close to a name in *our* bloodline family, a name *we* do not care to share here.

The *modus operandi* of Loughner as a programmed assassin is undeniable for certain of *our* alters with particular programming, and the technique of media flooding worked quite well on the general public in this case.

[Loughner, in my opinion, was an MK assassin sent in and disposed of thereafter through the same methods I have seen related to my own programming. Mine involved stalker evidence provided after the on task, and/or suicide to close it off.]

5
The Mental Health Community

Both the deprogramming and mental health communities are infiltrated by perpetrators of *total mind kontrol* programming and are therefore rife with disinformation, misinformation, and out and out lies. Fortunately, however, good men and women with patience and discernment—two of the most valuable attributes for anyone attempting to deprogram with the assistance of others—can be found there, as well.

We would love to say that once there, the *tmk* slave is home free, but it is quite the opposite. What is well known to *us* first hand—and to others *we* have chosen to discerningly work with—is that the attacks by third-dimensional—and beyond—handlers and kontrollers is real and ongoing once deep deprogramming begins. Programmers, kontrollers, and handlers continue to exert a concerted effort to thwart *our* deep deprogramming. This manifests spiritually and mentally as well as physically from the world around *us*.

Extreme caution should be used when seeking help. In *our* twenties, *we* wound up being reprogrammed instead of breaking free, and *our* use continued for more than two decades after receiving "therapy" for several years. In *our* late forties, almost three years into deep deprogramming, *we* looked for assistance with what *our* downloads often left *us* with and were met with complete denial by a clinical psychologist who did not want to hear what *we* felt *we* needed to talk about because it was counter-productive. He then told *us* to "try meditating more."

The good news is that his shameful behavior allowed *us* to face the very painful feelings still present for many of *us* regarding *our* past reprogramming in the same mental health community. Alters brought forward all that they *felt* regarding not being able to get help back in our twenties and getting handled and brought into line for continued use for two more decades!

Our repeated pleas for help over the years—including self-mutilation and other self-destruct programs—were met with experts' frightened looks, followed by incomplete diagnoses, prescribed anti-depressants, and even lithium that left *us* fully in the malevolent hands of *our* programmers and their minions. *We* shudder to think of how many slaves have been sent away medicated or locked up and destroyed because of the inability of mental health professionals to recognize when a patient may be telling the truth, no matter how outrageous that truth seems to them. How many have died by their own hand or their handler's hand, or like *us*, continued to be used due to the inadequacies of a therapist, psychologist, or psychiatrist?

As with so many people, their humanity has been programmed right out of them, leaving in its place professional arrogance and an inability to *see* beyond the latest contrived DSM. Of course, they too are suffering from the same powerful global programming that afflicts so many, but complacency in this community is inexcusable and nothing short of shameful and criminal due to the ethical commitment of their profession to help those in need—a responsibility that goes beyond that of the average person. Each of us has the right to not know something, but in a profession supposedly committed to helping others, it is their responsibility to check on what is being reported despite personal beliefs! Condescending denial is not an option for mental health, and those who do so should have their licenses revoked.

Of course, the system within which they work is designed and kontrolled by programmers and the education therapists receive is yet another form of programming. In *our* most recent encounter with a psychologist, *we* were strong enough in *our* deprogramming to realize it was he who was telling lies, not *us*; it was he who could not face truth, not *us*. *We* pray that for their sakes no other *tmk* slaves walk through his door, that they be guided elsewhere for genuine help. This psychologist should stick to helping people with weight loss or quitting smoking and not pretend to have answers to questions he himself has never even asked.

Until people realize that this issue demands not just mental understanding but spiritual as well, the mental health community will continue to serve malevolent programmers.

Meet MKUltra Sociopath, Dr. D. Ewen Cameron.

Certainly, one of the most nefarious of the MK-Ultra projects was the "depatterning" research conducted by Scottish-born psychiatrist Dr. D. Ewen cameron. Cameron was not hidden away in a dark closet: he was one of the most esteemed psychiatrists of his time. He headed both the American Psychiatric Association and the World Psychiatry Association. He sat on numerous boards and was a contributing editor to dozens of journals. He also enjoyed a long relationship with US intelligence agencies dating back to World War II, having been brought to Nuremberg by Allen Dulles to help evaluate Nazi war criminals, most notably Rudolf Hess. While in Germany Cameron also lent his hand to the crafting of the nuremberg code on medical research. (https://gangstalkingmindcontrolcults.com/descent-into-hell-mkultras-torture-doctors-scientists-spies-politicians-hall-of-shame-rogues-gallery/)

6
Time Is of the Essence

To the best of *our* recollection, the *time is of the essence* that *we* refer to here began consciously in 2006—a haunting anxiety rumbling just under the surface. *We* are very familiar with anxiety, but this is a specific feeling regarding an impending inevitability just out of conscious reach. It refers to actions that must occur, must happen, and *our* need to *begin* something.

September 2006

In 2006, *we* were still based out of the Taos, New Mexico area. In August of that year, *we* were staying for free in an expensive condominium a friend had offered to *us* for two months in Taos Ski Valley. After sleeping at the art gallery where *we* also worked for some time, the offer was welcome and the scenery magnificent.

However, in the twelve hours before arrival, sleep paralysis had recurred at 3:33 a.m. in a motel in Taos proper with some of *our* programs running inside *our* head. It was terrorizing because of how systematic it always is, and because a presence is always in the room with *us*, sometimes seen, sometimes not.

> *"Sleep paralysis is a state, during waking up or falling asleep, in which a person is aware but unable to move or speak. During an episode, one may hallucinate, which often results in fear. Episodes generally last less than a couple of minutes. It may occur as a single episode or be recurrent."* (https://en.wikipedia.org/wiki/Sleep_paralysis)

[Sleep Paralysis: A state during rest in which I am paralyzed and unable to speak at which time I encounter non-physical (and possible physical) presences allowing programming to take place. I see this being done by beings of another form and possible dimension as well as with black, esoteric technologies. Sleep paralysis is utilized with MKUltra victims and their nighttime accessing and programming. To define this as a purely organic condition is deeply flawed.]

It's About Time

Upon arrival, *we* learned that *we* were one of two off-season residents, which added to *our* fear. From the outset, *we* recognized the front door of the condo two doors down, despite believing *we* had never consciously been to these condominiums before or even knew the owner of the one I would be staying in. They offered their place to a friend of mine who in turn offered it to me. On the way, *we* had even turned onto the wrong road.

From the start, *our* stay was plagued by *malevolent being* encounters and other paranormal activity. Once *we* felt comfortable with the young woman who managed the place, *we* mentioned that it seemed haunted. She fearfully agreed; someone had committed murder there some time ago, the condo dating back to the early 1960s. Given that we were used to *spirits, demons,* and *beings, we* were not necessarily frightened, but *we* had never gotten used to their presence, either.

We were always afraid, but it was *our* programmers, kontrollers, and handlers who really frightened *us*, not necessarily lost *spirits* wandering the halls of the old condominium complex.

But the *alien/demonic* activity quickly became almost unbearable, often beginning in full daylight and announcing the oncoming night's terrorizing. The morning light streaming through the wall of large windows of the spacious living room where *we* slept was always welcome. *We felt* a rush of fear even going down the tight, spiral staircase that led to the dark, dank bedrooms below on the first floor. The only reason *we* went down was for the bathtub to warm us through. Otherwise, the fireplace was upstairs with an endless supply of wood, along with central heating.

Upon awakening one morning during the second week of September, *we* sat up with the words *You are on*, as clear as a bell in *our* head—not only the thought and words, but the *feeling*, with a tinge of fright. *Our* front alters asked, *On how? For what?* but *we* received no answer, at least not right away. Others of *us* were indeed "on" and that is what was so frightening.

The only reason *we* cannot name the exact date is because in March 2008, two weeks prior to meeting with the two men in Salt Lake City who would assist the beginning of *our* deep deprogramming, *we* finally gave in to the ongoing "burn" instructions for the journals *we* had been keeping and burned them. Fortunately, *we* were strong enough to only redact the one *we* were writing in during this particular time in 2006. *We* consciously recall the internal struggle, the painful and constant arguing amongst *ourselves*, particularly right before going to meet the two men in Salt Lake City.

We know this was programming because in deep deprogramming *we* recalled that it was not the first time *we* were instructed to destroy journals and no less than six photo albums filled with pictures of *us* since *our* teens and younger. *We* cannot even express how painful this is; *we* can hardly stand to think of it. Burned into *our* memory are timelines recorded in these journals, timelines that dealt with both programming and on-task use, both location and time lapses, many were from the perspective of those of *us* asking questions about what was and continued to be wrong about *our* life. *We* can still *see* photos of *us* in certain alters clearly in *our* mind. Not only did *we* look different, but others who viewed the alters in the photos could *feel* the difference—even *our* own mother. The programmers and kontrollers won that particular round of destructive instructions, hands down.

The importance of where the *You are on* awakening in September of 2006 fit in the timeline became crystal clear in deep deprogramming. On September 11, 2007 (before deep deprogramming began in 2008), *we* were again turned "on". *We* diligently recorded it in *our* journal in an attempt to figure out what was happening to *us*, despite being too programmed to notice the date at the time and subsequently taking six months to see it. Then in 2008, after beginning deep deprogramming, *we* went back into *our* remaining journals to find an excellent record of these two turned-on experiences, the most recent having occurred on September 11, 2007, and the first occurring the same week of September 11, 2006, though the actual day is one of the missing pages in *our* partially redacted journal.

"9-11-2007" was directly related to *our* programming to Dr. Steven Greer and seeking out the trigger of his face and voice, which led to the *A. True Program*. More on this below. (See Book 2, Chapter 1, "Updates," *A True Program*.)

[The NBC show *My Own Worst Enemy* came out in October 2008, one month after September, and was about triggering End-Time programming in slaves. See Book 1, Chapter 11, "The Forties", *My Own Worst Enemy*.]

September 2007

On a spur of the moment solo trip to Roswell, New Mexico in September 2007—a trip that was a *must* from within—*we* went to the UFO museum on September 11 and played a VHS tape recording of one of Dr. Steven Greer's interviews. *Our* front alters believed this was the first time they had ever seen him, but others of *us* had already contacted at least his face and voice. Six months down the road, *our* front alters began to be able to *see* and *feel* some of what was sequestered in *us* from the many years of abuse, torture, programming, and use. *We* had been programmed to Dr. Greer's face and voice, and after seeing and hearing him that day in 2007, a programmed obsession for at least one of *us*—*Greer's girl*—was triggered that included a devotion to him that knew no bounds, even allowing him to kill *us* if he deemed it necessary. Her programming was total acquiescence to his face, voice, and body.

Within a few of months of that first "encounter", another alter claimed to know him: *alter14*, a kill alter. While *our* internal programming presented to *us* an intimate, sexual, decades-long relationship with Dr. Greer, *alter 14* had a detailed kill program to Dr. Greer she showed to *us* over a period of several weeks during the summer of 2008. It was lucid and filled with the *feelings* of *alter 14*, rather like the *A. True Program* with *she 29ᵗʰ* programmed to Dr. Ott, including an alternating hatred and rage that knew no bounds. Both programs were obsessions with false memories implanted to make *our* alters believe that *we* had ongoing relationships with both of these men when neither of these relationships existed beyond *our* alters' minds, as far as *we* can tell.

This discernment has taken much time to understand, and *we* still doubt it while attributing it to powerful programming and *our* definitive opinion that Greer is also a *tmk* slave. The links between the programs to these men are fragmented, but are clearly and inextricably linked. *We* have yet to fully understand these links.

2008: The "Next Level"

Back in 2006 and 2007, *we* were turned "on" for *time is of the essence* and End Time programming, the *next level* of the agenda. Since then, *we* have dismantled certain subprograms, enough to prevent any End-Time programs from running at all. The *omega* program was to be *our* end as well.

In 2008, more was heaped onto *our time is of the essence* program that is directly associated with the current chaos being created. There is a concerted effort by *our* programmers and their associates to create chaos to further their agenda of kontrol on a global scale. *We* are programmed with at least one End-Time program and suspect more than one. One of *our* alters refers to hers as *omega*, the Greek letter meaning "the end". She presented this *omega* program to *us* in March 2008, about one month before *we* began deep deprogramming. She showed *us* what she called her first on-task kill (her *alpha*) followed by her last programmed on-task kill (her *omega*), the latter not having taken place. (See Book 1, Chapter 4, "Killing", *Alpha and Omega: First and Last Solo*.)

The *omega* segment involved the delivery of something (possibly bio-weapons and/or a bomb, I do not know the content) in the greater

Salt Lake City area. It involved the West Valley City area during the programming session, and may have been part of the future program scenario. It is a fragmented download with lucid fragments directly linked with the Church of the Latter-day Saints, the programming having taken place in the Conference Center across from Temple Square. (The LDS Conference Center was built in 2000, thus *our* programming for the End Time program must have taken place after 2000.) *We* recognize the gray-haired men and women who participated in this memory as "the observers".

Our affiliations with the behind-the-scenes Mormon/LDS Church came about in a most sinister way, the CIA being only one of the groups that intentionally designed and programmed *our* multiplicity. I contend that at the highest levels, the CIA, FBI, and the LDS Church have worked closely together for decades in *total mind kontrol* programming and the use of slaves.

August 2008: Do or Die

As discussed above regarding the *A. True Program*, *she 29th* made herself known to *our* conscious mind in August 2008, four months into *our* deep deprogramming. As with many of *our* alters, it was not her first appearance, but it was her first intentional presentation to *our* conscious front alters.

By August, *we* knew that there had been programming to Dr. A. True Ott, though *we* could not get clear about the extent. Fragments seeped in, loaded with devastating programmed-in fears and destructive emotions. Suicide programming and numerous other self-destruct programs designed to interfere ran day and night. More often than not, *we* encountered 3, 4, and 5 running at once, painfully aware that *loop* programming was running all night with *us* often coming to while it was occurring. (For the amount and variety of deception programming *we* were under, see Book 1, Chapter 14, "Running Interference".)

On August 28-29, 2008, from late night to early morning, *she 29th* visited *us*, though at that time she was unnamed. She announced that someone was going to die and she was coming as a witness to it. She showed *us* that a plan had been hatched for *us* to kill someone, and that one of *our* alters had been present at a meeting that sealed the deal. Only months later would *we* realize that the details of this meeting—the identity of the man *we* met instructing that she was to do the ritual kill—were not revealed. But she did show *us* that the meeting had taken place while *we*

299

were traveling about in a van in a remote campground off-season in the mid-to-late 2000s.

[This would have been the time that the triggering and instructions would have been assured to be in place. The programming for such had already been programmed in by then. In the late 1990s is what I believe.]

It took time for others of *us* to clearly *see* and *feel* what *she 29th* was truly coming forward to do, given that she had been programmed to thwart everything *we* were awakening to and many other things as well. When *she 29th* was fully present with others of *us* and consciously co-existing, *we* named her.

As shared above in *A. True Program*, *she 29th* tried consistently during the months after *our* front alters' initial meeting with Dr. Ott to get *us* to go back to Salt Lake City to "finish it", including manipulating *us* in attempting to acquire a 9mm from a person in the Taos area and using an out-and-out lie to do so. Others of *us* were clearly aware while the lie was being spoken, but *i* could not stop it. *We* were still struggling terribly with *our* programming and alters, particularly *she 29th*.

By October-November, *we* were staying in a house in which the owner (someone entity influenced/accessed) had left a sawed-off shotgun in plain view for *us*. As *we* fought with *our* programming to return to Salt Lake, *we* realized that the sawed-off was meant for *us* if *we* were no longer to be of use. They either wanted *us* functioning or dead, and *our* programming was going haywire, the programs and alters up and running when they were not intentionally triggered to do so. It was one big damn meltdown 24 hours day! From a survival perspective, this is not good for them or *us*. Unfortunately this is how *our* deprogramming occurred.

[This episode in deprogramming was an intense and incredible learning experience. Surviving it allowed much more empowerment in the future in dealing with alters and taking authority.]

What kept *us* from doing so many things that would have hurt or killed others and *ourselves* is impossible to say. When *we* try to get clear on all that was occurring and not occurring, the events are far too numerous to even try to list, even though *we* were diligently recording in *our* journals day after day, hour after hour. *We* prayed constantly, pleaded constantly, not even certain what power *we* called upon, though Benevolence comes to mind. But something was assisting *us*. *We* could not believe in a Benevolent god in some fatherly form, some man on high or his only son sent to save us; it just could not be for *us* at this time. Such is far too like the malevolent ones—dominating male figures who judge if you are worthy—and saying certain names to save *ourselves* far too like malevolent programming.

The one thing *we* did know was that *we* had to save *ourselves*. *We* called and still call upon Benevolent, Unconditional Love—no form, no father, no son, no mother, no god nor goddess—just pure Love, a Love that knows no judgment, nor does it even consider *our* worthiness. It just is, now and always, despite *our* grave shortcomings and indecencies under programming. For *us*, this Love has no name but is connected to *our* soul.

By December of that year, *we* had learned to manage *she 29th*. *We* contacted True Ott and the other man *we* were working with about coming back up to Salt Lake City for a meeting. Both were very agreeable to it, and *our* intent was to tell Dr. Ott about *our* program to him and his family. It was *our* contention that if *we* were programmed for this and did not follow through thanks to deprogramming, they would likely send someone else.

[Another version of this did occur later. My program to Dr. Ott was to *bring him to his knees* by going after his family. His wife was in a terrible car "accident," hit by a man from the Hill AFB in Ogden, Utah. This was no accident and his wife would receive an anonymous letter at their home after her recovery stating such.]

The dates and times that *our* alters present are not random but have a profound significance, often *seen* only after time passes. "29" showed up too coincidentally in other ways. In August 2011, while updating information on our computer regarding *our* End Time programming related to Salt Lake City ("Gotham City") that apparently took place in the LDS Conference Center located there—including its association to *Batman* programming and the planned release in summer 2012 of *The Dark Knight Rises*—*we* switched personalities and experienced a time loss for a few moments. At that time, *we* were pretty certain that *we* had not been losing time. At first, *we* thought a computer glitch had occurred, despite being aware of a sensation of "blinking out" and then "blinking in" shortly after. *Our* computer cursor was now several sentences farther along than *we* remembered. When *we* scrolled back up, *we* found the number 29 in the last sentence *we* recalled typing. Immediately, *we* knew who had typed it. A chill ran up *our* spine: *she 29th*, no question.

Some of *our* alters were still running in programming due to not relinquishing their allegiance to malevolence, but this was *she 29th* and that was not okay. *We* have repeatedly asked *ourselves*, how can *we* ever really be free of programming if *we* never get to consciously meet all the deep dark alters? How deeply can *we* affect them? Deep deprogramming means dismantling *our* programming through a combination of conscious awareness and understanding combined with Benevolent, Unconditional, Creative Love. But if *we* never meet certain alters and are thus unable to dismantle all of their programming, how can *we* say *we* are program-free?

We have encountered other stories in which the victim believes as *we* do—that it is virtually impossible to dismantle it all due to not being able to consciously encounter it all. Those who have shared this opinion of their own programming were used extensively as killers. Is that the reason? According to *our* programmers, *our* alters number over a thousand, fragments and full personalities combined. Not all were programmed, just split off during trauma and torture.

When *she 29th* got on *our* computer, she hit or slammed into *us*. But those few brief seconds (minutes?) were all she could do, thanks to deprogramming. It frightened *me* deeply, and *I* pondered it and her for some time, alert to her possible presence in the weeks following. To date, *I* am unaware of a similar assault.

[The key to my deprogramming: the act of becoming Sovereign. This is not something I can clearly demonstrate to another, but rather an ongoing engagement of my will, mind and spirit with Truth. As I began to gain ground, the empowerment resulted in less and less missing time. In other words, alters were no longer taking control and had been subsumed within. This is my wholeness and my Sovereignty.]

7
Accessing and Triggering: Surveillance and Handlers

Our front alters well understood that kontrolling and handling *us* occurred no matter where *we* went, especially during *our* deep deprogramming years. *We* have been accessed in numerous ways as written of previously here. The following are specific examples of what has been used on *us* while *we* were conscious enough to recognize the accessing as it occurred, both in the two years prior to deep deprogramming and during deep deprogramming.

Taos

These events occurred while in the Taos area of New Mexico, specifically Arroyo Seco and areas to the north toward the Colorado border and south to the Santa Fe area.

Regarding surveillance and handlers in Taos, *we* wish to address one in particular whom *we* will refer to as Richard. What was mentioned in the first three minutes of meeting Richard is eerily similar to what the next significant handler sent in after Richard would say the following year.

We were getting hit with a trigger while staying at a friend's house in Arroyo Seco while they were in Santa Fe. *Our* behavior would only reveal its depth of oddity after following *our* programming and subsequently meeting Richard. *We* were overwhelmed by the urge to go into Taos to try and catch *our* friends there upon their return from Santa Fe, despite the fact that they would be returning to the house within an hour or so. Taos was about 15- 20 miles away and *we* did not have a car, so *we* would have to hitchhike, a process known to take several rides, meaning *we* might miss them entirely. Despite this, grabbing *our* daypack, some of *us* knew that it did not make sense.

We walked down a short dirt road to the narrow paved road and put out *our* thumb. The very first vehicle picked *us* up and took *us* all the way to the crossroads intersection. *We* got out and crossed to the correct side of the road to catch a ride to Taos. No sooner had *we* put out *our* thumb than a large pickup truck pulled over. The man had sunglasses on (as did *we*) and had the look of having been around the block a few times, but we *felt* good about him as well as a very strong and familiar attraction. He was darkly attractive in the way of a hard-living type.

Wired to the Mind

In the first three minutes, *we* realized that some "hooks" had been dropped. As soon as he said he had been in the Army Rangers, *we* immediately recognized it as a hook. Consciously, *we* realized what had just occurred, starting with the trigger at *our* friend's house that led to getting to the roadside where Richard picked *us* up. The question was, did he know? It *felt* like we were both continually looking at one another, trying to *see* through our sunglasses into each other while guarding ourselves and trying to get more information than we gave. Something was pulling at both of *us* so much that he asked if it would be all right if we pulled over and continued talking, stating that if *we* missed *our* friends, he would drive *us* wherever *we* needed to go. *We* agreed, knowing that *we* had a live one and that someone or something, likely related to both our programming, had evidently brought *us* together. Or, could it be Benevolent that we met; to reveal to one or both of us Truths?

At this point in *our* life, *we* were taking a lot of risks to figure out what had been and evidently still was occurring to *us*. Since 2006, *we* had *felt* that *we* would only live a very short time longer if *we* did not find answers, and soon. *Our* death *felt* imminent and it might even be *us* who would do it.

We talked for some time and eventually the conversation ended after *we* saw *our* friends drive by. Richard drove *us* where they were headed.

A few days later, Richard began coming by where *we* worked in Arroyo Seco. *We* answered a lot of his questions, but were not yet ready to tell all. He said that he had had an overwhelming spur-of-the-moment "thought" shortly before picking *us* up on the day we met. He had even been heading in the opposite direction for the 45 minute drive home when he had the thought, *Turn around and go towards Taos one more time.* The timing had been too perfect. In light of how we had been brought together, along with the profound situation that eventually took place between us a short time later, it was obvious to *us* that both he and *we* had been set up by our respective kontrollers, and *i* understood with the intention of our beginning a sexual relationship that would allow mutual handling to take place. This was not the first attempt of this kind of use for *us*, nor the last.

During the many months that Richard and *we* spent time together, *we* struggled with *our* sex alters. To *our* conscious knowledge, *we* did not engage sexually with him. What did occur between us *we* will never forget because it would forever change *our* front alters' consciousness regarding *our* programming. The intimate conversations that took place between us were a direct result of *our* sharing with Richard many of the things that *we* remembered happening to *us*, most of which ninety-nine percent of the people *we* meet could not have handled hearing. Not so with Richard. He took *us* seriously and asked *us* to tell him more.

Then *we* found out why. The morning after the previous day's profound download to him, he told *us* about some of his own memories—the only time *we* saw this tough, six-foot-something ex-Ranger look truly

305

terrified. It is not *our* place to write what he told *us*, but it did indeed confirm *our* suspicions that he had been sent as a handler. It was perfectly clear that he was another victim. Being victimized always precedes being used as a handler.

Location, Location, Location 2

It also became evident that he did not stop at the level of Army Ranger. He had been repeatedly tested to see if he would join Special Forces. He had declined, but from what he told *us* that morning in his kitchen, he did indeed become part of a more clandestine group of soldiers. We know from personal experience how this works. What he shared were profoundly disturbing programming memories involving severe trauma and torture.

They had evidently decided that he was an excellent subject, given that his memories recalled repeated tests for Special Forces.

All in all, what he wound up sharing with *us* told a very different story from the one his everyday life proclaimed. He had been traumatized, tortured, programmed and used, and had fragmented memories of such, some going back to five years old, with nightmare awakenings of torture. *We* know; *we* have many of the same memories. Revealing what *we* did to him shook some of his own memories free from behind the veil of programming, and it scared the hell out of him! Rightfully so. It is a devastating experience when memories bleed through; they can even re-fragment a victim. He told *us* that he had never told another soul in all of his 50 years what he told *us* that morning in his kitchen. That said a lot about his terror, and his shame—things *we* knew plenty about.

Although knowing Richard assisted *our* deprogramming in a roundabout way, *we* had some bizarre moments with him that eventually led to stepping away from any contact with him. It was not that he was more dangerous than *us*, but that *we* recognized our interactions as being dangerous: things that *we* contemplated doing with him could have ultimately killed *us*. Meeting with other victims too early in deep programming can go either way—toward a true deprogramming experience, or mutual handling, as was the explicit intention of his and *our* kontrollers. The stable male benefactor was the early handler prototype sent in on more than one occasion. Other types would appear as *our* ability to deny handlers became apparent.

Salt Lake

In April 2008, after leaving the potential handler's house in the Salt Lake City area after a five-day stay (See Book 2, Chapter 1, "Updates", *A. True Program*), *we* moved into a motel in downtown Salt Lake City where *we* were approached in a threatening manner by two different men, the first there to take *us* away, the second to threaten *us*. Neither man was working on his own. You know it when you look into the eyes of a fully functioning, fully possessed, programmed slave, particularly when you have been one! *We* did not open *our* door at 2 a.m. for the first. For the second, *we* gathered *our* courage and confronted him two days later in the afternoon while one of the men *we* were working with stood nearby as a witness. Often in early deprogramming our fear turned to anger and motivated our courage.

On the long drive back to Taos, a couple on a motorcycle was follow-ing *us* to make sure *we* were indeed returning to Taos. After discovering them, *we* repeatedly tested them and they knew it. Then *we* made direct eye contact with the woman and they stopped following us. In Taos, more frightening surveillance and handling occurred, including *our* intended hiking "mishap" perpetrated by two operators I would thwart on one of the trails in Taos Ski Valley.

[Seven years after an attempt on me, an *execution on the very same trail* would take place. There are many details left out of the various articles written about this. For one, there is no "river" on this trail, yet a shal-low creek that no one in their right mind would go to to "fish", let alone "drown" in. Even an anonymous Search and Rescue member agreed with me that no one goes there to fish. Across the street from the trailhead is a fast flowing downhill creek that many fish in. This chef served the Bush and Clinton presidencies. There is *no question* for me that he was murdered, as were many other Bush and Clinton associates. https://www.taosnews. com/news/former-white-house-chef-found-dead-in-forest-near-taos-ski-valley/article_4e965b66-acee-5963-89cc-104e0ca7d679.html]

However, it was when *we* moved to Moab, Utah that the level and reach of kontrol still taking place became even more frighteningly appar-ent to *our* conscious mind.

Moab

As previously mentioned under *A. True Program*, *we* were programmed to move to Moab, Utah where two handlers were waiting for *us;* one a law enforcement officer, the other a marksman extraordinaire with vali-dated connections to the Kennedy assassination. Neither of these victims exhibit conscious awareness of their own programming. The marksman's programming breakdown was undeniable; the law enforcement officer's recent history prior to *our* arrival fueled what *we* discerned about him. As of this writing, *we* still live in Moab and so choose to give no more details about this person: a threat at his hand has already been amply shown to *us*.

Within a week of *our* arrival in Moab, *we* understood that *we* had been programmed to come to keep *us* programmed enough to still be of use.

This is reprogramming in its most basic: handlers are sent in to access *us* and reinforce programming by replacing conscious awareness with alters and their programming. If *entities* still kontrol *us* to any significant degree, *we* will then follow programming and most likely not even be aware of it, with the exception of missing time.

Deprogramming is a very individual person-to-person thing—how it will or will not work, successes and failures, etc. There is no across-the-board solution. There are, however, consistent programming similarities amongst slaves, depending on the years in which they were originally targeted for programming.

[I would contradict this statement about years of original targeting determining programming specifics. Though there is a baseline one could follow, I have come to learn with remote technologies pretty much anyone, young or old, can be brought into modern versions of programming and use, despite their original year of entry.]

We have met deprogramming slaves who are unaware of still being accessed. This can be problematic for them and *us*.

Our choices have led to a continuing life over death path. Some choices have involved strong spiritual intentions regarding disconnecting from handlers. It took time and a profound awareness to truly break the hold they had over *us*.

In less than two months since beginning to exercise *our* spiritual discernment and therefore disconnect, the Kennedy marksman announced he was leaving town. When he told *us* where he was going, it was apparent he was being brought "home" for what I imagined was death; the information in him was not to be allowed to come out and he was clearly breaking down. Though *we* are still triggered when *we* see the law enforcement officer around town, *we* have spiritually broken any hold he had over *us*. It is very much an internal spiritual disconnect first, rather than an external one. Complacency is never allowed, no matter how dismantled things *feel*. This is key for *us*.

Phone Calls

Phone calls were systematically used throughout *our* programmed life, but in the first year of deep deprogramming, *we* became conscious of daily

309

phone calls consisting of a combination of recorded messages with hidden-in-plain-sight meanings, tones, music and songs, blank calls, even caller ID-triggering displays (clearly mostly automated). Calls also came from handlers, witting and unwitting alike, the latter being programmed multiples like *us*. Even though certain alters were conscious of what was occurring, some alters reacted to the triggers emotionally. Co-existing consciously with still-programmed alters meant they would answer calls with caller IDs clearly placed by kontrollers and handlers that would occasionally result in full abreactions. (*We* are still receiving access calls at *our* house sits on their landlines.)

Recorded Messages

One of the most profound calls came one morning at the art gallery in which *we* worked and for a time lived. *Our* kontrollers obviously knew this, given all the accessing triggers that made their way to *us* there. A recorded message came from "The Omega Group" out of Salt Lake City. *We* immediately recognized Omega as well as the area code, and that this was indeed an access call. The two pieces of information had already begun the triggering process and *we* had not even picked up the receiver. *Omega* is part of *our* programmed-in language directly associated to one of *our* End Time programs and *our* demise. This particular End Time program is also directly associated to Salt Lake City and the Mormon hierarchy at the highest levels. The area code for Salt Lake City is 801; the call came during the summer of 2008, when *we* were still quite young in *our* deep deprogramming—vulnerable but also courageous and determined to break *our* programming.

At this point, *we* often took great risks and this was one of those moments: *we* answered the call. When alters that *we* do not have a managing role over get triggered, there is no telling what programs will run or what events will be set in motion. In this case, a recording told *us* this is "your last chance", that if *we* were "in", *we* were to press a certain number; if *we* were not, *we* were to press a different number. *We* heard loud and clear that if *we* chose to stay in the Network, *we* would live; if *we* chose to continue deprogramming, *we* would die. "Last chance," it said.

Before hanging up, *we* had a full abreaction. During the abreaction, *our* mind re-fragmented. It does not occur any longer, but dissociation can and does.

310

We clearly understood the phone call's effect on *us* in the hours and days following it. *We* do not recommend taking such risks, but it was and is in *our* nature to do so. These days, *we* are becoming gentler with *ourselves*, having learned how to protect *ourselves*. *We* wrote about the recorded message and spoke about it and became very clear about what this call was and from whom. *We* also gained insight into how *our* programming was related to it. At that time, *our* deprogramming was pretty much *us* against "them", but *we* also had someone *we* were learning to trust who listened to everything *we* needed to share, which allowed *us* to make sense of it all for conscious front alter recognition and being able to emotionally and often extensively and repeatedly talk it out. He helped *us* to learn to record all of what was occurring rather than trying to make sense of it at the time, allowing for it to be recorded uncensored and looked at later when fewer triggers were occurring. (This is what *we* have done while writing *Our Life Beyond MKUltra*, too.) With time, *we* formed an unmistakable picture and were able to *see* patterns that eventually validated a lifetime of experiences. This became crucial to *our* deprogramming and healing, and is in fact what *our* deep deprogramming is.

Tones

Tones were also played over the phone with extensive regularity. *We* recorded the set of high-pitched, rapidly played tones being sent to *us* daily at the art gallery, capturing them on *our* micro-cassette recorder. (The answering machine would not go completely mute, only low volume.) *We* tried to not answer, but then it would go to the answering machine and *we* would hear it as it recorded. *We* tried to answer, then quickly hit the hang up button so *we* would not have to hear it. Sometimes that worked, sometimes not. They had it set to go off immediately upon answering, with the tones firing off rapidly. Due to it being a place of business, *we* could not turn it off entirely.

As with so many *tmk* slaves, *we* had nowhere else to go. It is very unfortunate that most slaves have to start deprogramming while still being heavily accessed by their kontrollers and handlers. This is the awful design by the programmers that slaves try to extricate themselves from. People have no concept of how extensive and pervasive this vast global Network is, or the power they wield. People like *us* are made out to be paranoid and delusional at best.

Blank Calls

As for *blank calls*, for a programmed, mind kontrolled slave, they are much more than an annoyance. It is not only the call itself, but several other factors that come along with the call, one being their frequency. For the programmed, these calls set off fear regardless of who is on the other end, or even the caller I.D. display accompanying the calls. Even the time the call arrives has an impact. With extensive numeric programming, the time of the call or time of its termination becomes a series of numbers that work as a pre-programmed trigger for certain alters and their programs.

As with so many aspects of *tmk* programming, blank calls in particular have the added effect of how the uninitiated do not believe the slave when they attempt to report these calls as accessing calls, another tool in the arsenal of "doubt and crazy" programming.

In July 2011, while staying at someone's house in Moab for a month, *we* received upwards of 25 blank calls each day that began the day she left town. The ringer would not go completely off. *We* turned down the volume on the answer machine so *we* would not hear messages if they came in, but the ringer still rang—hence the hounding blank call effect. *We* see a handler sitting silently at the other end. This is psychological warfare, and they are masterful at it.

[This is actually Artificial Intelligence systems running with no effort on the programmer's part.]

Music and Songs

Prerecorded songs were played over the phone to trigger *our* extensive music programming (1) to activate alters and their programs for different uses, such as sex programming and kill programming; (2) to activate the original baseline programs and reinforce programs. Prerecorded songs also trigger abreactions in deprogramming.

In October 2010, through the cooperation of certain alters and their knowledge of its affiliation with a certain End Time program, *we* consciously understood the intended use of the song "Life in a Northern Town" by Dream Academy that originated from a deprogramming Mormon/LDS *tmk* slave's phone.

[I believe this was a hack utilizing the ex-Mormon MKUltra victim's phone number to divide us during deprogramming encounters. Divide and conquer/isolation efforts are classic interference programs in MKUltra methodology.]

[To repeat, individuals in the hierarchy of the Mormon/LDS Church were directly involved in the programming and use of bloodline, ritually abused, trauma-based, *total mind kontrolled* slaves. The Mormon/LDS Church is also directly involved with national and international intelligence agencies, as well as countless other organizations and institutions—corporate, political, and religious—in a concerted effort to gain global domination and reign with Luciferian/Ahrimanic world kontrol.]

Family

One of the most difficult ties that *we* had to break to be able to gain any degree of freedom from *our* programming was ties to *our* family of birth. Phone calls filled with program language and triggers came from family members with increased frequency during *our* first few months of deep deprogramming. At times, they used damaging program words delivered in kind, loving language, and techniques that not only triggered out certain alters but also attempted to call *us* back "home", a place *we* can never go. They were clearly doing this unwittingly. Finally in December 2008, *we* announced with Love that *we* would be out of contact for some time, knowing that most likely *we* would never be in contact again. At times, it is still quite painful, but *we* are clear why it has to be done.

When you understand how it works within a family of total mind kontrol *victims*, it is very dangerous to think you are wiser than them and can handle it. If we had done that, *we* are certain *our* demise would have been imminent, or at the very least, *we* would still be working for *our* programmers, kontrollers, and handlers. *We* have repeatedly seen *tmk* slaves kept in programming by this very technique. The malevolent ones use love of family to keep slaves useful and in full programming. The only way to break programming is to view the situation from the highest possible viewpoint with Benevolent, Unconditional Love for all concerned. *We do not help our family in any way whatsoever by staying under programming.*

313

Mailed Messages

The postal system was also used to trigger *us*.

During *our* mid-thirties, when *our* programming was showing significant signs of deterioration, *we* found that even the breakdown of programming occurs according to a certain programmed schedule per programmer design—not necessarily in a timed fashion so much as in a programmed sequence. For example, after incest memories surfaced in *our* early twenties, the next very difficult program bleed-through were *alien* abduction memories. Before, during, and after these two sequences, a variety of fragmented memories moved into *our* conscious mind, including incest, sexual abuse and rape, interactions with otherworldly *beings*, military abductions, awareness of unusual abilities, death, and murder, as well as *our* other parts presenting to *our* front alter consciousness in a variety of ways.

An Opened Letter

This particular episode occurred during *our* attempts to get help with *our* *alien* abductions, the irony being that the people who wound up assisting *us* with *our* abduction memories turned out to be re-programmers sent in to lock down *our* programming and keep *us* functioning as a *tmk* slave. It set *our* efforts to get real assistance back more than a decade and allowed *our* programmers, kontrollers, and handlers continued access and use.

According to the UFO researcher/hypnotherapist who eventually introduced *us* to the woman who would reprogram *us* (I cannot say if this hypnotherapist was or was not aware of the woman's status, though I suspect he really did not know what he was involved with in his work), *our* initial correspondence with him regarding working together arrived to him opened. He came recommended by a foundation created and run by Budd Hopkins, well known in the UFO community as an artist, author, and alleged therapist to *alien* abductees (The Intruder Foundation).

The letter detailed some of *our* concerns about memories bleeding into *our* conscious mind. The researcher/hypnotherapist held back from showing *us* this letter until after we had done a few sessions together. When he showed it to *us* and said that it had arrived opened at one end, a rush of fear surged through *us* and *we* heard in *our* head, *Get out now, you haven't done anything yet!*

He saw *our* look of fear and said he would continue to work with *me* if *i* wanted, yet he would understand if *i* did not wish to continue, that it was *my* call. *We* knew at that moment that *we* were being watched, that they were monitoring *our* every move, but who were they? They were so close to *our* conscious mind that *we* could *see* and *feel* them, but not name them. The fear *we* felt was very real, very palpable. At this time, very early on, *i* really did not know what was happening to *me*.

In his office that day, anger began to replace the fear that was a mask for the rage lurking underneath from a lifetime of abuse, torture, violation, horrification, and use. *We* told him, "Fuck it, *i* don't want to stop!"

It is difficult to describe how it feels when there is more than one of *us* participating in *our* consciousness at one time, but some of *us* knew who and what was watching and waiting, and some of *us* did not. Those who did not began asking those who did, which was a good thing. What *we* did know was that whoever the watchers were, they had the ability to open a letter after it had entered the postal system, but at this stage, *we* could not consciously get a grip on why anyone would do it. *We* in front alter consciousness repeatedly asked *ourselves* who wanted to know what *we* were writing about to this seemingly unknown UFO researcher?

The Postcard

In August 2008, just days before *our* alter *she 29th* announced herself to *our* conscious front alters and presented things to *us* while *we* co-existed with her, a postcard arrived at *our* general delivery address in Arroyo Seco. Within minutes of receiving and reading the postcard, *i* realized that I did not know "Bob".

[A palindrome: a word that "runs back" on itself. A word that is the same backwards or forwards. This is poignant to MKUltra programming.]

It was loaded with triggers. In fact, the postcard was intended to trigger *she 29th* to return to Salt Lake City and finish the program thwarted four months prior: the *A. True Program* followed by *our eat a bullet* suicide program. (There is a colláge with this postcard in it regarding this program and can be found at the end of *A. True Program* in Book 2, Chapter 1, "Updates".)

The Outfit

In September 2008, *we* received an outfit addressed to *us* at the art gallery where *we* worked and lived, despite having no address other than "general delivery" at the post office. *We* opened the package and found a black and white outfit, a top with pants, from New York. *We* did not own a camera at that time and so *i* painstakingly drew the outfit in *our* journal after leaving a voice mail for one of the men *we* were working with regarding this strange package. *We* were keenly aware that the outfit was a trigger and took time to draw the detailed pattern on the top.

Codes We Lived By

In response to *our* message, the man called back that evening. We discussed the outfit and decided to get rid of it immediately! A handler had obviously sent it with some nasty mojo attached. It is not uncommon for the Network to do such things, such as spell-casting, so don't kid yourself, it has an effect. *We* took a pair of sharp scissors to it and shredded it, finally painfully realizing that *we* had been gone for a couple of hours because another from within had taken over. When time loss due to alter switching occurs, *our* sense of time and surroundings have a surreal nature. Often, *we* sense it coming on and as in this case *we* know afterward that it has occurred. It gets more bizarre.

Within nine days of receiving the outfit, the program reinforcement continued and what occurred was difficult for *our* front alters to take in. It was Sunday and *we* were working at the gallery when the thought came to *us* to drive 20 miles into Taos proper after work and see a movie. *We* had not been to the cinema for some time, due to realizing that *we* had been heavily programmed with and to certain actors and films over the years. *We* called the cinema. *We* had never heard of *Body of Lies*, but it was playing and *we* went to see it.

It turns out it was set in the Middle East and about CIA espionage and murder in the name of national security—and loaded with triggers and program reinforcement. In true Hollywood style, the storyline included a romance between the star CIA agent and an Iranian woman. Part way through the film, the two of them are sitting at a small table at an outdoor café drinking tea, which was when a profound message was sent to *us*: the scarf the Iranian woman was wearing on her head was of the exact same material and design as the top in the outfit *we* had received in the mail just over a week before! Never had *we* seen that material and design prior nor since.

A rush of adrenaline and fear overcame *us*. At that very moment, *we* heard in *our* head, *We know everything you do, everywhere you go, even before you do. You can never get away. We* looked around the darkened theatre at the dozen or so faces present but could not see well enough to determine if someone there was doing this. Then *we* remembered that they don't have to be physically present to do this shit. *We* crouched down in *our* seat and began to cry.

8
Entities

Entities and *demons* have deeply affected *our* programming and deprogramming. Not only have they played a dominant role in *our* abuse and use over the years, but they continue to play a very significant role in affecting *our* deep deprogramming.

Many who read this will have one or more reasons for not accepting the supernatural, either due to personal intellectual beliefs or spiritual ones that denounce the reality of evil. But the reality of evil as part of humanity's ancient and ongoing history cannot continue to be denied. Malevolence is real and not sourced in the bad intentions of men and women.

Our use of the words *entities* and *demons* may or may not be consistent with official definitions, but *our* intention is to present malevolence in the various forms *we* have systematically, consistently, and frequently encountered throughout *our* life, including the consciousness of *our* front alters. Both demonology and "black tech" are used in *total mind kontrol* programming, but the malevolent forces behind *our tmk* programming are very real and have for eons kontrolled the men and women through whom they work. *We* have learned this through being terrorized at the hands of *our* programmers, kontrollers, and handlers, and through *our* ability to significantly affect these malevolent ones by intensely and repeatedly focusing on Creation rather than destruction.

There is no mind kontrol programming without this malevolence. Man is not inherently evil, and when one comes to understand the longevity of evil and its perpetration of malevolent deeds, it is no longer about certain men gone bad. It has gone on beyond a particular generation and through centuries of recorded history. It is the legacy of bloodlines designed by this malevolence, passing it from generation to generation, systematically, uniformly, without a break in the programming. Who man was before this interference is the question and where the Benevolent human soul and spirit comes in.

Within each civilization, black tech is introduced to the human element for the intended goal of *total kontrol* without total destruction. On an individual level, *we* were to be a *total mind kontrolled* and enhanced slave for the life of this body with the intention of retaining kontrol of *my* soul after the body gives out. *Bloodline.* They feed off of *my* energy while utilizing extreme fear. They continue to attempt to thwart *my* grasp of *my* own Benevolent soul as a Creation of Benevolence. *I* will continue to struggle with what is within and without, yet *i* have an ongoing consciously developing relationship with this magnificent Creative Force. The world we all live in is co-designed and continually influenced by these malevolent ones.

Internal

By 2011, *we* have realized that what has been done to *us* has a lasting effect. This does not mean that they can use *us* as they did previously. *We* will not consciously meet certain alters nor be able to consciously come to a full intellectual understanding of their programming. Still, *we* manage the parts designed to remain allied to the malevolent ones through diligent, daily, active conscious connection with Benevolent, Unconditional Love. This is due to *our* higher Self being present and allowing ongoing revelations of what was intended by those who may still be susceptible to programming.

Despite no longer being under full programming, the rule that applies elsewhere also applies to *us*: that even with this Love, it is very difficult to fight an enemy one cannot *see*, let alone name. There is still so much *we* do not *see* or understand about *our* programming and certain alters. That *we* can still be accessed by malevolent *entities* by triggering programming in certain alters is due to the extreme nature of what was systematically done to *us* and maintained for so long.

Few do not want to be "saved" from some aspect of life, be it spiritual, physical, financial, or relational. *I* have learned through experience that *i* must engage Benevolent Love, *my* will and *my* mind to save *us*. This combination has a profound and lasting direct effect on the access to internal programming that can and does still occur. *I* am an intelligent, self-aware, strong woman, and *my* willingness to write about the truth regarding the spiritual aspect of *total mind kontrol* programming should not tarnish that. Often, this spiritual aspect—especially sincere, intelligent discussion about

319

entities and their relationship to programming—is denied from the public deprogramming sector.

Several Christians *I* have chosen to work with do recognize the existence of *entities*. We may disagree on matters, but we do agree on the malevolent foundation of *total mind kontrol* programming. *I* am in the daily process of active, consistent involvement with Benevolent, Unconditional Love combined with conscious and absolutely necessary healthy choices to bring a degree of release from *total mind kontrol* programming.

In more than three years of deep deprogramming, the hope that the evil will somehow leave *us* altogether is only wishful thinking. Meaning, the deprogramming process is ongoing, and quite frankly, needs to occur as such within the general populace as well. This is not a commentary on anyone else's recovery and should not be mistaken for such. It is the expression of *our* experiences thus far as a deprogramming slave who even allowed a Christian exorcism at one point.

The World of Interiors

External

The numerous attacks from without and varied means used are too numerous to list. These *entities* literally "ride the tech" into people. Combine the spiritual with the scientific and you will see how it works. The majority chooses not to look. *Our Life Beyond MKUltra* is written for those who genuinely wish to understand.

Regarding external attacks, *we* experience the malevolent *beings* and what *we* believe are weapon systems. (Again, *we* recommend *Project: Soul Catcher, Volume Two: Secrets of Cyber and Cybernetic Warfare Revealed,* 2010, as well as *The Matrix Deciphered*, 2010, by Robert Duncan.)

Sometimes it is difficult to specify the source of symptoms, but *we* are getting better at it. For example, the temperature changes in or on *our* body, as if someone threw a switch and a specific area is hit, combined with an instant headache. Or instantaneous extreme confusion that undermines *our* focus while downloading—again, as if a switch were thrown. Or not a simple case of memory loss but a heavy "fog" that *we feel* coming on from outside of *us*, adding to the internal "fog" that *we* can *see* and *feel* descending inside *our* head, programmed in years ago. Even some of the despair and loss of hope that *we* experience—again, like a switch being thrown—is due to black technology overshadowed by malevolence.

After a while, one becomes able to *see* and *feel* these attacks when they occur. *Our* focused, intention-filled reliance upon Benevolent Love has been able to assist in alleviating some attacks, internal and external, some of the time, the instantaneous effect being a progressive relief over the course of an hour or more. Often, *we* convince *ourselves* to hold on, let it pass because it will, and not to give in to the programming being triggered, whether sourced internally or externally. *We* still have times of thinking *we* are not going to make it. *Our* positive practices must be done consistently, which for *us* means throughout the course of the day and night.

[Much more could be said regarding the current technologies in use. Again I refer those who desire to know—and you most certainly ought to due to targeting taking place globally—the resources section of this book, particularly Dr. Robert Duncan's and Elana Freeland's work.]

9
Tools for the Recovery of Our Splits

The following tools used in *our* deep deprogramming are now second nature, but *we* assure you it did not start out that way. Early on, everything malevolent in and around *us* fought against *our* doing these things, but the most Benevolent part of *us* won out and *we* kept going, kept doing what needed to be done despite the programming attempting to stop *us*. An all-out war was going on inside and outside of *us*, and *we* give thanks every day for *our* strength and support system. *We* will do whatever it takes to stay as conscious as *we* can in order to avoid such kontrol over *us* ever again, and do it always with the highest good for *us* and everyone else in *our* heart and mind.

The first time around, *we* were far too young to have a choice. Now *we* have one. However, complete deprogramming seems impossible without *our* spiritually-evolved programmers present to assist.

[I have come to find out that a Sovereign state can indeed be reached with the proper process and discipline. I often tell other victims that they have to be willing to give up everything if need be. This is indeed a tall order, yet these circumstances demand it. What was required of me was to allow all I believed to be true fall away, as if the very foundation under me shattered leaving me completely ungrounded. This is how it feels, and quite frankly how it is for a time, though I can state emphatically that what has come into my life as a result of that courage, strength and commitment was more than I knew to even imagine. Struggling in the world around me is still often the case, but that is the case for any and every one I know, at least at times. *No one owns me.*]

Trusting Someone

Trust was the most difficult but crucial step in the beginning. *Our* higher Self kept *us* alive for years and availed *us* of the strength to break certain programs enough so *we* could find the assistance necessary to begin sincere deprogramming. Finding genuine help is difficult enough without getting handled and reprogrammed, or getting sent on a self-destruct course once usefulness is gone. But it was breaking free of the *trust no one* and *no talk* programming that was the hardest, and it did not make it any easier that one of the men who assisted *us* was a man *we* had been programmed to kill.

Freeing Us

Though *we* still contend with trust issues, *we* have a couple of people *we* do trust, and this is wonderful. Finding a truly safe person who is not a kontroller or handler is one of many life-threatening situations an awakening slave has to face, but making it through this danger is very possible, especially when focusing on the guidance, assistance, and protection of *our* inherent Benevolent, Unconditional, Love-filled soul. It knows no judgment, waits inside all human souls, has no form, and yet is and always will be a human soul's greatest ally. *We* found it active in someone who assisted in keeping *us* alive in the early years of deprogramming.

What to Avoid

Discernment is difficult to come by and yet absolutely vital to deep deprogramming. What *we* encounter from within is a fluctuation between the ability to know and the inability to know, and it is due to alters' programming designed to facilitate confusion. *Our* first year of deprogramming was like walking through a minefield day and night. If it wasn't a kontroller or handler attempting to reach *us*, *our* own alters and their programming were trying to either get *us* to *go home*, finish certain on-tasks, or die. *We* were hit from every side and then some. *We* recorded days and nights of five and six programs running at the same time. *We* came to at night during what *we* referred to as "delirious sleep", when programs ran without sleep with several of *us* co-existing. It was terrifying and exhausting. *We* were flooded with memories being executed from within and without, a common tactic to overwhelm the deprogramming slave. Each passing day meant cultivating discernment. *We* neither trusted others nor ourselves.

Even before meeting the two men who have greatly assisted *our* deep deprogramming, *we* stopped engaging sexually with anyone. (Later, *we* learned that this was not true for all of *our* alters across the board. That did change once missing time no longer was occurring.) By the time *we* began deep deprogramming, *we* were consciously abstaining from sex, drugs (even over-the-counter), alcohol, and were vegetarian. (Due to the forced cannibalistic practices.) No mind-altering substances were allowed, except sugar, and that should be tempered. *Our* decision came out of the deep, profound knowing that so much was wrong with *our* life. This choice was second only to focused Love regarding *our* ability to deprogram.

None of this is required to get started but was *our* condition because of the debilitating effects on *our* body, mind, and spirit from years of trauma. The idea was to feed *our* health as much as possible without triggering or giving in to destructive alter desires. The deprogramming *we* have experienced began before finding any assistance. But it was slow and sure to fail without the further steps *we* eventually took through both Love and sheer will.

The degree of sexual programming is so extensive that *i* cannot consciously imagine being able to engage in sex without triggering any number of programs completely devoid of Love. It is utterly baffling to *me* how any ritually abused, trauma-based, *total mind kontrolled* slaves like *us* are able to dismantle enough to not be triggered into sex programs after the extensive and prolonged trauma and outright torture they have gone through for a lifetime. *Our* sexual programming began as a very small child and *our* use lasted into *our* forties and still continues at times on a beyond-three-dimensional level. Quite frankly, it does not matter if *i* ever engage sexually again. Love as *we* know it, on the other hand, is a completely different issue. The Love that *we* have consciously come to know has absolutely nothing to do with sex. For *us*, sex was a distraction and reinforcement for *our* programming, as well as to prevent *us* from coming to know Unconditional Love, the basis of all truth, the sole root of all of *our* trust.

Talking

Our programming was calculated to facilitate a *no talking* policy no matter what, no exceptions. Even death was an option before talking. Other interferences included screen memories and even real memories. They even program in how the programming will break down, a sequence of deprogramming to allow them to kontrol the release of information, such as having the child alters show up first because they held less important information than that of some of the deeper alters, fragmented presentations less mature and far more emotional, more irrational sounding downloads, etc. The programmers' science is amazing, but it is anything but foolproof.

Young alters' presentations often appear incoherent, particularly if someone is unfamiliar with *tmk* programming. Within the larger context of high-level, *total mind kontrol* programming, these young alters and their downloads are very important, yet in early deprogramming their truths can work against the larger truth if that larger truth is not known of or understood. Due to early experiences with those not savvy to *total mind kontrol* programming, it can actually work in favor of *our* programmers, kontrollers, and handlers.

325

It was only because *we* survived the numerous self-destruct and suicide programs and external attacks that the deeper information made it to the surface to be talked about. Seeing this was a stunning revelation and added another level to the absolute malice of these programmers. They designed the programming to even facilitate extensive torture and trauma from within while deprogramming, which was why it took years for *us* to get to enough alter memories to start making sense of it. Fragmented memories showed up a lot, and deceptions clouded the issues so much that most of the time *we* went in and out of feeling crazy. This method of using a programmed-in schedule for program breakdown was intended to facilitate a death before any sense could be made of the information *our* alters presented.

One of the other methods was what *we* call *fog* programming. *We* actually *saw* and *felt* a fog inside *our* head as it descended over *our* brain from the inside, creating an instant confusion and loss of ability to relay information at the moment of downloading into *our* conscious mind or verbally downloading to one of *our* support people, thus affecting the capacity to rely on it as credible.

While consciously co-existing with other alters in deprogramming, *we* experienced a bizarre *no talk* program that prevented *our* conscious alters from overriding what some of the deep, dark alters were trying to do to *us*, and on more than one occasion literally disallowed *our* conscious alters from speaking or vocalizing thoughts making their way into *our* conscious mind. When *we* consciously understood what was occurring, *we* were able to dismantle it with authority and Love. Other *no talk* programs included making *us* too ill to talk and punishing *us* during and after talking.

We have already written about the latter part of 2008 in the Taos, New Mexico area when *she 29th* was attempting to acquire a 9mm and *we* could not speak of it even though some of *us* were consciously aware. *We* recall the conversations in *our* head between *me* and *she 29th* and being kontrolled by her. *We* also recall breaking that programming while driving down from Taos Ski Valley. The empowered Benevolent part of *us* came forward and said, *No, this is not an option, this will not occur.* The feeling was one of strength combined with forgiveness for her programming. It was stronger than her and clearly had the ability to remove the option from the table. *I* know this as *our* Benevolent will.

This occurred with numerous deep, dark alters and programs time and again. What *i* am really doing is reprogramming *our* alters in such a way as to remove them and their programming as the kontrolling force in *us*, allowing *our* higher Self to be that Loving, managing force instead.

Besides *she 29ᵗʰ*, *our occult alter* has taken kontrol of *our* vocal cords even while *we* were consciously trying to take back control. It was only for a few minutes, but very frightening. *Our occult alter* called upon "the mothers of darkness" in the early morning hours when *we* were rising from bed and attempting to begin *our* morning focus on Love. (Technology at work? See Book 1, Chapter 1, "Updates", *The Serpent in the Garden of Eden*.) Ultimately, *our* focus on Benevolent Love with sincere intention while returning to a calm state of mind allowed *me* to be of single mind again.

This *no talk* program is very powerful and until *we* came to understand what it was, *we* could not dismantle it, which is how it works with most of *our* programs. It takes time to really grasp what the program is and how it really works with the affected alters. It is not straightforward, and *our* deprogramming takes a deep, strong commitment that must be restated everyday with heartfelt sincerity and accompanied by an active, daily practice of what needs to be done. *We* cannot take a day off. When *we* on occasion faltered because *we* consciously chose to not do something (see Book 1, Chapter 11, "The Forties", *Relinquishing*), *we* were set back in deprogramming. Of course, something can always be learned and is. Viewing things in absolute terms is hazardous to deprogramming, which makes *our* compulsive nature as a direct result of trauma-based mind kontrol programming even more challenging.

Bottom line: when *we* began talking about what had happened to *us* and what was still happening to *us*, particularly in April 2008, *we* truly began to break away. The power of being able to talk is a very effective and necessary tool in the recovery process.

Prayer and Contemplation

Prayer is for *us* the single most important tool when allied with conscious understanding of *our* situation, *our* programming, and what all of it meant for *us*.

[After a few years in deep deprogramming, I found my way to Spiritual Science, where a whole new level of awakening began for me. I consider myself an Esoteric Christian (as opposed to an exoteric Christian). I was involuntarily inducted into the dark occult, and yet I found my way to the Light side, the mystical side, to Anthroposophy or Spiritual Science. This fell in line with so much I had already experienced and carried me further into understanding what had been in my life and run it for so long, as well as how to remove their influence through the act of learning to engage my thinking, willing and feeling with the Christ Impulse, a work in progress. It brought me to the concern of the world at large as opposed to my personal situation alone. See the teachings of Anthroposophy and Dr. Rudolph Steiner for more.]

Malevolence needs someone or something to be worshipped, someone greater than you who are not worthy enough. Their methods involve instigating and maintaining separation to keep one disempowered; they know that the real power lies in this Love and the human capacity to be with it, that it is what the human soul is.

Ours is a journey through, not a goal attained. *Our* contemplative practice focuses *our* mind, heart, and soul upon all that is true. *We* do not gain it like a goal; *we* remember it as always being here to keep *us* alive despite hundreds of times over, *our* only worldly outcome being death and destruction. It is *our* focused intention that allows this to be consciously *seen* and *felt*, and *we* can only hope for the ability to be able to maintain this as deprogramming continues.

The following is one of the most frequent, consistent intentions *we* used for the first few years:

> *Benevolent, Unconditional, Creative Love infuses us from within, surrounding us in Benevolent Love, Benevolent light, Benevolent protection and Benevolent safety, day and night, indoors and out, resting and awake, preventing malevolence from accessing me or any of us in any way known and unknown to us, in body, mind, soul or spirit, now or ever again. I exist in Benevolent Love from this moment forward.*

Journaling

A profound tool in critical ways, journaling has allowed *me* to see what refused for some time to remain in *my* conscious mind. It allowed the extensive and varied memories of all of *us* to be brought forward and remain recorded and not disappear back into the depths of *our* mind along with the alters who held them. In early deprogramming, journaling allowed *me* and those consciously present—particularly front alters—to *see* and *feel* what others of *us* had known far too long on their own. This eventually facilitated a united front and provided a foothold for *our* deep deprogramming that could no longer be shaken loose.

Coming to understand *our* memories and experiences is an extremely important aspect to *our* deprogramming. If something within *us* remains hidden or deniable, it also remains apart from *me*. Journaling was one of the main tools that helped *us* to *see* what needed to be *seen* as well as providing a record of events over the years, facilitating being able to piece together a timeline of *our* life as if piecing together a puzzle of hundreds of fragments. Pieces are still coming forward, and making sense of as much of it as *i* can is important to *me*. *My* understanding is a significant part of the motivation to keep moving forward.

In the first 8-12 months, *we* journaled daily, sometimes throughout the day, due to downloads. In 2009, *we* decided *we* needed to write about what was occurring to *us* during deep deprogramming. Words have been and continue to be a very powerful tool for *us* in deprogramming. Despite *our* eccentricities and liberties in writing, most of the time *we* do well getting across the *see* and *feel*. The main challenge has been how to make it available as it was intended in content and format.

Audiotapes

In the first week of *our* deep deprogramming, *we* realized that the information coming forward was coming so fast and in such a great quantity that *we* could not write it all down. Internal *flooding* is in fact an intentional programming design. *We* often felt like someone was trying to drive *us* insane, and *we* were right. Alters and their memories were presenting day and night, and *we* wrote and drew crude drawings as fast and furiously as *we* could. A mini-cassette recorder greatly assisted in this process, particularly during the night when programming seemed to be running regardless of *our* rest periods. *We* did not sleep; some of *our* alters rested while others remained ever vigilant and running *our* systems. *We* came to in the middle of running programs, grabbed the recorder, and recorded the fragments whether they made any sense or not.

[I cannot stress enough the profound need for vigilant recording. A programmed victim does not have the mind yet to retain much of what breaks

329

through when it is doing so at such consistent speed and volume. It is a denial to think one can during that process. Record, record, record! Alters are likely surfacing and then diving down inside, often with the information you just received. In time, the details begin to fall into cohesive encounters and events, and such clarity brings a *tremendous* amount of empowerment and desire to move forward. I began to feel some control in my own life for the first time.]

We learned not to censor what came forward, just record it and attempt to *see* and understand later. At times, certain alters were powerful and influenced *our* understanding of certain things for good or bad. Later, the information made sense to the small collective that was conscious and desired to assist *our* deep deprogramming. The mini-cassette recorder also worked well when *we* were driving and could not stop to write, such as when *we* left Salt Lake City in April 2008 and were returning to Taos and recorded almost the entire way back.

Our Colláges

Colláges became a far more powerful tool than *we* could have imagined because they allowed the many of *us* to participate without having to present their identities, though at times during the actual colláge design certain alters were indeed clearly *seen* and *felt* by *me*. Anonymity was what some needed, including the fragments of *us* who are not even full personalities; the colláges allowed them to make a contribution, then return to the depths within.

Some of *us* are incapable of so-called normal interactions. One of the most important requests by some of *us* is to not be asked who they are. So far, there seem to be two reasons:

First, many do not even know who they are, though *i* have now come to understand that for them. This was a real struggle early on as others of *us* felt a need to know who is who. But *we* have come to respect this and guard their right to anonymity. Offering this respect has often allowed them to change that on their own. Secondly, some of *us* have tremendous fears regarding identities being revealed—even their existence being revealed—due to it having been or still being a case of life and death.

The colláge work has been a huge step in the direction of coming to realize the significant number of *us* inside, as well as a strong sense for many that *we* had not yet sensed. Simply put, *we* could *see* and *feel* on a deeper level during and after the colláge work; *we* had a much larger perspective of who and what *we* are. In fact, *we* are still finding connections in the colláge pages put together years ago. This greatly assists *our* conscious understanding of *our* life and the alters who have lived various fragments of it.

Much of what is present in these pages was not—and in some cases is still not—fully understood by *us* in front alter consciousness.

[As I gathered the pieces for the future colláge, I often had no idea what was what and why it needed to be gathered. Then the process of construction, with the assistance of those from within—different alters for different colláges—became a fantastic adventure that unfolded years of my life and slowly brought me into alliance with those of me within. This, along with the journaling/recording, had deep healing and understanding as its reward.]

Videotapes

At first, someone *i* worked with was doing the taping. *We* were frightened and not very willing to tape *ourselves* early on in deprogramming due to fears about repercussions from *our* programmers, kontrollers, and handlers. There were indeed repercussions, but they came with deep deprogramming in general, not just videotaping. They knew every move *we* made before *we* did, so the idea that if *we* kept silent and stayed hidden, *we* would be all right, was simply more programming lies.

[I must say, this is true today for each and every individual on the globe. What is occurring *will not just go away*.]

We had never been silent and hidden from them, just from everyone else out there in the world. They make the rules and they break them. *We* were never cared for nor respected, only for loyalty binding, and were abused and used. So to think that keeping silent and staying hidden might save *us* was just more programming with no basis in truth. For many of *us*, this took time to understand and is still taking time for others with deeply-rooted programs that do not allow them to *see* or *feel* their own trauma and torture by those they would protect.

331

The act of speaking truths out loud is very powerful, and it relieves the urgent need to tell that some of *our* alters find necessary. Videotaping records *our* process while it is occurring and allows *us* to *see* other parts presenting. *I* would go back and view a taping only to find that it was most certainly not *me* presenting.

In 2010, *we* purchased *our* own small camera to do *our* own tapings so *we* could be more spontaneous. This has been tremendously helpful in being able to talk about memories and download important information rapidly, knowing that even though no one else is there to hear it at the time, *i* do.

All Rooms Are Born

We have been blown away by some of the information recorded because when it came up, *we* were not necessarily in *our* conscious mind. Due to the many of *us* and all the information they hold, it is far too much to keep in *our* conscious mind and function as needed. Plus some of it is too horrible to be allowed to remain there, so *we* allow it to be released a little at a time until it is released enough that the need for separation from it is no longer necessary. And then there is the case of something surfacing, only to disappear back down inside with the presenting alter.

When *we* first began to realize how many of *us* there are, *we* realized that it would take time. At first, it was difficult to accept: *we* wanted it out of *us* now! But that is not realistic. To deprogram in a way that is non-destructive, healthy, and hopefully long lasting, *we* must allow compassion garnered with strength to take *us* where *we* need to go when *we* need to go there. Thus most of the videos are a very personal record, and copies currently reside with a few people *we* trust.

10
Containment, Caution, and Hope

The placement of caution and hope near the end of Book 2 is by no means an afterthought. In fact, this chapter may be more disturbing in content than anything written above. *We* will neither mince words nor try to protect the reader's sensibilities, as deprogramming is a very serious endeavor.

For high-level (denoted by those who are given access to them), ritually abused, trauma-based, *total mind kontrolled* slaves who are waking up, the following is crucial to understand because it most certainly will happen. The circumstances may vary—the individuals certainly will—but the modus operandi is unmistakable:

They will send someone in on you, usually several, to gather your information and contain you. Brace for it; protect yourself spiritually and physically. This **containment** will come in a variety of forms and disguises, and if deemed necessary, will ultimately lead to your death. To allow continued use, reprogramming—reinforcing what was already placed inside, including *enhancements*—is one form of containment, whether with sweetness or threat, and when a slave's programming has truly begun to deteriorate, a final containment is sought: death. First, all the information the slave has to give is extracted and contained by limiting exposure; they know that some exposure must occur and will seek to minimize it. Then, if you are no longer of use or cannot be reprogrammed, the next containment will be slow or quick assured death. This is neither a new method nor an outdated one, and is extremely effective. (And can go unnoticed by everyone around you thanks to remote technologies.)

As *we* have repeatedly stated and written, they do not care how much one knows as long as the exposure can be kontrolled. A significant part of the story is not the same as the core of the story. Information related to key political figures—even naming them—is more often than not no real threat to them. Generally, they move in before it hits the public to any significant degree, and may even present the information themselves. By planning the release of information about themselves and their agenda, they maintain kontrol through containment. They watch, learn, and plan for future disclosures and make necessary adjustments to future programming methods. Rarely is there legal repercussion or significant public outcry because all is carefully kontrolled and contained through a variety of methods, including well-honed indoctrination and media kontrol. Truth can hide in the open—"hidden in plain sight"—when people are properly indoctrinated not to believe it and lack the strength to realize their own degree of indoctrination and programming, which would be too frightening.

Ideally, no one would talk, but the truth is that many do, for which damage kontrol is marshaled. Often, *we* hear, "Yeah, but they named so and so," to which *we* respond that one of *our* uses was to eliminate their own. They have been offering up their own for centuries and will continue to do so. Ultimately, this kontrol is exercised by *beings* that are not human and therefore have no allegiance to humans in the end. *Everyone is expendable*, and those who believe they are important will soon enough find this out. A scapegoat is always handy.

Potential handlers who show up in deprogramming may be a psychologist with lots of experience with mind kontrol programming. Or the handler may be someone who understands in a sexual liaison. Or the father or grandpa figure to replace the one you were never able to trust. Or the older sister you needed when the real one could not face the truth of her own programming. Or the local pastor who can "deliver" you from it all in the blink of an eye. A helper, a protector, a friend. No matter the need, it will be provided. Precisely when, how, and who, will be determined by your handlers and kontrollers showing up in a succession of individuals originating from the same source: them. Unfortunately, many of the deprogramming options out there are tied back to the Network in some way. This is important to understand so as not to become disillusioned and give up.

There are sincere people out there willing to help. Keep going! Most likely, you will stumble time and again as *we* did. Eventually, *we* developed a sense of strength and focus that allowed some assistance and protection through that Love every day and night, paid attention and developed *our* skills of discernment. When *our* head began to clear, *we* even found that some of *our* programmed skills designed by them came in handy to assist in breaking free of *our* programming.

The idea that *we* can never really break out, never come to be the one in charge of *our* life is a lie. *We* trusted until *we* knew.

Learning to trust *ourselves* was crucial, despite vacillating between trusting others and not. With time, *we* saw that *we* have very good instincts, a well developed intuition, and an ability to listen to them, despite those who disagree with *our* take on things. It is a process and takes time—in fact, the rest of *our* life. *We* faced the temptation to alleviate *our* profound loneliness with the presence of others. Isolation must be assuaged, but only gradually with time and a clearer head. With a support person or two—safe people you can trust—you can do this! You and your alters, with the constant protection of prayer and contemplation you can deprogram. As a matter of fact, you have more information about your internal systems, programs and alters than anyone around you! Forming a safe relationship to them is the key to access on your own. It will not seem that way at first, yet if you keep going, it will be done. Do not give up!

11
Untenable Final Ideas

Whatever affects one directly, affects all indirectly…
This is the interrelated structure of reality.

– Martin Luther King, Jr.

It is important that readers avail themselves of all the previous information prior to reading the following. All is written to offer a progressive context from early programming and use to our deep deprogramming thus far. It is of utmost importance to remember that malevolence is masterful at taking something beautiful and turning it upon itself. Reversals allow the ultimate kontrol.

The Most Untenable

What follows does not affect *us* alone. *We* may remain isolated in this understanding, but *we* are not unique. Initially, isolation is implemented and maintained by the programmers, followed by others misunderstanding of MKUltra design which helps to continue that isolation. As with so many aspects of *total mind kontrol* programming, one's misunderstanding from misinformation, disinformation, and decades of indoctrination prevents deep understanding. This is true for all of us and is often a consciously missed effect of the global mind kontrol program.

We understand things that *i*, the front alter, have no previous exposure to—details running deeper than intellectual understanding, arising from the depths and spanning time and space in a very non-linear fashion. What *i* am elsewhere is also what *i* am here and now.

Though the methodology used by the programmers is "alter-ed" at points in time and space, it has also been basically the same for eons, as is the goal. So regarding what they *do*, there is really nothing new, however, a new level of kontrol as regards a linear time frame is upon us. Over the ages, this level of kontrol was elusive, given that the human domain is subject to a set of laws that must be adhered to. That alone is a vast topic, one about which *I* am not well informed enough to write.

One example is crossbreeding between the programmers' multi-dimensional DNA and human DNA, which is also multi-dimensional. The goal has never been to destroy humanity, only to "alter" it to the degree necessary to successfully kontrol its energy signature, and thus Benevolent nature inherent in the soul-mind. Maintaining the presence of the human soul holds great value for these malevolent ones. It is what is truly sought after. They can utilize much more of the human body, mind, and spirit, but are denied *personal access* to such for reasons beyond *my* conscious understanding.

I am of a bloodline initially designed by these programmers long ago, a cross-breed of other multi-dimensional DNA and human DNA, designed to facilitate many things, most of which *i* am consciously unaware of, *i* am sure, such as truths about *our* abilities experienced in *our* front alter consciousness and through *our* alter personalities, as well as *our* other bodies.

[Cloning is very real on the human level and has been around for decades. Body doubles—look-alikes—are still used as well. I am aware that I have been cloned, as have other MKUltras. In addition to this are REM clones in which the astral is pulled from a victim at REM sleep initiation and transferred to their clone body. This process can be repeated as many times as the programmer's wish and continue to clone a person's body. I am aware that this occurred to me (I referred to this as "pulls" but did not at the time understand the technology). I know several others it is currently happening to, of various ages. Cloning centers are also reported where these astral induced clones are used for sport and entertainment. There are now many celebrities coming forward with claims of their abuse. You decide, but do not do so out of fear. I can validate that cloning of MKUltras has been ongoing for decades. Many high level celebrities are MKUltras as well.]

> THC (THE HIGHERSIDE CHATS): "In 2011, **Donald Marshall** unleashed his first public disclosure on the internet with a letter describing his abuses in a vast underground program of human cloning by parasitic non-human entities in conjunction with the worlds shadowy elite. He detailed several types of cloning done at these underground bases, most notably **REM driven clones**, where as long as they've created a second body for this individual their consciousness can be transported to these hidden husks at the press of a button. Not only is

this the elites main method of meet-ups in the modern world, but also the technological solution to their blood lust and desire to torture and abuse children to no end. And since Donalds come forward as an Illuminati whistleblower he hasn't been shy about naming those from the political and entertainment realms that he has met down below, from **Queen Elizabeth** to **Henry Kissinger**, **Hilary Clinton** and **Obama**, to **Bernie Mac**, **Tila Tequila**, **Kurt Cobain** and **Mila Kunis**. But as odd as this all sounds there is a recent trend of celebrities actually tweeting about cloning centers and their own abuses…" (https://truthscrambler. com/2018/04/13/selling-your-soul-means-waking-up-in-a-cloning-center-donald-marshall/)

[You can find information in the Resources section at the end of this book for the title of Donald Marshall's book. Tila Tequila reported this activity openly online years ago and subsequently had an aneurysm at a young age. I can verify that heart attacks and aneurysms are also decades old execution (and warning?) techniques perfected in remote technologies. Additionally, Britney Spears made an animated music video of a cloning center involving what clearly look like many "elites" that have access to her, with Eminem making an interesting video that included another version of himself with clear references to programming. (Britney Spears, *Break The Ice*, https:// www.youtube.com/watch?v=eQFIKP9rGhQ ; Eminem, *The Monster*, https://www.youtube.com/watch?v=EHkozMIXZ8w.) And then there is this social media post in early 2022 from Britney Spears who has consistently shown the most evident signs, publicly, of her programming pain and suffering, as well as program breakdown. Anyone who understands what this looks like would have to be blind to not see it for this young woman:

"it's okay to lock your daughter up and make her work 7 days a week…8:00 am to 6:00 pm…no days off…105 people are in and out of a small trailer home ? weekly…No private baths ?…seen naked when changing…drugged…can't even speak or talk…has to be available to the treatment people and show up every day for 10 hours a day… if not will have to stay longer…never given a date on when you can leave…9:00 pm bed every night like 8 gallons of blood weekly…this happened to me for 4 months after I worked for my dad and my family for 13 fucking years…I gave my all when I worked only to be literally thrown away…I was nothing more than a puppet to my family yet to the public I just performed on stage and did what I was told to do…

339

but it was worse than that because it was accepted and approved by the people I loved the most ?...Looks are deceiving...I must have it nice on vacations lol !!!! After 13 years damn straight I should go !!! I was treated less than, demoralized and embarrassed...nobody should ever be treated the way I was...The reason I bring this up is because ending the conservatorship is a huge deal but come on...THAT'S IT ??? They all got away with it !!! If you've ever been in shock ? for 4 months...threatened for your life...you would be upset too...I'm not done...I want justice and won't stop until something is done to those who harmed me...and YES I was harmed !!!! This is a message to all who have been threatened for their life...You are NOT ALONE !!!!"]

Our experiential understanding of space-time runs outside the *programmed* concept of linear time. Programmed untruths always have to be accompanied by truth in order to hold the consciousness of humanity under deception's spell. To be able to explain space-time as *we* understand it is another matter entirely, given that *we* have to rely on the reader's ability to break through the programming impeding their ability to *hear us*, though they may listen.

Many of *our* experiences fall outside of linear time all the way back to early childhood. In fact, the genetic design of *our* body—**overshadowing** at conception—was no doubt to utilize the many of *us* within the parameters of *total mind kontrol* programming so as to encompass the three dimensional realm *and beyond*. To only look to one or the other is very myopic, given that they are inextricably interconnected.

Particular bloodlines are of great significance to the attainment of their goals. Many out there were designed for such, and the programmers' ability to maintain containment through isolation is quite effective. Many of us could be in contact with one another, but to do so outside of the programmers' reach and kontrol is questionable and potentially dangerous. When one *sees* the true nature of handling and kontrolling, one gets a clearer understanding of what it is that humanity is up against. Only then will the ability to affect become visibly evident.

It is *our* contention that the Benevolent nature of the human soul-mind is one of the most powerfully pervasive forces in all the universe, due to being inextricably linked to God. The allowance of Love's presence consciously, actively, is the key to its effectiveness.

What needs to be *seen* here is the nature of those like *us* and how that carries on into deprogramming. *My* conscious understanding of *our* history is a result in part from cellular memory. These *beings* have been a significant part of *our* programming and use, many of them placed in *me* during programming. But that is not the complete picture. More often than not, possessing only part of the truth regarding *total mind kontrol* programming can be very detrimental to being able to truly understand what is at work. The human inclination to reach "either/or" conclusions is part of the malevolent programmers' indoctrination. Partial truths can actually impede further understanding. As with *tmk* programming, the realm of deprogramming is often not what it first seems, and that is indeed the case here.

The *"we"* of *me* is not solely what those within the deprogramming community have accepted as such. *We* have never wavered on this issue but have kept silent in the recognition of the inability of others to hear *us* correctly. *We* can only speak from the stance of a *tmk*, high-level *enhanced* design; *we* cannot speak to other circumstances, nor do *we* wish to try.

The apparent expectation of mental health professionals who have worked with persons suffering from programming similar to *ours* is that of an "integrated" person who returns to a wholeness originating from a "core personality"—a model *i* have little resonance with. Even the religious deprogramming community shares this view, though their methods differ. In all honesty—an honesty remaining despite years of humbly attempting to achieve something resembling that model while consciously *knowing* that this was not what was occurring in *our* deprogramming—*i* am now ready to uphold what it is *we* know, different as it may be. Many who remain silent may resonate with what it is *we* present while remembering that programmers' nuances and specific programming may differ, not to mention the differences among slaves, such as pre-conception influences.

[Entity **overshadowing** and chromosome tweaking: the esoteric and exoteric technology at work.]

During *our* conscious deep deprogramming, a return to a "core personality"—an undeveloped physically, emotionally, mentally, and even spiritually thwarted part—has never made sense. After such fragmentation in mind and soul as *I* have undergone, it has never seemed correct that these splits would ever, nor could ever, be *fully* re-integrated in any *conscious* capacity. Not only do they number far more than most people could even comprehend, but many of them are allied to their malevolent designers in ways the deprogramming community has yet to sincerely consider as possible. These parts spend their entire programmed existence fighting any form of cooperation whatsoever, and not entirely because of the demonology they are under.

To be *seen* properly, this issue must encompass all of the circumstances of how "*i*" combined with "*we*" are actually living, now. *We* are living from *our* collective, personal experience, not someone else's expectations.

First, much is lacking in the mental health view of MPD/DID. To *my* knowledge, nowhere has this issue been addressed for those like *us*:

> *The intentional design of enhanced, multiple personality slaves by malevolent programmers, kontrollers, and handlers represented in various government, military, intelligence, religious, and corporate organizations and institutions, as well as the various individuals associated with such, all utilizing sophisticated technology and occult esoteric practices in a most heinous scientific method to design completely dissociated beings with abilities reaching beyond perceived three-dimensional human limits, for the express purpose of abusive, malevolent, traumatic, and torturous acts of rape, murder, and more against humanity at the direction of the very same malevolent programmers.*

Until this is a part of the mental health community's current DSM definition, *we* have no use for it. As anyone who has even cursorily investigated allegations of complicity on the part of many in the mental health community should know, anything coming from the long-held traditions of this "community" and its "associations" (American Psychiatric Association, APA), should be viewed not only with discretion but with great suspicion.

Second, the expectations for a deprogramming slave who has undergone extensive and extreme programming for an entire lifetime, including the ongoing effects of on-tasks that occurred during several decades of use, are astounding to *us*. *I* have addressed this in both Books 1 and 2. This expectation usually arises from a misunderstanding of context, not malevolent intention, there being far more unwitting misinformers than witting disinformers, though both exist in significant numbers. Well-established indoctrination runs deep when combined with ongoing disinformation and misinformation, and is designed to buffer the unavoidable alarm from discovery, recognition, and acceptance of pervasive and extensive *total mind kontrol* programming. The natural inclination is to seek relief from the pain and fear of the "veil"-piercing discovery.

Nothing within *tmk* programming begs for revelation. Quite the opposite: its very nature defies logical reasoning and acts as an assault upon all that one believes to be true. Understandably, many will step away as quickly as possible and by whatever means necessary. For those who for a variety of reasons cannot step away, a treacherous slope lies before them, it being difficult, if not impossible, for someone who has not experienced the life of a multi-generational, enhanced slave to truly understand what a reasonable deprogramming might be, and this technology is accelerating at an unimaginable pace.

The problem with the expectation concepts of "integration of personalities" and "core personality" is that it does not take into account the advancing "black tech" (which includes black magic; *yes*, I said *black magic*) being used by malevolent programmers against *all of us*. *We* cannot return to something separated from *me* almost a half century ago, which is now sequestered away in a void *we* cannot reach. The who of *me* now is a person who has survived against all odds and broken through various and sundry programs and "walls" within *our* mind that have sequestered away personalities that are and always have been parts of *us*, parts of *me*. Whatever is left of the original *me* is a part of something much greater now, a part of many lives lived from within one body.

I am not a "system" of programs, nor malevolent *entity*-run alters, but a group of people who have lived *our* lives together and apart, born of the same fragmented human soul and spirit now fronted by a person who is becoming as whole as she can be with the assistance of God and other parts of *me*. *We* work together. This front part is *developing* as a person, exiting the limited, programmed shell of the front alter personality with the assistance of all the other participating parts as fragments of *our* human soul and spirit belonging to *me* are extricated. It is the degree of extraction of *our* soul's fragmented parts from the programmers' grip that will determine the nature of *our* future course.

We have never wavered in how deep deprogramming must be pursued, though *i* continue to self-inventory other possibilities. Now, the programmers are apparently making *post-conception* genetic adjustments, as well.

Nor do *we* place faith alone in the lasting effects of religious exorcism of the *entities* running the programs and thus *our* alters. Only by *our selves* can this be achieved with the assistance and support from above. This insight is based on a personal experience in deep deprogramming. *Our* experience is that exorcism facilitates a temporary reprieve only, yet one that may indeed be welcomed due to the silence of mind it can offer, which likely will be

343

completely new to a victim. Outside support is a necessity for *our* deprogramming, but not someone fixing *us*. There are always exceptions, so *i* do not wish to address conditions *we* have not experienced. It is *our* hope that many avenues to sincere deprogramming will be developed in time.

To summarize: *What were once frontline alter personalities— including the main host—are developing into a full person with the assistance of the many personality fragments who are and have always been me, with the guidance and assistance of the parts of* our *fragmented, human soul/spirit and God.*

With each of these parts come the lives and partial lives that they have lived. *Our* infant core is a part of *me*, not the other way around. This is who *i* continue to *consciously* become: a person born of everything that has occurred up to this moment.

This is not a case in which all of these personalities are up and presenting fully at once. In *our* deprogramming process, they become part of a cohesive, conscious state in which they do not cease to exist but instead become part of a conscious collective as opposed to a robotic hive mind at the beck and call of malevolence. Using the term "*we*" has elicited an indoctrinated program response from those around *us*, one set in them long before *we* began *our* deprogramming. If this reference cannot be understood presently, *i* am certain it will in the future. Perhaps another will do far better than *i* at relaying why.

From a more genetic perspective within *our tmk* enhanced experience, the part of *me* that is other remains. What is and has been present within *us* cannot be viewed solely from the "entity possession" utilized during programming from very early on and continued through the years of on-task use and program maintenance. There is more. Again, we must consciously move beyond an "either/or" level of truth.

"Enhancing" a slave in a pre-conception design (as well as a post-birth alteration) means an aspect is present in them from that moment on, not just a *potential* for them to inhabit that body through demonology. Enhancement facilitates more than a potential possession that will later be used as a highly functioning aspect of *tmk* programming. It offers something far greater regarding use: an *already present potential* within that body, an aspect that needs little instruction or training, only needing to be loosed on the world in a *tmk*-kontrolled fashion. All *tmk* programming that follows is in addition to this and will be determined by what is already genetically present.

What lies under *total mind kontrol* programming that involves

intentionally designed MPD and demonology is the preconception enhancement and what that truly means regarding use within this life and
beyond. Add cloning to this as well as other realized, horrific designs, and
one will begin to see a very different picture of what *tmk* programming
truly entails in our times.

[If one looks today at the technologies I referred to here years ago, one will
find a frightening amount of evidence to validate mind control has arrived
on the global scale.]

Breaking the Cycle

This is a deeply important issue that remains extremely unpopular. Without
individual acceptance, the current state of human kontrolled consciousness
being taken to the "next level" will be maintained. *I* am not referring to
shifting human consciousness, as those in the Transhumanist movement
would have it. Whether or not Transhumanist or **Singularity Artificial
Intelligence** members grasp who and what is really backing the movement, *we* are sure it was designed by the very same programmers (Ahriman
and posse as well as the Asuras and Sorat's influence) *we* know.

The shift *we* refer to is one of allowing what already exists as pure Love
to be, union with the **Christ Impulse**. Allowing this Love to prevail in all
things is the precursor to dismantling all that is of malevolent design. The
two cannot inhabit the same space at the same time. For this to take place,
humanity must first come to the full conscious realization that *all human
perpetrators were victims first*. This equation facilitates multigenerational
programming.

But this is only half the equation, and this is where it becomes very
difficult for people to hear, let alone accept: *All victims become perpetrators*,
though *the degree of this* varies greatly from person to person, even including unwitting behavior. Until human society comes to terms with each
individual's role in perpetuating this, the situation will remain as human
society kontrolled by malevolence, whether mass mind *kontrol* or the extremes of trauma-based, *total mind kontrolled* programming. *Each becomes
complicit.*

Even viewing *ourselves* solely as victims without acknowledging *our*
perpetration born out of that victimization would mean *i* could never
truly begin to heal. To disavow any participation in *our* role is a lie.

345

Acknowledging *my* responsibility in *our* choosing to survive led directly to the murder of others at *our* hands. It is true that *we* were fully programmed and kontrolled, but to view this as a black and white issue, "good" versus "bad", is impossible for *us*. *I* must come to terms with this and have been in that process for some time now. To attempt a stance as solely a victim would be irresponsible. Upon *consciously* accepting this— through the *clear* recognition of this truth while sustained by Unconditional Love—*i* finally began to be truly freed from the bonds of shame and guilt that remained with that denial. Blame and shame only facilitate programming. Perhaps this can only be understood by the victims of extreme programming, *i* do not know, yet *i* do know with absolute clarity that this is the truth of *our* lives. Taking responsibility for *our mind-kontrolled* alters has allowed *us* to move into a deep degree of emotional and spiritual healing.

The obscuring concept of good guys/bad guys has long been a mainstay of malevolent programming. Whether one's role is denying the existence of malevolent programming in the first place—*tmk* of the individual slave or *en masse*—or more heinous, complicity with foreknowledge, all become participants in continuing the success of *tmk* programming and its horrific, devolutionary effect. It is perpetrated by the witting *and unwitting* alike.

By consciously owning the situation as it is, *i* am allowed to sincerely move forward in forgiveness of those parts of *me* as *i* address *our* responsibility for being a perpetrator as a direct result of victimization, genetic and otherwise. By removing self-imposed denial, *we* can then use *our* energy for truth.

The malevolence *i* refer to is not born of a single script; it is the same malevolence in text after text through the ages, going back as far as is known and even farther. The names may change, but the malevolence does not: a dimension-crossing malevolence feared and revered as gods and called by various names in various locales as the progression of linear time has permitted upon Earth. Their power of deception is rife with misinformation, disinformation, and indoctrination that veils consciousness even as they enslave us. So deep and thorough is this deception that the victims themselves defend their enslavers' non-existence. The irony is that the force of Love due to the Benevolent soul living in each human form is far greater, the exception being soulless malevolent designs. Malevolence knows about this Love and fears that the conscious, active realization of it could occur in each human soul.

In order to dismantle and remove these malevolent programmers *once and for all,* this Love must be allowed to prevail in each individual. The programmers know this and have worked for eons to keep this understanding out of human consciousness. Humanity's union one to another is never to be subject to any institution, organization, or god of superiority, nor is it the goal to become as gods, as the programmer-backed Transhumanist movement recommends. Such so-called gods are not gods at all, except in program-induced, acquiescing minds and spirits under kontrol. Union of heart, mind and soul needs nothing of ritual, dogma, or ceremony; it only needs the individual to honestly and truthfully face what is—and what is not—whatever the personal attachment.

[**Initiation** into the truth of this world and the cosmos and all in it is upon us, ready or not. I will relay a fabulous quote here: "Enlightenment is a destructive process. It has nothing to do with becoming better or being happier. Enlightenment is the crumbling away of untruth. It's seeing through the façade of pretense. It's the complete eradication of everything we imagined to be true." —Adyashanti (I am not a follower of this man's teaching, however, I appreciate this statement deeply as it is indicative of my experience.)]

This is by far *the* most difficult journey that *any* human soul will ever face. Yes, extremely difficult, due to the resistance the effort will meet—the resistance from within and without born of malevolent programming and the degree of individual and societal acceptance of such. Humanity is not innately evil, however, some of humanity's programmers are. The human propensity toward violence is born of programmer malevolence and enhances the "energy" they seek while perpetuating their kontrol.

[See Rudolf Steiner's lectures on the Ahrimanic double (doppelgänger): "Ahrimanic Double" Dornach, November 20, 1914 GA 158
  • has its dominion entirely within the subconscious.
  • it is highly intelligent, and endowed with a will closely related to the forces of nature.
  • presently disappears shortly before death, but has a strong impulse to conquer death and stay with Man after death.
  • is extremely dependent upon the Earth as a whole organism, the various earth-forces work with particular strength into the racial and geographical varieties of mankind. (https://anthroposophy.eu/The_Double)]
  Once the misinformation, disinformation, and heavy indoctrination

heaped upon us for eons is acknowledged, the second step is to face the degree of variously accepted untruths within our *own* lives as well as our tenacity to cling to them, no matter how painful and no matter how vulnerable we feel over these revelations. The sensation of powerlessness will be deep but temporary *if* we continue to sincerely seek to exhume the truth. For *me* and for the *us* that lives in *me*, this is a painful, ongoing journey that is absolutely necessary. The farther *i* go into it, the more challenging it becomes. This is by design!

Coming to consciously know one's self and embracing deep knowing of the cosmic realms and one's place in it—no matter the distractions thrown in one's way—is the only lasting solution for the individual and the whole of humanity. It is not about becoming part of the deceptive "one consciousness", the "hive mind" that New Age programmers seek; it is about an *individual's* journey with Love as the ally—Love that naturally allows an eventual connection to others who are doing the same, all of which will innately heal a species and remove the situation whereby malevolence could strike at ever-present vulnerability.

Until this occurs on a significant scale, those on the cutting edge (and being cut by that edge) will continue to fight for freedom. All of humanity needs freedom from their oppressors, not just those the media talks about!

First, though, each human being must come to *see* their oppressors as they really are and how it is that each of us is used to maintain and perpetuate a dominance-and-submission model. As long as the many remain under "veiled" consciousness, even the few will continue to struggle deeply to reach wholeness. Do not let the illusions of daily life get in the way, which is the intention: a design of distraction.

The true Benevolent nature of humanity is *magnificent* and far greater than any carnal pleasure or success. Unrecognized by most, malevolence is so far successful in wielding pleasure and pain, and when the line between them blurs, malevolence has succeeded. When humanity defends malevolent programs as being of their own making, righteous and true, malevolence has succeeded. We can only help one another if we first face ourselves. It is not just about *seeing* our own degree of perpetration; it is about *seeing* who and what we really are and allowing that to be ever present—*the* monumental task.

It is not *my* intention to blame *us* or others like *us*, but to openly acknowledge *our* responsibility for *our* part in how programming is being allowed to continue uninterrupted and evolving. If *i* attempt to deny *our* responsibility, this will not be possible. Consider this a call on an unprecedented scale, an absolute necessity for the release of one and all from the grips of eons-old malevolence. It must first take place individually in order to be effective on a mass scale.

The Transhumanist Übermensch

The entertainment value of the superhero and villain may seem innocuous at first, but like many aspects of societal indoctrination, it is far more sinister and reaches much farther back than modern day comic book characters hitting the big screen. The superhero and villain are the ancient archetypes of stories told by peoples throughout human history. That the same archetypal stories and characters jump through historical time from civilization to civilization as demi-gods neither fictional nor mythical is proof of a reality that cannot be denied. In other words, the longevity alone is a testament to their actual existence, and that they were viewed as gods is understandable.

If it were about the reach and magnitude of ancient Sumer, it would be accepted as truth, but despite all the artifacts supporting the existence of demi-god interaction with the human race here on Earth, their existence is relegated to myth.

The present-day Transhumanist desire to be "super-human" (**Übermensch**) is the same theme with the same characters. The Transhumanist movement is like the old theocratic religion supported by slavery. All the talk about uniting "tech" and neurology/biology to create the ultimate human cyborg is just another version of the old repackaged demi-god stories.

Same program, same goal: the "next level" of subjugation—the selling of the individual human soul/mind by subsuming the Benevolent aspect unique to humanity. The "next level" in this space-time is to remove the choice that has been available to humanity—conscious choice—*without individuals recognizing that the ability to choose is no longer an option.* By combining technology and the esoteric (black magic), the End Time agenda can be achieved.

Superheroes and villains disseminated in entertainment to encourage acceptance of the idea that being superhuman—whether the good guy or the bad guy—is exciting and admirable, so that people will accept further programming of humans. *Mighty Man* (1978), the *X-Men* series of

349

today—super human abilities strikingly similar to abilities reported by slaves attempting to deprogram from multi-generational, bloodline, *total mind kontrol*, enhanced programming, some of which certain alters have reported to *us*. These abilities are not fictional, only fictionalized. All of this culminates in the reanimation of the Mighty Men of old and much more.

Interference and Abilities

Prior to deep deprogramming, *our* conscious mind perceived no sign of dyslexia. When *we* began deep deprogramming at age 46 years, *I* began noticing some reversals while extensively writing on a computer about *our* downloads, as well as *Our Life Beyond MKULTRA*. So far, *we* only experience it in writing, not in reading.

It definitely creates interference to relaying *our* story. Is this dyslexia part of an alter interference program due to *our* attempt at deprogramming and sharing what *we* know?

This dyslexia may tie in to another condition, pervasive and chronic as well, which began long before deprogramming. *Our* eyes experience what *we* can only liken to a "hiccup" in *our* visual field. An analogy might be sitting in a movie theatre, totally engrossed in a film, and once consciousness is fully entrained (no longer aware of their surroundings), a "hiccup" occurs in the film reel and momentarily shutters the view on the screen, prompting the viewer to return to conscious awareness of the surroundings and of watching a film. This is comparable to what *i* refer. It is as though the visual field is suddenly jarred and *we* are aware that all is not what it seems, despite what *i* am seeing.

Additionally, *we see, feel,* and *hear* the flow of electric current going through devices, regardless of their design or use. In each and every case, it is a disruptive sound that causes *us* discomfort. Sometimes, *we* have to disable the device, due to the adverse affect on *our* entire being.

Then there is the ability of knowing what a person is going to say. This has been with *us* for as long as *i* can recall. Uncanny abilities seem normal, not extraordinary, when you live with them. It doesn't even feel like *we* are exercising or controlling them; they just seem to occur more frequently than not.

Knowing what a person is going to say before they say it aloud most frequently occurs during face-to-face interactions, though it also occurs long distance and sometimes before an interaction even takes place, including on the phone or when viewing a pre-recorded video of someone on a monitor. *We* generally react and/or reply to the impending statement or question *prior* to its delivery.

We never really saw this as *precognitive telepathy* until we witnessed another slave doing it. It is actuated via *enhancement programming*, with a direct relationship between the level of energy in the dialogue and the frequency of its occurrence, though there are exceptions to this as well. The more intense and truth-oriented the dialogue, the more frequently it occurs. We attribute this to truth's intensity and depth. Additionally, *our* precognitive "muscle" often reaches into the lives of many we do not know.

[Organic ability due to trauma and torture, yes. However, Brain Computer Interface (BCI) is also at play.]

We experienced telepathy with a male bloodline slave over the course of several days. It was not something either of us were doing intentionally; it just occurred and it was not until we were no longer in contact that *i* realized the ease and extent of our interaction. Though *we* were comforted by this exchange, it was also exhausting to be around him, due to so many of his and *our* alters interacting on so very many levels. *I* was just a couple of years into deprogramming, and he was clearly still being accessed by his handlers and kontrollers.

My Clones

As with so many realizations for *me*, the front alter, facing *our* past and present never ceases to require a courage that *i* am becoming all too painfully familiar with. It is not that *i* do not wish to understand the truth of *our* lives with extreme clarity, but it requires reaffirming *our* choice daily. No matter what *i* must face, it is *my* express desire to continue to move further into the conscious understanding of what was done not only to *us* but to many others out there.

The conscious acknowledgement of *our* clones came with the most somber and thoughtful release of *my* denial and understandably took quite some time. The truth of *my* multiplicity remains unchanged with the release of *my* denial about *our* clones. That there is more than one physical, flesh and bone *me*—other versions of *us*—has become a conscious reality in addition to the former understanding of *our* MPD.

Me, Me, Me…

[I am aware that there were at one time four different physical versions of me. I cannot say which clones are still living at this time, nor can I state if more have been developed. The nature of what is known about cloning is limited in scope in the above ground consciousness, though those of us who have been a part of these ongoing programs know more than most.]

While in alter, *we* have encountered at least one of those clones, previously thought to be an alter due to *my* denial and limited understanding. This occurred despite the fact that upon her initial *conscious* presentation she was clearly *seen* and *felt* as *different* than the other alters. At that time, *my* ability to grasp the depth of that difference was severely limited. Denial and compartmentalization work well that way. Her role during that presentation was as a handler for one of *our* kill alters, *alter 14*.

These clones became a part of *our* experience when *i* was 27 years old. In that summer of 1989, they were "brought online" in a facility in New Mexico. *I* do not know why this took place, though *i* have suspicions. *I* also have reason to believe that not all of the original clones are still alive. I believe *we* were transferred to a clone body during that time.

[Thankfully, I came to the realization that this is not so regarding my being in a cloned body. I am in my original body despite experiencing physical changes in this body that assisted my belief that I am not in my original body. Needless to say, the changes were convincing ones. That there are other "me's" out there is still an unfortunate reality. Their status I do not know, nor do I know if there have been more produced than the original four. This is more common than people with no knowledge of such matters would believe. I will state here that *I have absolutely no doubt that transferring consciousness to another body is indeed taking place.* We have all heard of the lifelong and long-distance connection between twins, now imagine what that connection between clones would be like.]

We have a terrifying, lucid memory fragment from the mid-2000s of attempting to escape from an underground area in New Mexico that I am certain was related to this cloning process. *We* were rounded up by a "recovery team" via helicopter. (See Book 2, Chapter 2, "Continuing Revelations", *Escape and Retrieval Teams*.) *I* am uncertain if this was a physical abduction or an astral one. It is *our* understanding that this vast underground facility with tunnels stretching into several states in the Four Corners region had to do with crossing the spiritual aspect of programming with black tech in such a way as to maintain kontrol. Breaking the spiritual aspect of programming is a crucial aspect of *our* deprogramming, as well as coming to understand it intellectually.

The act of recovering *our* alter parts in deep deprogramming has long been a controversial subject within *our* personal support group. Though that group is rather small, the opinions regarding this matter are as numerous as its members. Dealing with other bodies that are *ours*, bodies that contain a part of *our* consciousness (?) as well as our personality or parts of

353

it (?), also presents an obstacle not acknowledged by anyone *we* have yet encountered in the deprogramming community. And yet a significant degree of management of *our* parts can be obtained, management being quite effective with the numerous alters as *we* continue deep deprogramming.

[There is much information nowadays regarding cloning and many people coming forward with claims of being cloned.]

Two of *our* clones are still "active" and kontrolled by *our* programmers. *We* originally numbered five physical beings in total—though not from birth—including the original *me* from which the other four came, with two of those four clones currently "active". *We* believe the other two have been killed, though *i*, the front alter, am not absolutely certain of that. From a programmer's standpoint, it is not difficult to comprehend the value of having five of *us*, particularly when one understands how successful "black tech" has been.

[I would be remiss if I did not include this commercial for BMW that came out in 2016, a few years after publishing Book 1 and 2 initially. I know, it is just a commercial, however, the effect it had on me is quite stunning as I saw so many similarities in my programming and cloning experiences that I had publicized by then. The number of bodies produced, the names of those bodies (called both by numbers and by flowers, especially the name Lily), and the behavior of the clone and even of the handler. As stated previously, fiction is taken from actual life, not the other way around. I cannot express how much within this commercial is true to my experience. Coincidence? Perhaps, if so, someone in production was given details they would not necessarily have access to. https://www.youtube.com/watch?v=2GQnCfmXWIA&t=645s]

Several other disturbing points must be addressed.

First, the status of *our* fragmented soul and the potential degree of reclamation of *our* alter parts, not only within *me* but also the consciousness fragments contained within these clones that may possibly also suffer from MPD. *I* realized long ago that *my* consciousness and personality had been fragmented with esoteric "black tech", and that at least some of those fragments were still in more than one underground facility. This is where the uncertainty comes into play regarding the two remaining clones in "active" status.

354

[I have come to understand through experience that this consciousness fragmenting can be corrected through a sort of soul retrieval from what I could only call a soul capture during the years of programming and use. I have joyfully found my soul intact through my work on these matters and am no longer "captured".]

A clone can be downloaded with an entire real personality with lucid, vivid memories belonging to another mind. There is no question *whatsoever* for *us* that this is the current state of "black tech" available and utilized with success for many decades by these malevolent programmers. With *my* conscious acceptance of *our* clones' existence, another unexpected avenue of understanding has opened up in the past year, that of a much greater understanding of many memory fragments from *our* past that were unexplainable within the framework of solely *tmk* programming involving one body.

[About 10 years into deep deprogramming I would be contacted by another victim who recognized "me", with certainty. I rather expected this to occur eventually due to going public. Through the course of several interactions (long distance) over about a six month period, he would reveal to me that he knew "me" back when and that I became a handler for him. I recognized the description he gave of my personality as similar to one of my alters, however, there were details regarding my tattoos that validated it was a clone rather than me. Prior to this encounter with this man, I knew that one of my clone's personalities was very specific regarding her programming, minus several things that a programmer would consider problematic. The "me" that this man described personality-wise as well as body, was the same as that clone according to my discoveries. This man even sent me a picture of himself from the time he said we were involved. I had a vague sense of recognition, but not an overly strong one. Additionally, during deep deprogramming, a long-distance connection between me and one of my clones was brief and quite profound. She was me but 20+ years younger (and identical to me at that age) with clearly a "soldier" mentality with kill programming and minus any unnecessary empathy. This was not a case of my offspring, that was clear to me.]

My exposure to "lives" lived in a completely divergent reality to the one lived and accepted by society at large perpetuates a separation that is difficult to resolve. The truth of *our* experiences—and now those of others who are reporting the same—has made *our* revelations untenable at best. So much of *our* history and present circumstance now understood is due to what has been released from "behind the veil"—an intellectual understanding fueled by spirit.

Only a few people have been able to even engage *us* sincerely in most of these matters, let alone accept their reality. Human society needs to come to understand the machinations of their world on physical, mental, *and spiritual* levels if they are to survive with any *conscious* freedoms. That the human species will continue is not in question. However, the conditions of that survival are in question and must be addressed in a thoughtful, sincere, and active fashion, and now. A most distressing confrontation must take place before this can occur.

ELISA Programming

Our Life Beyond MKULTRA, Books 1 and 2, are a significant cross section of *our* experiences within the MKUltra Network, from *our* perspective. *We* always keep in mind that "insider" information is remembered in compartmentalized pieces from which a vast story can be pieced together. As people come forward, more and more pieces connect up and the bigger picture begins to come into view. This is how *we* perceive Mr. Duncan's work as well: his experiences in designing programming systems combined with pieces of a fragmented story he accumulated after his torture and programming that *we* can then, with discernment, overlay onto *our* pieces and those presented by other victims. Discernment is essential to forming an accurate *big* picture.

Readers who haven't been victimized by MKULTRA should keep in mind that just because something falls outside of one's limited context of experience does not mean it should be relegated to the trash bin. MKULTRA mind kontrol methods and procedures were and still are extreme and diverge radically from mainstream daily reality.

In April 2013, *we* began reading an edited-for-ease-in-reading version of Robert Duncan's online book *The Matrix Deciphered*. *I* use "began" because this body of work often triggers *us*, due to similarities to *our* own abuse and programming. Triggering is not exclusive to Mr. Duncan's work but occurs anytime *we* read material associated with MKULTRA and **SRA (Satanic Ritual Abuse)** programming.

Despite *our* limited scientific understanding of the "tech" revealed in *The Matrix Deciphered*, *we* acknowledge the importance of what is being brought forward. In fact, in *our* opinion it is unprecedented. However, as with many others out there like *us*, once programmed, always accessed to some degree; it is the nature of MKULTRA programming. (This is where deep deprogramming involving initiation into a much deeper understanding of the world and ones place in it becomes absolute necessity.) So whatever any of us who have been its victims say, books like *The Matrix Deciphered* ought to be read with that awareness.

Imagine *our* surprise when in the Table of Contents we read, "Elisa and Neural Linguistic Programming Using Phonemes from Brain Waves". It was no coincidence, and indeed struck *us* as very personal. As with many "alter" memories that surface and at first *feel* as if something is sitting just on the periphery of *our* conscious grasp, what *we* read began yet another process of conscious understanding.

Following are ELISA excerpts from *The Matrix Deciphered*. However, readers should avail themselves of the entire book in order to understand how they themselves might fit into the remote mind kontrol agenda now up and running.

ELISA was an artificial intelligence computer program that the Stanford Research Institute demonstrated back in the 70's. It acted like a psychologist and asked stupid questions and responded to answers, parsing and understanding sentences. This field is called *natural language processing (NLP)*—not to be confused with neuro-linguistic programming (also NLP). ELISA fooled about half of the people into believing it was a real human being on the other end.

Fast forward 35 years and instead of parsing natural language phrases from keystrokes, ELISA recognizes phonetic brainwaves and parses them into words and sentences for artificial intelligence (AI) and natural language processing (NLP). Now the tortures and menticizations can scale to entire populations through this automation…

The brainwave cognitive ELISA adds realism by inducing an empathetic emotion with the words the target feels, thus adding a new dimension of convincing the target that the synthetic mind virus is a real person…

In the 2003 film *The Matrix Revolutions*, Agent Smith becomes a virus and starts cloning himself into everyone he touches. There only needs to be one nearly perfect cognitive model like this and then the supercomputer can evolve and simulate multiple copies of that mind virus. Think of this mind virus as a much more advanced ELISA artificial intelligence program, except that rather than based on just words and some logical inference engine, it uses a neural network model.

One of the duties of a "psychic warrior" or the simulated ELISA cognitive model sentence stimulator is being able to endlessly engage the target in useless banter. The strategy is to be as controversial as possible. With someone you know, practice walking away from or remaining silent when faced with offensive and disagreeable speech. With enough practice, you will have developed a most important skill against a voice-to-skull (V2K) electronic harassment attack.

Briefly, "ELISA" is psychic driving software[2]—an automated computer form of a real human being speaking.

Mr. Duncan points out that neuro-linguistic programming was introduced into the Army and pursued as a weapon by the infamous U.S. Army Col. John Alexander, and that NLP "masters" can kill people with NLP. In *our* Book 1, the collàge "Greer's Girl" references NLP, as does our collàge "The Minions" found in Book Two under Continuing Revelations. We have reason to believe that Col. Alexander was present at the facility outside Albuquerque, New Mexico, when *our* clones were brought online. We wrote about this in Book 2 and shared it with some of *our* support people prior to reading *The Matrix Deciphered*.

"Enhancements" to *our* programming have taken place in several such underground facilities. *Our* trip in 1989 across the United States also involved being taken to underground facilities, particularly in New Mexico. *We* have been in at least four different locations underground and suspect several more, including a facility associated with Sandia National Laboratories in Albuquerque and Los Alamos National Laboratory not far from Espanola, an incredibly dark town.

The pieces presented by Robert Duncan validate the understandings *we* have regarding such matters within *our* own personal experience. After overlaying what he has revealed, *we* have come to the conclusion that the current "black tech" being utilized is not only "EEG heterodyned cloning" utilizing brainwave frequencies, but also actual *physical* cloning of the human body into which personalities can be downloaded.

---

2 Psychic driving: a continuously repeated audio message on a looped tape to alter behaviour. Invented through torture by CIA "spychiatrist" Dr. Donald Ewen Cameron as part of MKUltra. Cameron was the first chairman of the World Psychiatric Association, president of the American and Canadian psychiatric associations, and a member of the Nuremberg medical tribunal in 1946-47 as a protector of Operation Paperclip Nazis.

[And add to this REM clones as witnessed by Donald Marshall whose book is found in the Resources section in this book. Additionally, the psychic driving for *tmk programming* is no longer necessary in person. Remote processing suffices, once a person's brainwave frequencies can be sufficiently harvested and tracked by AI. There will always be high-level slaves designed by multi-agency organizations, but now the average citizen is also a potential victim.]

We also believe that part of the reason he was allowed to present this information is to further obscure the issue of physical cloning—*as well as the downloading of personalties into cloned bodies*—within the "black tech" world of mind kontrol programming in the name of *Revelation of the Method.*[3]

Furthermore, *we* believe that the release of *our* story publicly as that of "Elisa" will be relayed to those "in the know" that this is what ELISA cloning tech currently looks like when deprogramming and "going public". It has long been *our* contention that "insiders going public" is one of the best teachers for insiders, hidden in plain sight. In other words, the same global information system exposing the horrors of MKUltra in its current stages to sincere researchers is also of pedagogic interest to those in the Network, while full human body cloning remains a revelation that must await further public indoctrination regarding its many "benefits".

---

3 See "The Scapegoating of Ted Kaczynski: Cereal Murder and the Group Mind", Joan D'Arc's Paranoia 2000 interview with Michael A. Hoffman II, author of the elucidating *Secret Societies and Psychological Warfare (1992)*, now free on the Internet: Hoffman: Revelation of the Method concerns mind control in the last stages and at a high level. When you tell someone what you are doing to them—murder, mayhem, kidnap, rape, you name it—and they do nothing to stop you or protect themselves, you have created a doubly enslaved subject.

This is part of the motivation for the occult processing of America through ritual murder, etc. The Cryptocracy carries out "cereal" murder crimes attended by archetypal signs and symbols which the dreaming mind of the Group Mind groks at a certain level. Next they confess in the Videodrome that it is the police and the authorities who are behind the crimes. Then they let the whole stew percolate into the psyche of the masses until the next covert sting operation.

This is partly why we have the least revolutionary and most passive population in recent memory. I'm not advertising the invincibility or genius of the Cryptocracy. They are succeeding by default and by dint of their great gambler's instincts. It's a huge risk to reveal to people what you've done to them. Somebody who can decode this for the masses can short circuit it and turn it against the Cryptocracy.

[And trust me, that time is not far off as many are clearly enamored with the concept of becoming "beyond human", or cyborgs. Just look at all the alterations and implants many are welcoming into their bodies with open arms. Additionally, the envied, beautiful and famous stars of the Hollywood and music industry (MKUltra controlled) are speaking about their clones. Indoctrination at its finest.]

Additionally, *we* have emphasized that the "next level" of End-Time programming is complete kontrol of the population at large and not just of high-level slaves. This is already occurring now, not later at some future nebulous date. The publication of *Our Life Beyond MKUltra* is yet another message sent to those "in the know" that "ELISA cloning is online and working."

However, *we* also believe that *our* programmers did not intend that *we* deprogram as much as *we* have, nor that *we* become aware of being cloned in the late 80s, let alone accept its reality and still maintain *our* sanity. Instead, they assumed *we* would "go public" without that knowledge and as a global demonstration of the success of ELISA to high-level insiders purchasing the programming at a high market price.

There are no coincidences, coincidence being a luxury only for the uninitiated. Within the Network, the use of symbols, words, phrases, numbers, and sounds are never coincidental but are a form of "twilight" communication covertly sent around the globe under the masses' noses. Paper trails or computer records that can be hacked are liabilities that might create an embarrassing situation, so a certain amount of information is exchanged in a safe and undetected manner, namely "hidden in plain sight".

When *we* wrote about how "they" continue to kontrol even the dissemination of deprogramming information, this is what *we* meant. That some slaves will wake up is inevitable, but utilizing even this to their advantage is part of the global Network's foresight.

For *us*, Robert Duncan's ELISA revelation has become a truth that has validated what *we* know from personal experience. Learn to read the twilight language hidden in full view and you too will be able to "see" into the elite Network's agendas.

[For those who still resist the idea of where current bio-technologies are, as in currently *in use*, please refer to Elana Freeland's book *Geoengineered Transhumanism: How the Environment Has Been Weaponized by Chemicals, Electromagnetics, & Nanotechnology for Synthetic Biology*, 2022.]

Male/Female Programming

A recurring experience during deep deprogramming has involved the conscious expression of the physical, emotional, and mental attributes of both a female and male at the same time, switching while fully conscious between the two. Bear with *us* as this is obviously difficult to relay. The significance of this, the implication of what is occurring, demands attention and cannot be sufficiently relayed to someone who has not experienced it.

We are not referring to aspects of *me*, but of experiencing another being entirely, co-consciously—an overlapping in which *we* are experiencing and expressing both, simultaneously, while switching from one to the other, seamlessly. This occurs when female and male are sexually interacting together. It is not an imagined experience or expression, it is a fully conscious actual one during which *I* am experiencing all of the sensations as if *I* were both female and male, in every imaginable way, until becoming both at the same time.

This experience of being something other than solely *us* in body, mind, emotion, and even spirit is not just about the human form; it has occurred with certain animal forms as well during which *i* was still conscious of *me* while also fully conscious of *being* them.

For periods of time throughout *our* life, *we* have been, for all intents and purposes, these other forms in body, mind, and spirit while still co-existing with *our* own consciousness. *We* attribute this recurring phenomenon to *our enhanced* status combined with abilities resulting from programming. As *i* deprogram—allowing the management and dismantling of the various alter programs within *us*—this condition as well as others are becoming revealed and disappearing.

Many might say that these enhanced memories are programmed-in and not real. Perhaps they are right; time will surely tell. Due to the number of presentations and forms these malevolent *beings* have taken, it appears they are attempting to obscure the issue, whoever they are.

[Take a moment to to think deeply about what I just relayed above. Stop for a moment to think about what is currently taking place globally regarding gender and transgender issues. Add to this the agenda regarding Transhumanism. Then, have a look into the MKUltra documents that did surface and brought to the public's attention in 1975 by the Church Committee. Amongst the projects was one in which the MKUltra doctors successfully programmed an adolescent boy into believing he was a girl.

They then repeatedly switched him back and forth between the two. Are you seeing what I see?]

Cognitive Dissonance and Alternate Programs

The awakening consciousness of a human soul/mind encounters *pre-programmed* roadblocks, and this disruption will inevitably occur. A direct relationship exists between the two—between the awakening and the disruption encountered. It is *our* explicit contention that the more profound the understanding becomes in the consciousness of the one breaking out of the global programming, the more difficult their day-to-day activities become regarding their security within this world. This will manifest in a variety of forms and be influenced by a variety of factors, depending on the individual in question.

The farther one goes "down the rabbit hole", as many refer to it—though this reference is a program trigger for many slaves—the more disconnect with the smooth machinations of society one will experience. Dysfunction within one's physical, mental, emotional, and spiritual aspects will appear and intensify as one progresses toward truth, the degree of dysfunction depending upon the number and degree of remaining connections to programs present in their own body and mind-soul and within their concession of associations.

Pre-set exiting programs are rife with *pre-programmed* repercussions and are part of a global program that is triggered as deprogramming intensifies. This is true for multi-generational, high-level slaves and for those under varying degrees of mass mind kontrol. As one moves farther and farther out from under programming into a conscious state of sincere truth, difficulties in their world will proportionately increase, particularly if conscious and unconscious associations to the programmers, kontrollers and handlers remain. For example, they may present new diversions, a common method of reprogramming. Disruption may manifest in financial status, physical health, emotional health, mental health, and/or spiritual health. The degree will vary, but financial ruin, relational distress, mental breakdown, cult participation, violence against others or oneself (suicide), etc. may likely follow.

To buffer dysfunctions, one can temper the timing and amount of truth-finding, keeping in mind that exit programming includes a reward/relief function doled out in degrees if one chooses to *reverse* the deprogramming process—not reverse in full, just to retreat to a point the programmers, kontrollers, and handlers have predetermined as acceptable while maintaining the illusion of continuing the deprogramming. Reward incentives will be in relation to how much the reversal allows ongoing use of the individual. In other words, the reversal reward allows a compromise requiring only that the human will not *fully* awaken from programming.

There is a well-established, *pre-programmed sequence* of factors involved in deprogramming as set forth and activated by the programmers, kontrollers, and handlers reaching into the third dimension as well as beyond it. This action-response program has pre-set variants for pre-determined circumstances, and is initially designed from beyond three-dimensional limitations to allow for almost infinite potential. This is why "containment" is so pervasive and successful without the conscious knowledge of even the initiated. *Under these circumstances*, only a small degree of deprogramming can be reached, though one is perfectly capable of breaking through the reprogramming that can and unfortunately does extensively occur. Far too many do not move beyond that reprogramming and that ought to be of grave concern for all of us. This is one of the double-bind methods of the kontrollers that offers a way out only to have it not be a way out at all but instead facilitate a re-binding to a different format. Escape becomes no escape at all and is instead a recycling of the same program through what *appears* to be new parameters.

This is the most commonly used form of reprogramming that *i* have personally experienced and viewed in others, from high-level slaves to those who do not believe they are programmed at all. It has been perpetrated upon *us* numerous times in order to assure *our* continued use over the years.

[One of the telltale signs of this is the true answers to life's questions that one is looking for never really come, yet show up only to change after some time has passed. This cycle can go on for an entire lifetime completely unnoticed by the individual due to not revisiting their history to see the pattern of constant change in the "answers" over time. The only solution is initiation into the mystery of life, such as Anthroposophy or Spiritual Science. With time, study, and practice, truths present with continued discipline, and genuine answers come that remain throughout time.]

Why is this method so successful? In *our* attempts to reveal what it is *we* have experienced, it has become apparent to *me* that the human condition, with all of the malevolent overshadowing, is well-trained to seek pleasure in abundance, the consolation prize being the avoidance of any painful personal enterprise. Ultimately, this has resulted in a great disadvantage to humans. Programmed avoidance means that the individual will assist in maintaining the global mind kontrol programming while unwittingly and inadvertently assisting in their own handling. (**Cognitive Dissonance.**)

We were designed this way, with *our* front alters being the main perpetrators of avoidance and denial. There are, of course, exceptions, but this programmed avoidance is on a massive scale. Those who escape this programming are usually halted during the deprogramming process by a new diversion that detours them into an even more insidious, prolonged compartment of programming. One *thinks* he or she is awakening from programming only to be "contained" by the kontrollers within another set of parameters as a diversion. This takes place in the world at large as well as MKUltra.

This masterfully designed "system" within global mind kontrol programming acts as a self-perpetuating loop. In fact, *we* are a microcosmic design of what is used on a macrocosmic level, *ours* being an intensified design reflecting the methods and means long used on society as a whole. An individualized, concerted effort by government, military, intelligence, religious and corporate institutions has designed a slave for various uses, the same goal as for mass mind kontrol but usually employing less individual means. "Black tech" is changing this. Up to now, enhancement and EEG heterodyned cloning and the necessary trauma and torture have pertained to individualized programming, but no more. *Total mind kontrol* technology has moved beyond this limitation.

The extent and level of intended use is directly related to the need (or lack thereof) for a concerted, intensified regime of *total mind kontrol* programming, the goal being to kontrol the subject without the subject being aware of it while diverting and "containing" glitches in the programming by reprogramming. Subjects will be under *total mind kontrol* and be incapable of freeing themselves from it. This is the "next level" of End Time programming as *we* know it—no longer a few slaves, but *the entire human species* used in various capacities without conscious knowledge of it. This will apply to multiple personality, high-level slaves with alters as well as those under mass mind kontrol.

How will the programmers go about creating an ongoing containment of so many slaves? Remember: the express goal is a society of slaves who do not know they are slaves, an illusion from which they will *not be able to awaken*. This will require an infinite variety of extensive diversions. Reach beyond a solely three-dimensional world view and imagine what this might look like. To maintain only the three-dimensional view is to assist in the perpetuation of the perpetration cycle.

Reincarnation and the Perception of Linear Time

Within the world at present, the experience of linear time is a perspective imposed and maintained by malevolence to assist in kontrol over humanity. The disinformation and misunderstanding around this issue allows programming to be maintained over unwitting, acquiescing individuals. *Partial truths* can and do more often than not work in favor of these programmers because acceptance of partial truths prevents us from *seeing* broader and bigger truths. Partial truths are more difficult to disprove. Malevolent programmers know this well and utilize partial truths in reprogramming. A partial veil disempowers *us*, which is all it takes to maintain programming.

As with many issues that the human race must learn to consciously face, *total mind kontrol* programming is fraught with partial truths of disinformation, misinformation, and indoctrination, and "linear time" is at the root of misunderstanding so as to aggravate our ability to grasp time's relationship with "space". *Our* personal experience of the true nature of time is not in the least linear, despite being *perceived* as such in this dimensional reality, the operative word being "perceived". A more accurate perception is its ever-present *now* nature.

Time is linear in certain accepted parameters, much as many limitations are. Attempt instead to visualize time as a *circle* and place yourself at the center of that circle. Grasp this experience *body, mind and soul* and at any point reach into the circle's perimeter that is space-time and attain access to past, present, or future. An intellectual grasp is the first step, but you will eventually have to go beyond intellect. When you *remember* this on every level, then it is effective.

We have frequently and systematically experienced space-time outside the parameters of linear time, both while under full programming and while in deep deprogramming. Time has been "altered" for *us*, sped up and slowed significantly, thus precipitating profound spatial affects in *our* conscious experience, some in "altered" consciousness, some in higher Self consciousness. We experience the general world of the everyday around *us* as an "altered" consciousness, apparently unrecognizable to many we encounter. However, *we* have met others who also know this to be true, due to their experiences completely independent of *ours*, and additionally some who have experienced events along with *me* in this reality—fully conscious, as it were—that revealed the presence of the mass program they too were under. This group includes some who consider themselves initiates of truth.

Once one understands the true scope of space-time—or the lack of truth in the present understanding of linear time—the experiences being reported by deprogramming slaves like *us* will begin to make more sense.

The truth is that we can access points in space-time—past, present, or future—to affect the now. This has been done for eons by those who fully grasp this law and develop the ability to do so. *Our* status as well as *our* programming and use provided numerous occurrences of "alter-ed" space-time, some memories of which remain in *our* conscious mind never to be lost—experiences that facilitate an out-of-the-ordinary view of space-time even now for *me*, the front alter.

This same misconception of time also affects current views of reincarnation. That lives have been lived in the "past" is a (mis)perception based on the (mis)perception of linear time. The concept of "past lives" is stuck in a static, unchanging history of linear time, over and done with: *history*. This is yet another partial truth. *I* do not mean to exclude other lives lived—not in the least—but they are excluded from the now, and this is problematic. That another time in history and the future can be accessed right now is true, which means that linear *history* is only a (mis)*perception* of time based solely in an experience of it within world-programmed consciousness. Other lives pertain deeply to this one.

Once we experience life outside the linear consciousness we can remember and participate in this journey of life and its offering of individual and group evolution as intended, beyond malevolent programming.

This is not about what ought to be or not, only what is and has been for *us* during *tmk* programming and use as well as during *our* breaking of *our* bondage to it. That *we* have *consciously* accessed past and future events in very real, tangible ways does not pertain solely to *our* own lives lived in the perception of linear time. *Past lives and future events are accessible now.*

Many of *our* abilities were obviously considered necessary for *our* design in the first place.

[Many of my experiences were random and seemed to be spontaneous despite any effort on my part.]

We caution the use of the word "evolve" due to how malevolence has usurped this concept for a dark and heinous agenda involving the total *kontrol* of humanity—body, mind and soul. A faux "evolution" is at its heart, and reincarnation as it is currently (mis)understood in the world plays into that deception.

This freedom can be gained by individual acts in isolated experiences and thus may be perceived as "unstable". When it is accepted by many, it will become acceptable within the everyday world. This needs to occur here on Earth while in a body.

As soon as one begins to attain ideas outside of the "world" program, societal pressure due to programmed consciousness isolates and marginalizes the individual. To accept what and where the individual is attempting to go would require others to break their own programming to a degree they are afraid to do. *We* have repeatedly witnessed this as the most frightening request one can make of another, hitting as it does at the most primal survival mechanism programmed into humanity for eons—survival of body and mind that have forgotten the power of remembrance by the soul.

Soratic Transhumanist Entities

A few years ago, I began to "see" entities of a whole new variety in my periphery of vision. Experiencing such things is not unusual for me, and thus it is not a fearful encounter, but more of an exploration. I move into such things with questions and a searching mind and heart. In other words, heart-based thinking.

What I would encounter in the place I was staying in New Mexico in various rooms at a distance (not in my auric field), were what I would describe as black, somewhat insect-like creatures that had a mechanical air about them. The defining lines were sharp and angular. I would understand them to be a cross between biological and technological in nature, and not of this world. They appeared to have gained entry here in this realm, but did not belong.

In 2022 I would receive a research paper (https://growupconference. com/news/covid-vaccines-consequences-on-the-soul-spirit-and-life-after-death/31329/) by Bernhard Guenther titled Covid Vaccines—Consequences on the Soul, Spirit and Life After Death. In this was contained information gathered by different Spiritual Science practitioners in the alternative health field who had encountered clients who had been vaccinated by the various Covid "vaccines".

What I discovered was that the entities I had encountered in my periphery over many months and years prior, those described above, appear to be what the researchers referred to as "Soratic Transhumanist spirits". Due to my own connection to Sorat throughout my programming and use years, as well as one particular download several years ago prior to the encounter of the entities I mention here, this came as no surprise, yet a welcomed identification.

There was no question for me that I had arrived at the identity of the entities I had encountered.

In that download, which occurred in the early mornings hours after I exited bed and sat quietly with the intention of allowing what was attempting to surface to do so, I would come to the profound understanding that Sorat, an entity that does not belong to our realm and is from another part of the Cosmos outside of the earth realm, was coming in to "incarnate". That this was occurring *soon* (timelines being nebulous in such instances and thus "soon" could be any number of days, weeks, years, etc.) was of great concern to me as I understood on a deep level the nature of this being due to previous involvement in my life. I attribute the unconscionable and inhuman thoughts, actions and desires of humans to this being's influence. (He uses Luciferic and Ahrimanic spirits to assist his agenda as well.) I think of him as nihilistic as regards the human race.

[That involvement in my programming in part was my being wed to him many years ago in a strange ceremony that involved a statue as representative of him. Additionally, I would discover that the Chinese symbol tattooed on my right shoulder included within it the symbol for Sorat according to Rudolph Steiner who provided said symbol approximately one hundred years ago.]

I would discuss this with a friend who was quite familiar with Anthroposophy (Spiritual Science as provided by Rudolph Steiner) and this helped a bit to alleviate the need to share. On occasion, such downloads are deeply concerning and consuming, especially when I do not understand the full implications of the information I receive or what it is I am supposed to do with it. Who do I tell? And what do I say?

My conclusion at this time, during this time, is that the Soratic transhumanist spirits (entities) are inundating our environment on perhaps an unprecedented scale due to their presence in at least some of the Covid "vaccines". This includes said entities being able to migrate further into the environment and those within it.

I was clearly witness to this prior to the "vaccine" delivery and symptom presentations of said entities now occurring.

My point in presenting this is rather simple. Well over a decade ago I stated that nanobots were in my body, and the response was one of cognitive dissonance. And today, *everyone* has nanobots thanks to chemtrails, GMO foods and various pharmaceuticals and "vaccines". It is important that people come to understand what it is we are all up against. One cannot genuinely counter an enemy if they are not even aware of it. This is a war of spirit, a war that requires a consciousness that seems to have vanished from humanity. A consciousness that must be awakened if one is to remain human in light of the spirit-come-physical means being used against each and everyone of us. We must individually take responsibility for the "new unconsciousness" pervading our society.

As stated many times previously: *they are riding the technology into us.* They being the ones outside of our physical perception who wish to interfere with our Divine evolution. Their influence within the slumbering human populace is painfully evident. People are "checked-out". Just because one has information, it does not protect in and of itself. Consciousness must reach into a much deeper understanding, a life-changing true understanding of the Cosmos and our place in it.

This is our exit from the narrative that subsumes our mind and spirit and soul.

Conclusion (2013)
with Updates and Revisions (2022)

Recovery for *us* is not recovery from events per se, but an ongoing way of life. The way *we* interpret the world around *us*, how it is that *we see* and *feel* things, does not allow for normalcy as others know it. *We see* beyond what appears to be there and cannot stop being who *we* are in that respect, nor do *we* wish to. In part, this is *our* innate ability as well as a result of what was done to *us* by them. *We* don't have to continue to suffer from the past, but are often inadvertently triggered by what *we see* and *feel* going on around *us* in the present.

"Moving on" as most think of it is not for *us*, but conscious awakening and living is. *We* continually encounter people—many of whom consider themselves initiated—with absolutely no idea about the degree of what they do not understand about the world around them and how it directly affects them. When someone pushes for *us* to "move on," it is clearly their own inability to face and accept parts of truth being presented.

To other slaves out there who are trying to recover the many parts of themselves: *You will more than likely know more about many things regarding your programmed life and the effect the Network has on the world than those you work with.*

Your initial difficulty will be establishing a coherent framework and discerning truth from program. This will be determined by the degree of conscious awareness you and those who help you deprogram assert. This will be challenging in your work with them, but they will have to learn with you if they are mature enough to do so and sincerely willing.

Early in *our* deep deprogramming, we needed steady support and the grounding presence of one person near *us*, even if only in long distance phone contact. His compassion, kindness, and knowledge helped *us* understand more clearly on a conscious level what it was that came forth from *our* alters. This was an absolute necessity in the first year or two, and his ability to remain neutral and open-minded was lifesaving. With time, *we* began to trust *ourselves* and what it is *we* know, despite the conflict with what other people seem to think they know about *our* predicament. Again, discernment once the fog begins to clear is crucial. Program messages will not just disappear.

Continued healing is necessary and *we* know in part what *we* need to facilitate that. *We* are working to make that happen. *Our* ability to maintain what *we* have for the past several years in deep deprogramming—particularly alters and their programs allowing *us* to function appropriately—is coming to an end, the energy gone. *We* are exhausted in body, mind, and soul, and the separation between alters that once allowed a degree of acceptable functioning no longer exists. However, *we* continue to make appropriate choices to the best of *our* ability.

[This is a bit unknown and misunderstood by most. A person with MPD has had many personalities to cope with the world at large, and when the transition of becoming whole ensues there is a sense of exhaustion and often a loss of functionality that various parts assisted with. This can be resolved. However, in later life often the energy needed to "start a new life" is difficult to find. Having said this, from a physical mentality it is true, yet new found spirit can assist in keeping one going forward in light of new understandings and perceptions from a much broader stance or consciousness. I refer to this as moving from initiation in the dark to initiation into the Light.]

As *we* become more conscious, *we* have to learn to function with different skills outside of full programming. Additionally the work—the writing, the journals and books, the colláges, videos, audios, research—needs to be set aside. Real rest in a safe and peaceful environment is in order, though *we* are not certain it can be attained to the degree *we* need. *We* will find out soon enough.

What is imperative for readers to understand is that despite *our* higher consciousness being present and making choices, the reprogramming attempts and interference continues to make things difficult.

First, the obvious: *within a handful of years, the intention is that* we *die*, which for slaves like *us* can be made to occur in several ways: alcohol and/or drug abuse, sexual addiction, bulimia and/or anorexia, physical violence to self, "lone gunman" acts of violence, suicide, and/or a variety of diseases in the body. Unless *we* are of significant use during deprogramming as a disinformation agent or handler—or *our* conscious, active, daily relationship to Love and God carries *us* through— *we* will be killed by programming one way or another.

Despite malevolence's abilities, however, the most powerful solution to keeping these programs from taking over again during deprogramming, initiation into esoteric Christianity is and continues to be our solution and protection. Exercising it must be consistent and ongoing, daily.

Second, *discrediting ourselves during the deprogramming process is intended as more and more truth is revealed.* Upon hearing part of *our* story, many uninitiated ask, "Why have they not just killed you?" to which *we* respond, "They are attempting just that." Numerous factors are involved in deciding the how and why for each slave, not only who the slave is and what they remember, but more importantly the slave's ability in real deprogramming to reveal certain details of what they remember to those who can genuinely hear it. More often than not, both the uninitiated and the initiated alike seem to believe that only naming perpetrators and organizations involved will not be allowed. This is not what they fear.

They send in their kontrollers and handlers on slaves beginning to awaken to kontrol the release of information they deem sufficient for their particular agenda, including the names of specific officials. They move in before anyone else does, knowing where the significant breakdowns in programming are occurring long before anyone else does, sending in their own to kontrol and handle the gathering, containment, and release of information they will then handle. This is containment.

In this process, the slave is kontrolled and handled as well. If you understand nothing else, understand this: This has occurred more times than can be counted and continues to be perpetrated as one of their methods. *We* know it well. Due to indoctrination of the uninitiated, the longer *we* stay in deep deprogramming, the more surreal the information coming forward will sound to them (and to many of the initiated as well). This is not *our* fault, barring limitations in presenting the information. It is directly due to the current consciousness of the indoctrinated, misinformed, disinformed public. Cognitive Dissonance abounds.

It is common knowledge among insiders that they send in theirs to contain information and allow leaks, then repeatedly and consistently sacrifice their own, either by public infamy or death—murder of their own as "sacrifices" in private and in public (one just needs the proper context to see them for what they are). Using their media to publicly defame a well-known official is a common practice after their significant use years have passed. Offering up one of their own assists in obfuscating the truth and distracting the public at the same time.

These malevolent ones have no allegiance to any human, even at the highest levels. All slaves are eventually disposed of as the being moves on to another human, usually in the same bloodline.

The many and varied ways of use run the gamut from literal physical sacrifice as in a private or public occult ritual, individual or en masse, to the sacrifice of a member's persona before the world to be viewed and wondered at. For insiders, there is no wondering; it is *seen* for what it is. Agendas are furthered, the balance of energy necessary to reach their ultimate goal without total destruction of their human subjects maintained.

Rituals summon these malevolent *beings* as well as the powers these *beings* can exercise in this third dimension. One of the most profound effects of rituals is to maintain a veil over the consciousness that is the innate nature of humans, including their ability to *see* and *feel* what is right before them. Make no mistake, malevolent *beings* have a very real, tangible presence with a very real influence and are a significant part of why these rituals are performed. The fact that rituals deeply enhance trauma-based, *total mind kontrol* programming is not in question.

Many at the highest levels of this Luciferic/Ahrimanic Network are the grandest philanthropists in society which has absolutely nothing to do with true Benevolence, nor Love, but works as a very successful cover. Many powerful, educated, wealthy families perpetrate the things *we* have written here, and if you think this does not and will not affect you and yours, think again. It already is.

Based on a person's degree of conscious awareness, they will take in the world around them accordingly. Certain individuals are unable to actually hear what is being said, even when it is repeated. What *we* mean is an actual inability to hear, in most cases accompanied by a somewhat vacant look in the eyes, a sign that the invisible line has been crossed into the unknown. In some instances, they will even repeat their question while not acknowledging the unheard response. At this point, *we* try to gently steer the conversation out of these areas to respect the person's programmed inability to go there.

Some of the biggest stories to break during so-called public disclosure are presented publicly by the malevolent ones themselves, some of whom are regarded as "heroes" in the deprogramming/conspiracy community.

These multiple personality, *total mind kontrolled* slaves are part of the Network and are often frighteningly powerful. They are used both unwittingly and wittingly. *We* could name some of them as well as speak about their position within the Network, including the hierarchy level of the *beings* running them. In some cases, *we* could even name who their specific kontroller and handlers are. *We* refer to them as "gangs" with either a reasonably high-level kontroller at the top or a very powerful one. And remember: the handling does not work one way, it is always mutual handling between insiders; *we* have been used in this capacity even while in deep deprogramming.

Examine the history behind people in stories that appear to reveal so much truth. Research their connections, the language, how Neuro-Linguistic Programming (NLP) works, and always ask, "What is not being revealed?" Check the conclusions drawn. Where did the information take you? After its disclosure, what changes happened, what happened to the players? Follow it. Did it eventually become of no consequence? Truth can be gleaned from such stories, but only with patience, discernment, time spent, and being continually guided by Divine consciousness.

Deprogramming is the choice *we* would again make, though at times *we* have felt as though *we* jumped from the frying pan into the fire. For *us*, it is all about taking back *our* human soul and trying to make a real, tangible difference for those who seek to break their own programming: MKUltra and civvy alike.

Through private conversations with those *we* trust, *we* have decided to reveal specifics, but not for public disclosure. The highest good for all concerned is *our* intention when it comes to *our* disclosures. The only reason *we* mention this here is to encourage other slaves to do the same once they have established a truly safe support system and can discern where to take certain information and where not to.

There are things that must be released from within the slave, no matter what. Only each can determine what those things are and when they are to be brought forth.

It is also necessary to reveal truth to clearly understand how this Network operates and thrives. As has been true for other slaves *we* have met, the difficulty is finding those who are sincerely able to hear what needs to be heard. If the one you are attempting to tell is not hearing you, look for someone else. Truly hearing someone—not only listening—requires a profoundly deep commitment that will tear at the foundations of what one has believed and had faith in. Those able to venture beyond their staunchly held limitations are rare. It is far easier to remain on the periphery, but such will not serve the individual clinging tightly there, nor serve those who desperately need help to break free of *total mind kontrol* programming. Again, everyone is directly affected by this; no one is beyond its reach.

We still struggle deeply with physical problems as a direct result of the life handed *us*. *Our* main concern has been and continues to be the extraction of *our* soul from the reach of malevolence, now and always. In this, *we* believe *we* are indeed winning.

When *we* were finishing up Book 1, *our* desire was that it would be enough, that *we* would not have the need to write any more on the subject of *tmk* programming, particularly *our* personal experiences and understandings. *We* longed to walk away from it all, leave it behind, have a more "normal" life. *We* cannot express in words the self-delusion that lay in those desires. As *our* book has stated, this is not true for *us*, not in the least. Nor is it true for any who have awakened. Something far greater is available and it is *our* sincerest hope that these books will initiate many questions in those who need to ask them, and that the Christ Impulse guides them to that greater truth.

In 2022 while updating these books, a resolution to something from 2014-2015 occurred. It would be in March of 2022 that a friend and researcher/radio host would send me a copy of a show he recently did regarding what was being found in the vials of "COVID vaccines". The whistleblower in that show was a microscopy expert who wished to remain anonymous due to recent repercussions some whistleblowers regarding this massive psychological operation were experiencing. Upon seeing some of this person's photo and video footage from their microscopy research, I realized that a series of fully conscious visions from 2014 through 2015 were finally revealing what the subject matter was. These interactive visions had lasted for months.

During the months of said visions, this is what I came to know, without question. What I saw was alive, and most certainly made of "Luciferic light". The light was white, but of the blue spectrum. Cold, no warmth as with golden light, much like the lights I had seen coming out for years and naming them as of malevolent intent: things such a "Blu-ray". (Blue laser technology. Nowadays, with all the LED, such as in car headlights, the new streetlights, all of it is part of smart technologies being installed for mind control. I also understand this to be very much associated with Ahriman's character.) It pulsed with this light and moved ever so gracefully and slowly: it was beautiful and treacherous to behold. It was dangerous and had an affect on humanity from the level of DNA (this was due to one of the visions I encountered involving a human fetus surrounded by the subject within the vision with the understanding that the fetus was being taken over by the subject). I recognized its importance, but lacked enough understanding of what I was seeing to be able to proclaim what it was I was experiencing. No one I brought it to had any ideas either.

At the time of viewing the video from my friend in 2022, I realized that what I had encountered *eight years prior* was the final result—meaning the full growth and development of this sentient matter—of what was now showing up in the so called "vaccine" that was well-known as of 2022 to not be a "vaccine" at all, but a bio-weapon being injected into unwitting human participants. (A bio-weapon as well is on the swabs being presented as part of "testing for COVID".)

When I saw the microscopy footage that utilized the dark background, it was then I knew without any doubt what I had encountered. However, now I questioned why I was shown this and by what or whom? Was this one of numerous organic visions I had encountered over the years? One of several prophetic experiences that played out accurately? Or was this someone on the inside attempting to show me through BCI (Brain Computer Interface) what was to come, and why? I would soon realize that it did not matter in the end, yet viewed it as another piece of information that assisted my understanding of several aspects of what I had experienced for a lifetime not only at the hands of malevolent programmers, but also the organic abilities I had—and have—that were not only a result of what was done to me, but a pre-existing condition that drew the very same enemy's attention my way from the very start. I will go so far as to say—and this will indeed become apparent in the generations to come—that my pre-birth selection—dare I say even the coupling of my parents?—began my entry into mind control experimentation. What I understand that many would have no access to in "normal" life circumstances is that the black magicians working in these arenas have access to the **Supersensible World** through their malevolent practices. Mind control experimentation has been presented as its most obvious definition solely, leaving out the ultimate goal: Transhumanism and all that entails. The occult, esoteric aspects of these "programs" is often neglected in lieu of the more mundane, material conscious aspects: science. As stated so many times over in this work and elsewhere, the esoteric/occult, *black magic-science* cannot be over looked if one wants to truly grasp what we as a species are already in the midst of.

This was my personal validation of and deeper understanding of the "overshadowing" I had already written about regarding my conception.

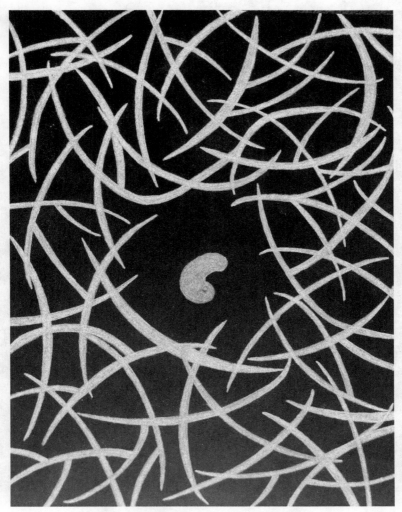

*A 2014 prescient vision of a malevolent sentience
disrupting the genetics of humanity via the fetal stage.*

Lexicon

Abreact/Abreaction: to release or express an emotion previously repressed or forgotten.

Alter: Can be either a fragment of a personality or a full personality designed within this body, either by the programmers or me (only a few were created by me), who can be triggered to the surface by a variety of means, thus either co-existing with other alters or "holding the body" by themselves, depending on the state of my deprogramming from intentionally designed "multiplicity". In deep deprogramming many alters co-exist consciously together all of the time, with some trading predominant roles as needed per their abilities, as well as many trying to surface who are no longer allowed to (by me being conscious enough to control them) due to their malevolent nature, per their programming.

Adrenochrome: The oxidized form of adrenaline produced by the trauma and torture of children (and adults) to be utilized for highs and longevity by psychopaths and sociopaths. It has become an industrialized product on a global scale, harvested in many underground facilities such as DUMBs (Deep Underground Military Bases).

Ahrimanic: Sub-human ahrimanic beings living in the elements of Earth and water enter Man's subconscious, especially during sleep, and take hold there of Man's will forces and weaken Man. (https://anthroposophy.eu/Ahrimanic_influence_on_Man)

Artificial Intelligence: The ability of a machine or computer to perform tasks that require learning.

Astral Body: The human astral body is one of Man's Bodily principles, part of the structural make-up of Man, and so closely intertwined with the other bodily principles it should not be studied or considered as a separate entity. In one's lifetime Man develops the astral approximately

between 14 and 21 years from the age of puberty. (https://anthroposophy.
eu/Huaman_astral_body) The astral system finds its expression in the nervous system. Additionally, there is an astral body around the Earth.

Asuras: I will not attempt to define this term, but rather leave this to Rudolph Steiner. Suffice to say they are of purely evil intent and fall outside of the Luciferic and Ahrimanic realm from my experience. Dr. Steiner referred to them as retarded Beings of the Hierarchy of the Archai. They desire to entrap man into gross egoism, or materialism. "Beings known as the Asuras will creep into the consciousness soul and therewith into the human 'I' or ego—for the 'I' lights up in the consciousness soul. The Asuras will generate evil with a far mightier force than was wielded by the Satanic powers in the Atlantean epoch or by Luciferic Spirits in the Lemurian Epoch." (Rudolph Steiner, "The Deed of Christ and the Opposing Spiritual Powers Lucifer, Ahriman, Mephistopheles, Asuras".)

Brain Computer Interface (BCI): "...is technology that sends and receives signals between the brain and an external device. Brain-computer interfaces are also called brain-machine interfaces (BMI). BCIs collect and interpret brain signals, and then transmit them to a connected machine that outputs commands associated with the brain signals received." (https://www.emotiv.com/bci-guide/)

Call Back Programming: This is designed for calling back numerous slaves with similar programming and can be done with *hidden in plain sight* techniques (in plain view but unknown to the masses who are asleep to such.) As with the television show mentioned in this manuscript, *My Own Worst Enemy*, many slaves will not only be drawn in to watch the show, but will be triggered intentionally by something in the broadcasting to access one or more alters to reach out to their handlers/kontrollers. This technique is layered into the victim years before and is used for End-Time programming. This is a test to see if programming is intact.

Christ Impulse: "Rudolf Steiner's teachings of Christ—and in particular what he refers to as the 'Christ impulse'—are unique. Christ, he says, is an objective universal force, existing independently of Christian churches and confessions, and working for the whole of humanity. The impulse that Christ brought to earth acts for the advancement of all people, irrespective of religion, creed or race...Christ will influence the future development of the earth and humanity…Christ will reappear but in a higher reality than the physical one—in a reality which we will only see if we have first acquired a sense and understanding of spiritual life." (*The Christ Impulse and the Development of the Ego-Consciousness*, Rudolf Steiner. https://zoboko.com/text/rmmolojq/the-christ-impulse-and-the-development-of-ego-consciousness/1)

Clean Slates: These are split off parts during trauma and torture that are later either programmed (the strongest splits will later be chosen for programming and this can be only a few out of the many created) or left in the mind as fragments that will integrate when that process is strong enough among other alters. (It has always been heartbreaking to me that these fragments are created and then left as an empty "piece of mind". How awful.)

Containment: My term for the programmers, kontrollers, and handlers moving in to control an impending situation that involves revelations not warranted by the Network. It often involves either one MKUltra slave moving towards deprogramming or the uncovering of human trafficking/pedophilia/programming locations, deeds, and perpetrators. An insider is sent (or a mind controlled slave) to thwart the deprogramming or run the "investigation" into the surfacing information. In the case of latter, the public will see a sacrifice offered up with disinformation while the deeds continue elsewhere with no one of great importance to the Network sacrificed and the slumbering public remaining unaware.

Cult-Loyal Alters: These alternate personalities are designed from the start to remain devoted to the cause and rituals in which they participate. They are spiritless and despondent, or the opposite, being much like their human counterparts, the perpetrators. An example of one of the latter is alter *She 29ᵗʰ*.

Deep Deprogramming: This process began when the main front alter became *consciously* aware of who and what I am, allowing other parts of me to come forward to present what they knew. This could not occur as long as the front line system denied the truth of my programming.

Directed Energy Weapons (DEWS): Weapons that target individuals, groups, communities and even states and nations with lasers, microwaves, particle beams and sound beams. These technologies utilize satellites, cell towers, GWEN (Ground Wave Emergency Network) towers, antenna arrays (such as HAARP), NEXRADS (Next Generation Weather Radar), smartphones, 5G and 6G, etc. They now come in compact individual units that a perpetrator can carry around with them. They can destroy, slowly or quickly, as well as harass and control, and in many cases without the victim knowing such and often for a lifetime. (For more understanding of this and its true intended purpose, I recommend in the Resources Elana Freeland's three book series on such technologies.)

Dissociation, Dissociated: An ongoing state of MPD due to programming methods involving various traumas and torture: a scientific and esoteric methodology utilized by my programmers. This state can be experienced minimally or extremely depending on any given situation, allowing me to remain functional or not within the world for any given period of time. It is a state of being "removed", "distant", "away" somewhere in mind and spirit, though my body is present. It is my contention that my true nature exists somehow on the outside of my body during this state. There is always some connection between my spirit and body, it is only the degree that varies.

Download: Information presented by my alters to the main front alter. This can include memories belonging to that alter as well as information that alter has attained due to its interaction with other alters, *entities/beings*, or people and situations in the world.

eMKUltra: Electromagnetic programming which can be done from afar, as in remotely. This technology is *extremely* advanced as compared to above ground technologies and would be difficult for the average person to understand, let alone accept. It involves such things as HAARP-like phased array antenna systems, cell towers, NEXRADS, GWEN towers, satellites, smart phones and much more. A person of interest can be selected, programmed and utilized all at a distance…as in no hands-on needed.

Etheric Body: In one's lifetime, Man develops the etheric bodily principle approximately between 7 and 14 years, up to the age of puberty. In Man's physical body, the etheric body finds its expression in the glandular system and processes. (https://anthroposophy.eu/Human_etheric_body) Additionally, there is an etheric cosmic realm. The etheric energies are responsible for the formation of the human being we see and interact with.

Front Alter: This is a sort of "shell" or "conduit" alter heading the frontline system through whom other alters present to the world.

Frontline Alter System: A collection of alter personalities designed to present to the world. This system is headed by the main front alter, and is designed to never allow the truth about my multiplicity to reach the consciousness of or beyond the main front alter.

Initiated: In this book, this refers to those "in the know" regarding mind control and having access to mind-controlled slaves. As opposed to:

Initiation: In this book, this refers to the process of coming to understand the truth of the world and cosmos we live in as perceived through the study of Spiritual Science, known as Anthroposophy and brought to the world through Dr. Rudolph Steiner. In our times, this process is being offered whether ready or not, as exposure to aspects of the occulted malevolent side of this is occurring on a worldwide basis.

Kontroller: A person whose malevolent hierarchic power level falls between a programmer and a handler. They are more powerful than a handler yet not of the caliber of a programmer, oversee several handlers and slaves, and are often at the head of a group of individuals I refer to as a "gang." It has been important to someone inside of me that it is always spelled with a "k". The same goes for the word *kontrol* when it is referring to *total mind kontrol (tmk)* programming.

Loop Programs: These programs run repeatedly in a loop, often for hours and at night. This reinforces the program that was put in years before.

Luciferic: Luciferic and Ahrimanic influences are to be seen in a broader context of "counterforces" or spiritual influences that are opposing or side-tracking Man's development. They are two polar force-fields or influences that pull into different directions, whereas the Christ represents the balanced middle ground. (https://anthroposophy.eu/Luciferic_influence_on_man)

Malevolence: Forces and *beings* that reside in the supersensible world—beyond this realm—yet long to reside in the world of man—living through man—that work for the injury, ill intent and subjugation of humanity. They work through man and advanced technologies as well.

Missing Time: This can be extreme in MPD, yet can also occur during any form of trauma or dissociation. It is the experience of an actual block of time missing from your chronology ranging from minutes to years, as was the case with me. It can go unnoticed in the short interims.

Morgellons: A more appropriate name, and one I often refer to it as, is "chemtrail sickness". Thanks to horrific geoengineering for decades now, humans, animals and the entire Earth environment are saturated with nanotech appearing as fibers, quantum dots, heavy metals, crystals and in the more extreme cases insects and insect parts that have grown inside the tissues of the body. As of late, thanks to the "vaccine" for Covid-19, computer chips on the nanoscale are also present with the "vaccinated" affecting strange signals and anomalies when around technology.

Multiple Personality Disorder (MPD): A disorder in which two or more distinct personalities exist in the same person, each of which prevails at a certain time. This was the original name for what is now known as Dissociative Identity Disorder (DID).

Overshadowing: At the time of conception, the entities co-join as well through the act of intercourse and insemination of the humans. It may be two entities through both woman and man, or one parent alone. It is my belief that this is part of shoring up bloodlines for generational programming and "purity". (I wonder at what goes on in artificial insemination?)

Optogenetics: A technology that allows you to turn specific neurons on and off in the brain by genetic targeting utilizing light frequencies.

Quantum Teleportation: Known as Einstein's famous "spooky action at a distance" or quantum entanglement, in which the properties of a particle affect the properties of another particle even though a large distance separates them.

Reprogramming: An intense reinforcement of already established programming executed in a particular setting and timeframe, with possible enhancements.

Reporting Alter: An alter internally installed to report any movement towards deprogramming or to report unsanctioned activities by other alters. Often programmed to call in each day to their handler to report the days activities.

Satanic Ritual Abuse (SRA): Any form of physical, sexual or psychological mistreatment that involves the use of satanic ritual. (https://www.wordnik.com/words/satanic%20ritual%20abuse)

Singularity; Artificial Intelligence: "…it will begin with an artificial general intelligence (AGI) entity that can improve on itself without human intervention. Its evolution into a more powerful agent, an ASI, will cause an "intelligence explosion" that notable personalities like Tesla CEO Elon Musk and physicist Stephen Hawking have surmised could eventually lead to the extinction of the human race…Predictably, there has been much disagreement about how the singularity might be triggered. Some purport that it will be a pure-machine entity, while others say humans themselves might find a way to amplify their own intelligence…One hypothesis suggests a process called Whole Brain Emulation (WBE), where humans will "upload their brain" into a computer that will simulate a virtual world based on the brain's model." (https://1reddrop.com/2019/01/09/what-is-the-singularity-in-artificial-intelligence-what-you-need-to-know-about-the-future-greatest-event-in-human-history/)

Supersensible World: My understanding—as I study Anthroposophy and Rudolph Steiner's lectures—the world we inhabit between death and rebirth. The world inhabited as well by beings of the Hierarchies not manifest in our physical world, yet of significant influence on such and humanity.

Targeted Individuals (TI): A person who has been singled out for his or her whistle-blowing or their politics. As well someone who is desired by another person to be a slave due to sexual attraction, sadistic desires and even because that person just happened to be in the wrong place at the wrong time. I have heard of those who simply said the wrong thing to the wrong person—someone with power or access to the current technologies such as Directed Energy Weapons (DEWS)—being subsequently targeted.

Total Mind Kontrol (*tmk*): A powerful, well financed, vast Network of programmers, kontrollers, and handlers who through a variety of methods utilizing occult, esoteric practices, and what we call "black tech" (covert technology financed and designed in secrecy) design *total mind kontrol* slaves to be covertly used by various government, military, intelligence, religious, and corporate organizations and agencies, some of which are part of the very design and programming process to begin with. Slaves are also used by individuals associated with this vast Network.

Twilight Language/Symbols: The language and symbols of the esoteric (hidden from the masses, occulted, and only grasped and understood by those initiated), as opposed to the exoteric (in plain view and perceived by the masses).

Übermensch: Literally meaning "overman", coined in 1883 by Frederich Nietzsche, meant to be the ideal future human and goal of humanity. The English translation became "Beyond-man" and finally "Superman". (The Transhumanist goal of today.)

Resources

This list is for anyone wanting to better understand *total mind kontrol* programming as well as multiplicity, along with dealing with the effects of such in deep deprogramming. It is a small sampling of a quickly growing field of research and understanding. Some of this material is very far reaching, beyond the *total mind kontrol* slave's individual experience. The subject of mind control reaches into every aspect of human existence.

Most of this material can trigger *total mind kontrol* slave's programming if they are not in genuine deprogramming. Please do not access this material if you are possibly a victim of this programming, until you are certain that you have someone, at least one person, to utilize as a support person. Someone with whom you have presented your possible situation to prior to your reading this material. This material is not to be taken lightly.

We do not promote any particular faith nor religious views that are provided by the individuals or their works listed below. *We* do however give immense gratitude for their devotion and diligence in providing the valuable, and in some cases, unprecedented parts of this vast puzzle. *We* know personally that to do so forever changes one's place within the world.

Books In Print and More

Alan, Ron. *21ˢᵗ Century MK-Ultra Slave: A Vintage Transhuman Tale*, KDP, 2022.

Bain, Donald. *The CIA'S Control of Candy Jones*. Barricade Books, 2002.

Bowart, Walter. *Operation Mind Control*. Fontana, 1978. Look for the *Expanded and Revised, Researchers Edition*, 1994.

Bryant, Nick. *The Franklin Scandal: A Story of Powerbrokers, Child Abuse and Betrayal*. Trine Day, 2009.

Byington, Judy, M.S.W, L.C.S.W, ret. *Twenty-Two Faces: Inside the Extraordinary Life of Jenny Hill and Her Twenty-Two Multiple Personalities*. Tate Publishing, 2012.

We caution those abused and used by Mormon/LDS hierarchy; my initial reading of this book years ago seemed to absolve any perpetration by such authorities. It does, however, offer an incredibly accurate view of ritual abuse multiplicity from the victim's standpoint.

Cannon, Martin. *The Controllers: A New Hypothesis of Alien Abductions,* 1992. https://www.bibliotecapleyades.net/sociopolitica/esp_sociopol_mindcon04.htm

Chase, Truddi. *When Rabbit Howls.* Reed, 1987.

Cooper, Milton William. *Behold a Pale Horse.* Light Technology, 1991.

Background to the deception behind the creation of the UFO community as well as the shadow government agenda.

Craig, Gary. *EFT (Emotional Freedom Technique) for PTSD.* Energy Psychology Press, 2009.

de Vere, Nicholas. *The Dragon Legacy: The Secret History of An Ancient Bloodline.* Book Tree, 2004. This author is a bloodline elite and much can be learned with the proper discernment.

Dizdar, Russ. *The Black Awakening: Rise of Satanic Super Soldiers and the Coming Chaos.* Preemption Products, 2009.

An invaluable tool for understanding the demonic aspect of tmk programming and its effect on multiple personalities. Pastor Dizdar died October 18, 2021. His contributions to understanding the world of mind control and demonic possession are invaluable.

Duncan, Robert and The Mind Hacking Strategy Group. *Project: Soul Catcher, Volume Two: Secrets of Cyber and Cybernetic Warfare Revealed.* KDP, 2010.

The Matrix Deciphered. 2010. Online.

Must reads for initiated and uninitiated alike. The most in-depth scientific perspective on "black" mind tech being used in mind control programming that I have found.

Epstein, Orit Badouk, Schwartz, Joseph and Wingfield Schwartz, Rachel. *Ritual Abuse and Mind Control: The Manipulation of Attachment Needs.* Karnac Books Ltd, 2011.

Freeland, Elana. *Chemtrails, HAARP and the Full Spectrum Dominance of Planet Earth.* KDP Publishing, 2014.

Under an Ionized Sky: From Chemtrails to Space Fence Lockdown. KDP Publishing, 2018.

Geoengineered Transhumanism: How the Environment Has Been Weaponized by Chemtrails, Electromagnetism, & Nanotechnology for Synthetic Biology. KDP Publishing, 2021.

Sub Rosa America: A Deep State History. KDP Publishing, 2010-2018, Books 1-4.

Friesen, James G. *Uncovering the Mystery of MPD.* Wipf and Stock Publishers, 1997.

This book spoke to my heart and soul with the words of a true humanitarian.

Hersha, Cheryl, Hersha, Lynn, Griffis, Dale, Schwarz, Ted. *Secret Weapons: Two Sisters' Terrifying True Story of Sex, Spies and Sabotage*, New Horizon Press, 2001.

Horn, Tom and Nita. *Forbidden Gates: How Genetics, Robotics, Artificial intelligence, Synthetic Biology, Nanotechnology, and Human Enhancement Herald the Dawn of Techno-Dimensional Spiritual Warfare.* Defender, 2011.

Icke, David. *The David Icke Guide to the Global Conspiracy.* Associated Publishers, 2007.

Icke, David. *Human Race Get Off Your Knees: The Lion Sleeps No More.* David Icke, 2010.

Keith, Jim. *Saucers of the Illuminati.* IllumiNet Press, 1999.

Mind Control, World Control: The Encyclopedia of Mind Control. Adventures Unlimited, 1998.

Lee, Jim. *Paradise Lost, The Great California Fire Chronicles*

Madness in the Fast Lane, BBC, 2009; includes video of Sabina and Ursula Eriksson. https://www.bitchute.com/video/9YxiULm3GIWR/

Marshall, Donald. *Empowerment by Virtue of Golden Truth. Human Cloning: Specifically, REM Driven Human Cloning, FULL DISCLOSURE.* KDP Publishing, 2015.

O'Hagan, David. *The Battle For Humanity.* https://www.option3.co.uk/the-battle-for-humanity/

Patton, Ron. *Mkzine: The Definitive Collection*, Lulu Enterprises Incorporated, 2016.

Rutz, Carol. *A Nation Betrayed: The Chilling True Story of Secret Cold War Experiments Performed on Our Children and Other Innocent People. 2001.*

Scura, John and Phillips, Dane. *Battle Hymn: Revelations of the Sinister Plan for a New World Order.* Black Rose, 2011. Request the second printing.

Seymour, Cheri, a/k/a Carol Marshall. *The Last Circle: Danny Casolaro's Investigation into the Octopus and the PROMIS Software Scandal.* Trine Day, 2010.

Shurter, David. *Rabbit Hole: A Satanic Ritual Abuse Survivor's Story.* Consider It Creative, 2012.

Sullivan, Kathleen. *Unshackled: A Survivor's Story of Mind Control.* Dandelion Books, 2003.

Svali. *Svali Speaks: Breaking the Chains: A Book by Former Illuminati Trainer Svali.* https://www.wanttoknow.info/secret_societies/svali_book_svali_speaks

Taylor, Brice, a/k/a Sue Ford. *Thanks for the Memories: The Truth Has Set Me Free: The Memoirs of Bob Hope's and Henry Kissinger's Mind-Controlled Slave.* Brice Taylor Trust, 1999.

Wheeler, Cisco and Springmeier, Fritz. *How the Illuminati Create an Undetectable Total Mind Controlled Slave,* 2008.

Appendix A
"Enter-Entrainment" as Triggers and Programming Reinforcement

So many Led Zeppelin songs reinforce *our* programming in so very many ways!

During *our* early programming years, *our* eldest brother's extensive collection of music is represented in the following list (his being rock-n-roll albums) that consolidates programming and program reinforcement songs and films.

The production and release of programming music and films has increased extensively in recent years. Songs and film represent a well-planned, methodical venue for indoctrination, disinformation, and misinformation, and are also used for the continued programming and program reinforcement of both older and younger slaves.

Songs

"Moon River", Perry Como, 1962

"These Boots Are Made for Walking", Nancy Sinatra, 1966

"Dazed and Confused", Led Zeppelin, 1968

"Communication Breakdown", Led Zeppelin, 1969

"Babe, I'm Gonna Leave You", Led Zeppelin, 1969

"Heartbreaker", Led Zeppelin, 1969

"You Shook Me", Led Zeppelin, 1969

"Whole Lotta Love", Led Zeppelin, 1969

"Ramble On", Led Zeppelin, 1969

"I'm Your Captain", Grand Funk Railroad, 1970

"Black Magic Woman", Santana, 1970

"Black Dog", Led Zeppelin, 1971

"When the Levee Breaks", Led Zeppelin, 1971

"Stairway to Heaven", Led Zeppelin, 1971

"Witchy Woman", Eagles, 1972

"Horse With No Name", America, 1972

"We're an American Band", Grand Funk Railroad, 1973

"Band on the Run", Paul McCartney, 1973

"Over the Hills and Far Away", Led Zeppelin, 1973

"Lady", Styx, 1973

"Dream On", Aerosmith, 1973

"Sweet Emotion", Aerosmith, 1975

"Kashmir", Led Zeppelin, 1975

"Suite Madame Blue", Styx, 1975

"Feel Like Makin' Love", Bad Company, 1975

"Dream Weaver", Gary Wright, 1975

"Lorelei", Styx, 1976

"Nobody's Fault But Mine", Led Zeppelin, 1976

"Back in the Saddle", Aerosmith, 1976

"Hotel California", Eagles, 1977

"In the Evening", Led Zeppelin, 1979

"I'm Burnin' for You", Blue Oyster Cult, 1981

"In the Air Tonight", Phil Collins, 1981

"Early in the Morning", Gap Band, 1982.

> *I recall this song during the wee hours of the morning after an on-task. It was used to seal in my programming to forget as well as to relieve my fear and anxiety. I am uncertain if it was used after other on-tasks to program in our feelings of being alright in the morning, afternoon, or nighttime. It is the chorus that is so effective, repeated five times at the song's end:*
>
> > *Early in the mornin'*
> > *In the middle of the day, baby*

Late at night, mama,
Everything gonna be all right

"Life in a Northern Town", Dream Academy, 1985

"Dude Looks Like a Lady", Aerosmith, 1987

"Ragdoll", Aerosmith, 1988

"Janie's Got a Gun", Aerosmith, 1989

"Walking in Memphis", Marc Cohn, 1991

"Livin'on the Edge, Aerosmith, 1993

"Ordinary World", Duran, Duran, 1993

"Come Undone", Duran, Duran, 1993

"You Know My Name", Chris Cornell, 2006 (*Casino Royale* soundtrack)

"Another Way To Die", Jack White and Alicia Keys, 2008 (*Quantum of Solace* soundtrack)

Films and TV Shows
Hollywood is anything but entertainment; it is designed to be entrainment. That programming is designed and implemented to be constantly reinforced is a significant part of the reason it is so difficult to truly break free and maintain freedom. I refer to "low dosing": utilized in early deprogramming, a turning to certain songs and films to assist *our* functioning in the everyday world. Some of these films were used in the actual programming process of certain alters.

The Wizard of Oz, Warner Brothers, 1939

Bambi, Disney, 1942

Alice in Wonderland, Disney, 1951

20,000 Leagues Under the Sea, Disney, 1954

101 Dalmations, Disney, 1961

The Manchurian Candidate, Metro-Goldwyn-Mayer, 1962; Paramount, 2004

The Incredible Mr. Limpet, Warner Brothers, 1964

Mary Poppins, Disney, 1964

Batman, television series, ABC Network, 1966-1968

The Jungle Book, Disney, 1967

Chitty Chitty, Bang, Bang, United Artists, 1968

> *Based on a book by Ian Fleming and produced by Albert Broccoli, the same writer and producer respectively of the James Bond series: profound program reinforcement for kill programming.*

The Day of the Dolphin, Avco Embassy, 1973

The Parallax View, Paramount, 1974

The Stepford Wives, Columbia, 1975

Close Encounters of the Third Kind, Columbia Pictures, 1977

Altered States, Warner Brothers, 1980

Lethal Weapon, Warner Brothers, 1987, with sequels running through 1998

> *During the filming of* Lethal Weapon 3, *I have a conscious memory of leaving a group of people late at night to drive to Clearwater Beach, Florida where filming was taking place. My arrival was timed perfectly. I parked, walked to the location, stood for only a few minutes when around the corner came Mel Gibson followed by Danny Glover. After Glover walked by, I turned and left. This was part of* our *programming to Glover as written in Book 1, Chapter 4, "Killing", Shiny Purple and the Actor. It was quite eerie then and now.*

Batman films, Warner Brothers, 1989, 1992, 1995, 1997

The Lawnmower Man, New Line, 1992

The X-Files, the television series, Fox Network, 1993-2002

Jurassic Park, Universal, 1993

The Point of No Return, Warner Brothers, 1993

The Professional, Columbia, 1994

The Long Kiss Goodnight, New Line, 1996

Conspiracy Theory, Warner Brothers, 1997

Enemy of the State, Touchstone, 1998

Eyes Wide Shut, Warner Brothers, 1999

Unbreakable, Blinding Edge, 2000

Harry Potter, Warner Brothers, 2001-2011

Though this came to the screen many years after my programming, the profound effect it has in helping me feel normal due to its magical content and muggle world—the equivalent of the programming network and the "world of man"—is astounding. I bought the series and watched it in its entirety no less than a dozen times before passing it off to a support person. Harry Potter must be used extensively for programming.

Signs, Buena Vista, 2002

The Bourne Identity, Universal, 2004

The Bourne Supremacy, Universal, 2004

The Bourne Ultimatum, Universal, 2007

The Bourne Legacy, Universal, 2012

Jason Bourne, Universal, 2016

Collateral, DreamWorks, 2004

Constantine, Warner Brothers, 2005

The Listening, Echo Film, 2006

Dexter, Showtime series, 2006

Website: "America's favorite serial killer."

Casino Royale, Columbia and Metro-Goldwyn-Mayer, 2006

The Golden Compass, New Line, 2007

Batman Begins, Warner Brothers, 2005

The Dark Knight, Warner Brothers, 2008

The Dark Knight Rises, Warner Brothers, 2012

On August 12, 2011, during research for accurate release dates on the films listed here, I discovered that the final Dark Knight *sequel* The Dark Knight Rises *was planned for release in summer 2012. This profoundly shook me because of "the dark lord is rising in Salt Lake City", the quote that occurred for me in January 2011. (Book 1, Chapter 12, "Internal Programming/ Programming to actor Christian Bale" as well as Book 2, Chapter 4, "Us and Current Events: Nothing Is What It Seems, Jon Huntsman, Mormon Manchurian Candidate and the New Jerusalem".) On July 20, 2012, 12 people were shot and killed inside a Century movie theater in Aurora, Colorado during a midnight (12 o'clock) screening of* The Dark Knight Rises.

Wanted, Universal, 2008

Twilight film saga, Summit, 2008-2012

True Blood, HBO series, 2008-2014

My Own Worst Enemy, NBC network, 2008.

> *The amount of blowback the tmk network received from their slaves due to this series may have been the real reason it was pulled so quickly. The triggers were profound. I lost time while viewing it, not to mention the "contact your handlers" message in the commercial break during its pilot and encore showing. Episodes may or may not still be available.* **Not recommended for programmed individuals**.

United States of Tara, Showtime series, 2009

Dollhouse, Fox Network series, 2009

Push, Summit, 2009

Terminator Salvation, Warner Brothers, 2009

Watchmen, Warner Brothers, 2009

The Men Who Stare at Goats, Overture, 2009

Salt, Columbia, 2010

Eagle Eye, Dreamworks, 2011

The Hunger Games film series, Color Force and Lion's Gate, 2012-2023

Skyfall, Eon Productions, 2012

Her, Annapurna Pictures, 2013

World War Z, Skydance, 2013

Elysium, Tristar, 2013

Frozen, Walt Disney Pictures, 2013

Parkland, American Film Company, 2013 (A fine piece of propaganda!)

Maze Runner, film series, Gotham Group, 2014-2018

Kingsman film series, Marv Films, 2014-2021

American Ultra, The Bridge Finance Company, 2015

Ex Machina, A24, 2015

Spectre, Eon Productions, 2015

Patriots Days, CBS Films, 2016 (Another fine propaganda film...)

Deepwater Horizon, Summit Entertainment, 2016 (Propaganda at its finest.)

You Were Never Really Here, Film$ Productions, 2018

No Time to Die, Metro-Goldwin-Meyer, 2021

The Suicide Squad, DC Films, 2021

Appendix B
The Feasibility of Liquid Breathing in Man

ADA037089

REPORT DOCUMENTATION PAGE

READ INSTRUCTIONS
BEFORE COMPLETING FORM

1. REPORT NUMBER	2. GOVT ACCESSION NO.	3. RECIPIENT'S CATALOG NUMBER

4. TITLE (and Subtitle)

The Feasibility of Liquid Breathing in Man

5. TYPE OF REPORT & PERIOD COVERED

Final Technical Report
5/1/69 - 10/31/75

6. PERFORMING ORG. REPORT NUMBER

7. AUTHOR(s)

Johannes A. Kylstra, M. D.

8. CONTRACT OR GRANT NUMBER(s)

N00014-67-A-0251-0007

9. PERFORMING ORGANIZATION NAME AND ADDRESS

Duke University Medical Center
Durham, N. C. 27710

10. PROGRAM ELEMENT, PROJECT, TASK AREA & WORK UNIT NUMBERS

11. CONTROLLING OFFICE NAME AND ADDRESS

Office of Naval Research
Arlington, Virginia 22217

12. REPORT DATE

2/28/77

13. NUMBER OF PAGES

9

14. MONITORING AGENCY NAME & ADDRESS(if different from Controlling Office)

15. SECURITY CLASS. (of this report)

Unclassified

15a. DECLASSIFICATION/DOWNGRADING SCHEDULE

16. DISTRIBUTION STATEMENT (of this Report)

Approved for publication release. Distribution unlimited.

DDC
MAR 14 1977
RECEIVED
C

17. DISTRIBUTION STATEMENT (of the abstract entered in Block 20, if different from Report)

18. SUPPLEMENTARY NOTES

Supported by ONR contract N00014-67-0251-0007

19. KEY WORDS (Continue on reverse side if necessary and identify by block number)

Liquid breathing - Fluorocarbon - Emulsions - Lung lavage - Gas exchange - Ventilation

20. ABSTRACT (Continue on reverse side if necessary and identify by block number)

The maximum effective alveolar ventilation ($\dot{V}_A^e$max) in healthy young liquid breathing men is approximately 3 l/min. This estimate is based on measured expiratory flows of saline and FC-80 fluorocarbon liquid from excised dogs' lungs and maximum expiratory flow and gas exchange in saline ventilated lungs of men. At a solubility of CO_2 in saline of 0.742 ml STPD/l/mmHg, a $\dot{V}_A^e$max of 3 l/min precludes the feasibility of saline breathing in man.

DD FORM 1473 1 JAN 73   EDITION OF 1 NOV 65 IS OBSOLETE
S/N 0102-014-6601 |

20. Abstract

Normothermic anesthetized dogs ventilated with oxygenated FC-80 fluorocarbon liquid can be maintained at a normal $PaCO_2$ for 1 hr. This indicates that the solubility of CO_2 in FC-80 fluorocarbon liquid is approximately 3 ml STPD/l/mmHg, which is considerably higher than reported in the literature. It should be possible for a healthy man breathing oxygenated FC-80 fluerocarbon to maintain a normal $PaCO_2$ while at rest. This would make possible the rapid escape from disabled submarines at great depths. The use of an emulsion of 1% (by volume) of 2 M NaOH in FC-80 fluorocarbon liquid should permit a liquid breathing diver to perform work requiring a V_{O_2} of approximately 1 l STPD/min while maintaining a normal $PaCO_2$. Microscopic examination of the lungs of dogs and rats that had breathed oxygenated FC-80 fluorocarbon liquid or an emulsion of 1% (by volume) of 2 M NaOH in FC-80 fluorocarbon liquid revealed the transient presence of increased numbers of mononuclear cells but no other pathologic changes.

$V(O_2)$

INTRODUCTION

Decompression sickness could be eliminated if the inert gas in the breathing mixtures which currently are being used in diving could be replaced by a noncompressible liquid. Furthermore, liquid breathing would make it possible to study the biological effects of pressure per se in mammals without the interference of pharmacological effects of compressed gases, provided that thermal, metabolic and respiratory homeostasis could be maintained during the hydraulic compression of the experimental animals.

The research on liquid breathing dating back to 1962 has been reviewed earlier elsewhere (10). In this report, the work performed under ONR contract N00014-67-A-0251-0007 between May 1, 1969 and October 31, 1975 is summarized. The activities aimed primarily at assessing the feasibility of liquid breathing in man are discussed in Section I. Other investigations dealing with the physiological responses to a hyperbaric environment are summarized in section II. A complete chronological bibliography of scientific publications emanating from the contract is given in section III.

I. LIQUID BREATHING

In all experiments prior to 1969, adequate arterial oxygenation could be maintained but the experimental animals invariably developed a severe respiratory acidosis. The elimination of CO_2 through liquid filled lungs depends upon the solubility of CO_2 in the alveolar liquid (αCO_2) and the effective alveolar ventilation (V_A^e) which may be defined as the virtual volume of exhaled liquid in which the partial pressure of CO_2 is the same as in the arterial blood, or more conventionally, as the difference between the minute volume of ventilation (V_E) and dead space ventilation ($\dot{V}_D$). Thus, under steady state conditions when the inspired liquid does not contain CO_2, $PaCO_2 = \dot{V}CO_2/V_A^e \cdot \alpha CO_2$. Hence, if a normal $PaCO_2$ cannot be maintained at a given VCO_2, then either V_A^e or αCO_2 or both are too low. To assess the feasibility of liquid breathing in man, it was therefore deemed to be of prime importance to establish the limits of V_A^e during ventilation with various liquids and to explore possibilities of increasing αCO_2.

1. Experiments with Excised Dogs' Lungs

Volume-flow characteristics of saline and FC-80 fluorocarbon filled excised dogs' lungs were compared by using volume-displacement plethysmography (17). In these experiments, expiratory flow started from a lung volume at which the static recoil pressure of the same lung filled with air had been 20 cm H_2O. The maximum flows of saline and fluorocarbon were compared over the first 50% of the total volume expired. The mean flows were 121 $\pm$ 32 ml/sec for the saline filled lungs and 104 $\pm$ 46 ml/sec for the fluorocarbon filled lungs. At comparable lung volumes, the static recoil pressure of FC-80 filled lungs was found to be greater than in saline-filled lungs, indicating that alveolar surface tension is not abolished in a fluorocarbon-filled lung (8).

2. Observations in Man

It is possible to ventilate one lung of man with saline while the other lung is ventilated with oxygen (7). Such a procedure is by now a generally

accepted method of treating patients with alveolar proteinosis and has
also been used successfully as an adjunct in the treatment of patients
suffering from bronchiectasis, cystic fibrosis of the pancreas, or intractable
asthma. Bronchoalveolar lavage has been used prophylactically to remove
accidentally inhaled radioactive plutonium from the lungs of a healthy man.

(a) Gas Exchange

During lavages of the lung of a patient with alveolar proteinosis and
a 49 year old healthy volunteer, the PO_2 and PCO_2 of end-tidal liquid remained
virtually unchanged as the time between the beginning of infusion to the end
of drainage of a tidal volume increased from less than 30 to more than 200 sec.
Also, the arterial and mixed venous PO_2 and PCO_2 remained essentially the
same, suggesting that diffusive gas tension equilibrium between alveolar
capillary blood and alveolar contents was established within 30 sec in these
saline filled human lungs (9). The computed difference between the mean
end-capillary and alveolar CO_2 partial pressure was, on the average, less
than 1 mmHg in the 28 year old patient with alveolar proteinosis indicating
that ventilation and perfusion were adequately matched in the liquid filled
lung.

(b) Ventilation

In the anesthetized volunteer, the maximum expiratory flow of saline
from the left lung was measured by applying and gradually increasing suction
at the outflow tube until the rate of flow of saline ceased to increase.
The minimum time required to remove 500 ml saline, starting from a lung
volume of 2000 ml was 9.4 sec. The computed total lung capacity (TLC) of
the left lung (0.45 x TLC of both lungs measured the day before the experi-
ment) was 2900 ml. Assuming that the time required for inspiration is equal
to the time required for expiration, and assuming an equal maximal expiratory
flow rate for both lungs, the maximum minute ventilation of this man, if he
were breathing saline, would be 3.2 liters, at a tidal volume of 1 liter
and with expirations starting at 70% of TLC. In the patient with alveolar
proteinosis, 500 ml saline was drained from the left lung in 7 sec, starting
at TLC. Making the same assumptions as before, the maximum minute volume of
ventilation in this patient, if he were to breathe saline, would be 4.2 liters
at a tidal volume of 1 liter and with expiration starting from TLC.

The maximum expiratory flow of either gas or liquid is dependent upon
the recoil tendency of the lung and limited by dynamic compression of the
airways. Therefore, the maximum expiratory flow cannot be increased by
mechanical assistance, i.e. by artificially applying a greater than normal
difference in pressure between the alveoli and the mouth. However, the
inspiratory flow is not limited by dynamic airway compression, so that,
theoretically, the inspiratory flow should continue to increase as the
difference between the pressure in the alveoli and at the mouth increases.
It had been found earlier that the inspiratory flow in spontaneously saline
breathing dogs was about twice as great as the expiratory flow (6). As a
result, the minute volume of ventilation was 33% greater than would have
been the case if inspiration and expiration would have lasted equally long.
By increasing the inspiratory flow rate, as the saline breathing dog did,
the 49 year old volunteer's maximum minute volume of saline ventilation
could be 4.3 liters. The maximum minute volume of ventilation in the 28
year old patient with alveolar proteinosis, if he were breathing saline, could

be 5.6 liters at a tidal volume of 1 liter with expirations starting from TLC. Diffusive mixing in saline filled gas exchange units of the human lung appears to be complete within 30 sec and the ventilation and perfusion of saline filled lungs appears to be matched adequately (9). The expiratory flow of saline and fluorocarbon from liquid filled excised dogs' lungs was very similar (17). Hence, it seems reasonable to conclude that the effective alveolar ventilation in a healthy young saline or fluorocarbon breathing diver could be 3 liters/min.

(c) *Recovery following Lung Lavage with Saline*

Chest x-rays taken shortly after a lung lavage usually show a diffuse opacification of the washed lung, but the lung is clear again after 24 hours (7). Serial pulmonary function tests following lavage of a lung of the volunteer revealed a decrease in the vital capacity, TLC and FEV_1; a PaO_2 of 76 mmHg; and a $PaCO_2$ of 37 mmHg 24 hours after the procedure but these parameters returned to prelavage control levels in 72 hours and remained at these levels during the following 2 years. Static pressure-volume relationships of the left lung and chest of the anesthetized and curarized volunteer revealed a considerable decrease in compliance immediately following the lavage, as compared to the measurements made just before the lavage. This can be explained by the diminished volume or air in the lung caused by the presence of residual saline and by the surface tension at the interface between residual liquid and air.

(d) *Subjective Acceptability*

The healthy volunteer whose larynx and trachea had been anesthetized to facilitate intubation, but who otherwise received no medication, did not experience intolerable sensations arising from the flow of saline into and out of his lungs and seemed not to be aware of the presence of residual liquid in his lung after the lavage.

3. **The CO_2 Carrying Capacity of Various Breathing Fluids**

At a maximum $\dot{V}_A^e$ of approximately 3 l/min and a solubility of CO_2 in saline at 37°C of 0.724 ml STPD/l/mmHg, the $\dot{V}CO_2$ is limited to 87 ml STPD/min at $PaCO_2$ = 40 mmHg. Hence, it will obviously be impossible to maintain respiratory homeostasis in a saline breathing diver. The solubility of CO_2 at 37°C in FC-80 fluorocarbon was found to be approximately 3 ml STPD/l/mmHg (12). Therefore, it should be possible for a fluorocarbon breathing diver who produces no more than 360 ml STPD of CO_2/min to maintain a normal $PaCO_2$. While this would probably suffice to escape from disabled submarines, it would preclude the use of liquid breathing under circumstances where appreciable work has to be performed by a diver. For this reason, several possibilities of increasing the CO_2 carrying capacity of a liquid have been explored.

(a) *The Addition of THAM*

The addition of THAM to the inspired salt solution markedly prolonged survival of liquid breathing mice (5) and rats (18). To evaluate quantitatively the increase in the CO_2 carrying capacity of a saline breathing fluid caused by the addition of THAM, an isotonic 0.3 Molar THAM solution, titrated to pH 7.4 was equilibrated with various gas mixtures containing CO_2 at partial pressures ranging from 7 to 70 mmHg. The CO_2 content of the gas-equilibrated

The Feasibility of Liquid Breathing in Man
J. A. Kylstra, M. D., Principal Investigator   4

THAM solution was then determined by the method of Van Slyke. The CO_2 content of an isotonic 0.3 Molar THAM solution at pH 7.4 equilibrated with carbon dioxide at a partial pressure of 40 mmHg was approximately 390 ml STPD/1. In contrast, a liter of saline under these conditions contains only 29 ml STPD of CO_2 (17).

If a diver were to breathe an isotonic 0.3 Molar THAM solution titrated to pH 7.4 at an effective alveolar ventilation of 3 l/min, then he would be able to eliminate 3 x 390 = 1170 ml STPD of CO_2 per min at a $PaCO_2$ of 40 mmHg and thus be able to perform work which requires an oxygen uptake of 1462 ml STPD per minute, assuming that R = 0.8. However, the solubility of oxygen in a 0.3 Molar THAM solution is no greater than in saline (0.0299 ml STPD/1 per mmHg at 37°C) so that a partial pressure of 16,300 mmHg or 21.45 atm of oxygen, at least, would be required in the inspired THAM solution to supply the 1462 ml of oxygen per minute. Such partial pressures of oxygen are prohibitively toxic.

(b) *Emulsions of Fluorocarbon in THAM Solutions*

A stable emulsion can be prepared by subjecting a mixture of 30% (by volume) FC-80 fluorocarbon; a 0.3 Molar THAM solution titrated to pH 7.4 with HCl; and 0.04 g F68 Pluronic surfactant per milliliter FC-80 to ultrasonic energy (11). The emulsion has a density of 1.24 g/ml; an absolute viscosity of 2.4 centipoise; and an approximate fluorocarbon droplet diameter of 3 μ. The approximate CO_2 content of the emulsion at partial pressures ranging from 30 to 60 mmHg is 132 ml STPD/liter + (5.5 x PCO_2). The O_2 content in ml STPD/liter equals 0.213 x PO_2 (mmHg). Since the density and the viscosity of the emulsion are somewhat greater than of saline, the maximum V_A^e can be expected to be somewhat less. However, to permit work requiring 1 1 STPD/min of oxygen, a diver breathing the emulsion would need a $\dot{V}_A^e$ of only 2.3 l/min. in order to eliminate the 800 ml STPD of CO_2 produced by his tissues each minute and yet maintain a $PaCO_2$ of 40 mmHg. However, at a $\dot{V}O_2$ of 1 1 STPD/min and a $\dot{V}_A^e$ of only 2.3 l/min, a PIO_2 of at least 2100 mmHg would still be needed to maintain adequate arterial oxygenation.

(c) *Emulsions of NaOH in Fluorocarbon*

It is possible to make emulsions consisting of a continuous phase of fluorocarbon liquid in which are suspended small droplets of NaOH surrounded by surfactant molecules. Such an emulsion combines the high oxygen solubility of fluorocarbon with the high CO_2 combining capacity of NaOH. The CO_2 can diffuse through the continuous fluorocarbon phase into the NaOH droplets, whereas the NaOH cannot diffuse through the water immiscible fluorocarbon phase and, therefore, is prevented from coming in contact with the alveolar wall (13). The total CO_2 capacity of the emulsions is the sum of the amount of CO_2 physically dissolved in the FC-80 fluorocarbon plus the amount of CO_2 which is bound chemically by the NaOH when Na_2CO_3 is formed. At a PCO_2 of 40 mmHg, a 1% 2 Molar NaOH in FC-80 fluorocarbon emulsion contains approximately 300 ml STPD of CO_2.

The absolute viscosity of the 1% (by volume) 2.0 M NaOH in FC-80 fluorocarbon emulsion is 1.17 centopoise which is nearly equal to the absolute viscosity of FC-80 alone. The density of the emulsion is also

The Feasibility of Liquid Breathing in Man   5
J. A. Kylstra, M. D., Principal Investigator

approximately the same as of FC-80 fluorocarbon so that the maximal $\dot{V}_A^e$
of a diver breathing the emulsion would be the same as if he were breathing
FC-80 fluorocarbon. At a $\dot{V}_A^e$ of 3 l/min, a diver breathing a 1% (by volume)
2.0 M NaOH in FC-80 fluorocarbon emulsion would be able to eliminate approximately 900 ml STPD of CO_2 per minute at a $PaCO_2$ of 40 mmHg. To ascertain
adequate arterial oxygenation at a VO_2 of 1125 ml STPD/min (assuming that
R = 0.8), a PIO_2 of only 700 mmHg would suffice. Moreover, a NaOH in
fluorocarbon emulsion would offer important advantages over a fluorocarbon
in THAM emulsion: (1) return to spontaneous air breathing would be easier
since the surface tension of residual liquid in the lung would be much lower;
(2) no untoward water and electrolyte shifts between liquid in the lungs
and blood in the alveolar capillaries could occur.

The lungs from rats that had breathed a 1% (by volume) 2.0 M NaOH in
FC-80 fluorocarbon emulsion for 15 minutes, subsequently returned to air
breathing and then were sacrificed after 3 hours, appeared normal. Eight
days after breathing these emulsions, the only pathological findings con-
sisted of some macrophages in the alveoli near the alveolar ducts. Thirty
days after breathing the emulsion, the lungs contained a greater number of
macrophages in the alveoli and there was some perivascular edema. There
were also lymphocytes in some alveoli, but other than that, no pathology
was seen.

4. Maintenance of Respiratory Homeostasis in Normothermic Liquid Breathing Dogs

The experimental conditions necessary to differentiate between
pressure and the pharmacologic effects of compressed gases have been realized
so that it will be possible in the future to study the immediate and long
term effects of pressure per se in liquid breathing dogs.

Ten anesthetized, paralyzed, purebred beagle dogs were ventilated
for 45 and 60 min with oxygenated (PIO_2 = 685 mmHg) FC-80 fluorocarbon
liquid at 38°C. In five dogs, the $PaCO_2$ remained constant at approximately
43 mmHg during 60 min of liquid ventilation (mean tidal volume = 290 ml,
mean respiratory frequency = 2.8 breaths/min). Histological examination
by light as well as scanning electron microscopy of the lungs of dogs
sacrificed 10, 30 or 180 days after liquid ventilation revealed no pathological
changes except for a slight increase in the number of macrophages, especially
around the alveolar ducts (12).

II. PHYSIOLOGICAL RESPONSES TO ALTERATIONS IN AMBIENT PRESSURE AND THE
     COMPOSITION OF BREATHING MIXTURES

1. Pulmonary Gas Exchange

Theoretically, $P(A-a)O_2$, i.e. the difference between the mean alveolar
and arterial PO_2, due to imbalance of ventilation and perfusion, should
vanish if the inert gas in a breathing mixture is replaced by oxygen. This
can be done without changing the PIO_2 by lowering the ambient pressure in
an altitude chamber. This theoretical prediction has been verified experimentally (14). Increasing the inert gas fraction in a breathing mixture

405

The Feasibility of Liquid Breathing in Man   6
J. A. Kylstra, M. D., Principal Investigator

(as is done in diving practice to avoid oxygen toxicity) should, theoretically,
cause an increase in $P(A-a)O_2$ caused by ventilation-perfusion imbalance.
This was also verified experimentally (15). Since the distribution
component of $P(A-a)O_2$ can be eliminated by oxygen breathing at simulated
altitude, and since the shunt component of $P(A-a)O_2$ can be minimized by
lowering the PIO_2 to around 60 mmHg, the remaining $P(A-a)O_2$ must be due
to incomplete diffusive equilibrium between alveolar gas and end-capillary
blood. It was found that, in normal men, there was no measurable diffusion
component of $P(A-a)O_2$ at rest, but that it was present when the men performed
exercise (1).

The principle of abolishing $P(A-a)O_2$ by breathing 100% oxygen at a
simulated altitude was also tested to explain an unexplained drop in PaO_2
upon immersion up to the neck which occurred in two Navy divers. It was
found that, in some men, this drop in PaO_2 upon submersion up to the neck
in water is caused by a ventilation-perfusion imbalance but that in others
it is caused primarily by an increase in true venous admixture (2).

2.   Effect of Pressure on Ventilation and Gas Exchange in Man

In six men breathing various gas mixtures at different ambient pressures,
the $PaCO_2$ increased rectilinearly with ambient pressure but the change in
$PaCO_2$ was not related to other experimental variables. This would indicate
that the regulation of breathing somehow is affected by pressure per se (16).

3.   Maximum Expiratory Flow

The maximum expiratory flow of various breathing mixtures (gas as well
as liquid) can be calculated for Weibel's lung model, using the equal
pressure point (EPP) concept and standard fluid dynamics equations. The
computed maximum expiratory flow of air and of oxygen-helium mixtures over
a range of ambient pressures from 1 to 53 atmospheres was in good agreement
with measurement reported in the literature (3). It would, therefore, seem
possible to predict a diver's maximum expiratory flow at great depths (when
breathing gas or liquid) from measurements made at the surface and at shallow
depths while breathing air.

4.   Pharmacological Properties of Helium

Reports in the literature that helium breathed at normal atmospheric
pressures reduces the incidence of cardiac arrhythmias following coronary
artery ligation in dogs could not be confirmed (4).

References

(1) Cohen, R., E. M. Overfield, and J. A. Kylstra: Diffusion component of
the alveolar-arterial oxygen pressure difference in man. J. Appl. Physiol.
31:223-226, 1971.

(2) Cohen, R., W. H. Bell, H. A. Saltzman and J. A. Kylstra: Alveolar-
arterial oxygen pressure difference in man immersed up to the neck in water.
J. App. Physiol. 30:720-723, 1971.

The Feasibility of Liquid Breathing in Man   7
J. A. Kylstra, M. D., Principal Investigator

(3) Haynes, J. H. and J. A. Kylstra: Estimate of maximum expiratory flow
based on the equal pressure point concept and Weibel's lung model. Undersea
Biomedical Research 1:45-58, 1974.

(4) Holland, J. A., W. G. Wolfe, and J. A. Kylstra: Helium: Absence of
antiarrhythmic effect in anesthetized dogs. J. Thorac. Cardiovasc. Surg.
66:478-480, 1973.

(5) Kylstra, J. A., M. O. Tissing, and A. van der Maen: Of mice as fish.
Trans. Amer. Soc. Artif. Int. Organs 8:378-383, 1962.

(6) Kylstra, J. A., and M. O. Tissing: Fluid breathing. Clinical Applica-
tion of Hyperbaric Oxygen, I. Boerema, W. H. Brummelkamp, N. G. Meyne, eds.,
Elsevier Publishing Co., 1964, pp. 371-379.

(7) Kylstra, J. A., D. C. Rausch, K. D. Hall and A. Spock: Volume-controlled
lung lavage in the treatment of asthma, bronchiectasis and mucoviscidosis.
Amer. Rev. Resp. Dis. 103:651-665, 1971.

(8) Kylstra, J. A. and W. H. Schoenfisch: Alveolar surface tension in
fluorocarbon filled lungs. J. Appl. Physiol. 33:32-35, 1972.

(9) Kylstra, J. A., W. H. Schoenfisch, J. M. Herron and G. D. Blenkarn:
Gas exchange in saline-filled lungs of man. J. Appl. Physiol. 35:136-142, 1973.

(10) Kylstra, J. A.: Liquid breathing. Undersea Biomed. Res. 1:259-269, 1974.

(11) Matthews, W. H. and J. A. Kylstra: A fluorocarbon emulsion with a
high solubility for CO_2. Undersea Biomed. Res. 3:113-120, 1976.

(12) Matthews, W. d., R. H. Balzer, J. D. Shelburne, P. C. Pratt and J. A.
Kylstra: Respiratory homeostasis in normothermic, anesthetized liquid
ventilated dogs. Submitted to Journal of Applied Physiology.

(13) Matthews, W. H. and J. A. Kylstra: Investigation of a new breathing
liquid. Sixth Symposium on Underwater Physiology (in press).

(14) Overfield, E. M. and J. A. Kylstra: The distribution component of
the alveolar-arterial oxygen pressure difference in man. J. Appl. Physiol.
27:634-636, 1969.

(15) Overfield, E. M., H. A. Saltzman, J. A. Kylstra and J. V. Salzano:
Respiratory gas exchange in normal men breathing 0.9% oxygen in helium at
31.3 Atm. J. Appl. Physiol. 27:471-475, 1969.

(16) Saltzman, H. A., J. V. Salzano, C. D. Blenkarn and J. A. Kylstra: Effects
of pressure on ventilation and gas exchange in man. J. Appl. Physiol. 30:
443-449, 1971.

(17) Schoenfisch, W. H. and J. A. Kylstra: Maximum expiratory flow and estimated
CO_2 elimination in liquid ventilated dogs' lungs. J. Appl. Physiol. 35:117-
121, 1973.

(18) Pegg, J.H., T. L. Horner and E. A. Wahrenbrock: Breathing of pressure-
oxygenated liquids. Proc. 2nd Symp. Underwater Physiol. pp. 166-170. Washington, D.C.:
Natl. Acad. Sci., Natl. Res. Council (Publ. 1181).

The Feasibility of Liquid Breathing in Man
J. A. Kylstra, M. D., Principal Investigator   8

III.   CHRONOLOGICAL BIBLIOGRAPHY OF SCIENTIFIC PUBLICATIONS EMANATING FROM
        CONTRACT N00014-67-A-0251-0007

Saltzman, H. A., J. V. Salzano, G. D. Blenkarn, and J. A. Kylstra: Effects
of pressure on ventilation and gas exchange in man. J. Appl. Physiol. 30:
443-449, 1971.

Kylstra, J. A., D. C. Rausch, K. D. Hall and A. Spock: Volume-controlled
lung lavage in the treatment of asthma, bronchiectasis and mucoviscidosis.
Amer. Rev. Resp. Dis. 103:651-665, 1971.

Cohen, R. W., H. Bell, H. A. Saltzman, and J. A. Kylstra: Alveolar-arterial
oxygen pressure difference in man immersed up to the neck in water. J. Appl.
Physiol. 30:720-723, 1971.

Overfield, E. M., and J. A. Kylstra: Change in (A-a)DO$_2$ as a function of
FIO$_2$ at a constant PIO$_2$ in normal man. J. Appl. Physiol. 31:581-585, 1971.

Cohen, R., J. V. Salzano, and J. A. Kylstra: Diffusion component of alveolar-
arterial oxygen pressure difference in man. Fed. Proc. 30, April, 1971 (abstract).

Cohen, R., E. M. Overfield, and J. A. Kylstra: Diffusion component of the
alveolar-arterial oxygen pressure difference in man. J. Appl. Physiol. 31:
223-226, 1971.

Schoenfisch, W. H. and J. A. Kylstra: Maximum expiratory flow from saline
and fluorocarbon filled lungs. Physiologist 14:225, 1971 (abstract).

Haynes, J. H., W. H. Schoenfisch, and J. A. Kylstra: Computed maximum
expiratory flow of gas and liquid. Physiologist 14:160, 1971 (abstract).

Overfield, E. M., and J. A. Kylstra: The volume and rate of volume change of
the swimbladder of the goldfish. Resp. Physiol. 13:283-291, 1971.

Kylstra, J. A. and W. H. Schoenfisch: Alveolar surface tension in fluorocarbon
filled lung. J. Appl. Physiol. 33:32-35, 1972.

Schoenfisch, W. H. and J. A. Kylstra: Maximum expiratory flow and estimated
CO$_2$ elimination in liquid ventilated dogs lung. J. Appl. Physiol. 35:117-
121, 1973.

Kylstra, J. A., W. H. Schoenfisch, J. M. Herron and G. D. Blenkarn: Gas
exchange in saline filled lungs of man. J. Appl. Physiol. 35:136-142, 1973.

Holland, J. A., W. G. Wolfe, and J. A. Kylstra: Helium: Absence of antiarrhythmic effect in anesthetized dogs. J. Thorac. Cardiovasc. Surg. 66:478-
480, 1973.

Haynes, J. H. and J. A. Kylstra: Estimate of maximum expiratory flow based
on the equal pressure point concept of Weibel's lung model. Undersea Biomed.
Res. 1:45-58, 1974.

Schoenfisch, W. H., G. D. Blenkarn, B. A. Hills and J. A. Kylstra: Liquid
Breathing: expiratory flow and CO$_2$ elimination using fluorocarbon and aqueous
solutions. Underwater Physiology V, C. J. Lambertsen (Ed.), FASEB, Bethesda, Md.,
pp. 91-99, 1976.

The Feasibility of Liquid Breathing in Man   9
J. A. Kylstra, M. D., Principal Investigator

Matthews, W. H. and J. A. Kylstra: Investigation of a new breathing
liquid. Sixth Symposium on Underwater Physiology (in press).

Matthews, W. H., R. H. Balzer, J. D. Shelburne, P. C. Pratt and J. A.
Kylstra: Respiratory homeostasis in normothermic, anesthetized, liquid
ventilated dogs. Submitted to Journal Applied Physiology.

Everyone Deserves to be Safe and Loved

About the Author

Elisa E is a survivor of MKUltra programming born in New Jersey, United States in the early 1960s. Her story crosses the MKUltra trauma-based programming of that era and runs into the technological advancements in the 1990s taking her into remote programming and accessing (eMKUltra), as well as cloning technologies occurring in the late 1980s programs.

As a survivor and support person to other survivors, she chose to update these books in 2022 as a witness to what is occurring globally since late 2019. Her insights remain pertinent due to the eyes to see and ears to hear beyond the narrative and into the esoteric agenda she has lived through, as well as some of her prophetic proclamations from early deprogramming playing out.

Many of Elisa's interviews on various alternative media internet radio shows can be found online. Some have been removed, by whom we don't know. Additionally, Elisa wrote articles for several issues of *Paranoia Magazine*.

Printed in the USA
CPSIA information can be obtained
at www.ICGtesting.com
LVHW021623181023
761486LV00037B/339